Scriptural Allusions and Exegesis in the Hodayot

Studies on the Texts of the Desert of Judah

Editor

Florentino García Martínez

Qumran Institute, University of Groningen

Associate Editors

Peter W. Flint – Eibert J.C. Tigchelaar

VOLUME LIX

Scriptural Allusions and Exegesis in the Hodayot

By
Julie A. Hughes

BRILL
LEIDEN · BOSTON
2006

This book is printed on acid-free paper.

Library of Congress Cataloging-in-Publication Data

Hughes, Julie, 1950–
   Scriptural allusions and exegesis in the Hodayot / by Julie Hughes.
     p. cm. — (Studies on the texts of the desert of Judah, ISSN 0169-9962 ; v. 59)
   Includes bibliographical references and indexes.
   ISBN 90-04-14739-X (alk. paper)
     1. Thanksgiving Psalms. 2. Bible O.T.-Criticism, interpretation, etc., Jewish.
   3. Allusions in literature. I. Thanksgiving Psalms. English & Hebrew. Selections. II. Title.
   III. Series.

BM488.T5H84 2006
296.1'55–dc22

                                                                             2005058217

ISSN 0169-9962
ISBN 90 04 14739 X

**© Copyright 2006 by Koninklijke Brill NV, Leiden, The Netherlands.
Koninklijke Brill NV incorporates the imprints Brill Academic Publishers,
Martinus Nijhoff Publishers and VSP.**

All rights reserved. No part of this publication may be reproduced, translated, stored in
a retrieval system, or transmitted in any form or by any means, electronic,
mechanical, photocopying, recording or otherwise, without prior written
permission from the publisher.

Authorization to photocopy items for internal
or personal use is granted by Brill provided that
the appropriate fees are paid directly to The Copyright
Clearance Center, 222 Rosewood Drive, Suite 910
Danvers, MA 01923, USA.
Fees are subject to change.

PRINTED IN THE NETHERLANDS

To Ray, Beth and Andy,
the most important people in my life;
and to Christine, because she listened.

CONTENTS

Acknowledgments xi
Abbreviations xiii

I. The Hodayot: A Brief Overview of Studies to Date 1
1. Introduction 1
2. 1QH^a and Early Hodayot Scholarship 2
3. The Reconstruction and Re-Ordering of 1QH^a 5
   3.1. Excursus on Numbering Systems 7
4. The Other Hodayot Manuscripts 9
5. A Survey of Significant Studies 12
   5.1. Textual Studies 12
   5.2. Early Views on Genre and *Sitz im Leben* 12
   5.3. Author 14
   5.4. Prosody 17
   5.5. Genre and *Sitz im Leben* Revisited 21
   5.6. A New and Distinctive Approach by Carol Newsom 24
      5.6.1. Community Hymns 27
      5.6.2. Hodayot of the Leader 30
      5.6.3. Differences and Areas of Common Interest 33
6. Objectives of This Study 34

II. Methodology 35
1. Introduction 35
2. Selection of Passages 35
3. How Does One Study Poetry? 36
   3.1. Terminology 38
   3.2. Metre, Parallelism and Structural Indicators 39
4. How Does One Study Allusions? 41
   4.1. Definition of an Allusion 42
      4.1.1. Quotation 42
      4.1.2. Allusion 44
      4.1.3. Idiom 46
      4.1.4. From Author to Reader 48

4.2. Identification of Allusions	50
4.2.1. Proposed Criteria	52
4.3. The Function of Allusions	54
5. How Does One Read Texts?	55
5.1. Intertextuality	56
5.2. Reader-Orientated Approaches	57
6. Outline of Method	58
6.1. Delimitation and Text	59
6.2. Translation	59
6.3. Analysis of Structure	60
6.4. Close Reading	61
6.5. Allusions	61
6.6. Intertexts	62
6.7. Observations and Comments	62
III. Two Dualistic Poems	63
1. Introduction	63
2. Two Ways: 1QH^a VII 21–VIII ?	63
2.1. Delimitation and Text	64
2.2. Translation	66
2.3. Analysis of Structure	68
2.4. Close Reading	71
2.5. Allusions	78
2.5.1. A Meditation on Jeremiah	81
2.6. Intertexts	82
2.6.1. Creation and Destiny	82
2.6.2. Jer 10:23	87
2.6.3. Two Ways	89
2.6.4. Is There an Underlying Exegesis?	91
2.7. Observations and Comments	93
3. "I" and "They": 1QH^a XII 6–XIII 6	95
3.1. Delimitation and Text	96
3.2. Translation	98
3.3. Analysis of Structure	102
3.4. Close reading	105
3.4.1. The Speaker and his Enemies	105
3.4.2. The Speaker and his God	116
3.5. Allusions	118
3.5.1. Correct and Incorrect Interpretation of Torah	119
3.5.2. A Prayer of Confession and Commitment	124

3.6. Intertexts	125
3.6.1. Spokesmen of Error and Plots of Belial	126
3.6.2. What is Flesh?	129
3.7. Observations and Comments	132

IV. A Poem in Three Movements ... 135

1. Introduction	135
2. Sustained Artistry: 1QH^a XVI 5–XVII 36	135
2.1. Delimitation and Text	136
2.2. Translation	140
2.3. Analysis of Structure	147
2.4. Close Reading	150
2.4.1. The Secret Garden Tended by the Speaker	150
2.4.2. The Afflicted Teacher	159
2.4.3. God the Compassionate Judge and Parent	163
2.5. Allusions	167
2.5.1. Preparation	168
2.5.2. Testing	171
2.5.3. Vindication	172
2.6. Intertexts	174
2.6.1. Another Long Hodayah and its Sequel	174
2.6.2. Garden Imagery	178
2.6.3. Suffering and Vindication	181
2.7. Observations and Comments	182

V. Two Eschatological Poems ... 185

1. Introduction	185
2. Three Images of Distress: 1QH^a XI 6–19	185
2.1. Delimitation and Text	186
2.2. Translation	187
2.3. Analysis of structure	189
2.3.1. Repetitions and Wordplays	192
2.4. Close Reading	194
2.5. Allusions	200
2.6. Intertexts	205
2.7. Observations and Comments	206
3. From the Depths to the Heights: 1QH^a XI 20–37:	207
3.1. Delimitation and Text	208
3.2. Translation	209
3.3. Analysis of Structure	211

3.4. Close Reading 213
3.5. Allusions 220
    3.5.1. Raised to the Heights, Living in the Midst of Evil ... 220
    3.5.2. Eschatological Destruction and Holy War 222
3.6. Intertexts 226
3.7. Observations and Comments 228

VI. Conclusions 231
1. Introduction 231
2. Diversity 232
3. A Literary Tradition 233
4. The Implied Speaker 234
5. Artistic Merit 235

Bibliography 237
Index of Authors 249
Index of Texts 253

ACKNOWLEDGEMENTS

This book is a revised version of my doctoral thesis, which was submitted to the University of Manchester in the Autumn of 2004. I would like to thank my supervisor, Professor George J. Brooke, for his encouragement and guidance. He has given his time generously, and his advice has been invaluable. His feedback has always been prompt and constructive. I have greatly enjoyed and profited from our discussions.

I would also like to thank Dr Charlotte Hempel for her advice and encouragement. I am grateful also to Professor Florentino García Martínez for accepting this study for the STDJ series, and for his constructive advice.

I am grateful to the Arts and Humanities Research Board for the postgraduate award which enabled me to undertake this research without financial worries. I value the friendship and inspiration provided by staff and fellow-students in the Department of Religions and Theology at the University of Manchester. Last, but by no means least, I could never have completed this project without the patient and loving support of my husband Ray.

ABBREVIATIONS

Abbreviations used are according to *The SBL Handbook of Style for Ancient Near Eastern, Biblical, and Early Christian Studies*. Edited by P.H. Alexander, J.F. Kutsko, J.D. Ernest, S.A. Decker-Lucke, and D.L. Petersen. Peabody, Mass.: Hendrickson, 1999.

Unless otherwise stated, biblical quotations in English are from *The Holy Bible New Revised Standard Version*. © 1989, Division of Christian Education of the National Council of the Churches of Christ in the United States of America.

All Hebrew Bible quotations are from *Biblia Hebraica Stuttgartensia*. Stuttgart: Deutsche Bibelgesellschaft, 1990.

CHAPTER ONE

THE HODAYOT:
A BRIEF OVERVIEW OF STUDIES TO DATE

1. *Introduction*

The aim of this study is to explore the use of scriptural allusions in the *Hodayot* by close examination of selected passages. It has long been agreed that the *Hodayot* make extensive use of biblical language. Possible biblical allusions have been noted by some commentators, notably Holm-Nielsen, and lists of verbal similarities with biblical texts have also been made.[1] However, the only attempts of which I am aware to distinguish between allusion and use of biblical language in the *Hodayot* have been by Kittel, Patte, and Schultz.[2] But it was not the main focus of those studies.

An attempt to analyse the effect upon the reader of the allusions in one poem has been made by Frechette.[3] He first analysed the structure and poetic devices of the poem before seeking to interpret the significance of the allusions. My study is very much in the spirit of what Frechette attempted to do, in that I also consider that the allusions cannot be understood except within the overall poetic framework. However, my analysis of this particular poem differs considerably from that of Frechette (see chapter five.)

---

[1] Svend Holm-Nielsen, *Hodayot: Psalms From Qumran* (ATDan II; Aarhus: Universitetsforlaget I Aarhus, 1960); Jean Carmignac, "Les citations de l'ancien testament, et spécialement des poèmes du serviteur, dans les hymnes de Qumran," *RevQ* 2 (1959–1960): 357–394; P. Wernberg-Møller, "The Contribution of the Hodayot to Biblical Textual Criticism," *Textus* 4 (1964): 145–173.

[2] Bonnie Pedrotti Kittel, *The Hymns of Qumran: Translation and Commentary* (Society of Biblical Literature Dissertation Series 50; Chico: Scholars Press, 1981), 48–55; D. Patte, *Early Jewish Hermeneutic in Palestine* (SBLDS 22; Missoula: Scholars Press, 1975), 247–269; Richard L. Schultz, *The Search for Quotation: Verbal Parallels in the Prophets* (JSOTSup 180; Sheffield: Sheffield Academic Press, 1999), 159–171.

[3] Christopher G. Frechette, "Chiasm, Reversal and Biblical Reference in 1QH 11.3–18 (= Sukenik Column 3): A Structural Proposal," *JSP* 21 (2000): 71–102.

There is thus to date no major study of the allusions in the *Hodayot*. Furthermore, much of the discussion that does exist is imprecise and impressionistic. I have sought to redress this gap in the scholarship by selecting several highly allusive poems for close study. In establishing a method for this study I have endeavoured to place the discussion of allusions within the *Hodayot* on a more systematic foundation. There are two main aspects to my method. Firstly, in order to assess the allusions as poetic devices, I have analysed the poetic structure of each poem. Secondly, I have sought to develop a less subjective method for identifying and understanding the allusions. To this end I have drawn upon insights from the field of comparative literature as well as the insights of biblical scholars.

In this introductory chapter I will give a brief description of the *Hodayot* and an overview of the relevant research. I will also indicate where this study fits into existing scholarship, and the new avenues that I wish to pursue. In chapter two I will describe some of the insights from comparative literature which have informed this study and set out the method that I have followed. Chapters three to five contain detailed analyses of selected compositions. In chapter six I summarize and comment upon the observations of chapters three to five. In particular I note that the poems vary considerably in both style and content and I comment upon their use of scripture and tradition. I also discuss whether this study has thrown any light upon who wrote the Teacher Hymns.

2. *1QH^a and Early Hodayot Scholarship*

A copy of the *Hodayot*, or *Thanksgiving Hymns*, was one of the first Dead Sea manuscripts to be acquired by Eleazar Sukenik. It was named *Hodayot* by Sukenik because of the distinctive opening phrase, אודכה אדוני, with which some of the hymn-like compositions begin. Subsequently another fragmentary copy from Cave 1 and six more copies from Cave 4 would be identified. The usage of the term has been further widened by the description of compositions contained in other works as "hodayah-like." But in the early years when scholars referred to the *Hodayot* it was 1QH^a that they had in mind.

Of the complete scrolls found in Cave 1, 1QH^a was one of those in the poorest condition. Sukenik assembled the sheets and fragments and they were photographed using infra-red technology, which helped bring out the image of some otherwise illegible writing. Sukenik published preliminary editions of some parts of the scroll in 1948 and 1950.[4] After Sukenik's death the complete edition, containing all the plates, a transcription and a translation in Modern Hebrew, was prepared for publication by Nahman Avigad. This was followed by an English edition in 1955.[5]

A number of scholars produced annotated translations of all or part of the text.[6] Their choice of passages was governed by the state of preservation of the text but other interests also played a part. From the outset translation and interpretation of the scroll was influenced by theological interests just as much as by literary or philological ones. For example there was a great deal of interest in 1QH^a XI 6–19 [III 5–18 in Sukenik's edition] because of its supposed messianic content. At first sight the poem contrasts the mother and birth of a "wonderful counsellor with his might" (cf. Isa 9:6) with the mother and birth of a "viper." The allusion to a verse with a possible messianic interpretation sparked great speculation; some thought that the author saw himself and his community as giving birth to a Messiah. The debate about this particular composition continues to the present day, encouraged by the fact that the Hebrew is very difficult to translate. I consider this poem in chapter five.

---

[4] Eleazar L. Sukenik, מגילות גנוזות סקירה רישונה (Jerusalem: Magnes Press, 1948) 27–33, pl. 10–13; Eleazar L. Sukenik, מגילות גנוזות סקירה שנייה (Jerusalem: Magnes Press, 1950) 22–39, pl. 7–10.

[5] Eleazar L. Sukenik, *The Dead Sea Scrolls of the Hebrew University* (Jerusalem: Magnes Press, 1955).

[6] Early translations of all or most of the text were done by Bardtke, Gaster, and Dupont-Sommer. The earliest thorough commentary was by Licht, but as this was in Modern Hebrew it was probably not as widely influential as two subsequent commentaries in English. These were by Holm-Nielsen and Mansoor. Other early translators and commentators were Morawe, Carmignac, Delcor and Vermes. See Hans Bardtke, "Die Loblieder von Qumran," *TLZ* 81 (1956): 149–154, 589–604, 715–724, and *TLZ* 82 (1957): 2–19; T.H. Gaster, *The Scriptures of the Dead Sea Sect* (London: Secker & Warburg, 1956) 131–217; A. Dupont-Sommer, "Le Livre des Hymnes découvert près de la mer Morte (1QH): Traduction intégrale avec introduction et notes," *Sem* 7 (1957): 1–120; Jacob Licht, *The Thanksgiving Scroll: A Scroll from the Wilderness of Judaea. Text, Introduction, Commentary and Glossary* (Jerusalem: Bialik Institute, 1957); Holm-Nielsen, *Hodayot*; Menahem Mansoor, *The Thanksgiving Hymns: Translated and Annotated with an Introduction* (STDJ 3, Leiden; Brill, 1961); Günter Morawe, *Aufbau und Abgrenzung der Loblieder von Qumran* (TA16; Berlin: Evangelische Verlagsanstalt, 1961); Jean Carmignac, "Les hymnes," in J. Carmignac and P. Gilbert, *Les textes de Qumran, traduits et annotes* (Paris: Letouzey & Ané, 1961) I. 129–282; Matthias Delcor, *Les Hymnes de Qumran (Hodayot): Texte hébreu, introduction, traduction, commentaire* (Paris: Letouzey, 1962); Geza Vermes, *The Dead Sea Scrolls in English* (London: Pelican Books, 1962).

The early concern with philological and theological matters was soon overshadowed by the strong interest and debate concerning the author of the *Hodayot*. The romantic possibility that the *Hodayot* provided a firsthand insight into the soul of the community's founder excited many scholars. This sometimes makes it difficult to disentangle the arguments about genre, *Sitz im Leben*, and author in the secondary literature. A significant number of scholars were also excited by the possible insights which the Dead Sea manuscripts might shed on early Christianity. It has been noted more recently that this may have caused a bias in early Qumran scholarship.[7] In the case of the *Hodayot* this is most marked in studies concerning the author, and appears to be an ongoing tendency.[8]

Three form-critical studies produced by scholars at Heidelberg University have been extremely influential in the debate about author and genre. They were not the first to identify two types of composition within 1QH^a, but their work reinforced the arguments for this distinction. They distinguished between Teacher Hymns and Community Hymns, names which are now generally used for the two types of composition. Jeremias in particular argued that the former type had been written by the Teacher of Righteousness, a figure referred to in some sectarian scrolls as particularly significant in the history of the community (see §5.3 of this chapter). However it should be noted that these studies were published in a series concerned with the New Testament and that their main areas of interest were historical and theological rather than literary.[9]

---

[7] See discussion in George W.E. Nickelsburg, "Currents in Qumran Scholarship: The Interplay of Data, Agendas, and Methodology," in *The Dead Sea Scrolls at Fifty* (ed. R.A. Kugler and E.M. Schuller; Atlanta: Scholars Press, 1999), 79–99.

[8] For example, in the work of Carmignac and Dupont-Sommer and, more recently of Charlesworth. See Dupont-Sommer, "Le Livre des Hymnes;" A. Dupont-Sommer, *The Essene Writings From Qumran* (trans. G. Vermes; Oxford: Blackwell, 1961); Jean Carmignac, *Christ and the Teacher of Righteousness* (Baltimore: Helicon Press, 1962), 115–158; Jean Carmignac, "Les éléments historiques des Hymnes de Qumrân," *RevQ* 6 (1960): 205–222; James H. Charlesworth, "An Allegorical and Autobiographical Poem by the Moreh HaS-Sedeq (1QH 8:4–11)," in *Sha'arei Talmon: Studies in the Bible, Qumran and the Ancient Near East Presented to Shemaryahu Talmon* (ed. M. Fishbane and E. Tov; Winona Lake: Eisenbrauns, 1992), 295–307.

[9] As the series title Studien zur Umwelt des Neuen Testaments suggests, the primary interest of these studies was in the relationship of the Qumran scrolls to the New Testament. Jeremias concentrated on the historical figure of the Teacher and Becker and Kuhn on theological concepts. Only Kuhn's study considered exclusively

Comparatively little attention was given to the order and the prosody of the *Hodayot*, although these topics were considered more important by later scholars (see §5.4 below). With the benefit of hindsight I think that an appreciation of these basic structural factors is indispensable to a proper understanding of the compositions.

3. *The Reconstruction and Re-Ordering of 1QH^a*

Before embarking upon any further discussion of 1QH^a it is necessary to consider the ordering and numbering of the columns. All of the early studies of 1QH^a used the column and line numbers assigned in the principal edition by Sukenik. However this numbering system has now been largely superseded by that of Stegemann and Puech. Although Stegemann had proposed a re-ordering of the 1QH^a scroll in his doctoral dissertation in 1963, this had not been published and was not widely known.[10] Thus, Puech later independently arrived at a reconstruction substantially identical to that of Stegemann. It was the publication in the late eighties of a paper by Puech which changed the perception of the structure of 1QH^a and led to a gradual adoption of the Stegemann/Puech reconstruction and re-numbering of the material.[11] In this thesis the two numbering systems will be distinguished by enclosing Sukenik's numbering within square brackets.

---

the *Hodayot*. Cf. the recent comments by Nickelsburg on the emphasis on theological rather than literary questions in Qumran Scholarship. See Gert Jeremias, *Der Lehrer der Gerechtigkeit* (SUNT 2; Göttingen: Vandenhoeck and Ruprecht, 1963); Jürgen Becker, *Das Heil Gottes: Heils-und Sündenbegriffe in den Qumrantexten und im Neuen Testament* (SUNT 3; Göttingen: Vandenhoeck and Ruprecht, 1963); Heinz-Wolfgang Kuhn, *Enderwartung und gegenwärtiges Heil: Untersuchungen zu den Gemeindeliedern von Qumran* (SUNT 4; Göttingen: Vandenhoeck and Ruprecht, 1966); Nickelsburg "Currents in Qumran Scholarship," 93.

[10] For a more recent summary of Stegemann's work see Harmut Stegemann, "The Material Reconstruction of 1QHodayot," in *The Dead Sea Scrolls: Fifty Years after Their Discovery. Proceedings of the Jerusalem Congress, July 20–25, 1997* (ed. L.H. Schiffman, E. Tov, and J.C. VanderKam; Jerusalem: Israel Exploration Society in cooperation with the Shrine of the Book, Israel Museum, 2000), 272–284; Harmut Stegemann, "Methods for the Reconstruction of Scrolls from Scattered Fragments," in *Archaeology and History in the Dead Sea Scrolls: The New York University Conference in Memory of Yigael Yadin* (ed. L.H. Schiffman; JSPSup8; Sheffield: Sheffield Academic Press, 1990), 189–220.

[11] Émile Puech, "Quelques aspects de la restauration du Rouleau des Hymnes (1QH)," *JJS* 39 (1988): 38–55.

Puech first noted that 1Q35, which had long been recognised as part of the *Hodayot*, actually contained text which overlapped with that of columns [VII] and [VIII] of 1QH^a and was therefore a second manuscript, 1QH^b. This identification enabled Puech to reconstruct some missing portions of the text of these columns. Following on from the work done by Carmignac,[12] Puech then made suggestions concerning the ordering of 1QH^a itself. Doubting Carmignac's hypothesis that there were two separate scrolls, he proposed to reconstruct the material as belonging to a single scroll. He took note that, as suggested by Sukenik, the pattern of damage and the change of scribal hand could be used as a guide. Thus columns [XIII] to [XVII] should precede columns [I] to [XII]. However, Puech also noted that the identification of columns [XIII] to [XVII] as one sheet of five columns was inconsistent with the evidence that the other sheets contained only four columns each. He proposed that column [XVII] did not belong to the same sheet as columns [XIII–XVI] but had preceded them. His proposed new order was

Sheet 1 (I–IV): three lost columns + Sukenik [XVII]
Sheet 2 (V–VIII): Sukenik [XIII–XVI]
Sheet 3 (IX–XII): Sukenik [I–IV]
Sheet 4 (XIII–XVI): Sukenik [V–VIII]
Sheet 5 (XVII–XX): Sukenik [IX–XII][13]

Puech then turned his attention to the fragments. He discussed various suggestions made by Carmignac and Stegemann and gave his own suggestions for placing various fragments amongst the preceding sheets. He disagreed with Sukenik's assembly of three large fragments as column [XVIII]. Using these and some of the remaining fragments he reconstructed the final two sheets as follows:

Sheet 6 (XXI–XXIV): each col. contained parts of [XVIII] + fragments
Sheet 7 (XXV–XXVIII): various fragments[14]

There are no substantial differences between the reconstruction arrived at by Puech and the earlier work of Stegemann. Stegemann in particular went on to develop and refine his methods on other fragmentary

---

[12] Jean Carmignac, "Remarques sur le texte des hymnes de Qumrân," *Bib* 39 (1958): 139–155; Jean Carmignac, "Localisation des fragments 15, 18 et 22 des hymnes," *RevQ* 1 (1958–1959): 425–430; Jean Carmignac, "Compléments au texte des hymnes de Qumrân," *RevQ* 2 (1959–1960): 267–276, 549–558.
[13] Puech, "Quelques aspects," 43.
[14] Puech, "Quelques aspects," 48–52.

manuscripts.¹⁵ Subsequently he has frequently been consulted by editors of Qumran texts.

The reconstruction of the scroll has several major benefits. Firstly, the accurate placing of adjacent fragments has enabled more portions of meaningful text to be recovered. Secondly, this method allows the original length of the scroll to be estimated as twenty-seven or twenty-eight columns of forty-one to forty-two lines each. The average length of lines is also known. Stegemann estimates that the original scroll contained at least twenty-eight, at most thirty-four different compositions. However, his upper estimate is based on combining some sections of text which have previously been considered as separate poems.[16]

Thirdly, it is now possible to investigate the overall structure of the collection, particularly when the data from the Cave 4 manuscripts is also considered (see §4 below). For example, it is now realised that all of the compositions identified as thanksgiving psalms by Holm-Nielsen are located in the central section of 1QH^a. This group contains all of the compositions identified as Teacher Hymns by Jeremias, Becker and Kuhn and therefore strengthens the argument that they represent a distinct group by a single author.

3.1. *Excursus on Numbering Systems*

The column numbers of Puech coincide with those of Stegemann. These column numbers are now widely used, but confusingly there is less agreement over the numbering of the lines within the columns. Stegemann and Puech assigned line numbers according to their reconstruction of the original columns. These often differ from the line numbers used by Sukenik. However, there has been a tendency in recent publications to use the new column numbers but to retain the line numbers of Sukenik wherever possible.[17]

---

[15] Stegemann, "Methods," 189–220; See also Annette Steudel, "Assembling and Reconstructing Manuscripts," in *The Dead Sea Scrolls after Fifty Years* (ed. P.W. Flint and J.C. VanderKam; Leiden: Brill, 1998) 1. 516–534.
[16] Harmut Stegemann "The Number of Psalms in 1QHodayot^a and Some of Their Sections," in *Liturgical Perspectives: Prayer and Poetry in Light of the Dead Sea Scrolls. Proceedings of the Fifth International Symposium of the Orion Center for the Study of the Dead Sea Scrolls and Associated Literature, 19–23 January, 2000.* (ed. E.G. Chazon with the collaboration of R. Clements and A. Pinnick; STDJ 48; Leiden: Brill, 2003), 191–234.
[17] This policy has been adopted by, among others, García Martínez and Tigchelaar, Newsom, and Abegg. However Douglas, Schuller, Puech and Stegemann all use the new line numbers. See Florentino García Martínez and Eibert J.C. Tigchelaar, *The*

A major drawback to this practice is that in some cases it obscures valuable data arising from the reconstruction of the scroll. Of particular relevance to this study is the fact that some manuscript lines which have been lost due to damage are not accounted for by the old line numbering. Because analysis of the structure of individual poems is crucial to this study it is important to take account of these lines. By extrapolating from the average length of poetic lines I am able to estimate the number of poetic lines within lacunae.

For example, there is considerable damage to the end of the long poem in 1QH^a XII 6–XIII 6 [IV 5–V 4]. I consider this poem in chapter three. In my translation I have indicated that there are a number of missing poetic lines corresponding to damaged portions of the last three manuscript lines of column XII and the first six lines of the next column. This leads me to postulate that the poem has a short concluding sub-section, thus giving a more balanced structure to the poem.

The very existence of the first two lines of the reconstructed column XIII, possibly six poetic lines, is obscured by the numbering system of Sukenik. The impact of this can be clearly seen if, for example, one compares my translation of this poem in §3.2 of chapter three with that of Newsom. Newsom has one stanza where I discern three or more.[18] For this reason I have decided to use the numbering proposed by Stegemann throughout this study. However, for ease of comparison with other studies, I will also give the Sukenik numbering in square brackets.[19]

Dead Sea Scrolls Study Edition (2 vols.; Leiden: Brill, 1997), 146–203; Carol A. Newsom, *The Self as Symbolic Space: Constructing Identity and Community at Qumran* (STDJ 52; Leiden: Brill, 2004); Martin G. Abegg, Jr. with James E. Bowley and Edward M. Cook and in Consultation with Emanuel Tov, *The Dead Sea Scrolls Concordance, Volume 1* (Leiden: Brill, 2003); Michael C. Douglas, "Power and Praise in the Hodayot: A Literary Critical Study of 1QH 9:1–18:14" (Ph.D. diss., University of Chicago, 1998); Eileen M. Schuller, "Hodayot" in *Qumran Cave 4.XX: Poetical and Liturgical Texts, Part 2* (ed. E. Chazon et al.; DJD 29; Oxford: Clarendon, 1999), 69–254; Émile Puech, *La croyance des Esséniens en la vie future: immortalité, résurrection, vie éternelle?* (Etudes Bibliques 22. Paris: Librairie Lecoffre, J. Gabalda, 1993); Stegemann "The Number of Psalms in 1QHodayot^a".

[18] Newsom, *The Self as Symbolic Space*, 312–315. Newsom is however not unaware of the problem, as she estimates the number of missing poetic lines in another composition; op. cit., 300.

[19] A table showing the relationship between the two systems may be found in Stegemann, "The Material Reconstruction of 1QHodayot," 280.

4. *The Other Hodayot Manuscripts*

As previously mentioned, 1Q35 was eventually recognised as a separate manuscript of the *Hodayot* and designated as 1QH^b, yielding some new text. Although some commentators alluded to the fact of several Cave 4 copies as evidence of the importance of the *Hodayot* at Qumran, these manuscripts did not otherwise affect opinions on the *Hodayot* until Schuller published a preliminary description in 1993/4.[20] Schuller commented that apart from one sentence she knew of no other publication on the subject by their former editor, Strugnell.[21] In 1990 Strugnell had handed over his unpublished notes to Schuller along with responsibility to publish the principal edition of these fragments. Schuller also had the benefit of Stegemann's work, done in collaboration with Strugnell, but also unpublished. The principal edition finally appeared towards the end of 1999.[22]

The Cave 4 materials consist of over one hundred fragments from six manuscripts designated 4Q427–432 (4QH^{a-f}). Most of these are fairly small, preserving just a few letters, with only twenty-five fragments containing ten or more words. The following is a summary of the basic characteristics of the manuscripts.[23]

Manuscript	Frg. total	Palaeographical Dating
4QH^a (4Q427)	16–22	75–1 BCE (late Hasmonaean/early Herodian)
4QH^b (4Q428)	59–69	100–50 BCE (Hasmonaean)
4QH^c (4Q429)	6	late Hasmonaean/early Herodian
4QH^d (4Q430)	1	early Herodian
4QH^e (4Q431)	2	early Herodian
4QpapH^f (4Q432)	22–24	early Herodian

Most of the material overlaps with that already known from 1QH^a and has not yielded much new information. The variations between overlapping pieces of compositions within the existing manuscripts from Caves 1 and 4 are mainly orthographic and in Schuller's opinion do not show any evidence of different recensions.[24] Despite Schuller's comment that the Cave 4 material provides "limited evidence" she does

---

[20] Eileen M. Schuller, "The Cave 4 Hodayot Manuscripts: A Preliminary Description," *JQR* 85 (1994): 137–150.
[21] Schuller, "The Cave 4 Hodayot," 88 n. 6.
[22] Eileen M. Schuller, "Hodayot" in *Qumran Cave 4.XX: Poetical and Liturgical Texts, Part 2* (ed. E. Chazon et al.; DJD 29; Oxford: Clarendon, 1999), 69–254.
[23] See Schuller, "Hodayot."
[24] Schuller, "The Cave 4 Hodayot," 90.

point to some significant finds. These are the material from 4QH^a and 4QH^b yielding substantial new portions of two compositions, and the evidence derived from reconstruction of the manuscripts.[25]

The new material from 4QH^a appears to be a version of the "Self-Glorification Hymn," also attested in the very similar version in 4Q471b, and the different but related version in 4Q491c.[26] This hymn is not part of this study, but it needs to be noted that its existence in more than one form reinforces the opinion that the compositions in the *Hodayot* collections have been subject to redaction. There are also several small portions of new text from 4QH^b. However, that which has aroused the greatest interest is from fragments 9 and 10 (formerly known as frgs. 6 and 7),[27] which overlap with columns XV [VII] and XVI [VIII] of 1QH^a. It enables the significant reconstruction of a hymn.[28]

The application of reconstruction methods to the Cave 4 scrolls has also yielded valuable new data which suggests that the Cave 4 manuscripts do not contain identical collections to that of 1QH^a. Only 4QH^b appears to be of a similar order and length to 1QH^a. Schuller notes that the order of the hymns in 4QH^a is different from the order of 1QH^a. This is most clearly demonstrated by the contents of fragment 8 (formerly known as frg. 3).[29] Fragment 8 II 10–21 corresponds with the composition in 1QH^a XX 7–21 [XII 4–18]. In fragment 8 of 4QH^a this hymn is preceded by a hymn not attested in 1QH^a whereas in 1QH^a it is preceded by a hymn which is partially preserved in fragment 3 (formerly known as frgs. 2+11) of 4QH^a.[30] Also, as reconstructed, 4QH^a is shorter than 1QH^a and has no preserved text corresponding with the known contents of columns X [II]–XVIII [X] of 1QH^a. Stegemann has suggested that 4QH^a may not have contained the compositions usually referred to as Teacher Hymns. Schuller has also noted a strong doxological, liturgical element in the compositions preserved from 4QH^a, with an emphasis on the union of humans and angels in praise. She

---

[25] Schuller, "The Cave 4 Hodayot," 98.
[26] Schuller, "Hodayot," 96–108.
[27] For changes in fragment numbers of 4QH^b see Schuller, "Hodayot," 132.
[28] Eileen M. Schuller, "A Thanksgiving Hymn from 4QHodayot^b (4Q428 7)," *RevQ* 16 (1995): 527–541; É. Puech, "Restauration d'un texte hymnique a partir de trois manuscrits fragmentaires: 1QH^a xv 37–xvi 4 (vii 34–viii 3), 1Q35 (H^b) 1, 9–14, 4Q428 (H^b) 7," *RevQ* 16 (1995): 543–559; Schuller, "Hodayot," 140–144.
[29] For changes in fragment numbers of 4QH^a see Schuller, "Hodayot," 88.
[30] Schuller, "The Cave 4 Hodayot," 97; "Hodayot," 109–116.

observes that of the only three hymns in 1QH^a to contain "we" language, two are preserved in this manuscript.

4QH^c survives in six fragments giving remains of eight columns. The writing is large, and the columns are short (twelve lines) and narrow; this physical evidence suggests that the scroll was not long enough to contain as many compositions as 1QH^a. All the surviving compositions overlap with columns XIII [V] and XIV [VI] of 1QH^a. Schuller suggests it may have been a collection of Teacher Hymns.[31] There is a similar possibility with 4QpapH^f, although it also preserves the creation hymn found in column IX [I] of 1QH^a. Schuller suggests that this composition had a special character and may have been included as an introduction to the Teacher Hymns.[32]

4QH^e preserves only a single composition which coincides with one of the Community Hymns. The reconstruction of the length of the scroll again suggests that it did not contain all the compositions of 1QH^a. Possibly it was a collection of Community Hymns, though as Schuller points out, with only one surviving composition we cannot even be sure that it was a manuscript of the *Hodayot*.[33] The smaller collections are later in date than 1QH^a. This leaves open the possibility that they were extracted from a larger collection, but Schuller thinks it more likely that they are copies of two earlier collections which were combined to form the collection preserved in 1QH^a and 4QH^b.

Also included in the same DJD volume are a number of poetic fragments which are too small to identify clearly. Strugnell and Schuller examined such fragments to see whether any of them could possibly represent further *Hodayot* manuscripts. Most of them were eliminated on grounds of form, vocabulary or content (e.g. the *Hodayot* do not refer to ישראל or use the divine name). The authors concluded that the identification of the few remaining manuscripts as possibly *Hodayot* was hardly worth the effort put in.[34]

---

[31] Schuller, "The Cave 4 Hodayot," 92–93; "Hodayot," 177–194.
[32] Schuller, "The Cave 4 Hodayot," 93–94; "Hodayot," 209–232.
[33] Schuller, "The Cave 4 Hodayot," 91; "Hodayot," 201–208.
[34] John Strugnell and Eileen M. Schuller, "Further 'Hodayot' Manuscripts from Qumran?" in *Antikes Judentum und frühes Christentum: Festschrift für Harmut Stegemann* (ed. B. Kollmann, W. Reinbold, and A. Steudel; Berlin: De Gruyter, 1999) 51–72.

5. *A Survey of Significant Studies*

5.1. *Textual Studies*

The principal edition of 1QH^a remains that published by Sukenik. There are also editions of the text by Licht, Haberman, and Lohse. These however need to be supplemented by information on the reconstruction published by Puech and Stegemann. There is as yet no critical edition of the full reconstructed text. The study edition of the scrolls by García Martínez and Tigchelaar provides a useful transcription of the Hebrew text which takes account of the reconstruction work. However, the line numbering within columns mainly follows Sukenik, though this is not always possible. I have used this text for ease of reference, checking it against the other available transcriptions and against the photographic plates of the scroll as published in Sukenik and in the CD-Rom edition of the scrolls corpus.[35]

Commentaries on the text as it is found in Sukenik are provided by Licht, Holm-Nielsen and Mansoor. But no-one has produced comparable commentaries on the reconstructed scroll. While not a commentary, Puech includes much useful information about his readings of damaged text in his study of the beliefs of the Qumran Community. I have made use of all these, particularly the work of Holm-Nielsen and Puech.[36]

The principal edition of the Cave 4 manuscripts was published fairly recently in the DJD series. I also refer to earlier preliminary studies published by Schuller.[37]

5.2. *Early Views on Genre and Sitz im Leben*

The fact that so many copies were found in Cave 4 (the nearest cave to the settlement and possibly a working library) suggests that the text had an ongoing function in the life of the community; but there was

---

[35] Sukenik, *The Dead Sea Scrolls of the Hebrew University*; Licht, *The Thanksgiving Scroll*; A.M. Haberman מגילות מדבר יהודה (Tel Aviv: Machbarot Lesifruth, 1959); Eduard Lohse, *Die Texte aus Qumran: Hebräisch und Deutsch*, (Darmstadt: Kösel-Verlag, 1964); Puech, "Quelques aspects"; Stegemann, "The Material Reconstruction of 1QHodayot"; García Martínez and Tigchelaar, *The Dead Sea Scrolls Study Edition*; Timothy H. Lim in consultation with P.S. Alexander. *The Dead Sea Scrolls Electronic Reference Library, Vol. 1* (Oxford: Oxford University Press and Leiden: Brill, 1997).

[36] Licht, *The Thanksgiving Scroll*; Holm-Nielsen, *Hodayot*; Mansoor, *The Thanksgiving Hymns*; Puech, *Croyance*.

[37] Schuller, "The Cave 4 Hodayot;" Schuller, "Hodayot."

no consensus as to what that might be. The two main positions were represented by Bardtke and Holm-Nielsen.

Bardtke's examination of genre led him to the conclusion that the *Hodayot* could not be understood as examples of individual thanksgivings or laments as in the canonical Psalter. He considered that they needed to be regarded in light of other late Jewish psalmody which, although imitating the style of the canonical psalms, did not have a cultic origin. In his opinion, late Jewish psalmody was composed in Jewish wisdom circles.[38] Bardtke gave as an example 1QH ͣ XIX 6–17 [XI 3–14] which he believed summarises the ideas of the *Rule of the Community* in similar ways to a catechism. He also mentioned the individualistic use of "I" and the address to God in the second person as evidence that the psalms were meant to be recited by the individual.[39] There are undoubtedly some wisdom elements in these compositions, as the study by Tanzer shows.[40] One of the eight compositions identified by Tanzer as having strong wisdom elements is discussed by me in chapter three (see especially §2.6.1).

The main supporter of a liturgical use was Holm-Nielsen. His arguments should be seen in the context of his already expressed views on the function of late Jewish psalmody in general. He argued for a developing compositional art of psalmody connected to cultic use by analysing some late psalms which had been included in the canonical Psalter. His argument defined cult more widely than the traditional temple occasions, to include later developments in temple practice and developments outside the temple, in synagogues for example. He also argued that it is misleading to make a sharp distinction between learning and worship.[41]

Holm-Nielsen made a particular case for the connection of some of the *Hodayot* with the covenant renewal ceremony described in 1QS. Amongst other passages, he quoted "All those who are gathered in thy Covenant enquire of me" (1QH ͣ XII 24–25 [IV 23–24]) and "Thou hast made me a father to the sons of grace, and as a foster father to men of marvel" (XV 23–24 [VII 20–21]). He also quoted passages which use a

---

[38] Hans Bardtke, "Considérations sur les cantiques de Qumrân," *RB* 63 (1956): 220–233.
[39] Bardtke, "Considérations," 231, 227.
[40] Sarah Jean Tanzer, "The Sages at Qumran: Wisdom in the 'Hodayot'" (Ph.D. diss., Harvard University, 1986).
[41] Svend Holm-Nielsen, "The Importance of Late Jewish Psalmody for the Understanding of Old Testament Psalmodic Traditions," *StTh* 13 (1960): 1–53.

terminology similar to 1QS.⁴² He did not rule out instructional use but thought that this would be a secondary or subsequent use and not the primary one.

Murphy-O'Connor notes that both Becker and Kuhn distinguished the *Sitz im Leben* of the Community Hymns from that of the individual thanksgivings. Becker considered that the Community Hymns were part of the daily prayers and liturgies of the community. Kuhn identified the key formal elements of the Community Hymns as a "soteriological confession" and a "meditation on misery" and hence connected them to the annual covenant renewal ceremony. He reclassified 1QH^a XI 20–37 [III 19–36] as a Community Hymn (see discussion in chapter five).⁴³

Apart from those cited above, the overwhelming impression given by most scholars regarding the *Sitz im Leben* was one of confusion and inconsistency. Their arguments tended to be obscured by their interest in other aspects such as the authorship of the hymns. By a close reading of selected compositions I hope to gain some insight into how a reader may have interpreted them, and hence into their possible *Sitz im Leben*. For a discussion of the contribution of Kittel and Nitzan to this debate see §5.5 below.

5.3. *Author*

As already noted in §2, studies by Jeremias, Becker and Kuhn sought to distinguish between Teacher Hymns and Community Hymns. Their lists, though overlapping, were not identical and were arrived at by differing criteria. All the poems included in the three lists of Teacher Hymns come from the group identified by Holm-Nielsen as "thanksgiving psalms" and by Morawe as "Danklieder."⁴⁴ The publication of these three studies reinforced on form critical grounds the conclusions of Morawe and Holm-Nielsen that the *Hodayot* can be divided into two distinct groups. Most scholars have since worked with this basic assumption, the two groups commonly being referred to as the Teacher

---

⁴² Holm-Nielsen, *Hodayot*, 328, 344.

⁴³ Becker, *Das Heil Gottes*, 126–128; Kuhn, *Enderwartung*, 29–33, cited in Jerome Murphy O'Connor, "The Judean Desert," in *Early Judaism and its Modern Interpreters* (ed. R.A. Kraft and G.W.E. Nickelsburg; Atlanta: Scholars Press, 1986), 119–156.

⁴⁴ Jeremias, *Der Lehrer*; Becker, *Das Heil Gottes;* Kuhn, *Enderwartung*; Holm-Nielsen, *Hodayot;* Morawe, *Aufbau*.

Hymns and the Community Hymns, while begging the question of any implications these titles might have regarding authorship or *Sitz im Leben*.

Davies put forward a new option regarding the author of the *Hodayot*. He dismissed the possibility of establishing the identity of the author or authors in favour of the more realistic option of establishing "the beliefs of the compilers, readers and users about their content."[45] In Davies' opinion it was likely that the Qumran community believed that the *Hodayot* had been written by the Teacher of Righteousness. In support of this tendency to link compositions to the life of a significant person he used the attribution of the psalms to David at Qumran.[46] Furthermore, he set out to show that the pesharim were dependent on the *Hodayot* and that therefore any correspondence between them could not be taken as evidence of historical reliability (see my discussion in §3.6.1 of chapter three). The importance of Davies' work is that he has demonstrated the flimsy foundations upon which the theory of the Teacher's authorship rests. However, if the situation was indeed similar to the attribution of the psalms to David then one wonders why no allusion to the Teacher's writing activities comparable to those for David have come to light.

More recently, Michael Douglas has reopened the debate on authorship with an examination of the literary evidence for the authorship of the Teacher Hymns.[47] His study falls into three parts. In the first instance he seeks to show by means of literary analysis that there is a block of poems within 1QH^a which were composed by a single author. Starting with a distinctive phrase found in several of the compositions, he identifies a substantial number of similarities between some of the poems. His argument is that these literary affinities are evidence for a block of poems which had a single author.

Next Douglas argues that the poems would have been understood by the readers, and thus meant by the author, as representing the leadership claims of a particular individual. In my opinion he does not distinguish clearly between the author and the implied speaker of the texts. I also consider that the possibility of discerning an author's intention

---

[45] Philip R. Davies, *Behind the Essenes* (Brown Judaic Studies 94; Atlanta: Scholars Press, 1987), 88.
[46] Davies, *Behind the Essenes*, 89–90.
[47] Michael C. Douglas, "Power and Praise in the Hodayot: A Literary Critical Study of 1QH 9:1–18:14" (Ph.D. diss., University of Chicago, 1998).

is more problematical than Douglas suggests. I discuss these concepts in chapter two. Both Davies (discussed above) and Newsom (see below) have offered alternative perspectives on the leadership claims of these poems.

Finally, Douglas argues that the author was not just an unidentified individual leader but that he was the Teacher of Righteousness. Using these poems and the pesharim he constructs a possible historical scenario and correlates this with a model of social conflict developed by V. Turner.[48] He considers that this supports his view that the poems reflect "social reality."[49] He further argues that Turner's model applies to the early phase of the movement and not to a later institutionalized phase. He thus identifies the implied speaker as the Teacher of Righteousness and not some other later leader.

This is a very impressive and significant major literary study of a large portion of the *Hodayot* compositions. The purpose and focus of Douglas is different from mine and I find his arguments about authorship unconvincing. I remain agnostic about the possibility and value of investigating the author(s) of the *Hodayot*. However, Douglas' literary observations are detailed and illuminating; they have provided the main source of comparison by which to measure my own analyses.

A very different view from that of Douglas is put forward in a recently published study of the *Hodayot* by Carol Newsom. I discuss her main arguments in §5.6 below. Newsom devotes several pages to a discussion of the arguments about the author and implied speaker of the Teacher Hymns. Her position is that it is not possible from the available evidence to either prove or disprove that these poems refer primarily to the Teacher of Righteousness. She proposes instead that they present a "leadership myth" which applied to whoever was the current leader of the community. The conclusions of my study lend weight to this position.[50]

---

[48] Victor Turner, *Schism and Continuity in an African Society* (Manchester: Manchester University Press, 1957); "Social Dramas and Stories about Them," in *On Narrative* (ed. W.J.T. Mitchell; Chicago: University of Chicago Press, 1981), 137–164.
[49] Douglas, "Power and Praise," 344.
[50] Newsom, *The Self as Symbolic Space*, 287–300.

5.4. *Prosody*

Most of the early commentaries concentrated more on the content than on the style of the compositions. In general they judged the poetry to be inferior to that of the biblical psalms. Licht, for example, commented that the scroll "does not seem to possess any high degree of literary merit. It is also very repetitive, to the point of monotony."[51] During the nineteen-fifties and sixties very few individual studies were produced on the poetic style of these compositions. This is possibly to be attributed to the assumption that they were to be understood in terms of the conventions of biblical poetry. Vast quantities of ink were used in deliberating upon the theological ideas they contained; little consideration was given to the possibility that an appreciation of the medium might contribute to an understanding of the message.

A second consideration which, although noted by Cross, did not at the time excite interest was that these poems might offer an opportunity for a better understanding of the development of Hebrew poetic techniques in the late Second Temple period.[52] The earliest specific study of the prosody of these poems was produced by Kraft, a scholar with a background in the study of the canonical psalms; he did see the *Hodayot* as valuable in tracing the development of late canonical poetry. He based his study on a selection of the best preserved and delineated compositions.[53] Kraft found that the compositions did not conform to his expectations about metre and parallelism drawn from studies of biblical poetry. He found that the metre varied so much that he described it as "metrical chaos" and wondered whether the poet considered metre to be of "no consequence." He also found a "freedom in the use of

---

[51] Licht, "The Doctrine of the Thanksgiving Scroll," 1.

[52] Frank Moore Cross, *The Ancient Library of Qumran and Modern Biblical Studies* (Garden City, NY: Doubleday, 1958, 1961), 122. See also James H. Charlesworth, "A Prolegomenon to a New Study of the Jewish Background of the Hymns and Prayers in the New Testament," *JJS* 33 (1982): 1–21.

[53] 1QH^a X 22–32 [II 20–30], XI 20–37 [III 19–36], XII 6–39 [IV 5–38], XIII 7–21 [V 5–19], XV 29–36 [VII 26–32], XIX 6–17 [XI 3–14]; five of these compositions were also chosen by Kittel for her study; see her discussion of Kraft's observations. Charles F. Kraft, "Poetic Structure in the Qumran Thanksgiving Psalms," *BR* 2 (1957) 1–18; Kittel, *The Hymns of Qumran*, 15–17.

parallelism" with "no rigid rules cramping one's style."[54] Kittel has criticised Kraft's work for imposing a parallelism which is not justified by the Hebrew.[55]

Carmignac was less inclined to impose upon the compositions ideas from biblical poetry. Organising his study in ascending size of unit, he considered first the stich then the couplet and finally the strophe. Using parallelism, rhyme, repetition, etc. to identify the stich, he recognised that unlike biblical poetry, where the stich was usually two or three words, the *Hodayot* contained stichoi of up to seven words. Carmignac also observed that although three-stich couplets were common, the poems employed longer combinations of four, five, seven or eight stichoi. Exceptionally even eleven or fourteen could be used, as in 1QH[a] XIX 13–17 [XI 10–14] and XX 6–12 [XII 3–9]. For delineating the strophes he used spaces left by the scribe as clues; he also noted that new units often began with an independent pronoun.[56]

Thiering also studied the compositions. Perhaps even more than Carmignac she was prepared to depart from the Old Testament model. She noted that when judged by such standards an impression was given of "very poor poetry characterised by irregular metre, rather weak use of parallelism, frequent and monotonous repetition of words, and the apparent absence of any firm principle of construction."[57]

Unlike previous commentators who had judged the poetry to be free form, Thiering believed that her study had shown evidence that they were in fact "more formally constructed than most OT poetry." She took as her starting point that very repetition of words which others had judged to be monotonous and based her study upon identifying the repetition of particular words in order to identify chiastic and chain structures. I believe that Thiering was correct in her observation that the repetition of words was a significant structural device. However, she overemphasised its significance and did not sufficiently pay attention to the other indications of structure, such as parallelism and the use of independent pronouns. Thus, for example, she missed the stanza divisions of the poem in 1QH[a] X 22–32 [II 20–30] which had been noted by both Kraft and Carmignac.[58]

---

[54] Kraft, "Poetic Structure," 16–17.
[55] Kittel, *The Hymns of Qumran*, 15–16.
[56] Jean Carmignac, "Étude sur les procédés poétiques des Hymnes," *RevQ* 2 (1959–1960): 515–532.
[57] Barbara Thiering, "The Poetic Forms of the Hodayot," *JSS* 8 (1963): 189–209.
[58] Noted in Kittel, *The Hymns of Qumran*, 19.

In 1981 Kittel published a groundbreaking study of the poetic techniques used in the *Hodayot*.[59] Unlike previous authors whose background had led them to analyse the poetry in terms and categories drawn from the study of canonical poetry, Kittel tried to approach the text with as few presuppositions as possible. In order to be able to analyse the overall structure of complete compositions Kittel chose eight compositions whose beginning and endings could be established with certainty.[60] For each composition she provided a transcription of the Hebrew set out into poetic lines and stanzas and a translation reflecting her observations on the prosody. She then gave a detailed description and analysis of the poetic devices upon which her layout was based. She concluded each analysis with observations on theology and imagery, including any relevant comments on genre etc.

Kittel started with the recognised techniques of canonical poetry including parallelism, lists, repetition and chiasm, and the use of strategically placed independent pronouns and particles. Because of the common use of series of infinitive phrases in other sectarian documents, she judged that this would also be a useful indicator of possible units within a composition.[61] Regarding the use of metre, Kittel concluded that whatever metrical system the compositions employed remained unknown and she instead used a system of counting syllables based on the vocalisations of Lohse and Haberman.[62] Although she recognised that any such count could only be approximate, it enabled Kittel to assess whether the poetic units she proposed displayed a "rhythmical balance."[63]

For most of the poems which she analysed Kittel observed that, as far as the overall structure and rhythmical balance was concerned, the opening formula and opening stanza were set apart from the main body of the composition; she likened this to an antiphon. The opening formula was followed by four lines introduced by the particle כי giving the reason for thanksgiving. The verb was usually in the second person masculine singular with a first person object. The structure of this

---

[59] Kittel, *The Hymns of Qumran*.
[60] X 22–32 [II 20–30]; XI 20–37 [III 19–36]; XIII 7–21 [V 5–19]; XV 9–28 [VII 6–25]; XV 29–36 [VII 26–33]; XVII 38–XVIII 14 [IX 37–X 12]; XIX 6–17 [XI 3–14]; VI 19–33 [XIV 8–22]. See Kittel, *The Hymns of Qumran*, 26.
[61] Kittel, *The Hymns of Qumran*, 28.
[62] Eduard Lohse, *Die Texte aus Qumran: Hebräisch und Deutsch* (Darmstadt: Kösel-Verlag, 1964); Haberman, מגילות מדבר יהודה.
[63] Kittel, *The Hymns of Qumran*, 30.

opening stanza was similar to the openings of the biblical psalms.[64] The opening stanza was rarely balanced by a closing stanza.[65]

Although the opening stanza usually exhibited a fairly standard parallelism the main body of each poem had a much freer structure. A number of different poetic devices and structures were employed and Kittel found no evidence of any single dominant pattern.[66] As well as parallelism between two or three lines, the compositions also employed parallelism within a line. They also used an "envelope form" consisting of four lines, the inner two of which were parallel. Other devices used included lists and series of infinitive clauses.[67] Overall structural devices included chiasms and inclusios and the use of thematic link words.[68] As others had noted, the compositions employed longer line lengths than biblical poetry. Kittel observed that a standard line consisted of between nine to thirteen syllables. A shorter and a longer line length were also used as well as a "double line" at strategic points.[69]

A limitation of Kittel's study, which she herself noted, was that the eight poems she studied were all shorter ones. She recognised that the longer poems might differ in style.[70] I have included two of these longer poems in my study (see chapter two and chapter four). I have indeed found that the structure of these poems differs somewhat from the shorter ones. However, many of Kittel's observations at verse and stanza level have been confirmed by my study.

A more recent study by Williams gives a line by line analysis of the parallelism in the well-preserved portions of 1QH^a. I have found some of his observations helpful in determining line and verse divisions. However, as the scope of Williams' study does not include a consideration of the overall structure of compositions the points of comparison are limited.[71]

---

[64] Kittel, *The Hymns of Qumran*, 155–158; see also 56, 86, 101, 171.
[65] Kittel, *The Hymns of Qumran*, 103; see page 44 for an example of a closing stanza.
[66] Kittel, *The Hymns of Qumran*, 28.
[67] Kittel, *The Hymns of Qumran*, 59f.
[68] Kittel, *The Hymns of Qumran*, 37, 77ff, 103f.
[69] Kittel, *The Hymns of Qumran*, 172, 45. For examples of "double line" see op. cit., 42, 92.
[70] Kittel, *The Hymns of Qumran*, 155.
[71] Gary Roye Williams, "Parallelism in the Hodayot from Qumran" (Ph.D. diss., Annenberg Research Institute, 1991).

5.5. *Genre and* Sitz im Leben *Revisited*

Apart from its intrinsic interest Kittel believed that analysis of poetic structure could shed light on other questions concerning the *Hodayot*. Her book is in many ways an implicit criticism of those who attempt to extract theological, historical or other information from these compositions without regard to poetic structure.[72] Of the eight compositions analysed by Kittel, four had been categorised by Holm-Nielsen as hymns and four as thanksgiving psalms. Kittel considered that her analysis supported Holm-Nielsen's categorisation. She found that, of the eight compositions, the hymns shared certain poetic features not present in the others. She referred to the fact that they tended not to combine verb forms in a single line, their use of lists and the rhythmic stability of the lines.[73]

Regarding the possible *Sitz im Leben* of these compositions, Kittel made plain from the start that she believed her study supported Holm-Nielsen's view that at least some of the compositions had a cultic function.[74] In fact she quoted Holm-Nielsen quite extensively. Kittel also agreed with Holm-Nielsen regarding the authorship of the *Hodayot*. Her criticisms of the "circular argument" of those who suppose the author to be the Teacher of Righteousness are quite scathing. She favoured the view that the "I" of the thanksgiving psalms could have been understood as referring to the whole community.[75] For example, regarding 1QH^a X 22–32 [II 20–30], she commented that the view of Carmignac and Delcor that this was a biographical poem "deprives the poem of its power and theological insight." In her view the poet universalises his experience by the use of apocalyptic imagery. The contrast between "I" and "they," the poet's enemies, is a key structural device of the poem, which is also capable of universal appropriation.[76] It is my opinion that Kittel's study demonstrates the importance of poetic analysis for a proper understanding of the meaning and function of these compositions.

The debate about *Sitz im Leben* had subsided for a while. However, a large number of further poetic and liturgical texts were steadily being

---

[72] See, for example, Kittel's comments about whether the *Hodayot* contain the concept of immortality in Kittel, *The Hymns of Qumran*, 78.
[73] Kittel, *The Hymns of Qumran*, 165.
[74] Kittel, *The Hymns of Qumran*, 4–5.
[75] Kittel, *The Hymns of Qumran*, 9–10, n. 7.
[76] Kittel, *The Hymns of Qumran*, 46–47.

published. This enlarged corpus allowed a wider perspective on the *Hodayot*. In the context of a study of most of the poetic texts published by 1990, Nitzan took a fresh look at the *Sitz im Leben* of the *Hodayot*. She devoted the final section of her book to a "confrontation" between the *Hodayot* and prayer texts from Qumran. In it she put forward a formidable list of comparisons with some of the recently published liturgical texts to support her argument that the *Hodayot* were not intended for use as fixed prayers.[77] Firstly, she observed that many of the liturgical texts included rubrics indicating their specific function, or headings indicating the days for which they were intended.[78] She then drew the conclusion that the custom at Qumran was to identify in a work its intended function or the occasion for its use. She argued that since 1QH^a appears not to contain such information it must instead have been intended for individual use.[79] She went on to discuss differences in form and content under the headings of formal characteristics, contents and prosody.

Regarding formal characteristics, she had sought in the previous chapters of her book to demonstrate that in general the liturgical texts exhibit "order, model, pattern, and formula." She observed that, although the poems in the *Hodayot* begin with the formula "I thank you, O Lord" or "Blessed be you, O Lord," they then do not follow any standard model or pattern; they do not exhibit any liturgical characteristics, such as formal ritual recitation, concluding blessing, or liturgical response.[80] Regarding the contents, she considered that the *Hodayot* reflect specific situations and theology; in contrast, liturgical texts tend to be more general in nature expressing religious ideas and identity developed over generations. In this respect she seems to have adopted the assumption of Licht that the compositions reflect the experiences of an individual.[81] However she made no reference to studies which differentiate between the Teacher and Community Hymns.

---

[77] Bilhah Nitzan, *Qumran Prayer and Religious Poetry* (Leiden: Brill, 1994), 320–355.

[78] Nitzan's examples of the former included the covenant ceremony in 1QS I 16–II 25, the Ritual of Marriage (4Q502) and the Ritual of Purification (4Q512); her examples of the latter included the Prayers for the Festivals (4Q507–509) and Songs of the Sabbath Sacrifice (4Q400–407; 11QShirShabb). See Nitzan, *Qumran Prayer*, 321 nn. 1–3.

[79] Nitzan, *Qumran Prayer*, 321.

[80] Nitzan, *Qumran Prayer*, 323–324.

[81] Nitzan, *Qumran Prayer*, 326 n. 17.

Nitzan also referred to the polemical nature and sectarian identity of the *Hodayot*. In her opinion this differentiates them from the liturgical texts from Qumran which do not distinguish between different kinds of Jew but tend to express themselves in terms of the national and religious identity of Israel. She quoted as examples of non-polemical works the *Words of the Luminaries* (4Q504–506) and the *Festival Prayers* (4Q507–509).[82] However, as Chazon has pointed out, Nitzan failed to take into account the possible non-sectarian provenance of these texts. Chazon further argued that some prayer texts do indeed express sectarian sentiments.[83]

Nitzan also considered that the long speculative and theoretical theological sections contained within the *Hodayot* differentiate them from the prayer texts. This accords with her earlier statement that, the expression of the particular world view of the authors had led to the conversion of the biblical thanksgiving genre into the "theoretical-didactic poem" represented by the contents of the *Hodayot*. She also referred to the compositions as "apocalyptic-mystic thanksgiving songs"[84] in which the biblical expression of thanks for deliverance from tangible physical difficulties had been developed to include subjective, theological and mystical themes.

Regarding the style of the poetry, Nitzan accepted that research such as Kittel's has shown that the *Hodayot* are "first and foremost poetic creations."[85] In contrast she stated that most of the prayer texts are written mainly in metric prose and that the poetic sections are characterised by a simple rhythm.[86] She also contrasted the *Hodayot* and prayer texts according to the type of descriptive language used. In the *Hodayot* extensive use is made of metaphors and strong imagery often combined in a complicated way, whereas the prayer texts use much simpler language.[87]

However, Nitzan did not distinguish at all between possible categories in the *Hodayot*, some of which might be closer to her criteria for prayer texts. To support her claim that the *Hodayot* are more com-

---

[82] Nitzan, *Qumran Prayer*, 328–329.
[83] Esther Chazon, "Review: B. Nitzan, *Qumran Prayer and Religious Poetry*," *DSD* 2 (1995): 361–365.
[84] Nitzan, *Qumran Prayer*, 28–29.
[85] Nitzan, *Qumran Prayer*, 345.
[86] Nitzan, *Qumran Prayer*, 344–348.
[87] Nitzan, *Qumran Prayer*, 348–354.

plicated rhythmically, Nitzan referred to Carmignac and Kittel's observations about length of poetic lines, etc. Although in a footnote she referred to more rhythmic units noted by Licht, she did not take note of Kittel's observation that the hymn type is characterised by a more stable rhythm.[88] Nitzan gave several examples which illustrate her opinion that the *Hodayot* employ elaborate language. However they are all examples of the thanksgiving psalm type drawn from columns X [II] to XIII [V]. It is likely that her contrast would seem less marked if she had chosen examples from the hymn type.

To summarise, Nitzan certainly highlighted some distinct differences between the *Hodayot* and other texts which are recognisably liturgical. The main weakness of her argument was in assuming that the *Hodayot* is a uniform collection. Holm-Nielsen, Kuhn and Kittel had already shown this not to be the case. The evidence from Cave 4 for different collections, published after Nitzan's study, now adds further support to their view. I intend in this study to add further evidence concerning the diversity of these poems. In addition, as Chazon pointed out, Nitzan may also have assumed too great a uniformity within the prayer texts, in particular that they were all of sectarian origin.[89]

5.6. *A New and Distinctive Approach by Carol Newsom*

In chapter two, in a brief discussion of the reader-oriented approach to texts, I refer to an article by Carol Newsom. In this article she argued that the *Hodayot* contributed to the shaping of a distinctive sectarian identity.[90] Newsom has now expanded upon her ideas in a book, which came too late for me to comment upon in my original thesis. As Newsom's book represents a significantly new approach to reading the *Hodayot*, I welcome the opportunity to discuss it here.[91]

Newsom devotes two extensive chapters to analysis of passages from the *Hodayot*. She includes four of the five compositions considered in detail by my study. The long poem analysed by me in chapter four is not covered by Newsom, but she does analyse another long poem upon which I comment briefly in that chapter. I will discuss Newsom's

---

[88] Nitzan, *Qumran Prayer*, 344 n. 59; Kittel, *The Hymns of Qumran*, 165.
[89] Chazon, "Review: B. Nitzan, Qumran Prayer and Religious Poetry."
[90] Carol A. Newsom, "The Case of the Blinking I," *Semeia* 57 (1992): 13–23.
[91] Carol A. Newsom, *The Self as Symbolic Space: Constructing Identity and Community at Qumran*, (Leiden: Brill, 2004).

observations about specific compositions in the relevant chapters. In the rest of this section I will discuss her general approach and its similarities to and differences from that of my own.

Newsom's study analyses selected passages from the *Rule of the Community* and the *Hodayot*. But, unlike the studies I have already mentioned, Newsom's primary interest is not in author, genre or *Sitz im Leben*. Her stated objective is "to model a way of reading the sectarian texts that draws attention to how the discourse of the community creates an alternative figured world and self-identity, thereby critically engaging other forms of contemporary Judaism."[92]

Newsom utilises ideas from discourse analysis to investigate how the Qumran community created itself within, and distinguished itself from, the wider social context of Second Temple Judaism. As the title of her book suggests she argues that "the self emerges as a particularly productive symbolic space in the sectarian world."[93] Some major influences on her work are Mikhail Bakhtin, Michel Foucault and Kenneth Burke.[94]

Her assumption is that, whatever their *Sitz im Leben* may have been, the sectarian texts contributed significantly to the formation of community members. She considers that the *Rule of the Community* was probably "a guide for the community's teacher, the Maskil" and that its "function has more to do with formation than information."[95] Her working hypothesis for the *Sitz im Leben* of the *Hodayot* is adopted from Reike; she conjectures that hodayot were recited at communal meals in a similar way to the description by Philo of hymns sung by the Therapeutae.[96]

---

[92] Newsom, *The Self as Symbolic Space*, 21.

[93] Newsom, *The Self as Symbolic Space*, 19.

[94] Mikhail M. Bakhtin, *The Dialogic Imagination* (trans. Caryl Emerson and Michael Holquist. Vol. 1, University of Texas Press Slavic Series; Austin, TX:University of Texas Press, 1981); Kenneth Burke, *Language as Symbolic Action: Essays on Life, Literature, and Method* (Berkeley, CA: University of California Press, 1966); *A Rhetoric of Motives* (Berkeley, CA: University of California Press, 1969); *The Rhetoric of Religion: Studies in Logology* (Berkeley, CA: University of California Press, 1970); Michel Foucault, *Discipline and Punish: The Birth of the Prison*. (Trans. Alan Sheridan. New York: Random House, 1995); "Technologies of the Self" in *Technologies of the Self: A Seminar with Michel Foucault* (eds. Luther H. Martin, Huck Gutman and Patrick H. Hutton; London: Tavistock, 1988), 16–63.

[95] Newsom, *The Self as Symbolic Space*, 102–103.

[96] Newsom notes that Reike's theory applied to the Community Hymns. She is less explicit about the Teacher Hymns but seems to assume that they had a similar *Sitz im Leben* but were recited by a leader of the community. See Bo Reike, "Remarques sur l'histoire de la form (Formgeschichte) des textes de Qumran," in *Les manuscrits de la mer Morte: Colloque de Strasbourg 25–27 Mai 1955* (ed. Jean Daniélou;. Paris: Paris University Press, 1957), 38–44; Newsom, *The Self as Symbolic Space*, 202–203.

Further, Newsom considers that the *Hodayot* was possibly "a collection of models for oral performance."[97] She suggests that the composition and recitation of such prayers was part of the "practices, utterances, and symbolic enactments" contributing to the "formation of subjectivity at Qumran." Newsom defines subjectivity as "the culturally specific ways in which the meaning of one's self is produced, experienced, and articulated."[98]

In common with most scholars, Newsom identifies two main categories of hodayot, the Community Hymns and the Teacher Hymns. She considers these two categories separately for their effect upon the sectarian reader. Newsom also considers that the category of Community Hymns is not a homogeneous collection. She singles out a subset of five hymns which possibly refer to the Maskil.[99] Even so, she understands the "I" of all these poems as representing an ordinary community member. To explain this she distinguishes between the character of the Maskil, represented in these poems as an ordinary sectarian, and his particular leadership responsibilities.

While giving due weight to the possibility that certain of the compositions may refer to a particular historical leader, she is more convinced by the possibility that they refer to the leadership office rather than to a particular individual. She thus calls them the "Hodayot of the leader" rather than the Teacher Hymns. I have also set out to study the poems without making assumptions about their authorship or the identity of the implied speaker. This makes my position much closer to Newsom's than to that of Douglas, who argues that a subset of the *Hodayot* were indeed composed by and refer to the Teacher of Righteousness.[100]

---

[97] Newsom gives as an example of a similar phenomenon the construction of a personal story in an Alcoholics Anonymous meeting, citing Dorothy Holland. See Newsom, *The Self as Symbolic Space*, 203; Dorothy Holland et al., *Identity and Agency in Cultural Worlds* (Cambridge, MA: Harvard University Press, 1998), 66.

[98] Newsom, *The Self as Symbolic Space*, 192, 195.

[99] 1QH^a V 18 [XIII 1], VII 14 [XV 11], XX 7 [XII 4], XXV 10 [frg.] all include the phrase "to/for the Maskil." Newsom notes Puech's suggestion that they may be section headings rather than headings for particular compositions. She also suggests that 1QH^a VI 19–33 [XIV 8–22] "describes responsibilities that the Serek ha-Yahad assigns to the Maskil" See Newsom, *The Self as Symbolic Space*, 198.

[100] Douglas, "Power and Praise," 7–8.

5.6.1. *Community Hymns*

In a chapter entitled "What do Hodayot do?" Newsom offers readings of several Community Hymns.[101] Drawing upon the work of Emile Benveniste and Kaja Silverman, Newsom argues that when a reader (the "spoken subject") hears or recites one of these poems he is implicitly invited to identify with the "I" (the "subject of speech") of the poem. This process of identification ("suture") encourages the formation of a particular sectarian "self."[102] This self is constituted both in relation to God (the vertical axis) and in relation to others (the horizontal axis).

In her discussion of the vertical axis, Newsom focuses upon the frequent declaration "I know" in the *Hodayot*. This phrase is usually qualified in some way to indicate that the speaker's knowledge is given by God. But Newsom points out that the knowing self thus formed is also the object of knowledge, speaking about its own nothingness in relation to God. In the very act of speaking what he knows, the speaker experiences himself as a created being incapable of understanding. Newsom had already noted this paradoxical experience in her analysis of the Maskil's hymn found in 1QS IX 12–XI 22. She describes this experience as "the cultivation of the masochistic sublime." Since this appears to be a key concept in Newsom's understanding of the *Hodayot* it is worth quoting her description in full.

> Reciting the hymn creates a vertiginous experience that might well be described as the cultivation of the masochistic sublime. The positive pleasure of seeing oneself as constituted and destined for heavenly reward by means of the overwhelming power and mercy of God is grasped and intensified precisely by perceiving and articulating one's natural human sinfulness and loathsomeness.[103]

Newsom has selected for her prime examples of this effect three poems that, following Tanzer and Merrill, I also link together in my study. These are 1QH^a VII 28–37 [XV 15–24], V 18–39 [XIII 1–22], and IX 9–36 [I 7–34]. Tanzer linked these poems because of their wisdom content and Merrill because of their theme of creation and predestination. Newsom only notes these features in passing. However, I suggest that the subjective crisis that she describes can also be viewed as

---

[101] Not all of the poems Newsom includes are undisputed Community Hymns.
[102] Emile Benveniste, *Problems in General Linguistics* (trans. Mary Elizabeth Meek; Miami Linguistics Series 8; Coral Gables, FL: University of Miami, 1971), 217–230; Kaja Silverman, *The Subject of Semiotics* (New York: Oxford University Press, 1983), 45–53, 194–201; cited in Newsom, *The Self as Symbolic Space*, 198–199.
[103] Newsom, *The Self as Symbolic Space*, 173.

a manifestation of the theological tension between predestination and responsibility; I discuss the possible exegesis and consequent theological tension of these poems in chapter three.

In one final short example of the vertical axis, 1QH^a XVII 38–XVIII 14 [IX 38–X 12], Newsom turns her attention to the form of rhetorical question which implies an answer in the negative; Burke calls this an "is not" construction and Newsom refers to it as "creation through negation."[104] Such rhetorical questions also occur in the previous three poems and in the Maskil's poem in 1QS IX 12–XI 22. Although she does not explicitly state it, these questions seem to be the quintessential expression of Newsom's "masochistic sublime."

In Newsom's own words, "The more the negative of the self is insisted upon, the more the self is grasped as the site of divine activity." She states that this experience of God leads on to a realisation of God's power in the cosmos.[105] However, in chapter three I argue that an almost reverse process can be detected in the previous three poems considered by Newsom; the realisation of God as creator leads to an experience of one's own nothingness. Newsom describes the self characterised by this internal conflict as unstable. She then goes on to discuss three poems which externalise the conflict, astutely observing that this produces a much more stable sense of self.[106]

In discussing the horizontal axis Newsom focuses on three compositions of conflict and deliverance, 1QH^a X 22–32 [II 20–30], XI 2–19 [III 1–18] and XI 20–37 [III 19–36]. Newsom acknowledges that it is disputed whether these are Community Hymns or Teacher Hymns, but includes them here because she considers that they "address the problem of the formation of sectarian subjectivity."[107] This suggests to me that the compositions can be categorised in a variety of ways, depending upon the reader's interests. In chapter five of my study I examine two of these hymns from yet another perspective and come to the conclusion that the categories of Teacher Hymns and Community Hymns are inadequate to encompass all the facets of these poems.

In her discussion of these three poems Newsom concentrates much more on the use of image and allusion. There is thus some common

---

[104] Burke *Language as Symbolic Action*, 469–479; *Rhetoric of Religion*, 17–23, 273–316 cited in Newsom, *The Self as Symbolic Space*, 232 n. 57.
[105] Newsom, *The Self as Symbolic Space*, 230–231.
[106] Newsom, *The Self as Symbolic Space*, 240.
[107] Newsom, *The Self as Symbolic Space*, 233.

ground between our observations. However, Newsom does not do equal justice to all the images and allusions in the poems, concentrating upon those which add weight to her argument. I therefore differ from Newsom in my identification of their main emphasis. Nevertheless, I consider that our readings are complementary rather than mutually exclusive.

A summary does not do justice to Newsom's detailed and cumulative arguments. However, the main thrust of her observations on these three poems seems to be that the speaker understands himself to be situated within a cosmic conflict in which his enemies are identical with the enemies of God. Newsom comments that in 1QH^a X 22–32 [II 20–30] the speaker is characterised as a passive battleground rather than as an agent in the battle. However, Newsom observes that this externalisation of the negative temporarily relieves the internal conflict she had described earlier. She identifies the crisis in 1QH^a XI 2–19 [III 1–18] and XI 20–37 [III 19–36] as being instead an anxiety over the similarity between the righteous and the wicked.[108]

This leads Newsom to a consideration of the moral discourse of the *Hodayot*, using 1QH^a IV 29–37 [XVII 17–25] as an example. Newsom considers how the *Hodayot* uses the same moral language as the dominant Second Temple discourse but gives it a new meaning within the context of a "predestined drama." This arises from the "perfecting"[109] of the idea of divine sovereignty. In particular she considers that, because the righteousness of the individual is dependent upon the graciousness of God rather than upon his own autonomous moral agency, the term righteousness has been "reaccented" with the non-traditional meaning of "acts of grace."

Newsom argues that this distinctive use of language is a powerful polemical tool for shaping an identity which is estranged from the dominant discourse. She illustrates this re-accentuation of traditional language by comparison with Ps 119 and Sir 15:11–16. She notes that Psalm 119 speaks of being humbled, but that the speaker assumes that he has the power within himself to perform moral acts, rather than attributing these to God. She states that Sir 15:11–16 appears to go even further in explicitly making a case for humankind's free moral

---

[108] Newsom, *The Self as Symbolic Space*, 241.
[109] Newsom borrows this term from Burke, meaning taking a concept to its logical conclusion. See Newsom, *The Self as Symbolic Space*, 267; Burke, *Language as Symbolic Action*, 16–20.

choice. She argues that the sectarian use of language, which attributes righteousness and choice to God alone, "stakes out the moral high ground of humility" making other discourses seem seriously wanting to the sectarian mind.[110]

Newsom's point is, in my opinion, a very valid one. The subtle distinctions in meaning attributed to words by a community undoubtedly shape identity. This is a view that she ably argues in chapter two of her book. She also makes it clear that here she is using these passages for illustrative purposes only, and that a sectarian reader would undoubtedly have read Psalm 119 through the interpretive lens of his own community's conventions.[111] She has of course chosen passages which best illustrate the comparison she is trying to make. On the other hand, in chapter three I compare the view of predestination in the *Hodayot* with a different passage from Ben Sira and question whether the theological contrast is as marked as it seems at first sight.

In her discussion of this poem, 1QH^a IV 29–37 [XVII 17–25], and of her final example of the chapter, 1QH^a VI 19–33 [XIV 8–22], Newsom refers back to her discussion of 1QH^a VII 28–37 [XV 15–24]. She makes the connection between these poems and the language of the *Rule of the Community*. This is a connection that I have discussed in chapter three. I am less convinced by her argument that this is a hodayah of the Maskil and therefore rhetorically justifies the authority of that office.[112] It does however lead Newsom neatly into her consideration of the "Hodayot of the leader," which is the topic of her next chapter.

5.6.2. *Hodayot of the Leader*

Newsom devotes a separate chapter of her book to the "Hodayot of the leader." She takes as her working hypothesis that these compositions "articulate the leadership myth of the existing community."[113] She considers that, just as the Community Hymns shaped the individual member's identity, so these poems shaped the leader's self-understanding. But the main focus of her attention is their contribution to "nurturing community solidarity and discipline."[114]

---

[110] Newsom, *The Self as Symbolic Space*, 269–273.
[111] Newsom, *The Self as Symbolic Space*, 272–273.
[112] Newsom, *The Self as Symbolic Space*, 278.
[113] Newsom, *The Self as Symbolic Space*, 289.
[114] Newsom, *The Self as Symbolic Space*, 286.

In her chapter on the Community Hymns Newsom noted several links between them. In particular she referred back several times to 1QH^a VII 21–38 [XV 8–25]. This is an aspect which appears to be lacking in this chapter, despite some obvious parallels between 1QH^a XII 6–XIII 6 [IV 5–V 4] and the language of the Community Hymns.[115] This may be because Newsom wishes to focus on the leadership myth represented in these poems. I consider that it may also in part be a reflection of the power that the categories of Teacher and Community Hymns exert upon interpretation. In an attempt to subvert this influence I have downplayed these categories even more than Newsom does. I have placed 1QH^a VII 21–38 [XV 8–25] and 1QH^a XII 6–XIII 6 [IV 5–V 4] together in chapter three where I discuss the parallels between them.

Newsom analyses three compositions; these are 1QH^a X 5–21 [II 3–19], XII 6–XIII 6 [IV 5–V 4], and XIII 22–XV 8 [V 20–VII 5]. She sees the first two poems as being closely related.[116] This close relationship has been noted by other commentators, as I discuss in chapter three. I too have suggested that the importance of these poems lies not in possibly unrecoverable links with historical individual(s) or circumstances, but in what they tell us about the sectarians' understanding of themselves and their leaders. Our independently arrived at observations on these poems are thus in broad agreement. Newsom's main focus is upon how the poems themselves reinforced and shaped sectarian identity. I have concentrated upon the possible underlying use of scripture. Both approaches assume the significance of the written and spoken word in the formation of the community's self understanding.

Newsom describes 1QH^a X 5–21 [II 3–19] and XII 6–XIII 6 [IV 5–V 4] as mapping the "social world" of the sect and "an ideology of truth" respectively. This concept of mapping is an illuminating one, reinforced by Newsom's provision of diagrams showing the relationships that the poems describe. With regard to the social world, Newsom argues that both the horizontal relationship between the sectarians (repentant ones) and the outsiders (sinners) and the vertical relationships between each of these groups and God is defined by their relationship to the speaker. She comments that this gives the speaker a central and powerful position.

---

[115] Newsom refers back just once to her discussion of negation in chapter 5 of her book. Newsom, *The Self as Symbolic Space*, 324.
[116] Newsom, *The Self as Symbolic Space*, 311.

In chapter two of her book Newsom has already outlined the central role of torah in the competing discourses of Second Temple Judaism. In her discussion of the second poem she cites Fredric Jameson for her understanding of the needs of an ideology to resolve complexities in the real world which threaten its own view.[117] She argues that the problem addressed in this hodayah is that God's people, Israel, reject the truth possessed by the sect. The poem solves the problem by blaming it upon the deliberate seduction perpetrated by rival teachers.

Newsom therefore counsels caution in identifying these symbolic rivals in the text with any particular group of actual rivals. In her preceding discussion (of 1QH^a X 5–21 [II 3–19]) Newsom also argued against the specific identification of "seekers of smooth things" with the Pharisees.[118] I consider her arguments to be persuasive. Apart from a passing reference to the use of language from the biblical Psalms, Newsom does not specifically comment upon the many scriptural allusions in this composition.[119] My study of the allusions in 1QH^a XII 6–XIII 6 [IV 5–V 4] supports her stance by suggesting that the sectarians were drawing upon exegetical resources to construct an image of their rivals and themselves.

Likewise, in her treatment of 1QH^a XIII 22–XV 8 [V 20–VII 5],[120] Newsom eschews linking the poem to any specific person or period in the sect's history. She considers that this poem deals with the problem of disaffection, which can be assumed to be a potential problem throughout the history of the sect. In this poem it is treated in a very personal manner, as disloyalty to the leader, which has prompted the theory that it refers to an early charismatic leader of the sect. According to this theory the discourse of 1QS reflects a later more institutional period.

Newsom argues against this assumption by contrasting this poem with 1QS VII 15–25 which also deals with the problem of disaffection. She argues that the two representations of the community and its leaders, one highly personal and the other impersonal and rule-based, are in fact complementary. The legal language "is every bit as much a

---

[117] Fredric Jameson, *The Political Unconscious: Narrative as a Socially Symbolic Act* (Ithaca, NY: Cornell University Press, 1981), 47–49, cited in Newsom, *The Self as Symbolic Space*, 311 n. 19.
[118] Newsom, *The Self as Symbolic Space*, 308–309.
[119] Newsom, *The Self as Symbolic Space*, 318–319, 308.
[120] Newsom, *The Self as Symbolic Space*, 325–346. I discuss this poem in §2.6.1 of chapter four.

rhetorical act as the highly charged words of the Hodayot."[121] Newsom considers that the former creates an effect of assurance and stability and that the latter is a call to solidarity. She once again illustrates how a reader-oriented approach challenges some of the socio-historical suggestions of other commentators.

5.6.3. *Differences and Areas of Common Interest*

Although the emphasis of her study is different from mine, Newsom is interested, as am I, in the impact of these texts upon their readers. Thus we both set out to model a way of reading rather than ask questions about authorship and *Sitz im Leben* per se. We are both concerned with the way these texts use language. We also both seek to place the texts within their wider cultural context by reference to other texts originating in Second Temple Judaism.

In contrast with the study of Douglas,[122] we both treat the *Hodayot* as an anthology, in that we select individual compositions for study on the basis of our particular interest. In grouping, comparing or contrasting compositions we are more concerned with their possible impact upon sectarian readers than with conjecture about their redactional history or the overall structure of the collection.[123]

There are also differences between our approaches. Informed by studies in comparative literature, I ask the question "how would the reader interpret the text?" Drawing upon insights from anthropological and cultural studies, Newsom asks the question "what would the text do to the reader?" However, I see these questions as complementary rather than mutually exclusive. The subjectivity of readers will affect their interpretations and vice-versa.

It is a premise of reader-oriented approaches that every reader brings their own experience and assumptions to the reading of the text. Both Newsom and I have tried to put ourselves into the position of a sectarian reader, while acknowledging that this reader is a construct based very much upon the texts themselves. Unlike some previous approaches the reader-orientated approach recognises the multi-valent nature of texts and of reader viewpoints. It thus invites multiple non-exclusive

---

[121] Newsom, *The Self as Symbolic Space*, 331.
[122] See the introduction to his dissertation; Douglas, "Power and Praise," 1–14.
[123] Newsom says "I am concerned with representative motifs within individual hodayah rather than with the principles of organisation of the collections themselves." See Newsom, *The Self as Symbolic Space*, 198.

readings each of which illustrates the richness and aesthetic effects of these poems. In my PhD thesis I stated that the literary observations of Douglas had provided the main source of comparison for my own study. However, the focus and method of Douglas' study was very different from my own. In this revised publication I am pleased to also have the reader-orientated insights of Newsom against which to measure my own observations.

6. *Objectives of This Study*

As noted above, the evidence from the Cave 4 manuscripts has reinforced the view that the *Hodayot* is not a uniform collection. Therefore, one of the working assumptions of this study is that the *Hodayot* is an anthology. Each composition will be studied as an individual unit without making prior assumptions based on its inclusion in the 1QH^a collection. Only after this initial analysis will comparisons or connections be made with other *Hodayot* compositions and other Dead Sea texts. Another assumption of this study is that the compositions are poetic, and I will seek to further the work of Kittel in understanding their poetic structure and the devices used. In particular I will be treating allusion as a poetic device. I consider that a greater understanding of how the allusions function within the composition will make it easier to identify any possible underlying exegesis.

I am, of course, interested in the questions raised by other students of the *Hodayot*. However, I consider that the questions and assumptions that some commentators have brought to their study may have prevented the compositions from speaking for themselves. It is my intention, as far as possible, to approach these compositions as an informed reader and to hear their authentic voice. Of course every reader, including the earliest readers of this text, brings their own unique experience and perspective to the task. I hope that my reading will help both to draw attention to this aspect and help other readers to appreciate the texts for themselves. If along the way some light is shed upon the historical and theological questions, then that indeed will be a bonus.

CHAPTER TWO

METHODOLOGY

1. *Introduction*

As stated in chapter one, the aim of this study is to explore the use of scriptural allusions in the *Hodayot* by close examination of selected passages. In this chapter I will consider the relevant methodological issues and set out my method of study. Firstly I will describe how the passages for study were selected. Secondly I will discuss the implications of reading the compositions as poetry. I will then explore how scriptural allusions are to be defined and studied. Following this, I will discuss the more general topic of how texts are read and interpreted. Finally I will outline the method I have used.

2. *Selection of Passages*

The text available for study consists of the eight manuscripts 1QH^a, 1QH^b, and 4QH^{a-f} (4Q427–432). The first criterion for selecting passages is that the text must be complete enough to enable the passage to be studied in suitable detail. Because of the fragmentary nature of the Cave 4 manuscripts the majority of passages satisfying this criterion come from the main Cave 1 copy. The possible exceptions are the "Self Glorification Hymn" (4QH^a 7, 4Q471b)[1] and the reconstruction of a hymn from the three manuscripts 4QH^b, 1QH^a and 1QH^b.[2]

In order to analyse how the allusions function within the text it is necessary to select complete compositions wherever possible. This is the second criterion. It is not, however, always possible to tell where

---

[1] Schuller, "Hodayot," 96–108; Esther Eshel, "Self-Glorification Hymn," in *Qumran Cave 4.XX: Poetical and Liturgical Texts, Part 2* (ed. E. Chazon et al., DJD 29; Oxford: Clarendon, 1999) 421–436.

[2] Schuller, "A Thanksgiving Hymn from 4QHodayot^b;" Puech, "Restauration d'un texte hymnique."

one composition ends and another begins. The main markers are blank spaces left by the scribe and the introductory formulae אודכה אדוני or אודכה אלי (I thank you, O Lord/my God) and ברוך אתה אדוני (Blessed are you, O Lord). The assumption made by Kittel, that when these two markers coincide the start of a new composition may be inferred, is the most reliable indicator but other indicators such as content and style will not be ruled out.[3]

Thirdly, the choice of composition has been limited to those that have been identified by commentators as making considerable use of allusions. The final consideration in selecting compositions was to ensure that a range of different types of composition were chosen, including examples of features which have attracted interest and debate among scholars.

Using these criteria I have chosen the following compositions. In chapter three I analyse 1QH^a VII 21–VIII ? [XV 8–25+frg. 10+frg. 32] and 1QH^a XII 6–XIII 6 [IV 5–V 4]; these two poems have a very dualistic outlook. In the fourth chapter I consider 1QH^a XVI 5–XVII 36 [VIII 4–IX 36]; this is a very long poem which has attracted considerable interest for its possible autobiographical content and also for its suffering servant motif. In chapter five I consider 1QH^a XI 6–19 [III 5–18] and 1QH^a XI 20–37 [III 19–36], two adjacent short poems with an eschatological flavour; the first of these has attracted much interest from commentators. In the introduction to each poem I will describe in more detail my reasons for including it in the study.

3. *How Does One Study Poetry?*

This study assumes that the *Hodayot* are poetic compositions, but this raises several issues. Firstly, there is no universally agreed definition of poetry. Secondly, some features of classical Hebrew poetry are not clearly understood. There are also clear differences between the structure of the *Hodayot* and the poetry of the Hebrew Bible, resulting in

---

[3] Stegemann has recently proposed that the criteria for deciding the start of a new composition need to be revised. In particular he considers that some shorter blanks at the end of a line indicate a new section rather than a new composition. Of the poems chosen for this study his observations affect only the first poem in chapter three. See Kittel, *The Hymns of Qumran* 25–26; Stegemann, "The Number of Psalms in 1QHodayot^a," 191–234.

some questioning of the poetic status of the former. In considering how to analyse these poems I have therefore consulted general studies on the reading of poetry as well as studies concerning classical Hebrew poetry.

The distinction between poetry and prose is far from clear-cut in most literary traditions. This is because many of the features thought characteristic of poetry, such as the use of elevated language, parallelism and figurative imagery, are also found in prose compositions. Furniss and Bath are of the opinion that poetry is an umbrella term that is essentially unstable.[4] However two of their other observations are indicative of fruitful avenues in the search for a workable definition.

Firstly, the idea expressed by Furniss and Bath that "poetry achieves its emotional power by working the resources of the language to the limit"[5] has been seen by some as a key concept. Lotman describes a poetic text as being "semantically saturated."[6] In Eagleton's explanation "Each word in the text is linked by a whole set of formal structures to several other words, and its meaning is thus always 'overdetermined', always the result of several different determinants acting together."[7]

Thus a word or phrase may be connected to another by a combination of syntactic, semantic, phonological or other equivalencies. These types of equivalencies occur in non-poetic texts but in poetic texts they are dominant and dense. The term parallelism is often used of such equivalencies; this encompasses, but is wider than, the traditional use of the term for biblical poetry. Adele Berlin in her study of biblical parallelism notes that parallelism does not occur only in poetry but that in poetry, unlike prose, it is the "constitutive"[8] or "construc-

---

[4] Tom Furniss and Michael Bath, *Reading Poetry: an introduction* (Harlow: Pearson Education, 1996).

[5] Furniss and Bath. *Reading Poetry*, 10.

[6] Yury Lotman, *The Structure of the Artistic Text* (Ann Arbor: University of Michigan, 1977); Yury Lotman, *Analysis of the Poetic Text* (Ann Arbor: Ardis, 1976) cited in Terry Eagleton, *Literary Theory: An Introduction* (Oxford: Blackwell, ²1996), 88.

[7] Eagleton, *Literary Theory*, 89.

[8] Berlin quotes Jakobsen, "Equivalence is promoted to the constitutive device of the sequence." The work of Russian Formalist, Roman Jakobsen is a major influence in the recognition and study of parallelism. Berlin provides a discussion of Jakobsen's ideas in relation to biblical parallelism. See Adele Berlin, *The Dynamics of Biblical Parallelism*, (Bloomington and Indianapolis: Indiana University Press, 1992), 7–17; Roman Jakob-

tive"[9] device of the text. In the opinion of Berlin parallelism is the key to "comprehending a poem's structure, its unity" and, hence, its meaning.[10] Therefore, in this study I will be paying close attention to parallelism in its widest sense. I will be seeking to identify repetition of and correspondences between words and phrases and patterns of all kinds.

The close structuring of poetry is reflected in a second observation of Furniss and Bath that the only watertight distinction is that poetry is arranged in lines.[11] In modern printed works the very fact that a text is set out in such lines will prompt a reader to attempt to read it as poetry. Of course the *Hodayot*, in common with much classical Hebrew poetry, were not set out in poetic lines on the page (stichography) but the use of parallelism as a structural device lends itself to the lineation (stichometry) of the text.[12] Thus, in this study the Hebrew text will be set out according to the manuscript lines but the translation will be arranged in poetic lines, using parallelism and various other linguistic clues as a guide.

3.1. *Terminology*

Before proceeding to further discussion of method it is necessary to define the terms for the basic structural units to be considered. Unfortunately there is, among scholars of Hebrew poetry, a considerable lack of consistency regarding terminology. This is in part due to the appropriation of terms used to describe classical Greek poetry, even though the units of Hebrew poetry are not exactly equivalent. The following definitions are based on the textbook on Hebrew poetry by G.W.E. Watson; commonly used alternative terms are given in brackets.[13]

---

son, "Linguistics and Poetics," in *Style in Language* (ed. T. Sebeok; Cambridge, Mass.: MIT Press, 1960), 358.

[9] Berlin, *The Dynamics of Biblical Parallelism*, 11. Here Berlin is citing L. Waugh, "The Poetic Function and Nature of Language." *Poetics Today* 2/1a (1980): 64–65.

[10] Berlin, *The Dynamics of Biblical Parallelism*, 17.

[11] Furniss and Bath, *Reading Poetry*, 12.

[12] I borrow this distinction from Watson who adopted it from Kugel. See Wilfred G.E. Watson, *Classical Hebrew Poetry: A Guide to its Techniques* (JSOTSup 26; Sheffield: JSOT Press, 1984), 15; James L. Kugel, *The Idea of Biblical Poetry: Parallelism and its History* (New Haven and London: Yale University Press, 1981).

[13] Watson, *Classical Hebrew Poetry*, 11–15.

The line[14] (colon, verset,[15] stich, stichos, hemistich[16]) is a single line of poetry. A number of lines are grouped into a verse (strophe) which forms a semantically independent unit comparable to the level of the sentence in prose. The most common verse is the couplet (bicolon) consisting of two lines, but other combinations exist such as single line (monocolon), triplet (tricolon), quatrain (tetracolon), etc. A stanza is a sub-division of a poem consisting of one or more verses. In describing classical Greek poetry the verse (strophe) and stanza are considered to be regular units but in Watson's usage such regularity is not a requirement. There is very little consensus on the use of "strophe" and "stanza" beyond the agreement that strophe is a subdivision of stanza is a subdivision of poem.

I propose to use the following terms, in ascending order of size: "line" (=colon), "verse" (=monocolon, bicolon etc) and "stanza." For ease in discussing the structure, I will also divide poems into "sections" and "sub-sections" consisting of one or more stanzas. In cases where confusion might occur with other uses of the word "line" a modifier will be used (e.g. poetic line, line of manuscript).

3.2. *Metre, Parallelism and Structural Indicators*

As stated above there is still much that is disputed about the nature of classical Hebrew poetry. Perhaps the most disputed area is the part, if any, played by metre. It may prove impossible to ever resolve this dispute because of lack of knowledge about the pronunciation of classical Hebrew. Furthermore, Kittel's study has demonstrated that in the *Hodayot* the length of poetic line varies considerably and has a greater range than that of biblical poetry. However, Kittel was of the opinion that once the structure of a poem had been determined, approximate syllable counts indicated a "rhythmical balance" between sections.[17] Because of the uncertainties, in this study metre will not be considered nor will I engage in syllable counting. I have sometimes used num-

---

[14] Watson adopts the terminology "line" instead of "colon" in Wilfred G.E. Watson, "Hebrew Poetry" in *Text in Context: Essays by Members of the Society for Old Testament Study* (ed. A.D.H. Mayes; Oxford: OUP, 2000), 261.
[15] Robert Alter, *The Art of Biblical Poetry* (Edinburgh: T&T Clark, 1990), 8.
[16] While noting this usage Watson takes hemistich to be a subdivision of a colon. Watson, *Classical Hebrew Poetry*, 11–12.
[17] Kittel, *The Hymns of Qumran*, 30, 172.

ber of manuscript lines as a very rough guide for comparing section lengths, in chapter four for example.

In identifying line and verse structure Kittel's observations on the *Hodayot* have formed my starting point. I have already outlined these in the previous chapter, and where relevant will refer to particular observations of Kittel in the footnotes to the detailed analyses of poems. Although the prosody of the *Hodayot* differs in many respects, it does also make use of devices found in biblical poetry. The studies of Watson have therefore provided many useful observations and illustrations on the poetic techniques of biblical poetry.[18] Where relevant these also will be footnoted in the detailed analysis.

In recent years much attention has been focussed upon the syntactical and semantic elements of parallelism. Studies by T. Collins, E. Greenstein, and M. O'Connor concentrated upon syntax as a means of identifying structure. S. Geller and D. Pardee combined syntactical and semantic approaches.[19] I have consulted the study by Williams,[20] which does employ such an approach. However, because of the seemingly freer form of the *Hodayot*, and because the emphasis of this study is on interpretation, I have adopted the less formal and more descriptive approach of close reading. In this I have been influenced by Robert Alter's study of biblical poetry.[21]

---

[18] Watson, *Classical Hebrew Poetry*; Wilfred G.E. Watson, *Traditional Techniques in Classical Hebrew Verse* (JSOTSup 170; Sheffield: Sheffield Academic Press, 1994).

[19] Terence Collins, *Line-Forms in Hebrew Poetry* (Rome: Biblical Institute Press, 1978); Stephen A. Geller, *Parallelism in Early Biblical Poetry* (Missoula: Scholars Press, 1979); M. O'Connor, *Hebrew Verse Structure* (Winona Lake, Ind.: Eisenbrauns, 1980); Edward L. Greenstein, "How Does Parallelism Mean?" in *A Sense of Text*, (JQR Supplement; ed. S. Geller; Winona Lake: Eisenbrauns, 1982) 41–70; Dennis Pardee, *Ugaritic and Hebrew Poetic Parallelism: A Trial Cut ('nt I and Proverbs 2.)* (VTSup 39; Leiden: Brill, 1988); all cited in David M. Howard Jr., "Recent Trends in Psalms Study" in *The Face of Old Testament Studies* (ed. D.W. Baker and B.T. Arnold; Baker Books, 1999) 329–368.

[20] Williams, "Parallelism."

[21] Robert Alter, *The Art of Biblical Poetry* (Edinburgh: T&T Clark, 1990).

4. *How Does One Study Allusions?*

As noted above, a characteristic of poetry is that it is "semantically saturated."[22] One way of achieving this density of meaning is the use of allusion. So I will now turn to a consideration of the use of allusion, particularly in poetic texts. Firstly I will discuss how to define allusions. Then I will establish some criteria for identifying allusions. Finally I will discuss how allusions work to create meaning within a text.

Many of the methodological issues have been considered in a study by Richard Schultz concerned with verbal parallels in the biblical prophets.[23] Schultz observed that although these parallels had been studied extensively there was no methodological consensus, and often methodological issues had not been adequately addressed. In order to inform his own methodological proposals he conducted a survey of studies of quotation and allusion in (i) ancient Near Eastern literature, (ii) Sirach and the *Hodayot* and (iii) modern literary theory. It should be noted at the outset that I do not consider it possible to remove completely the subjective element from the study of allusions. Instead my aim is the more modest one of setting out parameters within which this study will operate. Schultz' observation is pertinent:

> The proper assessment of quotation is inherently problematic. The confusion in comparative literary theory regarding terminology and methodology demonstrates that the difficulty surrounding prophetic quotation is not due solely to the nature of biblical literature but is rather due largely to the nature of quotation itself.[24]

Some of the problems which concerned Schultz regarding prophetic literature are less of a problem for the *Hodayot*. Because of the uncertainty over the relative dating of texts, Schultz needed to discuss criteria for deciding which text was the dependent one. It is assumed in this study that the scriptural texts, in some form, predate the text of the *Hodayot*. Likewise, the availability of the quoted texts and the familiarity of the readers with them can be assumed from the extensive scriptural library at Qumran and the emphasis on scripture study in the sectarian texts.

---

[22] Lotman, The Structure of the Artistic Text; Lotman, *Analysis of the Poetic Text*; both cited in Eagleton, *Literary Theory*, 88.

[23] Richard L. Schultz, *The Search for Quotation: Verbal Parallels in the Prophets* (JSOTSup 180; Sheffield: Sheffield Academic Press, 1999).

[24] Schultz, *The Search for Quotation*, 205.

4.1. *Definition of an Allusion*

So far I have used the term allusion without further clarification, but it is the terminology and the criteria for identifying allusions that present the greatest methodological issues. As noted by Schultz, there is no consensus on terminology, even within the extensive methodological corpus of modern literary theory. Within biblical studies there is a large corpus on the use of the Old Testament in the New. Stanley E. Porter has discussed the terminological and methodological confusion that prevails in this area. His discussion illustrates the difficulty of arriving at consensus on terminology and method; he recommends instead that each study clearly formulates its goal and then defines "the categories under discussion."[25] I will therefore begin by discussing my usage of the terms "quotation," "allusion" and "idiom" in preparation for establishing a method for analysing the poems.

4.1.1. *Quotation*

There is considerable overlap between the use of the terms quotation and allusion. For example, Schultz uses the term quotation in a wider sense than I propose in this study, using it to cover instances which I would consider allusion.[26] Many scholars differentiate between these two terms on the basis that quotation is a direct use and allusion an indirect use of a text. However, as this distinction is far from objective some scholars limit their discussion to explicit quotations; an explicit quotation is one which is clearly marked in some way, usually by an introductory formula.[27] There are many instances of this type of quotation in the Dead Sea literature[28] but it is not a feature of the *Hodayot*.[29] Explicit quotation is also marked in Dead Sea texts by the use of the pesher format.

---

[25] Stanley E. Porter, "The Use of the Old Testament in the New Testament: A Brief Comment on Method and Terminology" in *Early Christian Interpretation of the Scriptures of Israel: Investigations and Proposals* (ed. C.A. Evans and J.A. Sanders; JSNTSup 148; SSEJC 5; Sheffield: Sheffield Academic Press, 1997), 79–96.

[26] Schultz, *The Search for Quotation*, 216–221.

[27] Scholars often use the term *citation* interchangeably with this restricted use of the term quotation.

[28] For a discussion of these see Joseph A. Fitzmyer, "The use of Explicit Old Testament Quotations in Qumran Literature and in the New Testament," *NTS* 7 (1961): 297–333.

[29] The only probable instance occurs in 1QHª IV 24 [XVII 12].

Yair Hoffman has considered the rarity of explicit quotations in the literature of the

Fitzmyer also uses the terminology "implicit" or "virtual" quotation to describe phrases that lack an explicit formula but are "obviously intended to be quotations."[30] He does not elaborate and other scholars have also had difficulty in being more precise. Porter uses Phil 1:19 as an example of a difficult case. This passage contains five words that are identical to a phrase found in Job 13:16 LXX. Although often overlooked in discussions of quotations by Paul, Porter argues that this passage should be included in such discussions.[31] Porter proposes a definition of quotation that focuses on "formal correspondence with actual words found in antecedent texts."[32] One problem with this definition is the difficulty of identifying the specific text quoted, particularly in the case of different recensions. The second difficulty is that in the ancient world the accurate reproduction of the actual words of the quoted text does not appear to have been a priority.

These problems reflect the fact that it is difficult to avoid bringing modern preconceptions to the task. In most modern literature quotations are clearly marked by punctuation and often the source is acknowledged in a note. This is not so in ancient texts and the use of introductory formulae within Jewish texts seems to have been a gradual historical development.[33] Furthermore, the access to standardised texts made possible by modern technologies means that quotations are easier to define, produce and identify; the concept of verbatim quotation is potentially anachronistic when applied to the ancient world, where texts were copied by hand with multiple minor variations.[34]

A variation on the idea of quotation that avoids emphasis on knowing the source text is found in the work of both Gordis and Fox on Wisdom literature.[35] They include in their definition any statement that

---

apocrypha and suggested that in the case of wisdom and psalms texts this is due to the conventions of these genres. Y. Hoffman "The Technique of Quotation and Citation as an Interpretive Device," in *Creative Biblical Exegesis: Christian and Jewish Hermeneutics through the Centuries* (ed. B. Uffenheimer and H.G. Reventlow; JSOTSup 59; Sheffield: JSOT Press, 1988), 71–79.

[30] Fitzmyer, "The use of Explicit Old Testament Quotations," 304.
[31] Porter, "The Use of the Old Testament in the New Testament," 90–94.
[32] Porter, "The Use of the Old Testament in the New Testament," 95.
[33] Hoffman "The Technique of Quotation and Citation," 71–79.
[34] For a discussion of the factors affecting ancient conventions of quotation see Christopher D. Stanley, "The Social Environment of 'free' Biblical Quotations in the New Testament" in *Early Christian Interpretation of the Scriptures of Israel: Investigations and Proposals* (ed. C.A. Evans and J.A. Sanders; JSNTSup 148; SSEJC 5; Sheffield: Sheffield Academic Press, 1997), 18–27.
[35] Robert Gordis, "Quotations in Wisdom Literature," *JQR* 30 (1939/40): 123–147;

is marked in some way as not being made by the main speaker of the composition; they seek to identify this by detecting a change of voice or viewpoint. This would seem to be a useful definition of an implicit quotation that encompasses Fitzmyer's examples.[36]

Thus I would define a quotation as a phrase which is marked, explicitly or implicitly, as referring to the words of a speaker who is not the implied speaker of the composition. The identity of the referent may or may not be known. The words may or may not be quoted verbatim. According to this definition Phil 1:19 is not a quotation in this technical sense although it reproduces the words of Job 13:16. Is it therefore an allusion?

4.1.2. *Allusion*

Phil 1:19 certainly contains a verbal parallel to another text, but a reader unaware of this may satisfactorily explain the phrase as referring to Paul's plight. It is only an allusion if it also refers to the phrase in Job. C. Perri, a scholar of English literature, has elaborated this distinction in a study of allusion. In her view the crucial characteristic of allusion is that it "has at least a double referent." Thus the words have a non-allusive meaning within the text as well as referring allusively to one or more other texts. She adds a second requirement that "the alluding text directs our attention to one or more aspects of the source text necessary to comprehend the meaning of the allusion."[37]

Thus as readers we may perceive that Phil 1:19 alludes to Job only if it points to a specific aspect of the Job text thereby adding meaning. There seems to be no such specificity in this case and therefore the most that can be said is that Phil 1:19 echoes or is influenced by the passage in Job.[38] This example also illustrates the inadequacy of appealing to

---

Robert Gordis, "Quotations as a Literary Usage in Biblical, Oriental and Rabbinic Literature," *HUCA* 22 (1949): 157–219; Michael V. Fox, "The Identification of Quotations in Biblical Literature," *ZAW* 92 (1980): 416–431.

[36] E.g. Fitzmyer, "The use of Explicit Old Testament Quotations," 304, cites Heb 10:37–38 as an implicit quotation. In this case the speaker has obviously changed from Paul to God.

[37] Carmela Perri, "On Alluding," *Poetics* 7 (1978): 295–296.

[38] Richard Hays discusses possible "resonances" of Job in Phil 1:19, but describes the effect as a "subtle echo" rather than an allusion. See Richard B. Hays, *Echoes of Scripture in the Letters of Paul* (New Haven & London: Yale University Press, 1989), 21–23. Critiques of Hay's book together with his response can be found in Craig A. Evans and James A. Sanders, eds., *Paul and the Scriptures of Israel* (JSNTSup 83; Sheffield: JSOT Press, 1993).

the author's intention. In this case we have no way of knowing whether the verbal parallel was deliberate or unconscious. I will return to a consideration of the relevance of the author's intention later in this chapter.

Perri also, with others, compiled an annotated bibliography of works on allusion[39] on which she comments that "we have found, in the main, that the work done on allusion as a technique of style is confined to studies of specific artistic uses, with no or little theoretical discussion."[40] This still seems to be the case. It is worth therefore quoting Perri's working definition in full:

> Allusion in literature is a manner of signifying in which some kind of marker (simple or complex, overt or covert) not only signifies un-allusively, within the imagined possible world of the alluding text, but through echo also denotes a source text and specifies some discrete, recoverable property(ies) belonging to the intension (*sic*) of this source text (or specifies its own property(ies) in the case of self-echo); the property(ies) evoked modifies the alluding text, and possibly activates further, larger inter- and intra-textual patterns of properties with consequent further modification of the alluding text.[41]

A premise of this study is that the type of reference described by Perri is found extensively in the *Hodayot*, whereas commentators agree that quotations, as defined in the previous sub-section, are not.[42] Thus, although Perri's definition theoretically allows that a quotation may also be an allusion, it is a possibility which need not concern us. Another point made by Perri's definition is that allusion is a sophisticated literary device distinguishable from mere echo or influence. The term allusion is also widely used of references to a non-literary source such as a person or an event (it is in this wider sense that Perri uses the term "text"), but this study will be limited to allusions to written texts.

At this point it is necessary to comment on the assumption, widely shared by biblical scholars, that a literary allusion necessarily involves

---

[39] Carmela Perri et al., "Allusion Studies. An International Annotated Bibliography, 1921–1977," *Style* 2 (1979): 178–227.

[40] One exception is the article by Ben-Porat, which is cited frequently by other writers on the topic, and by Perri herself. Perri, "On Alluding," 289 n. 1; Ziva Ben Porat, "The Poetics of Literary Allusion," *PTL* 1 (1976): 105–128.

[41] Perri, "On Alluding," 295; note "intension" is a technical term for the group of attributes, and properties connoted by a term.

[42] The only instance noted by commentators on the *Hodayot* of a possible quotation in this limited sense of which I am aware is that of Ps 26:12 in 1QH^a X 32 [II 29] as noted in Kittel, *The Hymns of Qumran*, 35 n.C.

some kind of verbal parallel as the marker. It is this type of allusion that is most readily identifiable and upon which I will be concentrating in this study. Thus, unless otherwise stated, when in this study I refer to allusion some degree of verbal parallel is implied. However, it is theoretically possible to allude to a text by using a similar structure, narrative sequence, or combination of ideas, without using the same vocabulary.

4.1.3. *Idiom*

An example that illustrates several points I wish to make is the expression יצר החמר ומגבל המים (creature of clay, kneaded with water) variations of which occur several times in the *Hodayot*.[43] This is not a biblical phrase and in fact the second part of the expression is an example of emerging Mishnaic Hebrew.[44] However its content could be taken as alluding to the account of the formation of man in Gen 2:7[45] even though the only common vocabulary is the use of the verb יצר (to form). For reasons given below I am doubtful whether every occurrence of this phrase can be considered as an allusion. However, this discussion enables me to make the point that there is more to allusion than mere similarity of vocabulary.

Conversely, the existence of verbal parallels is not a sole sufficient indication of an allusion. On closer examination the aforementioned example has similarities of language to the scriptural passages Job 10:9, 33:6, Isa 29:16, and Isa 41:25. But such multiple use of a phrase is more easily explained as the use of an idiom; the biblical idiom may have originated in an allusion to the tradition contained in Gen 2:7 and/or a word play on the relationship between the verb "to form" and the occupation of "potter." (The first poem considered in chapter three contains a possible instance of such word-play.)

The expression "creature of clay, kneaded with water" is likewise best regarded as an idiom. It may have developed from the biblical idiom,

---

[43] 1QH^a IX 23 [I 21], XI 25 [III 24], XII 30 [IV 29], XVII 16 [IX 16], XIX 6 [XI 3], XX 29, 35 [XII 26, 32], XXII 10 [1 8], XXIII 13 [XVIII 12], [2 I 8], [3 18], [11 7]; 4Q428 5 6, 20 2; see also 1QS XI 22.

[44] According to J.C. Greenfield, in Mishnaic Hebrew גבל means 'to mix mortar' and is not used for the act of building itself. J.C. Greenfield, "The Root 'GBL' in Mishnaic Hebrew and in the Hymnic Literature from Qumran" *RevQ* 2 (1959–1960): 155–162, cited in Holm-Nielsen, *Hodayot*, 24 n. 43.

[45] According to Jastrow, גבל is used of the creation in rabbinic literature. M. Jastrow, *A Dictionary of the Targumim, the Talmud Babli and Yerushalmi, and the Midrashic Literature, Vols. I and II*. (New York: Putnam's, 1886, 1903), cited in Holm-Nielsen, *Hodayot*, 24 n. 43.

or independently from similar traditions. Thus Holm-Nielsen describes this phraseology as "technical terms in DSS for man's sinfulness as contrasted with the divine character."[46] In some occurrences in the *Hodayot* it appears to be used in this way and it is unlikely that it would have recalled the scriptural passages to a sectarian reader in such a way as to affect his interpretation. However the following example from 1QH[a] XX 29–38 [XII 26–35] indicates that this is not always the case.

29 חושך ותשובת עפר ליצר חמר בקץ [...]. בעפר
30 אל אשר לקח משם ומה ישיב עפר ואפ[ר ... ומה י]בין
31 [במ]עשיו ומה יתיצב לפני מוכיח בו .[... ק]ודש
32 [...] עולם ומקוי כבוד ומקור דעת וגבו[רת פל]א והמה לוא
33 [יוכל]ו לספר כול כבודכה ולהתיצב לפני אפכה ואין להשיב
34 על תוכחתכה כיא צדקתה ואין לנגדכה ומה אפהו שב אל עפרו
35 ואני נאלמתי ומה אדבר על זות כדעתי ׳דברתי׳ מצירוק יצר חמר ומה[47]

> And THE RETURN TO THE DUST for the *creature of clay*
> at the time of [… … … … …] into the dust
> (30) to the place FROM WHICH HE HAS BEEN TAKEN.
> And how shall dust and ash[es] reply? [...]
> [And how] shall it understand (31) his [wo]rks?
> And how shall he stand before the one who reproves him?
> [… h]oliness (32) [...] eternal
> And collections of glory, and wellspring of knowledge, and stren[gth of wond]er.
> And they, they [can]not (33) recount all your glory
> Or stand before your anger.
> And there is nothing to reply (34) to your reproof
> For you are just and there is no-one before you.
> What is he, THE ONE WHO RETURNS TO HIS DUST?
> (35) And I, I have kept silence for what can I say about this?
> In accordance with my knowledge /I spoke/
> Spat saliva, a *creature of clay*.

In this passage the expression "creature of clay" is combined with others in a clear evocation of Gen 3:19.[48] The specific aspect recalled in this case is that in the very beginning God himself drew attention to human created-ness and mortality as justification of his power and right to judge.

---

[46] Holm-Nielsen, *Hodayot*, 24 n. 43.
[47] García Martínez and Tigchelaar, *The Dead Sea Scrolls Study Edition*, 192 (line numbers amended).
[48] "By the sweat of your face you shall eat your bread until you return to the ground, for out of it you were taken; you are dust, and to dust you shall return." (Gen 3:19).

Expressions that are known to occur commonly in literature found at Qumran, scriptural or otherwise, will therefore be considered as examples of idiom unless there are other strong indications for thinking otherwise.

4.1.4. *From Author to Reader*

Before turning to the question of identifying an allusion it is necessary to consider the problem of authorial intention that I raised in the above discussion on Phil 1:19. Perri's definition is text-oriented but many scholars define allusion in terms of the author's intention. Furniss and Bath distinguish allusion from accidental similarity between texts in terms of the author's intention. They introduce the terms "influence" and "echo" to describe similarities due either to conscious or unconscious imitation of another's work, but not intended as a deliberate poetic device.[49] They refer to the work of John Hollander who defines an allusion as a similarity between texts which is meant to be detected by readers; he defines an echo as one which is not meant to be detected. Hollander explicitly states that the author must have intended an allusion whereas an echo may or may not have been intended.[50]

Hollander's opinion is contrary to that of Wimsatt and Beardsley. In an article that has become the classic statement of the "intentional fallacy" position[51] they denied that the intention of the author was a legitimate concern of the literary critic. They distinguish between data that is internal to the poem and that which is external. They state that only the former, i.e. the text itself, should be used as evidence for the meaning of the poem.

Wimsatt and Beardsley suggest that allusions work even when the reader does not recognise the source. They seem to mean by this that they work by a recognisable difference between the voice of the poem and the voice of the allusion. In an example from Eliot's notes to *The Waste Land*, they appear to suggest that Eliot's attribution of an allusion would work even if he had invented the alleged source.[52] In my opinion they do not adequately consider that allusions rely upon

---

[49] Furniss and Bath, *Reading Poetry*, 308.
[50] John Hollander, *The Figure of Echo: A mode of allusion in Milton and after* (Berkeley: University of California Press, 1981), 64.
[51] W.K. Wimsatt Jr. and Monroe C. Beardsley, "The Intentional Fallacy," in *The Verbal Icon: Studies in the Meaning of Poetry* (ed. W.K. Wimsatt; Lexington: University Press of Kentucky, 1954).
[52] Wimsatt and Beardsley, "The Intentional Fallacy," 15–16.

the reader being able to supply an unquoted context. However, they offer a needed corrective to too much emphasis upon external data; they are right to emphasise that the meaning of a text should be sought primarily in the text itself.

Nevertheless, the very meanings of words are dependent upon external factors and change with the years. It would therefore seem impossible to completely rule out external factors in interpreting a text. The shift from author to text has been followed by a shift to consideration of readers. This shift recognises that it is the act of reading that imparts meaning to a text. How an allusive reference works will depend upon the skills and background of the reader. Perri, having defined allusion in terms of the text, goes on to discuss the concept in terms of both the author and the audience. She utilises speech act theory to describe firstly the illocutionary rules of the act of alluding and secondly the perlocutionary effect on the audience.

The first description is given in terms of both author and audience, but the second is in terms of audience only. In the latter Perri outlines five steps by which a reader processes an allusion. Firstly, the reader *comprehends* the ordinary un-allusive meaning of the allusion marker. Then the reader *recognises* the allusion-marker as referring to a specific source text and *realises* that this requires interpretation. The reader therefore *remembers* aspects of the source text and *connects* them to the alluding text, thereby interpreting the meaning of the allusion.[53]

In my opinion it seems likely that most references recognised by readers as an allusion would have been intended by the author. However, it is possible that intended allusions may go unnoticed and that phrases not intended as allusions may be so interpreted by a reader. For practical purposes it seems preferable to bracket the notion of intention and regard as an allusion any reference which works as such for a reader. This approach recognises that real readers, and therefore interpretations, differ. This study will leave aside the issue of whether all interpretations are equally valid. However, particularly in cases of literature that is being considered across cultural boundaries (linguistic, historical, etc.), it seems important to state the perspective from which it is being viewed.

In the case of allusions the concept of an implied reader, "the reader encoded by the text's strategies,"[54] is a useful one. For example the

---

[53] Perri, "On Alluding," 301.
[54] For this definition see Margaret Davies, "Reader Response Criticism," in *A Dictio-*

Hodayot assume that the reader understands biblical Hebrew, is familiar with scriptural texts, has knowledge of and is in agreement with the beliefs expressed in this and other sectarian documents. It becomes a legitimate exercise to interpret a text with the implied reader in mind. However, it needs to be recognised that the greater the "distance" between the critic and this conceptual reader the more provisional any such interpretation must be. With this proviso in mind, I will approach the interpretation of allusions in the *Hodayot* having in mind a late Second Temple Jewish reader who is familiar with the sectarian literature found in the Qumran caves.[55]

4.2. *Identification of Allusions*

The major problem comes not in defining the concept of an allusion but in the practical task of identifying specific cases. The contributory factors to this problem are the aforementioned difficulty of ascertaining authorial intention and the fact that no two real readers are likely to perceive the textual allusions identically. In effect the critic constructs an ideal reader who "catches" every possible meaning and nuance which can be ascribed to the text within its cultural context. As expressed by Robert Fowler, this is "the implied reader writ large."[56] No real reader, first-century Jew or modern critic, corresponds exactly with this idealised construct.

Furniss and Bath note that the assumption of the existence of an ideal reader also involves the concept of a literary tradition or canon, and that the use of allusions contributes to the formation and maintenance of such a tradition.[57] Thus one criterion for identifying an allusion would be whether the proposed literary source was part of such a literary tradition. As already mentioned, this is an assumption which seems reasonable in the case of the use of scripture by the *Hodayot*. Fishbane notes that a similarity between texts does not necessarily point to a direct relationship between them; it may be due to the use of a fund of tradition or to a common vocabulary. However, he specifi-

---

nary of Biblical Interpretation (eds. R.J. Coggins and J.L. Houlden; London: SCM, 1990); see also Robert M. Fowler, "Who is 'The Reader' in Reader Response Criticism?" *Semeia* 31 (1985): 5–23.

[55] Recognising that this too is a construct, based on the Dead Sea Scrolls, archaeology, and literature of the period.
[56] Fowler, "Who is 'The Reader'," 16.
[57] Furniss and Bath, *Reading Poetry*, 307.

cally comments that "Since we have a large register of explicit biblical citations in manuscripts from Qumran, there is a strong presumptive likelihood that what appear to be biblical allusions or phrases in the *Hodayot*-Psalms, for example, are in fact anthologised reuses of the vast biblical thesaurus, and not just terms picked from the spoken environment."[58]

However, the use of common biblical vocabulary, while constituting a general allusiveness to scripture does not necessarily constitute allusion to a specific scriptural passage. Some commentators such as Carmignac, and to a lesser degree Holm-Nielsen, have been too eager to take coincidences in vocabulary as recognisable allusions. Kittel discusses the issue in an excursus on the use of Biblical language. Kittel lists seventeen instances from 1QH^a X 22–32 [II 20–30] cited by Holm-Nielsen and Carmignac as quotations and gives a brief analysis of each. Only in approximately seven of these does Kittel find some sort of correspondence which could be described as allusion or quotation. The remainder she attributes to "free" or "deliberate" use of biblical idiom, imagery and vocabulary rather than allusion to a specific passage.[59] She suggests that in cases of uncertainty a further requirement for a common phrase to be regarded as an allusion is that "the context, meaning, and the idiom itself must converge on one text, or must have incomplete convergence reinforced by surrounding references to the same passage."[60]

An important criterion discussed by Furniss and Bath for distinguishing between allusion and influence is whether there is evidence of a literary device; i.e. whether the identification of an allusion contributes to the interpretation of the poem's meaning or significance. This includes recognising ways in which the poem has reworked the original source.[61] (This corresponds well to Perri's definition of allusion as directing the reader to a particular aspect of the source text.) Thus identification of an allusion includes the element of interpretation. Furniss and Bath include an extended discussion of the ideas of Harold Bloom who argues that all poets struggle with the problem of being original in light of the tradition that they have inherited. This "anx-

---

[58] Michael Fishbane, *Biblical Interpretation in Ancient Israel* (Oxford: Clarendon Press, 1985), 9.
[59] Cf. The terms "influence" and "echo" used by Hollander, *The Figure of Echo*.
[60] Kittel, *The Hymns of Qumran*, 48–55.
[61] Furniss and Bath, *Reading Poetry*, 308–313.

iety of influence" becomes a greater problem as the tradition grows. Bloom defines a "strong poet" as one who successfully "misreads" the tradition, thus making his own original contribution.[62]

Although biblical scholars might baulk at using the term "misreading" as a description of exegesis, the type of creative transformation that Bloom describes has similarities with Fishbane's description of exegesis. In his discussion of aggadic exegesis Fishbane introduces two criteria for establishing an "implicit" or "virtual" citation of one text by another. These are:

(1) "Multiple and sustained lexical linkages"
(2) The second text uses the first in a "lexically reorganised and topically rethematised way."[63]

In elaborating on the first criterion Fishbane points to the presence of "clusters of parallel terms" and "analogous contexts" as being important.[64] But he gives examples to show that linguistic similarity alone should be viewed with caution. The additional presence of some exegetical transformation makes the identification more certain. Schultz' criteria also require something more than mere verbal similarity. His first criterion requires both verbal and syntactical correspondence and his second criterion is that of awareness by the adoptive text of the context of the adopted text.[65]

4.2.1. *Proposed Criteria*

To summarise the above discussion, a working definition of an allusion is a reference which is recognised by a reader as referring to a textual source, knowledge of which contributes to the meaning for the reader. In this study the reader is assumed to be the implied reader outlined in the above discussion on authors and readers. Taking account of all the above observations, I propose to use the following two criteria. If a passage satisfies both criteria then it will be deemed to be a certain allusion. If it satisfies only the first criterion, then it will be noted in the first instance as the use of scriptural language or as a weak allusion.

---

[62] Harold Bloom, *The Anxiety of Influence* (Oxford: Oxford University Press, 1973); *A Map of Misreading* (Oxford: Oxford University Press, 1975), cited by Furniss and Bath, *Reading Poetry*, 315.
[63] Fishbane, *Biblical Interpretation in Ancient Israel*, 285.
[64] Fishbane, *Biblical Interpretation in Ancient Israel*, 287.
[65] Schultz, *The Search for Quotation*, 222–227.

The initial criterion for considering that a phrase might be an allusion is identifying the marker. I will in the first instance be seeking to identify verbal similarity to a scriptural passage. I will however bear in mind the possibility of other more subtle markers, as discussed above. Verbal similarities which merit consideration as possible allusion markers would include the following:

(1a) A correspondence with a hapax legomenon in the Hebrew Bible (including any variant readings found in Qumran biblical texts).
(1b) A group of words which stand in a similar syntactical relationship in both passages and occur in this combination in only one identifiable scripture passage (e.g. Isa 9:6 "wonderful counsellor ... mighty/might").
(1c) A more commonly occurring phrase which nonetheless has similarities of meaning or context with one identifiable scripture passage. This would include the case where other more certain allusions to this particular scriptural passage or book have been identified within the poem. (An example of the latter are the multiple allusions to Jeremiah in the first poem discussed in chapter three.)
(1d) In the case of (1b) or (1c) the requirement of "one identifiable scriptural passage" may exceptionally be stretched to include a group of passages if a case can be made for some exegetical or other relationship between them, which would enable them to be viewed as an entity.

The second criterion is that discussed in different ways by Schultz, Perri, Furniss and Bath, Bloom, and Fishbane; i.e. the indication that the poem (the adoptive text) directs the reader to a particular interpretation of the adopted text. This criterion may be satisfied in one of the following ways:

(2a) Awareness of the context of the adopted passage contributes to the meaning/significance of the adoptive passage; i.e. the contexts may be compared or contrasted in some way.
(2b) The use of a poetic device such as word play, irony, variation of wording, juxtaposition with other texts or contexts. (For examples of this see the first poem discussed in chapter five.)
(2c) Evidence of an underlying exegesis of the adopted passage found in other texts present at Qumran and therefore presumably recognisable by the ideal reader. (For an example of this see the discussion on "way of his heart" in chapter three.)

(2d) Evidence of use of an exegetical method used in other Qumran texts.

(2e) Any other justifiable indication that knowledge of the adopted text adds meaning to the adoptive text.

It is hoped that bearing these criteria in mind will help to guard against the charge of "parallelomania."[66] Nonetheless, these criteria are given as a working basis rather than watertight rules. This is because the nature of poetic artistry is to surprise the reader. The vagueness of condition 2(e) indicates my intention to leave room for artistic judgement.

4.3. *The Function of Allusions*

An important factor to be considered is the function of the allusion within the composition, i.e. its effect upon a reader. I will assume that, in general, the use of scriptural allusions lends authority to a composition. Another important function is referred to by Stanley as creating a sense of solidarity; i.e. recognition of the allusion implicitly reinforces feelings of belonging to a particular community.[67] Newsom has aptly described how this may have worked to foster a particular kind of self-understanding in the sectarian community associated with Qumran:

> This sort of intertextual allusion both trains the sectarian (one begins to listen differently, alert for the double resonance of phrases) and it rewards the increasingly proficient reader with the evidence that he is indeed one who knows.[68]

However, I will also be looking for other functions which are specific to the choice and manner of use of the adopted text. A useful overview and discussion of the literature on the function of allusions in western literature has been provided by Schultz.[69]

---

[66] Samuel Sandmel, "Parallelomania," defines parallelomania as "that extravagance among scholars which first overdoes the supposed similarity in passages and then proceeds to describe source and derivation as if implying literary connection flowing in an inevitable or predetermined direction."

[67] Christopher D. Stanley "The Rhetoric of Quotations: An Essay on Method," in *Early Christian Interpretation of the Scriptures of Israel: Investigations and Proposals* (ed. C.A. Evans, and J.A. Sanders; JSNTSup 148; SSEJC 5; Sheffield: Sheffield Academic Press, 1997), 44–58.

[68] Newsom, *The Self as Symbolic Space*, 214.

[69] Schultz, *The Search for Quotation*, 192–207.

I propose to use the following terminology from the discussion of Michael Wheeler. The "gnomic allusion" may serve mainly as the fitting encapsulation of an idea or theme. This type of allusion borders on the proverbial or idiomatic saying and recognition of the adopted text adds only minimally to the meaning. The "shorthand notation" however is a way of concisely referring to a typical scenario, characterisation, set of concepts, etc. to be found in the adopted text. This is a maximal use of allusion, where knowledge of the source is crucial to understanding the marker. The "pointer" to plot or theme alerts the reader to expect certain developments on the basis of the adopted text's context ahead of their specific unfolding in the adoptive text. A "structural allusion" invites a reader to draw major parallels between the overall structure or theme of the adopted text and that of the adoptive text.[70] In addition, I will use Greene's concept of the "dialectical allusion" to describe the way in which the reader experiences the adopted and adoptive text in an interpretative dialogue, each affecting the interpretation of the other.[71]

5. *How Does One Read Texts?*

Although I have already touched upon the shift in literary theory from author to text to reader, most of the discussion so far has been based on methodology drawn from formalist, structuralist and rhetorical schools of criticism. These methods are basically text-orientated, with some consideration of reader interpretation. That is, they assume that certain strategies of reading are fairly universal, as are certain literary tropes.[72] In addition they assume that a literarily competent reader will be familiar with the particular stylistic conventions and literary tradition in which the composition stands. In this section I will deal in more detail with two other important reader-orientated approaches to the reading of texts. These are the ideas of intertextuality and of reader response.

---

[70] Michael D. Wheeler, *The Art of Allusion in Victorian Fiction*, (London and Basingstoke: The Macmillan Press, 1979), 20–25.
[71] Thomas M. Greene, *The Light in Troy: Imitation and Discovery in Renaissance Poetry* (New Haven: Yale University Press, 1982), 38–46, cited in Schultz, *The Search for Quotation*, 198.
[72] For a discussion of the strategies a reader uses to make sense of a text see Jonathan Culler "Prolegomena to a Theory of Reading," in *The Reader in the Text* (eds. S. Suleiman and I. Crosman; Princeton: Princeton University Press, 1980), 46–66.

5.1. *Intertextuality*

Allusion is not to be confused with the wider phenomenon of intertextuality. This concept, developed by Julia Kristeva and also widely written on by Roland Barthes,[73] is a theory that denies that the meanings of texts are stable because texts are continually interacting with one another to produce new meanings. "Texts" include not just literary texts but the whole world of cultural discourse. This reader-oriented approach, unlike the tracing of influences between texts, is independent of the relative date of composition of the texts. It also means that potentially any two or more texts familiar to the reader may be read intertextually. Fittingly then, given its origins in post-structuralist ideas about the instability of meaning, the term is often used very imprecisely as an umbrella term encompassing many approaches to the relationships between texts.

This study will use the concept in a limited sense to consider how a reader's interpretation of the *Hodayot* may have been influenced by his knowledge of other literary texts in the Dead Sea scrolls corpus and vice versa. I have preferred the term intertextuality to emphasise that I will be concentrating upon questions of reader interpretation rather than direct influence between texts. In other words I will be looking for similarities or contrasts between texts which may have encouraged readers to interpret them in light of one another. Under this heading I will consider texts which allude to one or more of the same passages or seem to reflect a common exegetical tradition. For example, in chapter three I discuss a number of different texts which possibly allude to Jer 10:23, or to an exegetical tradition connected with this verse. Other similarities which might provoke comparison are those of theme and genre.

---

[73] Roland Barthes, "From Work to Text," in R. Barthes, *Image-Music-Text* (trans. S. Heath; London: Fontana, 1977), 155–164, cited in Furniss and Bath, *Reading Poetry*, 324 n. 22; Julia Kristeva, *Desire in Language: A Semiotic Approach to Literature and Art* (ed. L.S. Roudiez; trans. T. Gora, A. Jardine, L.S. Roudiez; New York: Columbia Univ., 1980); Julia Kristeva, *Revolution in Poetic Language* (trans. M. Waller; New York: Columbia Univ., 1984), cited by Timothy K. Beal "Glossary," in *Reading Between Texts: Intertextuality and the Hebrew Bible* (ed. D.N. Fewell; Louisville, KY: Westminster/John Knox Press, 1992), 21–24.

5.2. Reader-Orientated Approaches

The above section on intertextuality considers how a reader's interpretation may be affected by other literary texts. However the sociohistorical factors which affect reader response are much more difficult to discern.

An example of such uncertainty of interpretation is the phrase "I know by your insight." Would a sectarian reader interpret this as referring to a special revelation, or to the insight gained by group study and teaching? Further, would he interpret the "I" as referring to a particular individual, a particular class of individuals, or to any member of the community? (These interpretations are not all mutually exclusive, as revelation given to a leader becomes insight shared by the whole group via teaching.) The interpretation of this first person phrase would in turn affect the reader's response. For example, it could be a state to be admired and respected, aspired to, or identified with. It could consequently reinforce hierarchical differences, reinforce certain theological beliefs (e.g. dependence upon God), encourage certain activities and practices (e.g. study), encourage certain feelings and attitudes (e.g. gratitude, group loyalty) and so on. Again not all of these are mutually exclusive.[74]

Two schools of reader-orientated theory address these concerns. The school of reception theory represented by Hans Robert Jauss[75] is concerned to chart the varying "horizons of expectation" which affect readers in different historical periods. However, sociological study has shown that even within a single historical period there are differing groups of readers.[76] The theories of Stanley Fish deny that texts have meaning apart from those that individual readers give them. But the extreme subjectivity of this position is made workable by Fish's idea of "interpretative communities" which allow groups of readers to attain

---

[74] Carol Newsom has discussed this and similar phrases found in the Community Hymns in the context of their juxtaposition with self-effacing language. She relates this "discourse of the self" to the disciplined life of the Qumran community as described in 1QS. Her thesis is that the community life required its members to exercise speech in the community assemblies but that this speech must also be submissive to the protocols of the community. Carol. A. Newsom, "The Case of the Blinking I," *Semeia* 57 (1992): 13–23. See also Newsom, *The Self as Symbolic Space*.

[75] Hans Robert Jauss, "Literary History as a Challenge to Literary Theory," trans. E. Benzinger, *New Literary History* 2 (1970): 7–37.

[76] Jacques Leenhardt "Towards a Sociology of Reading," in *The Reader in the Text* (ed. S. Suleiman and I. Crosman; Princeton: Princeton University Press, 1980), 205–224.

some degree of agreement in interpreting a text.[77] A premise of this study will be that the group(s) associated with the corpus of literature found at Qumran formed such an interpretative community.[78]

The major source of knowledge about this community is its literature. Other archaeological and literary data from the period may also provide clues. In order to attempt to uncover the social knowledge that these texts assume in their readers, historical, sociological and anthropological theories and models are pressed into service by scholars. Even when all this is done large uncertainties remain; as Susan Suleiman comments, we need to be "more wary about our general theories and more humble about what we can never know."[79] For example, both Douglas and Newsom take this approach, but with different models and very different conclusions.[80] While not ignoring the possible socio-historical influences on reader interpretation, in the spirit of the above comment by Suleiman I will approach such discussion with caution.

6. *Outline of Method*

To summarise then, the method and chapter layout for the study of each individual composition is as follows. For each composition I will give a brief introduction indicating the main points of interest. I have subdivided the analysis of each composition into seven sections. These sections approximate the order and stages of the analysis, although in practice each task has been reviewed and revised in the light of subsequent stages.

---

[77] Stanley Fish, "Interpreting the Variorum," *Critical Enquiry*, reprinted in *Modern Criticism and Theory: A Reader* (ed. D. Lodge; London: Longman, 1988); Stanley Fish, *Is There a Text in this Class?* (Cambridge, MA: Harvard University Press, 1980).

[78] The use of the term "Qumran community" begs the question of how the group altered over time and whether there was more than one geographical group associated with the movement.

[79] Susan Suleiman "Introduction: Varieties of Audience-Orientated Criticism," in *The Reader in the Text* (ed. S. Suleiman and I. Crosman; Princeton: Princeton University Press, 1980), 38.

[80] Douglas, "Power and Praise;" Newsom, *The Self as Symbolic Space*. See my discussion in §§5.3 and 5.6 of chapter one.

6.1. *Delimitation and Text*

The first task was to establish the textual basis, which is represented as a transcription of the manuscript lines. Because of the lack of a principal edition of 1QH^a taking into account the reordering of the fragments, the text contained in the Study Edition of the scrolls by García Martínez and Tigchelaar was used as a preliminary guide. This was checked against the principal editions, the official photographs, and relevant published articles. Where compositions are preserved in more than one manuscript these were also compared. Thus the final choice about textual uncertainties is a matter of personal judgement. Lacunae are indicated by square brackets and the source/justification for restorations and reconstructions is indicated in footnotes.[81]

6.2. *Translation*

I have endeavoured to set out the chosen passages in lines, verses, and stanzas, using as a guide the observations of the various studies cited in §3 of this chapter. The method was iterative, starting with a rough lineation based on the most obvious syntactic and semantic features and proceeding through progressive stages of amendment and refinement. The text was divided into roughly one grammatical clause per line, bearing in mind Kittel's comments that more than one verb per line is rare.[82] Another useful guide was Kittel's observation that strategic particles, such as כיא, independent pronouns, and interrogative particles, often mark the beginning of a new unit.[83] Any blanks left by the scribe were also taken into account. The recognition of parallelism and other poetic devices played a useful part at this stage, but has been analysed more fully at subsequent stages.

In order to emphasise that this is an interpretation and analysis, the poetic lineation is indicated in the translation rather than in the Hebrew text. To facilitate discussion I have adopted a very literal approach to the translation, reflecting as much as possible the original

---

[81] The publications consulted at this stage were García Martínez and Tigchelaar, *The Dead Sea Scrolls Study Edition*; Sukenik, *The Dead Sea Scrolls*; Schuller, "Hodayot;" Stegemann, "The Material Reconstruction of 1QHodayot;" Lim and Alexander, *The Dead Sea Scrolls Electronic Reference Library, Vol 1*; Licht, *The Thanksgiving Scroll*; Puech, *Croyance*.

[82] Kittel, *The Hymns of Qumran*, 163.

[83] Kittel, *The Hymns of Qumran*, 27.

word order. I have also endeavoured to use, where context allows, the same translation for a Hebrew root each time it occurs. This results in a somewhat wooden translation but enables structural devices, word plays, etc. to be indicated in the translated text.[84] The main structural features are indicated by the use of numbers and letters in the left hand column. These labels, rather than the manuscript line numbers have been used in the majority of the discussion.

6.3. Analysis of Structure

At each stage I have read through the poem noting poetic devices, beginning with simple repetitions of words or phrases and progressing to more complex devices. Helpful suggestions and examples of this type of method have been outlined by W.G.E. Watson.[85] Some of these repetitions and patterns indicate parallelism between adjacent lines or other poetic devices at line and verse level. Others may indicate correspondences at stanza level.

Repetitions may also indicate key structural devices at the level of the complete poem, such as keywords or inclusios. The overall structure of the poem is discussed in the third section of the analysis, whereas poetic devices at verse and stanza level are discussed in the close reading. At the start of this third section an outline summary of the structure is given, referring to the labels in the left-hand column of the translation. This is followed by a more detailed description of the structure.

Much of the discussion in this study revolves around the use of key words and phrases used as structural devices or as allusion markers. For this reason I have adopted the slightly unconventional practice of using italics rather than quotation marks for words or phrases under discussion from the poem being analysed. This also allows me to indicate such marker phrases within biblical quotations.

---

[84] The translation is my own, but I am particularly indebted to the commentaries of Holm-Nielsen and Mansoor for their many useful observations upon the possible meanings of words and phrases. Holm-Nielsen, *Hodayot*; Mansoor, *The Thanksgiving Hymns*.

[85] Watson, *Classical Hebrew Poetry* 15–20.

6.4. *Close Reading*

The close reading is a verse by verse description, demonstrating how the various poetic devices function within the text. Because allusions are being considered as poetic devices, it was first necessary to identify and classify all the possible allusions. I have used the lists compiled by Holm-Nielsen, Wernberg-Møller, and Carmignac[86] as a starting point for identifying possible allusions, using database software to collate the three lists. I have also made use of computer software to search within the Hebrew Bible for individual words and phrases which could be allusion markers.[87] I have also attempted to identify any relevant textual variants from the MT which have been identified in Qumran manuscripts.[88]

The allusions have been assessed according to the criteria set out in §4.2.1 of this chapter. In ascertaining the context and possible interpretations of the scriptural texts I have made use of available biblical commentaries. The certain allusions have been singled out for particular attention regarding their function. However, the close reading will also give an opportunity to reconsider other less certain possibilities of allusion in the light of the overall structure and theme of the passage. This section will also include some preliminary discussion of the effect upon a reader, which will be expanded upon in the following sections.

6.5. *Allusions*

In this section of the analysis I summarise and evaluate the allusions discussed in the close reading. Most of the markers and connotations will have been mentioned in the close reading, but I elaborate upon these where appropriate. In the close reading I have considered how each allusion functions within the verse or stanza in which it occurs. In this section I endeavour to assess the overall effect of the allusions. In particular I discuss any structural allusions or links between allusions. I also discuss any possible underlying exegesis.

---

[86] Holm-Nielsen, *Hodayot*, 354–359; Carmignac, "Les citations de l'ancien testament;" Wernberg-Møller, "The Contribution of the Hodayot to Biblical Textual Criticism."

[87] *Nelson's Electronic Bible Reference Library*[TM] (Nashville: Nelson Electronic Publishing[TM], 1997).

[88] Martin Abegg Jr., Peter Flint, and Eugene Ulrich, *The Dead Sea Scrolls Bible* (Edinburgh: T&T Clark, 1999), and relevant principal editions.

6.6. *Intertexts*

In this section I consider texts other than those alluded to which may have informed the reader's interpretation of the text or shed light on possible underlying exegesis and traditions. In keeping with the premise that the *Hodayot* is an anthology possibly drawn from a variety of sources, I first consider other *Hodayot* compositions. I also consider other literature from the Dead Sea corpus, and other literature from the late Second Temple period. In order to identify other Dead Sea texts which contain similar allusions, themes and vocabulary, I first made use of the concordances of Kuhn and of Charlesworth. During the course of this study a more extensive concordance by Martin Abegg has been published, which has greatly improved the ease of identifying such passages.[89]

6.7. *Observations and Comments*

In this final section I summarise the most significant observations arising from my analysis. I seek to highlight any general implications or areas for further investigation. I also compare my findings with those of other studies.

---

[89] Karl Georg Kuhn, et al., *Konkordanz zu den Qumran Texten* (Göttingen: Vandenhoeck & Ruprecht, 1960); James H. Charlesworth et al., *Graphic Concordance to the Dead Sea Scrolls* (Tübingen/Louisville: Mohr, 1991); Abegg, et al., *The Dead Sea Scrolls Concordance, Volume 1*.

CHAPTER THREE

TWO DUALISTIC POEMS

1. Introduction

In this chapter I will consider two compositions which have considerable features in common. One has generally been regarded as a Community Hymn and the other as a Teacher Hymn.[1] Both are dualistic in outlook and both contain similar vocabulary with possible literary dependence between them.

2. Two Ways
1QH^a VII 21–VIII ? [XV 8–25+frg. 10+frg. 32]

Although this composition is damaged the text preserved in 1QH^a VII 25–34 appears to be a discrete sub-unit. It is of interest because, although part of a Community Hymn, it nonetheless has a considerable number of allusions. Holm-Nielsen considered that the use of scripture is much stronger in the thanksgiving psalms than in the hymns. However, he also noted the apparent distinctiveness of this hymn.[2] It also appears to be fairly intricately structured, another feature not associated by most commentators with Community Hymns. Finally, this poetic segment has interesting connections with other poems within the corpus, particularly the poem in 1QH^a XII 6–XIII 6 [IV 5–V 4], which is considered later in this chapter.

---

[1] Becker, Jeremias and Kuhn classify 1QH^a VII 14–39 [XV 1–26] as a Community Hymn and XII 6–XIII 6 [IV 5–V 4] as a Teacher Hymn. Becker and Kuhn consider XII 31b–XIII 6 to be an addition to the latter. See Becker, *Das Heil Gottes*, 50–56; Jeremias, *Der Lehrer*, 204–217; Kuhn, *Enderwartung*, 21–26; Holm-Nielsen, *Hodayot*, 313.

[2] Holm-Nielsen's categories of thanksgiving psalm and hymn approximate to the categories Teacher Hymn and Community Hymn. He singles out 1QH^a VII 14–39 [XV 1–26] as not having any clear references to the community, but being closer to an instructional poem. See Holm-Nielsen, *Hodayot*, 312–313.

This composition has not received as much attention from commentators as the others in this study. H.-W. Kuhn considered it in his work on the Community Hymns. Because of its treatment of predestination it has attracted some comment by others, in particular by Merrill. Other studies which have analysed it in some detail are those of Tanzer, Puech, and more recently, Newsom.[3]

2.1. *Delimitation and Text*[4]

This composition can be found on Sukenik plate 49. Sukenik numbered it as XV 8 onwards but Stegemann and Puech have reassigned it as VII 21 onwards. The top ten lines of column VII, about one quarter of its length, are completely missing. The next ten lines are badly damaged but have been partially restored by the placing of fragments 10, 34, and 42 (Sukenik plates 56, 57). There is a blank space at the end of line 20 which gives reasonable confidence that a new composition started in line 21. Based on the first two or three letters most commentators have assumed that the damaged line 21 begins with the formula ברוך אתה. Stegemann reconstructs the beginning of the line as ברו]ך אתה אל הרחמים ב[שיר מזמור למש[כיל.[5] However, Puech has reconstructed this as a rubric בי]ו[ץ]את מ[עמד ⟨מזמור⟩ למש[כיל].[6]

The bottom of column VII is damaged, giving very little text in lines 39–41. A few letters at the beginning of lines 40 and 41 can be restored from fragment 32 (Sukenik plate 57). Lines 1–7 of column VIII are completely missing. This damage makes it impossible to know where this composition would have ended. Although it is possible that it may have ended in the first lines of column VIII (Sukenik plate 50), the partial restoration, by Stegemann and Puech, of lines 8–16 from fragments 12 and 13 (Sukenik plate 56) now make this less likely. This is because there is no indication from these restored lines that a new hymn has begun. Furthermore, Stegemann now argues that the

---

[3] Kuhn, *Enderwartung*, 103–112; E.H. Merrill, *Qumran and Predestination: A Theological Study of the Thanksgiving Hymns* (STDJ 8; Leiden: Brill, 1975), 16–23; Tanzer, "The Sages at Qumran," 42–47; Puech, *Croyance*, 385–389; Newsom, *The Self as Symbolic Space*, 209–216.

[4] Unless otherwise stated, references in this section are to Sukenik, *The Dead Sea Scrolls*; Stegemann, "The Material Reconstruction of 1QHodayot," 280; Puech, "Quelques aspects," 41–43, 45–46.

[5] Stegemann, "The Number of Psalms in 1QHodayot^a," 197.

[6] Puech, *Croyance*, 385.

formula ברוך אתה which appears in line 26 of column VIII is not the start of a new poem.[7] If this is the case then the poem possibly continues until the very end of column VIII.

Lines 11–20 of column VII overlap with 4QH[a] 8 I 1–12, but the poem which follows this in 4QH[a] is a different poem from the one found in lines 21ff. of 1QH[a] VII.[8] There is no known overlap between this latter poem and the Cave 4 manuscripts.

1QH[a] VII 21–41 [XV 8–25 + frg. 10 + frg. 32]

21 ב . [ ] [.. ב*מזמור* למש[ ] [[9]רנה] [
22 [יא[הבו[10] אותך כול הימים וא[ ] [
23 אמ[ ] ואהבכה בנדבה ובכול לב ובכול נפש בררתי . .][[[11]
24 הק[י]מותי לבלתי]סור מכול אשר צויתה ואחז'קה על רבים מ.] [לבלתי][12]
25 עזוב מכול חוקיך *vacat* ואני ידעתי בבינתך כיא לא ביד בשר] [ולא ל][13]אדם
26 דרכו ולא יוכל אנוש להכין צעדו ואדעה כי בידך יצר כול רוח]וכול פעול[תו
27 הכינותה בטרם בראתו ואיכה יוכל כול להשנות את דבריכה רק אתה]ברא[תה
28 צדיק ומרחם הכינותו למועד רצון להשמר בבריתך ולתהלך בכול ולה[גיל][14] עליו
29 בהמון רחמיך ולפתוח כול צרת נפשו לישועת עולם ושלום עד ואין מחסור ותרם
30 מבשר כבודו *vacat* ורשעים בראתה ל[ ]קץ [ח]רונכה[15] ומרחם הקדשתם ליום
הרגה
31 כי הלכו בדרך לא טוב וימאסו בבריתכ[ה אמת]ך תעבה נפשם ולא רצו בכול אשר
32 צויתה ויבחרו באשר שנאתה כי ל[16] [ ]ך הכינותם לעשות בם שפטים גדולים
33 לעיני כול מעשיך ולהיות לאות ומו[פת לדרת[17]]עולם לדעת כול את כבודך ואת
כוחך

---

[7] Stegemann, "The Number of Psalms in 1QHodayot[a]," 197, considers that line 26 is not the beginning of a new poem because the scribe left no blank space at the end of the previous line.

[8] However, Schuller notes that line 13 of 4QH[a] 8 I and line 11 of 1QH[a] 10 could be considered as overlapping. Schuller also notes that the orthography of 1QH[a] 10 is different from the rest of the first 8 columns of 1QH[a]. It is possible therefore that 1QH[a] 10 is misplaced. See Schuller, "Hodayot," 111 nn. 51, 52.

[9] This line is reconstructed from frg. 10, reading מזמור instead of Sukenik מבין. See Sukenik, *The Dead Sea Scrolls*, pl. 56. Note also the alternative readings by Puech and Stegemann which I included earlier in this chapter.

[10] Puech, *Croyance*, 385–389, reads ו]אהבה.

[11] Licht reads בררתי חפץ ר[צוני ובכול נפשי]; Puech reads בחרתי]ביראתך ועל (מאד) [רוחי. See Licht, *The Thanksgiving Scroll*, 194–199; Puech, *Croyance*, 385–389.

[12] Licht, *The Thanksgiving Scroll*, 194–199, restores מו]ראך ומשפטיכה לבלתי.

[13] Licht, *The Thanksgiving Scroll*, 194–199, restores as אורחותיו ולא ל].

[14] For this reading see E. Qimron "A New Reading in 1QH XV 15 and the Root GYL in the Dead Sea Scrolls," *RevQ* 14 (1989–1990): 127–128.

[15] Licht, *The Thanksgiving Scroll*, 194–199, reads ל[קצי חר]ונכה.

[16] Sukenik, *The Dead Sea Scrolls*, reads כול.

[17] Using short form (cf. MT Gen 9:12), for fit. Licht, *The Thanksgiving Scroll*, 194–199, restores as לקצי.

66 CHAPTER THREE

34 הגדול ומה אף הוא בשר כי ישכיל [באלה ויצ]ר[18] עפר איך יוכל להכין צעדו   vacat
35 אתה יצרתה רוח ופעולתה הכינות[ה] מקדם עולם [ומאתך דרך כול חי ואני ידעתי כיא
36 לא ישוה כול הון באמתך ואי[...] ק[ודשך[19]]ואדעה כי בם בחרתה מכול
37 ולעד הם ישרתוך ולא תקב[ל שוחד לעולה]ולא[20] תקח כופר לעלילות רשעה כיא
38 **אל**[21] אמת אתה וכול עולה ת[שמיד [22]]לא תהיה לפניך ואני[23] ידעת[י]
39 כי לך דר[ך] כ[ו]ל חי וברצונך אתה [תשפט כול] מעשה ואי[כ[24]] ל[   ]
40 קודשך [   ]
41 כי ב[   ]

2.2. *Translation*

IA (21) [… … … … … … … … … … …]
    [… … … … … … … … … … …][25]
    (22) [… They lov]e you all the days

IB And [I … … … … … … … … … …]
    [… …] (23) [… … … … … … … …]
    And I love you freely and with all (my) heart.
    And with all (my) soul I have purified […]
    [And …] (24) I have bou[nd myself]
    [so that I may not] turn aside from all that you have commanded.
    And I will hold fast to (the) many [… … … …]
    [so that I may not] (25) depart from all your statutes.   *Blank*

IIA1a And I, I know by your understanding
       that not by the hand of flesh [… …]
       [and not for]a human (26) his way
       nor can a man *direct* his steps.

IIA1b But I know that by your hand (is) the FORMATION[26] of every spirit
       [and all] its [works] (27) you *destined* before you CREATED it.

IIA1c And how can anyone change your decrees?

IIA2a Only you, you [CREATED] (28) the righteous one
       and from the womb you *destined* him for the period of approval:

---

[18] Following Puech; Licht restores [ברזיך ויצר] See Puech, *Croyance*, 385–389; Licht, *The Thanksgiving Scroll*, 194–199.
[19] Licht, *The Thanksgiving Scroll*, 194–199, reads קודשך בעדת לבוא ואוי[תי.
[20] Licht reads [תק[בל שוחד עולה; Puech reads (with unedited frg.) ולא תקבל שוחד [למעשי רע ולא] See Licht, *The Thanksgiving Scroll*, 194–199; Puech, *Croyance*, 385–389.
[21] This word is written in ancient Hebrew script.
[22] Licht reads [ת[שמיד לעד וכול דרך רשעה; Puech (with unedited frg.) תשמיד ל[עדו]רשעה See Licht, *The Thanksgiving Scroll*, 194–199; Puech, *Croyance*, 385–389.
[23] Licht, *The Thanksgiving Scroll*, 194–199, has לפניך אני.
[24] For this reconstruction see Puech, *Croyance*, 385–389.
[25] The reconstruction of this line of the MS is too uncertain to translate. It probably contained a rubric and/or introductory formula.
[26] "Formation" fits the context better than "inclination."

IIA2b	To keep (himself) in your covenant and to walk (uprightly) in all (things).[27]
IIA2c	And to [rejoice] over him[28] (29) in the multitude of your compassion and to open all the constriction of his soul for eternal salvation and peace everlasting and without lack. Thus you will raise (30) above flesh his glory. *Blank*
IIB1a	But the wicked you CREATED for [the time of] your wrath and from the womb you consecrated them for the day of slaughter.
IIB1b	(31) For they have walked on a way (that is) not good and they reject your covenant [and]y[our truth] their soul has detested nor have they delighted in all that (32) you have commanded and they choose that which you have hated.
IIB1c	For [… … … … … … … …] you have *destined* them to enact against them great judgements (33) for the eyes of all your works and to be for a sign and a por[tent for] eternal [generations] so that everyone may know your glory and your (34) great strength
IIB2a	And what then itself (is) flesh that it understands [these? And a FORMATI]ON of dust how can it *direct* its steps? *Blank*
IIB2b	(35)You, you have FORMED the spirit and its works you have *destined* [from before eternity].
IIB2c	And from you (is) the way of every living being.
IIIA	And I, I know that (36) no wealth can compare to your truth and … [… … … … … … … …] your holiness. And I know that them you have chosen above all (37)and forever they will serve you. And you do not acce[pt a bribe for injustice] nor take a ransom for wicked acts. For (38) the *God*[29] of truth you (are) and all injustice you [destroy] [… … …] will no longer exist in your presence.
IIIB	And I, [I] know […] (39) that to you [belong the ways of all living] [and that in your good pleasure, You, you judge all work] [And how … … … … … … … … …]

---

[27] I follow Holm-Nielsen, *Hodayot*, 230 n. 15, for the words to complete the sense of this line.

[28] Puech translates "qu'il s'en réjouisse à cause de l'abondance de tes tendresses," with the righteous one, not God, as the subject (Puech, *Croyance*, 386).

[29] This word was written in ancient Hebrew script.

```
          [... ... ... ... ] (40) your holiness
          [... ... ... ... ... ... ... ... ... ...]
          [... ... ... ... ... ... ... ... ... ...]
          [... ... ... ... ... ... ... ... ... ...]
          (41) For [... ... ... ... ... ... ... ... ... ...]
          [... ... ... ... ... ... ... ... ... ...]
          [... ... ... ... ... ... ... ... ... ...]
```

2.3. *Analysis of Structure*

I. Declaration of Loyalty	VII 21–25a [8–12a]
A. Introductory Stanza?	VII 21b–22a
B. Declaration (I love, I hold fast)	VII 22b–25a
II. Wisdom Poem	VII 25b–35c [12b–22c]

  A1. Introduction
    a. not by the hand of flesh … can a man *direct* his steps
    b. by your hand is the FORMATION of every spirit … *destined* … CREATED
    c. final emphatic line
  A2. The righteous
    a. CREATED … from the womb *destined* for the period of approval
    b. keep your covenant and walk (uprightly)
    c. you will raise above flesh his glory
  B1. The wicked
    a. CREATED … from the womb consecrated for the day of slaughter
    b. walked on a way not good and reject your covenant
    c. you have *destined* them … so that everyone may know your glory
  B2. Reprise
    a. what is flesh? … a FORMATION of dust, how can it *direct* its steps
    b. you have FORMED the spirit … *destined*
    c. final emphatic line

III. Confession of Faith? (I know)	VII 35d–? [22d–?]
A. The holiness and justice of God	VII 35d–38
B. ???	VII 39–?

Because of the damaged portions of this composition any description of its overall structure must be very tentative. However, for ease of reference I have divided it into three sections. The initial few lines possibly consist of a rubric and introductory stanza, which I have labelled IA. The main body of the poem probably begins with the conjunction and independent pronoun *and I* in line 23. This stanza, labelled IB, though damaged, appears to be a declaration of loyalty to the community.[30]

---

[30] Tanzer, "The Sages at Qumran," 46, observes that it "has the tone of a pledge."

Section II consists of two sub-sections, A and B. The opening words of these are indicated by short blanks in lines 25 and 30 respectively of the manuscript. There is also a short blank space at the end of line 34. Puech makes this the end of the stanza.[31] However, after some vacillation I have decided, following Tanzer, to include most of line 35 in this stanza. My reasons for doing this are as follows. Firstly, this completes the symmetry of this section. Secondly, the following sentence begins with the phrase *I know* (ואני ידעתי); such a combination of independent pronoun and perfect verb is often an indication of a new stanza and would match the identical phrase at the beginning of IIA1. Finally, there appears to be a change of subject at this point, to the use of wealth.

As mentioned, section II has a symmetrical structure so that the two outermost stanzas, IIA1 and IIB2, correspond with each other as do the two inner ones, IIA2 and IIB1. The outer stanzas introduce and recapitulate the basic theme and the inner stanzas elaborate it. This section is also unified by the use of the root כון which occurs six times, translated as *direct* or *destine*.[32] Closely associated with this are the roots ברא and יצר, which occur three times each[33] and are translated CREATE and FORM respectively. I have emphasised these key words in the translation and the structural table. I will now elaborate on the symmetrical features.

There are considerable lexical correspondences between the opening and closing stanzas. It is easier to see these in the Hebrew than in the English translation. The final phrase, *How can it direct its steps?* (איך יוכל להכין צעדו) picks up two phrases from the opening verses. These are the phrase להכין צעדו, which is translated as *direct his steps* in IIA1a, and the phrase ואיכה יוכל, which is translated as *How can* in IIA1c. The term *flesh* (בשר) is also used in both stanzas.

There are also some non-identical but corresponding phrases. *I know by your understanding* corresponds with *that it understands* and *creature of dust* corresponds with *human/man*. Couplet IIA1b corresponds very closely with IIB2b in sense and vocabulary, the main difference being grammatical. Both stanzas end with a single poetic line.

---

[31] Puech, *Croyance*, 385, 387.
[32] Holm-Nielsen, *Hodayot*, 17, 23 n. 27, translates as "ordained," noting that "mete out" is another possible translation.
[33] One of these is a restoration in line 34.

The correspondences between the two inner stanzas are easier to spot. Stanza IIA2 deals with the *righteous* person in contrast with IIB1 which deals with the *wicked*. The contrast is emphasised by the fact that the righteous person is a single individual whereas the wicked are anonymously plural. In IIA2a and IIB1a we see that both have been *created* by God *from the womb* but there the similarity ends. The righteous are *destined* for *the period of approval*, whereas the wicked have been *consecrated* for *the day of slaughter*.

Their behaviour is likewise contrasted in IIA2b and IIB1b. The righteous *keep your covenant* and *walk (uprightly)*, whereas the wicked *reject your covenant* and *walk on a way that is not good*. Unsurprisingly the wicked are more interesting than the righteous. Their bad conduct is further elaborated giving additional lines in part IIB1b. IIA2c and IIB1c contrast the *compassion* and *salvation* shown to the righteous with the *judgements* awaiting the wicked. God will raise the *glory* of the righteous but will demonstrate his *glory* by the judgement of the wicked.

In section III, the threefold repetition of *I know*, suggests that this is a confession of faith.[34] The first stanza is fairly complete. It seems concerned with the *holiness* and *justice* of God with a particular emphasis on the right use of *wealth*. The next stanza, labelled IIIB, is largely missing, although Puech has offered a tentative restoration of part of it.[35]

The poem may have ended somewhere in the first seven lines of column VIII or, as Stegemann suggests, it may continue until the end of column VIII. If indeed the poem is much longer than originally thought,[36] this may modify my analysis of its structure. However, the analysis as it stands gives a balanced structure with this unit at its centre. I read the content of column VIII as dealing with a new topic of confession, forgiveness and God's holy spirit. I think the likelihood is that these are consecutive poems of moderate length rather than

---

[34] Newsom, *The Self as Symbolic Space*, 211, similarly observes that in the *Hodayot* the expressions beginning "I know" "have something of the quality of a confessional statement rather than a cognitive one."

[35] Puech, *Croyance*, 387.

[36] My analysis of the poem was completed before seeing Stegemann's most recent analysis of the number and division of the poems, which suggests that the poem continues to the end of col. VIII. This is because the reconstruction means that there are now only 7 missing lines where a new poem could have started. Stegemann observes that the remainder of col. VIII continues the topics of col. VII making it likely that it belongs to the same poem. See Stegemann, "The Number of Psalms in 1QHodayot[a]," 197.

one long one. The following comments will be restricted to the second section of the poem, which is well preserved and appears to form a unit.

2.4. *Close Reading*

The first verse, IIA1a, begins with the independent pronoun *I* which emphasises the speaker as distinct from the generality of humanity being discussed and also in contrast with God who is addressed by the independent pronoun *you* in IIA2a. The idea that knowledge is a gift from God is expressed in the *Hodayot* in various ways and the expression *I know by your understanding* occurs also in 1QH^a IX 19 [I 21][37] and 1QH^a VI 24 [XIV 12].[38] In this case the addition of the expression *by your understanding* extends the opening phrase into a complete poetic line from which to hang the following three matching negative statements. Newsom perceptively notes that the addition of a qualifying expression also draws a reader's attention to what would otherwise be a hardly-noticed conventional introductory phrase, I know. She also sees the qualifying expression as indicative of the elusive nature of the speaker's own identity apart from God. However this reading is in light of her overall interpretation of the poem.[39] In my opinion, the main function of the phrase is to introduce and reinforce the didactic and wisdom tone of the section.

The first line is followed by three lines each beginning with *that not/and not*. The repetition of the particle לא emphatically reinforces the message that human beings are not in control of their own destiny. This verse contains clear markers to Jer 10:23.[40] As in Jeremiah the verse

---

[37] Merrill notes 56 occurrences of the phrase "I know." Commenting on 1QH^a IX 19 [I 21], Holm-Nielsen says that this expression in the *Hodayot* represents knowledge arrived at by divine revelation, available to members of the community. Ringgren and Licht also take this view. See Merrill, *Qumran and Predestination*, 16 n. 2; Holm-Nielsen, *Hodayot*, 24 nn. 40, 41; H. Ringgren *The Faith of Qumran: Theology of the Dead Sea Scrolls* (Expanded edition; New York: Crossroads, 1995), 114–120; Licht, "The Doctrine of the Thanksgiving Scroll," 1–13, 89–101.

[38] cf. 1QM X 16 "we know by your understanding." Ringgren, *The Faith of Qumran*, 114–120, notes that in the Qumran texts "the entire arsenal of synonyms for 'wisdom' and 'insight' from the biblical wisdom literature are used." This includes to know (ידע), knowledge (דעת דעה), insight (שכל), understanding (בינה), and less often wisdom (חכמה), prudence (ערמה).

[39] Newsom, *The Self as Symbolic Space*, 212, 221.

[40] ידעתי יהוה כי לא לאדם דרכו לא־לאיש הלך והכין את־צעדו (Jer 10:23).

begins with the phrase *I know* (ידעתי) addressed to God. The following clause continues with *that not* (כיא לא), and includes the phrases *a human his way* (ל[אדם דרכו]) and *a man (to) direct his steps* (אנוש להכין צעדו).

The second verse by contrast expresses the same thought in a positive way. It informs us that it is God who determines the course and outcome of each human life. This verse also begins with *I know* but in the imperfect state, contrasting with the earlier perfect verb.[41] Newsom points out that the repetition of the phrase *I know* is a common feature of Qumran literature. She argues convincingly that the second occurrence usually introduces a specifically sectarian meaning for the more ordinarily expressed sentiments introduced by the first occurrence.[42] The phrase *by your hand* contrasts with the earlier *by the hand of flesh*.[43] What humanity cannot do God can and does.

The second line of this verse has a lacuna, a plausible restoration[44] of which is given by comparison with a similar phrase in line 35 (IIB2b). The word translated *works* (פעולת) can mean either the work itself or the wages. Bearing in mind the emphasis on judgement which follows the reader is encouraged to understand both meanings. There are only fourteen occurrences of this word in the Hebrew Bible, but there are no other markers to indicate a specific allusion.[45]

In matching stanza IIB2b, *you have formed the spirit* seems parallel to *and its works you have destined*. If this is the case here, then the clause *before you created him*[46] is a ballast variant[47] balancing the clause *I know that*. However, it is more than a mere filler because it allows the poem

---

[41] As noted by Berlin, alternating perfect and imperfect forms of the verb is a recognised technique in biblical parallelism. See Berlin, *The Dynamics of Biblical Parallelism*, 35–40.

[42] Newsom, *The Self as Symbolic Space*, 212.

[43] The phrase hand of flesh is not found in the HB. The phrase arm of flesh is found twice in contrast to the power of God. "With him is an *arm of flesh*; but with us is the LORD our God." (2 Chr 32:8) "Cursed are those who trust in mere mortals (באדם) and make mere *flesh their strength* (בשר זרעו), whose hearts turn away from the LORD." (Jer 17:5). Cf. "The Egyptians are human, and not God; their horses are flesh, and not spirit. When the LORD stretches out his hand, the helper will stumble, and the one helped will fall, and they will all perish together." (Isa 31:3). References to the hand of the LORD are numerous, but see below on Job 12: 9–10.

[44] Suggested by Licht and followed by Holm-Nielsen and Puech. See Licht, *The Thanksgiving Scroll*, 196; Holm-Nielsen, *Hodayot*, 230 n. 10; Puech, *Croyance*, 386 n. 245.

[45] The references are Lev 19:13; 2 Chr 15:7; Ps 17:4, 28:5, 109:20; Prov 10:6, 11:18; Isa 40:10, 49:4, 61:8, 62:11, 65:7; Jer 31:16; Ezek 29:20.

[46] Cf. 1QH^a V 25 [XIII 8], IX 9 [I 11].

[47] See Watson, *Classical Hebrew Poetry*, 343–348; Watson, *Traditional Techniques in Classical Hebrew Verse*, 30.

to introduce the key verb CREATE (ברא) in parallel to FORMATION (יצר).⁴⁸ This brings to mind a whole complex of associations to do with the use of these two roots in the Hebrew Bible, in particular in the first two chapters of Genesis and also in Isaiah.⁴⁹

In both Jeremiah and Isaiah the root כון (establish, direct, destine) is also associated with creation. For example Jer 10:12 states "It is he who made the earth by his power, who established the world by his wisdom, and by his understanding stretched out the heavens."⁵⁰ Note that in this verse creation is also linked to wisdom and *understanding*. Thus by the juxtaposition of the key verbs create, destine and form and by subtle association with biblical ideas the poem sets out its theme of the link between creation and destiny.

The word translated as formation (יצר) is related to the word for an artisan (יוצר), particularly a potter. Clay in the hand of the potter is a biblical metaphor used for God's creation of and control over humanity as, for example, in the following passage.

> Woe to you who strive with your Maker (את־יצרו), earthen vessels with the potter! Does the clay say to the one who fashions it (ליצרו) "What are you making"? or "Your work has no handles"? ... Thus says the LORD, the Holy One of Israel, and its Maker (ויצרו): Will you question me about my children, or command me concerning the work of my hands (פעל ידי)? I made the earth and created humankind upon it; ... (Isa 45:9–12)

The metaphor is developed at most length in Jer 18:1–12. A play on this complex of ideas may be behind the phrase *by your hand is the formation* used instead of the more straightforward *you formed*, as in IIB2b. This then explains the addition of the phrase *not by the hand of flesh* to the allusion from Jer 10:23.⁵¹ However, when this phrase is compared with the matching phrases in IIB2 two other possible allusions come to light.

---

⁴⁸ יצר can also be translated as "inclination," as in Late Jewish literature, designating the two inclinations of man for good or evil. However the context weighs against this translation. Holm-Nielsen, *Hodayot*, 230 n. 10, cites examples where this is the meaning, but also comes down in favour of the translation "formation."

⁴⁹ For a biblical example of these two verbs in parallel see Isa 43:1, 7.

⁵⁰ See also Jer 33:1, 51:15. Isa 45:18 uses all three verbs. "For thus says the LORD, who *created* the heavens (he is God!), who *formed* the earth and made it (he *established* it; he did not *create* it a chaos, he *formed* it to be inhabited!): I am the LORD, and there is no other."

⁵¹ Holm-Nielsen, *Hodayot*, 230 n. 9, notes "Ring. assumes that there is a direct quotation from Jer 10:23, and thinks that the variation from MT is due to some variation of text or to a conscious departure from it for some unknown reason."

In IIB2b *you formed the spirit* marks an allusion to Zech 12:1, "Thus says the LORD, who stretched out the heavens and founded the earth and *formed the human spirit* within" (ויצר רוח־אדם בקרבו).[52] This is followed by a reference to *the way of every living being* (דרך כול חי). The use of the term *way* makes *living being* equivalent to *flesh* (בשר), *human* (אדם), and *man* (אנוש=איש) in IIA1. However the phrase can also be considered as parallel to *spirit* in IIB2b. This combination constitutes a probable marker to Job 12:9–10. Here, in the midst of a wisdom passage which stresses understanding, we find a rhetorical question which combines the vocabulary and sentiment of IIA1 and IIB2.

> Who among all these does not *know* (מי לא־ידע בכל־אלה)
> that the hand of the LORD has done this? (כי יד־יהוה עשתה זאת)
> *In his hand* is the life of *every living thing* (אשר בידו נפש כל־חי)
> and the *breath* of every *human being*. (ורוח כל־בשר־איש)

The third verse, IIBA1c, consists of a single line rhetorical question. This signals the closing of this stanza and also has an emphatic effect.[53] The question implies a response in the negative; written as a statement it would read "no-one can change your decrees."[54] It therefore matches the negative form of the statements in the first verse.

In stanzas IIA2 and IIB1 we move from the general to the particular. The common wisdom motif of the *righteous* and the *wicked* is used to characterise two alternative destinies for human beings. The literary device of referring to the righteous in the singular and the wicked in the plural is similar to Psalm 1 in the Hebrew Bible. It has the effect of emphasising the importance to God of each righteous individual, whereas the wicked are consigned to judgement as a group, their destiny being of no more concern. The two key verbs *create* (ברא) and *destine* (הכין), which were introduced together in IIA1b, are here repeated. The phrase *period of approval* corresponds with the parallel phrases *time of your wrath* and *day of slaughter* in stanza IIB1.

The use of the phrase *from the womb*, may be an allusion to Jeremiah's call in Jer 1:5. Although the expression is commonly used in the Hebrew Bible in the sense of "before I was born" or "ever since his birth," the

---

[52] The phrase "formed the spirit" is distinctive and the context of God as creator is similar. The only other possible fit for the marker is Amos 4:13, but the reference is probably to "wind" not to the spirit of a human.

[53] See Watson, *Classical Hebrew Poetry*, 170–172, 341–342.

[54] Cf. 1QH\u1d43 VI 26 [XIV 15] וכול יודעיך לא ישנו דבריך (and all who know you do not change your decrees).

noun בטן is the more often used for this expression. Of eleven occurrences of מרחם only three (Jer 1:5; Ps 22:10; Ps 58:3) use the expression in a similar sense to the way it is used here.[55] In Jer 1:5 the nouns are in parallel thus:

> Before I formed you in the belly I knew you (בטרם אצרך בבטן ידעתיך), and before you came forth from the womb I consecrated you (ובטרם תצא מרחם הקדשתיך). (Jer 1:5 NRSV, amended)

"Before I formed you in the belly" can be considered equivalent to the expression *before you created him* used in parallel to *formation* in IIA1b. The use of the word "before" is significant for the thought being expressed here, as well as being a marker to Jer 1:5. Lundbom comments thus on this verse in Jeremiah:

> No other prophet has such an advance appointment as Jeremiah. Moses —who in Deuteronomy is the prophet *par excellence*—and Samuel were destined for special ministry from birth (Exodus 2; 1 Samuel 1). The "servant" of Second Isaiah is also said to have been "formed in the womb" (Isa 44:2, 24; 49:5), and "called from the womb" (Isa 49:1).[56]

The phrase *for the period of approval* (למועד רצון) does not occur in the Hebrew Bible, but a similar phrase occurs in Isa 49:8 (בעת רצון), Ps 69:13 [14] (עת רצון) and Isa 61:2 (שנת רצון).[57] In the latter verse the year of favour is coupled with the day of vengeance (יום נקם). Thus in Isaiah the day of the LORD is good news for the righteous but bad news for the wicked. This correlates well with the similar contrast in this poem between the *period of approval* and *[the time of] your wrath/day of slaughter*.

In stanza IIA2 there follow four infinitives describing the righteous person. The first two relate to conduct and correspond to the descrip-

---

[55] It is used here in a temporal sense rather than in the sense of origin. In the HB, of 18 occurrences of מבטן and 5 occurrences of בבטן, the following are used in a similar context, including the three mentioned above where the expressions are used in parallel. (Judg 13:5, 7, 16:17; Job 31:18; Ps 22:9, 10, 58:3, 71:6, 139:13; Isa 44:2, 24, 46:3, 48:8, 49:1, 5; Jer 1:5; Hos 9:11).

[56] J.R. Lundbom, *Jeremiah 1–20: A New Translation with Introduction and Commentary* (The Anchor Bible; New York: Doubleday, 1999), 231. The word 'before' (טרם) occurs only 9 times in the HB. Here and twice in Gen 2:5 it is in the context of creation. See also Gen 27:4; Ex 1:19, 10:7; Num 11:33; 1 Sam 3:7; Hag 2:15. The phrase 'formed in the womb' occurs in the HB only in Jer 1:5, Isa 44: 2, 24 about Israel, and Isa 49:5, used of God's servant.

[57] "Thus says the LORD: In a time of favor I have answered you, on a day of salvation I have helped you" (Isa 49:8); "to proclaim the year of the LORD's favor, and the day of vengeance of our God" (Isa 61:2); "At an acceptable time, O God, in the abundance of your steadfast love, answer me" (Ps 69:13).

tion of the conduct of the wicked in IIB1b. The second two infinitives probably have God as the subject, although this is not altogether clear. They would then correspond with IIB1c which recounts the fate of the wicked. IIA1 ends with a reference to *glory* which matches the use of the word at the end of stanza IIB1.

There is a considerable use of biblical sounding terminology in IIA2c, but no clear markers to a particular text.[58] The one exception[59] to this is the phrase *the multitude of your compassions* (המון רחמיך). This combination of words occurs in the Hebrew Bible only in Isa 63:15. Moreover it occurs frequently in the *Hodayot*, and once in the Mysteries text 4Q301.[60] Holm-Nielsen considered it to be a stereotyped expression.[61] I will be comparing its usage here and in two other poems (see §3.6.2 in this chapter and §2.5.3 in chapter four) to see if there is any common link.

I will now turn to the wicked people. Ironically, although as individuals they are of little concern, their crimes merit a much fuller description than the virtues of the righteous. Again the key verb create (ברא) is used, but instead of the verb destine (הכין) we read *you have consecrated them* (הקדשתם). This is part of an allusion to Jer 12:3, in which the writer laments the prosperity of the wicked and calls upon God to "consecrate them for the day of slaughter." In this poem the plea has been changed to an established destiny which contrasts with the positive consecration of Jeremiah from the womb already alluded to.

Then follow five lines describing the crimes of the wicked. This takes the form of one introductory line beginning with כי, *for they have walked on a way that is not good*, followed by four lines in chiastic parallelism.

---

[58] For "constriction of soul" see Gen 42:21; Job 7:10; 2 Sam 4:9; 1 Kgs 1:29; Ps 31:7, 143:11; Prov 21:23. For "to rejoice over ... in" see Zeph 3:17. For "eternal salvation" see Isa 45:17, 51:6. For "peace everlasting" see 1 Kgs 2:33; Ps 72:7. For "without want" cf. Judg 18:10, 19:19; Ps 34:9; Prov 28:27.

[59] The expression "to open all the constriction of his soul" is similar to 1QH[a] XIII 35 [V 33] (ואת אלי מרחב פתחתה בלבבי ויוספוה לצוקה) and 1QH[a] XVII 28 [IX 28] (ורחוב עולם בצרת נפש[י]). There is a slightly stronger case for these two phrases being allusions to Ps 31:7–8, "you have taken heed of my adversities (בצרות נפשי), and have not delivered me into the hand of the enemy; you have set my feet in a broad place (במרחב)."

[60] 1QH[a] XII 37, 38 [IV 36, 37], XIII 4 [V 2], XIV 12 [VI 9], XV 33, 38 [VII 30, 35], XVII 8, 34 [IX 8, 34], XVIII 23 [X 21], 4Q301 3a–b 5; 4Q428 10 2. Note, in some cases I have adjusted the line numbers given by Abegg to agree with Stegemann's numbering. See Abegg, et al., *The Dead Sea Scrolls Concordance, Volume 1*, 227; Stegemann, "The Material Reconstruction of 1QHodayot," 280.

[61] Holm-Nielsen, *Hodayot*, 139 n. 12.

Reject and *detest* are parallel to and contrast with *choose* and *delight* respectively. The introductory line is a probable allusion to Isa 65:2, with strong connotations of God's judgement; although the idea of *a way not good* occurs elsewhere in the Hebrew Bible, only in Isa 65:2 is it used with the verb to walk (הלך).[62]

The next verse describes the destiny of the wicked. The introductory line again begins with כי, and it uses the key verb destine (הכין). The repeated use of the preposition ל adds a rhythmic quality to the verse. The phrase *to enact against them great judgements* uses biblical language, reminiscent of Ezekiel and Exodus.[63] The next phrase, *to be for a sign and a por[tent for] eternal [generations]* is a close match to Deut 28:46. As an allusion it implies that the judgement upon the wicked is the fulfilment of the curses for disobeying the covenant.[64] It seems that this poem is concerned primarily with judgement on those who see themselves within the Mosaic tradition. However, attached to each of these phrases are words with a more universal feel. The judgement upon the wicked in Israel will demonstrate God's glory *for the eyes of all your works*, and with the purpose that *everyone may know your glory and great strength*.

The final stanza, IIB2, returns to the key allusion to Jer 10:23 and the use of another rhetorical question. The implied answer is no. Humans do not control their own destiny. God does. The structure of this stanza matches that of the first stanza of the unit, IIA1, similarly ending with a single poetic line.

---

[62] cf. Ps 36:4, Prov 16:29, Ezek 36:31. Of the other two possible allusions noted by commentators, one is highly improbable because of its context (Ps 107:18). The other, *all that you have commanded*, should probably be explained as the use of common biblical phraseology rather than as an allusion. Although only in Jer 32:23 is there an exact lexical correspondence this is because both passages are 2nd person singular addressed to God in prayer.

[63] The phrase *enact judgements* occurs 9 times in Ezekiel. See Ezek 5:10, 15, 11:9, 16:41, 25:11, 28:22, 28:26, 30:14, 19. The phrase 'great judgements' occurs in Exod 6:6, 7:4.

[64] "All these curses shall come upon you, pursuing and overtaking you until you are destroyed, because you did not obey the LORD your God, by observing the commandments and the decrees that he commanded you. They shall be among you and your descendants *as a sign and a portent* forever. (והיו בך לאות ולמופת ובזרעך עד־עולם)" (Deut 28:45–46) The pair "sign and portent" occurs 18 times in the HB, the phrase "for a sign" occurs 14 times, but "for a sign and a portent" occurs only here. Additional markers "to be" and "eternal" make this allusion certain, with a phrase corresponding to "among your descendants" likely within the lacuna. The context of judgement also confirms the allusion.

2.5. *Allusions*

I will only summarise here the case for the most probable allusions, as the detailed arguments are described in the close reading. Those which have clear markers to a specific passage and clear contextual links (criteria 1 and 2) are Jer 10:23, Jer 12:3, Zech 12:1, Job 12:10, and Deut 28:46. Although the markers are not so clear-cut, the case for also including Jer 10:12 and Jer 1:5 is strong because of the other allusions to Jeremiah.

There are also three possible markers to verses in Isa 61–65. In the case of Isa 63:15 the marker is clear, but its frequency of use elsewhere in the *Hodayot* might suggest an idiomatic usage. While the contextual links are good, the markers to Isa 61:2 and Isa 65:2 are slightly less clear but the coincidence of verses from Isa 61–65 tips the balance in favour of these allusions. Finally, while there is no strong marker to any of the fourteen individual biblical verses using the term *works*, there is a cluster of these in Isa 61–65 where the context is similar.[65]

Jer 18:1–12 and Isa 45:9–19 are included on the grounds of being examples of the underlying potter metaphor. This metaphor, explicitly described in these passages is strongly implicit in much of Isaiah and Jeremiah. The idea that God created the world and then formed human beings, as a potter shapes clay, is also a connotation of the allusions to Zech 12:1 and Job 12:10 (cf. Isa 42:5, 44:24, 45:12). A further connotation is that, because human beings are the work of his hands, the Lord also has the power to order their lives as he sees fit.

The problem implicit in the Job allusion and in Jeremiah's complaint (Jer 12:1–4), that the wicked prosper while the righteous suffer, is solved in the prophets by the idea of the "day of the Lord;" on this day the righteous and wicked will be rewarded accordingly. This is an added connotation of the Zech 12:1 allusion. It lies behind the allusion to Isa 61:2, which refers to the judgement of God in terms of the year of approval and the day of vengeance.

---

[65] For I the Lord love justice, I hate robbery and wrongdoing; I will faithfully give them their recompense (פעלתם), and I will make an everlasting covenant with them. (Isa 61:8); The Lord has proclaimed to the end of the earth: Say to daughter Zion, "See, your salvation comes; his reward is with him, and his recompense (פעלתו) before him." (Isa 62:11); because they offered incense on the mountains and reviled me on the hills, I will measure into their laps full payment (פעלתם) for their actions. (Isa 65:7). Cf. Isa 40:10, Isa 49:4, Jer 31:16.

The innovation of this poem is in its taking these ideas about God as creator and judge and, via an exegesis based mainly upon Jeremiah, arguing that the life-choices and consequent judgement of the righteous and the wicked were destined for them by God. The sense of Jer 10:23 and similar sayings in the book of Proverbs[66] seems to be that a person cannot plan his own future circumstances but that God punishes or rewards as he sees fit. But verse IIA1b modifies this meaning in two ways. Firstly it projects God's purpose back beyond an individual's birth; secondly it implies that an individual's nature, rather than just his circumstances, is determined by God.

The phrase *from the womb*, in IIA2a and IIB1a, is too general a phrase to stand on its own as an allusion. However, in the light of the other allusions to Jeremiah, it may well be interpreted as alluding to Jeremiah's call in Jer 1:5. The possible allusion to the use of the potter metaphor in Jer 18:1-11 and Isa 45:9-19 similarly becomes more plausible.[67]

In effect the initial allusion to Jer 10:23 alerts the reader to further allusions to Jeremiah. Using the terminology proposed by Wheeler, the overall effect of the pattern of allusions is structural in that it invites the reader to draw extensive parallels between the two contexts.[68] Thus Jeremiah may represent the typical righteous person surrounded by wicked enemies, Jeremiah's call illustrates that God's choice operates before birth, Jeremiah's oracles indicate that the reward of the righteous and the punishment of the wicked have been destined by God.

Stanzas IIA2 and IIB1 elaborate upon the lifestyle and judgement of the righteous and the wicked, in a manner familiar from the wisdom tradition. As already mentioned, there are several allusions to verses in Isa 61-65 which together also constitute a structural allusion. There are also similarities between the passage in Isaiah and passages alluded to from Jeremiah. The allusion to Isa 61:2, as well as providing the basis for the phrase *the period of approval*, contains in it the idea that this is a day of vengeance for the wicked who oppress God's people. This latter corresponds to the *day of slaughter* in the allusion to Jer 12:3.

---

[66] E.g. "The human mind plans the way, but the LORD directs the steps." (Prov 16:9).
[67] "Just like the clay in the potter's hand, so are you in my hand, O house of Israel." (Jer 18:6, cf. Isa 29:16, 45:9, 64:8).
[68] Wheeler, *The Art of Allusion*, 20-25, as cited in §4.3 of chapter two.

Chapters 61 and 62 of Isaiah promise that God will bring recompense (פעלה), and an eternal covenant (ברית עולם) to his people.[69] Isa 63:15–64:12 contains a prayer similar to that in Jer 10:23–25 asking God to temper his anger, alluded to by the phrase *the multitude of your compassions*. This prayer also mentions the potter motif.[70] In contrast, Isa 65:1–16 gives God's reasons for judgement upon those who *have walked in a way not good*. God promises to recompense them for their *works*[71] and that they shall bow down to the slaughter. Although a different word for slaughter is used in the hodayah, there is a link via the use of a related word in Jer 12:3.[72] The condemnation of the people for not heeding God's words and going after other gods occurs in both Isa 65:1–16 and in Jer 11:1–17.[73]

The punishment of the wicked is elaborated by a certain allusion to Deut 28:46, that they will be *for a sign and a por[tent for] eternal [generations]*. The context of the passage in Deuteronomy is that of the covenant renewal ceremony at Mount Ebal with its blessings and curses. The punishment befalling the wicked is thus identified with the covenant curses. The poem has already referred to the keeping or rejecting of the *covenant* as a distinguishing the *righteous* from the *wicked*. Jer 11:3–5 also alludes to the covenantal curses, using the phrase ארור האיש אשר (cursed be anyone who) in imitation of the words of Deut 27:15–26. Of the twenty-one occurrences of the word *covenant* in Jeremiah, five are in this chapter.

---

[69] "I will faithfully give them their recompense, and I will make an everlasting covenant with them." (Isa 61:8).

[70] "Yet, O Lord, you are our Father; we are the clay, and you are our potter; we are all the work of your hand." (Isa 64:8[7]).

[71] "I will measure into their laps full payment (פעלתם) for their actions." (Isa 65:8).

[72] "and all of you shall bow down to the slaughter (טבח); because, when I called, you did not answer, when I spoke, you did not listen, but you did what was evil in my sight, and chose what I did not delight in." (Isa 65:12). Cf. "Pull them out like sheep for the slaughter (טבחה), and set them apart for the day of slaughter (הרגה)." (Jer 12:3).

[73] E.g. "They have turned back to the iniquities of their ancestors of old, who refused to heed my words (לשמוע את־דברי); they have gone after other gods to serve them; the house of Israel and the house of Judah have broken the covenant that I made with their ancestors." (Jer 11:10); "because, when I called, you did not answer, when I spoke, you did not listen (דברתי ולא שמעתם), but you did what was evil in my sight, and chose what I did not delight in." (Isa 65:12).

2.5.1. *A Meditation on Jeremiah*

Based on the above, I propose that this poetic unit may be regarded as a meditation upon Jer 10–12 supplemented by other allusions mainly from Jeremiah and Isaiah. This is, in fact, an example of what Greene calls a dialectical allusion, in which the reader experiences the adopted and adoptive text in interpretive dialogue.[74] Newsom, though she uses different language, appears to have noticed the same effect. The fact that Newsom, in a work not primarily concerned with allusion, has singled out this particular instance for extended comment reinforces my own observations about its significance.[75] Thus a reader familiar with Jeremiah will use it to fill out the context of this poem, but conversely will also be prompted to read Jeremiah through the interpretive lens of this composition.

In Jer 10–12 the coming exile is portrayed as God's inevitable judgement. Wisdom language is employed in a prayer which, while pleading for mercy and vindication, acknowledges God's right to thus punish his people. God is in control of human affairs. Like a latter day Moses, Jeremiah calls upon the people to obey the covenant. He testifies that the impending punishment is the fulfilment of the covenantal curses upon those who disobey. Jeremiah sees himself as an innocent suffering for God's cause at the hands of wicked opponents. He calls upon God to vindicate him and to punish the wicked.

In its interpretation of this passage our poem sees Jeremiah as the archetypal righteous person and his opponents as the archetypal wicked people. The key verse about God directing a human's way is interpreted by reference to a whole complex of ideas linked to God as creator and fashioner of humankind. These are key themes in both Jeremiah and Isaiah, the two main sources for allusions. The key terms are destine (הכין), create (ברא), and form (יצר).

Endorsed by the use of wisdom language in Jeremiah, the poem also co-opts another wisdom theme, that of the contrast between the righteous and wicked. This universal theme is here identified with the narrower contrast between those who obey and those who reject God's covenant. This is reinforced by the allusion made here and in Jer 11:3–5 to the covenantal curses of Deuteronomy.

Jeremiah's plea that the wicked be punished is transformed here into an inevitable outcome. In an extrapolation from Jeremiah's call both

---

[74] Greene, *The Light in Troy*, 38–46.
[75] Newsom, *The Self as Symbolic Space*, 212–214.

the righteous and the wicked are seen as fulfilling the destiny they were made for. They are mere artefacts in the hands of the heavenly potter. God will be glorified both by the vindication of the righteous and by the punishment of the wicked.

2.6. *Intertexts*

This hodayah has considerable parallels with other hymns. It has similarities with two hymns which speak of God as creator pre-ordaining everything. These are 1QH^a V 12?–VI 18? [XIII 1–XIV 7] and 1QH^a IX 3–41 [I 1–39]. I discuss these and other texts containing similar ideas in §2.6.1. In §2.6.2 I consider three other hymns (1QS X 1–XI 22, 1QH^a XV 29–36 [VII 26–33], and 1QH^a XII 6–XIII 6 [IV 5–V 4]) which contain a possible allusion to Jer 10:23. Finally, in §2.6.3 I discuss the idea of two ways or two spirits, which occurs frequently in the Dead Sea scrolls corpus and elsewhere.

2.6.1. *Creation and Destiny*

Tanzer places this poem in a group of eight hodayot with strong wisdom elements, all of which may be classified as Community Hymns. Discussion of the hymns in Tanzer's group of eight is complicated by the subsequent reconstruction and renumbering of the scroll. I will therefore give the numbering used by Tanzer in curly brackets.[76]

Two of Tanzer's group, 1QH^a V 12(?)–38 {13:1–21(?) with frgs. 17 and 15 1b} and 1QH^a IX 3–41 {1:1–2:2}, employ similar language to that used here concerning God's creation and direction of human beings. I discuss them further below. Tanzer has noted the similarities between these two hymns, including the element of predestination.[77] She has placed them in a different sub-category to that of 1QH^a VII 21–39

---

[76] Tanzer's eight wisdom compositions are, 1QH^a V 18–38 {13:1–21(?) with frgs. 17 and 15 1b}; VII 21–39 {15:8–26}; IX 3–41 {1:1–2:2}; XV 29–36 {7:26–33}; XVII 38–XVIII 15 {9:37–10:12}; XIX 7–18 {11:3–14}; XIX 31–XX 39 {11:29–12:36}; XXI 2–29 {18 16–33 with frg. 3}. Tanzer particularly associates this hodayah with one in column XXI [XVIII] in the subcategory concerning "Salvation only through God's Covenant and Statutes." See Tanzer, "The Sages at Qumran," 17–56.

[77] Tanzer groups these two hodayah together as "Compositions about Creation", which contain the following three features: "(1) The central theme of the compositions is the creation and ordering of the universe (including mankind); (2) God is portrayed as Creator, as having a purpose for each of his creations, and as one who reveals a knowledge of the mysteries of creation to mankind; (3) Finally, God has a predetermined plan for his creation and for man." See Tanzer, "The Sages at Qumran," 28–36.

{15: 8–26} because of the centrality they give to the creation theme. However, as shown in my close reading and also noted by Tanzer,[78] 1QH[a] VII 21–39 {15: 8–26} also has a strong underlying creation motif, and uses the verb ברא.

Tanzer categorises 1QH[a] VII 21–39 {15: 8–26} as a hymn concerning "salvation only through God's covenant and statutes," grouping it with 1QH[a] XXI 2–29 {18 16–33 with frg. 3}. She notes that both use the terms *covenant* and *statutes* (חוקים), and both use rhetorical questions, including the phrase *what is flesh?* She also comments that of her eight wisdom compositions, "they alone do not portray God as a revealer of his secrets or mysteries." However, if one includes 1QH[a] XXI 2–29 as part of a larger composition starting in column XX, as Stegemann does, then this observation does not hold.[79] Because of the fragmentary nature of the text and uncertainty about its delimitation, I will not consider the latter composition in any detail here.

The initial portion of the latter-mentioned unit Stegemann places at the end of another of Tanzer's eight poems, 1QH[a] XIX 7–18 {11:3–14}. Tanzer groups this with 1QH[a] XV 29–36 {7:26–33} as "hymns about the salvation of the elect."[80] I do not consider that these poems have any particular similarities with the poem being studied. This leaves 1QH[a] XVII 38–XVIII 15 {9:37–10:12} from Tanzer's group of eight wisdom poems, which, according to Tanzer, defies categorization.[81] This estimate by Tanzer may have been different if, as Stegemann does, she had continued the poem to 1QH[a] XIX 5 [XI 2]. This longer poem does seem to have elements of predestination and dualism. It also mentions the covenant and right use of wealth. However there are insufficient similarities to warrant a detailed consideration here.

---

[78] "Further, it should be noted that the composition found in col. 15 also partially shares the distinguishing features of the 'compositions about creation.'" Tanzer, "The Sages at Qumran," 42.

[79] According to Stegemann, 1QH[a] XXI 2–29 [XVIII 16–33 with frg. 3], and most of another unit, 1QH[a] XIX 31–XX 39 [XI 28–XII 38], identified by Tanzer as one of her eight wisdom compositions are actually part of the same poem. Tanzer does discuss whether the rubric-like statements beginning in XX 7 "originally began a distinct hodayah", but she considers the lack of an opening formula beginning either ברוך or אודכה as a problem. See Stegemann, "The Number of Psalms in 1QHodayot[a]," 279; Tanzer, "The Sages at Qumran," 43, 48–53.

[80] Tanzer, "The Sages at Qumran," 37–42.

[81] Tanzer, "The Sages at Qumran," 24–27. Newsom has also analysed this poem. Newsom, *The Self as Symbolic Space*, 230–232.

To summarise, Tanzer places this composition in a group of eight wisdom poems. All but two of these (1QH^a XV 29–36, and 1QH^a XIX 7–30 with XIX 31–XX 6) appear to have some similarities with the poem under consideration. Three others (1QH^a XVII 38–XVIII 15 with XVIII 15–XIX 5, 1QH^a XX 7–39, and 1QH^a XXI 2–29) I will not discuss in further detail, for reasons given above.

This leaves the poems categorised by Tanzer as compositions about creation, namely 1QH^a V 12(?)–38 {13:1–21(?) with frgs. 17 and 15 Ib} and 1QH^a IX 3–41 {1:1–2:2}. As noted in chapter one, these two poems and 1QH^a XVII 38–XVIII 15 {9:37–10:12}, which is also one of the poems in Tanzer's strong wisdom group, are grouped together by Newsom. With 1QH^a VII 21–VIII ? [XV 8–25], the main poem under consideration here, they are Newsom's prime examples of the effect which she calls the "masochistic sublime."[82] By this she means those passages in which the speaker experiences his own nothingness in relation to God. She also discerns this effect in the Maskil's Hymn in 1QS IX 26–XI 22.[83] She also makes a connection with the Treatise on the Two Spirits in 1QS III 13–IV 26.[84] I discuss this further in §2.6.3 below. The phrase "what is flesh" is also associated with this effect. I discuss this further in §3.6.2 of this chapter.

The poem 1QH^a V 12(?)–VI 18(?) [XIII 1–XIV 7(?)] has been restored by Puech from a number of fragments. It appears to start with a heading in lines 12–14, which in Puech's opinion applies not just to this hymn but to those following.[85] Puech also notes the dualism and predestination apparent in this hymn. He has also noted considerable similarities between this hymn and 1QS III–IV and CD II (see below, §2.6.3). If Puech is right about the heading in V 12, then perhaps this is the beginning of a series of didactic poems for the instruction of members of the community. This would account for the similarities with 1QS III–IV and CD II, which also seem to have a didactic purpose.[86]

---

[82] Newsom, *The Self as Symbolic Space*, 209–227.

[83] Newsom, *The Self as Symbolic Space*, 172–173. In §5.6.1 of chapter one I discuss Newsom's description of this effect.

[84] Newsom, *The Self as Symbolic Space*, 217, 278; for Newsom's discussion of 1QS III 13–IV 26 see Newsom, *The Self as Symbolic Space*, 77–90.

[85] Puech notes headings in 1QH^a V 12 [frgs. 15, 17, 21], XX 7 [XII 4], and XXV 34 [frgs.], with another possible heading in frg. 10 11=VII 21(?). See Puech, "Quelques aspects," 53–55; É. Puech, "Un hymne essénien en partie retrouve et les béatitudes: 1QH V 12–VI 18 (= col. XIII–XIV 7) et 4QBéat.," *RevQ* 49 (1988): 59–88.

[86] Newsom, *The Self as Symbolic Space*, 217, starts her analysis of this poem by noting that the heading evokes the teaching 1QS III–IV.

Merrill, in his study on predestination in the *Hodayot*, considered that the idea of God as creator was an important foundation for this doctrine.[87] The poem in column IX [I] is a hymn to God as creator. It expresses the idea that just as God has established and ordered all of nature, so he has ordered the lives of human beings. But the poem in column IX [I] is also thought to have been composed as an introduction to the Teacher Hymns. One can only speculate as to the purpose of this introduction. But possibly it is in part meant to emphasise that, whatever the exalted status of the speaker in the following hymns, this is not because of his own merit but in order to serve the purposes of God.

Before going on to consider literature attested outside of the Dead Sea scrolls I will briefly note two coincidences of language with 4Q301. As noted in the close reading, 4Q301 is the only Dead Sea text apart from the *Hodayot* to use the phrase *multitude of compassion*. Another similarity of language is the phrase *what is flesh that* (מה בשר כיא) which occurs in 4Q301 5 3. This is another possible link with wisdom traditions, the significance of which I discuss in §2.7. I will now consider the idea of creation and destiny in some other literature from the Second Temple period.

The idea that God the creator ordained all things from the beginning also runs throughout the book of *Jubilees*, with frequent references to everything having been "ordained and written" on the heavenly tablets. *Jubilees*, although probably not a sectarian document, was found at Qumran in several manuscripts, and is possibly referred to in CD XVI 2–4. It is generally considered to predate and to have influenced the sectarian literature.[88] The following passage expresses a sentiment close to that of this hodayah.

> And the judgement of everyone is ordained and written on the heavenly tablets, and there is no injustice in it: all who stray from the path marked out for them to follow, and do not follow it—judgement is written down for them, for every creature and for every kind of creature. And there is nothing in heaven or earth, or in light or darkness, which will not be judged; and all the judgements are ordained and written and engraved. (*Jub.* 5:26)[89]

---

[87] Merrill, *Qumran and Predestination*, 24–32.
[88] For a detailed study of the similarities between Jubilees and Qumran literature see James C. VanderKam. *Textual and Historical Studies in the Book of Jubilees*. Missoula: Scholars Press, 1977.
[89] C. Rabin, "Jubilees," in *The Apocryphal Old Testament*. (ed. H.F.D. Sparks; Oxford: Clarendon, 1984), 26.

The potter metaphor for God the creator is also found in other literature from the Second Temple period. In a polemic against idol worshippers in the Wisdom of Solomon we find the following lines:

> A potter kneads the soft earth
> and laboriously molds each vessel for our service,
> fashioning out of the same clay
> both the vessels that serve clean uses
> and those for contrary uses, making all alike;
> but which shall be the use of each of them
> the worker in clay decides.
> With misspent toil, these workers form a futile god from the same clay—
> these mortals who were made of earth a short time before
> and after a little while go to the earth from which all mortals are taken,
> when the time comes to return the souls that were borrowed.
> ... ...
> Their heart is ashes, their hope is cheaper than dirt,
> and their lives are of less worth than clay,
> because they failed to know the one who formed them
> and inspired them with active souls
> and breathed a living spirit into them. (Wis 15: 7–8, 10–11)

In Ben Sira the concept is set in the context of a dualism.

> Why is one day more important than another,
> when all the daylight in the year is from the sun?
> By the Lord's wisdom they were distinguished,
> and he appointed the different seasons and festivals.
> Some days he exalted and hallowed,
> and some he made ordinary days.
> All human beings come from the ground,
> and humankind was created out of the dust.
> In the fullness of his knowledge the Lord distinguished them
> and appointed their different ways.
> Some he blessed and exalted,
> and some he made holy and brought near to himself;
> but some he cursed and brought low,
> and turned them out of their place.
> Like clay in the hand of the potter,
> to be molded as he pleases,
> so all are in the hand of their Maker,
> to be given whatever he decides. (Sir 33:7–13)

As noted by Di Lella, this is in contrast to the remarks about free will in Sir 15:11–20. Indeed, Newsom quotes Sir 15:11–16 as an example of a contrasting perspective to that of the predestination presented by the hodayah analysed here.[90] Di Lella observes that the passage quoted above "*seems* to imply that God predestines some people for blessing and others for cursing." He concludes however, that "Ben Sira stops far short of attributing human sin to God and of saying that divine predestination destroys human freedom to choose between good and evil."[91] He also remarks on the complexity of the problem of reconciling human freedom with God's foreknowledge, which still taxes theologians today.

This should counsel against too easy an assumption that the sectarian authors of the Dead Sea Scrolls, despite their emphasis on destiny, had a theology which did not also encompass human responsibility and choice. As can be seen from the above references, the idea that God has ordained and knows everything was a fundamental one in late Second Temple Judaism, varying mainly in the emphasis it was given. I therefore disagree with Newsom, who appears to take the view that any resemblance to such traditional discourse is merely superficial. Newsom argues that the *Hodayot* present the denial of human agency as a "perfecting" of the notion of divine sovereignty. This ensured that the concept did not seem wholly strange to its readers; but by comparison other interpretations would then have seemed flawed and inadequate.[92]

2.6.2. *Jer 10:23*

There are several other compositions which appear to contain an allusion to Jer 10:23.[93] These are 1QS X 5–XI 22, 1QH^a XV 29–36 [VII 26–33], and 1QH^a XII 6–XIII 6 [IV 5–V 6]. The affinity with the Maskil's Hymn, 1QS X 5–XI 22 is particularly striking as the following two extracts illustrate:

---

[90] Newsom, *The Self as Symbolic Space*, 271–273.
[91] Patrick W. Skehan and Alexander A. Di Lella, *The Wisdom of Ben Sira* (The Anchor Bible; New York: Doubleday, 1987), 81–83, see also 399–401.
[92] Newsom, *The Self as Symbolic Space*, 266–273.
[93] There are many other verses in the HB which express a similar sentiment. In particular the following verses should be noted, as they employ a very similar vocabulary. "The steps of a man (גבר) are directed by the Lord, and he delights in his way." (Ps 37:23) "The heart of a human (אדם) plans his way; but the Lord directs his steps." (Prov 16:9) "The steps of a man (גבר) (are) of the Lord; so a human (אדם), how does he understand his own way?" (Prov 20:24).

כיא ל(וא ל)אדם דרכו ואנוש לוא יכין צעדו כיא לאל המשפט ומידו תום הדרך
ובדעתי נהיה כול ודול[94] הויה במחשבתו יכינו ומבלעדיו לוא יעשה

> For (not) to Adam his way, and humankind does not establish his steps. For to God (belongs) the judgement, and from his hand is perfection of the way, and by his knowledge all that will be, and all that is he establishes by his plan, and without him nothing will work. (1QS XI 10b–11c)

ומי יכול להכיל את כבודכה ומה אף הואה בן האדם במעשי פלאכה וילוד אשה מה
י(ח)שב לפניכה והואה מעפר מגבלו ולחם רמה מדורו והואה מצירוק המר קורץ
ולעפר תשוקתו מה ישיב חמר ויוצר יד ולעצת מה יבין

> And who can grasp your glory? And what indeed is the son of Adam in the works of your wonder? And one born of a woman, what shall he be reckoned before you? And he, from dust is his kneading, And bread of maggots his dwelling, And he is spit of clay moulded, And for the dust his longing. What will the clay and the formation of hand reply? And for counsel what will he understand?" (1QS XI 20–22)

In 1QS XI 10 the similarity to Jer 10:23 is unmistakable, although the scribe has omitted the word לא, probably in error, and the word אנוש has replaced the words איש הלך. The wording of the allusion here and in the poem under consideration is very similar. There are also other similarities, which suggest that underlying them is a common exegesis of the Jeremiah verse.

Firstly, there is a common theme of predestination. Secondly, the idea of predestination is linked to the idea that the righteous are destined for *perfection of way* (תום הדרך) by the *judgement* (המשפט) of God. Similar wording is found in 1QS XI 2 and 17.[95] The corollary of this, not stated explicitly in this poem, is that the wicked too are destined by God. We thus have implicitly in this poem the idea of the two ways, of those destined for salvation and those destined for punishment. See below for a further discussion of the two ways theology.

Thirdly, 1QS XI 20–22 uses rhetorical questions as a means of expressing the unworthiness of the speaker, as do IIA1c and IIB2a of this poem. This is of course a fairly common feature of the *Hodayot*. However the phrase "formation of hand" (ויוצר יד) resonates particu-

---

[94] Final form ך corrected from ע.
[95] "But I, to God (belongs) my judgement, And in his hand (is) the perfection of my way, With the uprightness of my heart. And in his righteous acts he shall blot out my sin." (1QS XI 2) "For without you (is) not perfection of way, And without your pleasure nothing will work." (1QS XI 17).

larly with IIA1b and supports my conjecture that the potter imagery of Jeremiah lies behind IIA1.

There is also a possible allusion to Jer 10:23 in 1QH^a XV 29–36 [VII 26–33]. This composition has been restored by both Schuller and Puech using 4Q428 and 1QH^b.[96] The relevant line, as reconstructed by Schuller, reads:

כיא לוא[לאד]ם דרכו כ[ול אלה לכבדכה עשיתה]

For not [for a huma]n his way; a[ll these for your glory you have done.])

In this hymn the speaker thanks God for establishing him in the way of his heart, in spite of his own unworthiness. The implication is that it is not because of any merit on his part, but because of God's sovereign choice. There is another possible allusion to Jer 10:23 in the Teacher Hymn in 1QH^a XII 6–XIII 6 [IV 5–V 6]. It now seems more likely to me that this is not a direct allusion but has been mediated in some way by the exegetical ideas outlined above. I discuss this further in §3.6.2 of this chapter.

The idea that all the steps of a man are ordained by God, when combined with the contrast between righteous and wicked produces a deterministic dualism. I will consider this aspect of the poem next.

2.6.3. *Two Ways*

As mentioned already, the idea of two ways occurs in the Hebrew Bible both in a covenantal context and in a wisdom context. In a covenantal context there are blessings for those who keep the covenant and curses for those who do not. Keeping the covenant is described as walking in God's ways, whereas those who do not keep the covenant are described as turning aside or being led astray. A typical statement of this is found in Deut 30:15–20. A typical wisdom passage in which the ways of the righteous and wicked are contrasted is Prov 4:10–27, which ends with the admonition: "Keep straight the path of your feet, and all your ways will be sure. Do not swerve to the right or to the left; turn your foot away from evil."

It is unsurprising then, that two ways imagery occurs frequently in texts originating in late Second Temple Judaism. However, in most of these texts the two ways are represented in terms of a warning or

---

[96] Schuller, "A Thanksgiving Hymn from 4QHodayot^b," 527–541; Schuller, "Hodayot," 141–144; Puech, "Restauration d'un texte hymnique," 543–558.

admonition concerning the choice between two opposing lifestyles.[97] The strongly deterministic dualism which combines two way terminology and ideas about predestination seems to be a distinctive feature of the sectarian Dead Sea scrolls. The most explicit exposition of this dualism is found in 1QS III 13–IV 26, commonly known as the Treatise on the Two Spirits.

Much of 1QS III 13–IV 26 is taken up with an elaboration of the two spirits, and corresponding two ways, and their final outcome. But from the outset the treatise is at pains to place this dualism within the control of the one God and creator. Thus both the Prince of Lights and the Angel of Darkness, with all those in their dominion, are subject to God's rule. This emphasis is expressed in language similar to that found in the *Hodayot*.

מאל הדעות כול הויה ונהייה ולפני היותם הכין כול מחשבתם[98] ובהיותם לתעודותם
כמחשבת כבודו ימלאו פעולתם ואין להשנות בידו משפטי כול והואה יכלכלם בכול
חפציהם

> From the God of knowledge comes all that is and that shall be. *Before they came into being he destined all their plans*; and when they come into existence in their fixed times according to his glorious plan they carry through *their tasks. Nothing can be changed. In his hand are the judgements of all things* and he supports them in all their affairs. (1QS III 15b–17a)

Newsom in particular has explored the language of the two spirits section of 1QS and that of the *Hodayot*. In a short chapter on the Treatise of the Two Spirits she relates the sectarian idea of knowledge to historical circumstances.[99] She also makes a connection between the language of the Two Spirits Treatise and 1QH^a V 18–VI 18 [XIII 1–XIV 7]. This is one of several poems, including the poem under consideration here, that Newsom identifies as being associated with the office of the Maskil.[100] She does not include any of these in the category of Teacher Hymns, but includes discussion of three of them in her chapter entitled

---

[97] In his discussion of the two-ways theology of 1QS, Nickelsburg mentions *The Wisdom of Solomon* 1–5, *The Testament of Asher*, *The Didache* 1–6, *Barnabas* 18–20, *Doctrina Apostolorum* 1–5, and The Mandates in *The Shepherd of Hermas*. However, with the possible exception of *The Testament of Asher*, the use of two-ways terminology in these later documents is not connected with predestination. See George W.E. Nickelsburg. *Resurrection, Immortality, and Eternal Life in Intertestamental Judaism.* (Harvard Theological Studies 26. Cambridge: Harvard University Press; London: Oxford University Press. 1972), 156–165.

[98] Probably emend to מחשבתם.

[99] Newsom, *The Self as Symbolic Space*, 77–90.

[100] 1QH^a V 18–VI 18 [XIII 1–XIV 7], VII 14–37 [XV 11–24], XX 7–39 [XII 4–36],

"What do Hodayot do?"[101] She therefore seeks to differentiate between the office of Maskil and the leadership role described in the Teacher Hymns.

In discussing the poem under consideration here and the associated one in V 12(?)–VI 18(?) [XIII 1–XIV 7(?)], Newsom focuses on describing how they construct the self in relation to God as "one who knows." She calls this self the "blinking I" because, she argues, in the very act of knowing the self tends to be lost, becoming an object of knowledge rather than a subject.[102] This effect that Newsom is describing seems therefore to be associated with the ideas about dualism and creation which I have described above. I have described these in terms of scriptural allusion and exegesis, whereas Newsom approaches the same phenomenon from a sociological and anthropological perspective.

There is also a strong dualism evident in the Admonition of the *Damascus Document* (CD I–VIII, XIX–XX). This is, as one would expect, sometimes expressed using walking and way images. Those whom God has led in the way of his heart (CD I 11) and walk perfectly on all his ways (CD II 15) are contrasted with those who stray from the way (CD I 14) into the ways of the wicked (CD II 3). However there is no sustained exposition of the two ways in the *Damascus Document*.

2.6.4. *Is There An Underlying Exegesis?*

In the discussion so far I have suggested that the sectarians connected ideas about dualism and predestination in a distinctive way. Furthermore, these ideas seem to be associated in several texts with an allusion to Jer 10:23. I suggest that there may have been an underlying exegesis which combined the idea of the two ways and the idea of creation and destiny and for which Jer 10:23 was pivotal. Such an exegesis, if it existed, is probably unrecoverable. However I will attempt to summarise the ideas which seem to converge around allusions to this verse.

The first phrase of Jer 10:23 states that the way of a human is not under his own control. In context it probably refers to plans and circumstances rather than to conduct. However in these allusions the

---

XXV 10 [frgs.], with VI 19–33 [XIV 8–22]. See Newsom, *The Self as Symbolic Space*, 299, 277.

[101] 1QH^a V 18–VI 18 [XIII 1–XIV 7], VII 14–37 [XV 11–24], VI 19–33 [XIV 8–22]. See Newsom, *The Self as Symbolic Space*, 209–221, 277–286. In Newsom, *The Self as Symbolic Space*, 165–174, she also discusses the Maskil's hymn, 1QS IX 12–XI 22.

[102] Newsom, *The Self as Symbolic Space*, 77–90, 209–221.

interpretation appears to be that a person's mode of conduct is predetermined. In 1QS XI 11 the phrase *perfection of way* appears in close proximity to an allusion to Jer 10:23. The phrase occurs twice more in column XI, and frequently throughout 1QS in connection with the conduct of life expected of those in the community. I suggest an underlying exegesis which contrasts the *perfect way* with the *way not good*. The latter, possibly idiomatic, term is found in IIB1b of the poem being studied and also in Isa 65:2, Ps 36:4 and Prov 16:29. Perfection of way or of heart is a common theme in the Hebrew Bible, so that it is not possible to positively identify an allusion. However, because of other similarities of language and style,[103] a good candidate is Ps 101:2–3.

אשכילה בדרך תמים מתי תבוא אלי אתהלך בתם־לבבי בקרב ביתי:

לא־אשית לנגד עיני דבר־בליעל

> I will study the way (that is) perfect; when shall I attain it? I will walk with perfection of heart within my house; I will not set before my eyes anything that is base (of Belial).

The second phrase of Jer 10:23 states that it is "not for the man who walks to direct his steps." This seems to have been interpreted in the light of the whole complex of ideas regarding creation and destiny (see §2.6.1), with the link being provided by the common use of the root כון. The root is used in the Hebrew Bible of God's establishing of creation in, for example, Jer 10:12, 33:2; Ps 119:89–91.[104] In *Jubilees* creation and destiny also seem to be linked in this way.

The final piece in the exegetical jigsaw is provided by the idea of the creator God forming humankind as a potter shapes clay. Of Jeremiah and the Isaiah servant figure it is also said that God formed them in the womb. This idea is supported by the use of the root יצר in many of the scriptural texts concerning creation, such as in Zech 12:1 and by the references to human beings as the work of God's hands, as in Job 12:10. Although the potter metaphor in Jer 18:1–10 in context seems

---

[103] Use of the verb שכל, and of the noun בליעל and of the first person are all features of the *Hodayot*.

[104] "It is he who made the earth by his power, who established the world by his wisdom, and by his understanding stretched out the heavens." (Jer 10:12); "Thus says the LORD who made the earth, the LORD who formed it to establish it—the LORD is his name." (Jer 33:2 cf. Isa 45:18); "The LORD exists forever; your word is firmly fixed in heaven. Your faithfulness endures to all generations; you have established the earth, and it stands fast. By your appointment they stand today, for all things are your servants." (Ps 119:89–91).

to imply that repentance is possible, and that God's judgement is not irrevocable, it can also lend itself to varying degrees of deterministic interpretation (cf. Sir 33:13; Wis 15:7; Rom 9:21).

2.7. *Observations and Comments*

In my study of this poem I have been led to confirm some of the conclusions of previous studies and to question some others. Firstly, the close reading has shown that this poem is highly allusive and well-constructed. This runs counter to the general observation by commentators that the Community Hymns are not very allusive or poetic. As this is the only undisputed Community Hymn considered in this study it remains to be seen whether the observation is wrong or whether this poem is an exception to it. Holm-Nielsen does seem to suggest that this poem may be of a different type from most others in the *Hodayot*.[105]

However, his analysis is based, as is mine, upon the best preserved section and not upon the whole poem. A superficial analysis of the other parts of this poem suggest that they do conform much more to expectations about Community Hymns. It could be that this unit of the poem has been incorporated from elsewhere, either existing as an independent tradition or as part of a larger work. Tanzer has already postulated that some hodayot are "hybrid" compositions. However she suggested that some of the Teacher Hymns had been edited to include elements of Community Hymns.[106] I am here suggesting that the Community Hymns themselves may also have been subject to a similar process.

Secondly, this study confirms another of Tanzer's observations, namely that there are strong wisdom elements to this poem. I have discussed Tanzer's observations in §2.6.1. It is apparent that this poem combines wisdom and covenant elements. For example it contrasts the prosperity of the righteous and punishment of the wicked; it also uses the metaphor of walking for conduct of life. These themes feature in both the Deuteronomistic literature and in wisdom texts such as Proverbs. The tendency to identify Wisdom and Torah is already apparent in some biblical texts (e.g. Ps 1:2; Job 28:28) and in some Second Temple literature (e.g. Sir 24:23, 4Q525 2 II 3–4, 4Q185).

---

[105] Holm-Nielsen, *Hodayot*, 312–313.
[106] Tanzer, "The Sages at Qumran," 148–150.

As noted by Tanzer, the theme of creation is also strong in hodayot with a strong wisdom content. In this poem creation is also very clearly related to ideas of predestination and dualism, ideas which are found elsewhere in Qumran sectarian literature. God is described as having *destined* all the acts of a person before he CREATED him. Like a potter, God has FORMED man from the dust. This link between creation and destiny in the Dead Sea corpus has also been noted by Merrill, although he did not discuss the connections with wisdom literature. More recently Armin Lange has explored this whole area. On 1QH^a IX 3–41 [I 1–39] he comments "That God's wisdom is mentioned, both in the context of the world's creation and in the context of the pre-destined fate of men, shows that the pre-existent order of the world described in this text is at least of sapiential origin."[107]

The similarities of language between this poem and 4Q301 also reinforce the link with wisdom traditions. Lange considers 4Q301 in the study mentioned above. He considers it to be a manuscript of 1Q/4Q*Mysteries* which he classes together with 1Q/4Q*Instruction* as non-sectarian sapiential texts.[108] 4Q301 is also considered by Frey in a study on the antithesis between flesh and spirit in the NT letters of Paul and in the Dead Sea sectarian scrolls. He argues that both developed from non-sectarian sapiential traditions attested by 1Q/4Q*Instruction* and 1Q/4Q*Mysteries*.[109] Perhaps then, section II of this hodayah originated as an independent non-sectarian wisdom composition.

The third of my observations about this poem is that it suggests a strong influence from Jeremiah in the formulation of the doctrine of predestination. I believe that this has not been noted before and in fact, there has been little discussion by scholars of the possible influences of Jeremiah in the scrolls.[110] In the close reading and the discussion of

---

[107] Merrill, *Qumran and Predestination*; Armin Lange, "Wisdom and Predestination in the Dead Sea Scrolls," *DSD* 2 (1995): 350.

[108] Lange, "Wisdom and Predestination," 343–346.

[109] Jörg Frey, "Flesh and Spirit in the Palestinian Jewish Sapiential Tradition and in the Qumran Texts: An Inquiry into the Background of Pauline Usage," in *The Wisdom Texts from Qumran and the Development of Sapiential Thought* (eds. C. Hempel, A Lange and H. Lichtenberger; BETL 159; Leuven: Uitgeverij Peeters, 2002), 385–400.

[110] Brooke has written an overview of the use of Jeremiah in the Dead Sea scrolls. Nitzan has discussed connections in Qumran literature between Deuteronomistic covenantal renewal, the new covenant in Jeremiah and Ezekiel, and wisdom. See George J. Brooke, "The Book of Jeremiah and its reception in the Qumran Scrolls," in *The Book of Jeremiah and its Reception* (eds. A.H.W. Curtis and T. Römer; BETL 128; Leuven: Uitgeverij Peeters, 1997), 183–205; Bilhah Nitzan "The Concept of the Covenant in

allusions I have argued that three concepts all found in Jeremiah have been combined exegetically to support the doctrine of a predetermined dualism. These are the concept of God's absolute control over his creation as expressed in the metaphor of the clay in the hands of the potter, the idea that God's choice of particular individuals such as prophets operated before their birth, and the wisdom concept that the steps of both the righteous and the wicked are ordered by the Lord. This argument is supported by the further observation that there are allusions to the key verse Jer 10:23 in other Qumran texts, also in the context of predestination.

To summarise, this poem is a strongly allusive passage which brings together wisdom ideas about creation with two ways teaching from both wisdom and covenantal traditions. It does this by means of an exegesis based on the book of Jeremiah, but also utilising other biblical texts. Although it is part of a Community Hymn it stands well on its own and may have once been an independent unit. From the deterministic dualism of this poem I turn now to another dualistic composition. This second poem has a much more personal feel to it and has generally been classed as a Teacher Hymn. However, as I will discuss, the two compositions have some strong similarities.

3. *"I" and "They"*
1QH^a XII 6–XIII 6 [IV 5–V 4]

Although many of the compositions in the *Hodayot* assume that humanity is divided into two distinct groups, this poem exhibits that dualism more clearly than most. With its repeated use of the independent pronouns *I*, *they* and *you* (referring to God) this distinction could be said to be the main theme of the poem.

My other main reason for including this poem is that a recent major study of the *Hodayot* makes it the lynch-pin of its arguments concerning authorship of the *Hodayot*. Douglas states three things which lead him to consider that this poem is "the most important in the Hodayot." Firstly, he considers that, of all the compositions, this one contains the likeliest reference to the history of the Teacher of Righteousness. Secondly, it contains two occurrences of the phrase "you exerted your

---

Qumran Literature" in *Historical Perspectives: from the Hasmoneans to bar Kokhba in light of the Dead Sea Scrolls* (ed. D. Goodblatt; Leiden: Brill, 2000), 85–104.

might through me" (הגבירכה בי). Douglas argues that this "signature phrase," which occurs in other poems, is sufficiently distinctive to have originated from a single author. Thirdly, Douglas notes that the final part of this poem has many similarities to compositions which are usually considered to be Community Hymns. He comments that this may call into doubt any assumption that the Teacher Hymns and Community Hymns originate from different authors.

Another more recent study by Newsom has also analysed this poem in some detail. Newsom describes it as mapping out the sectarian ideology. She discusses the dualism of the composition, calling it a "binary scheme." She also discusses the central role that knowledge of Torah played in establishing the claims of the sectarian ideology against other discourses.[111]

This hymn has attracted only a moderate amount of interest from other commentators. Tanzer did not analyse this poem in detail, but made some observations on its relation to other hodayot. She also noted the strong dualism. Puech has considered a few selected parts of the poem relevant to his study of beliefs about the after life.[112]

3.1. *Delimitation and Text*[113]

This composition can be found on Sukenik plates 38 and 39. Sukenik numbered these as columns IV and V but Stegemann and Puech have reassigned them as columns XII and XIII. They have also restored a small lacuna in XII 18 [IV 17] using frg. 43 (Sukenik plate 57). The start of this composition in 1QH^a XII 6 [IV 5][114] is clearly marked by a blank space followed by the introductory formula אודכה אדוני כיא. There are no other blank spaces discernible until XIII 6 [V 4]. This is followed by an introductory formula signifying the start of a new composition. As there are substantial lacunae at the bottom of column XII and the top of column XIII it is just possible that a very short composition begins and ends in these lines. However this seems unlikely. Apart from the above mentioned small section the text is well preserved.

---

[111] Newsom, *The Self as Symbolic Space*, 311–325.

[112] Tanzer, "The Sages at Qumran," 108–116; Puech, *Croyance*, 363–366.

[113] Unless otherwise stated, references in this section are to Sukenik, *The Dead Sea Scrolls*; Stegemann, "The Material Reconstruction of 1QHodayot," 280; Puech, "Quelques aspects," 41–43, 46.

[114] Douglas, "Power and Praise," 100, numbers this as XII 7.

TWO DUALISTIC POEMS

Lines 14–20 of column XII overlap with 4QH[d] 1 1–7.[115] There is also some small overlap between column XII and 4QpapH[f]. Lines 36–37 overlap with 4QpapH[f] 10 1–2.[116] Lines 11 and 23 possibly overlap with 4QpapH[f] 8 1 and 4QH[f] 9 1 respectively, but both of these fragments have only two or three readable letters.[117]

1QH[a] XII 6–XIII 6 [IV 5–V 4]

6   vacat אודכה אדוני כי[א] האירותה פני לבריתכה ומ[ ]‎[118]
7   בכל לבי[ ]‎[119] אדורשכה וכשחר נכון לאו[ר]תו[ם] הופעתה לי והמה עמכה [ ]
8   [כיא דב]רים החליקו למו ומליצי רמיה התעום וילבטו בלא בינה כיא[עשו]
9   בהולל מעשיהם כי נמאס(ת)ו[120] למו ולא יחשבוני בהגבירכה בי כי[א] ידיחני מארצי
10   כצפור מקנה וכול רעי ומודעי נדחו ממני ויחשבוני לכלי אובד והמה מליצי
11   כזב וחוזי רמיה זממו עלי {בין}[121] בליעל להמיר תורתכה אשר שננתה בלבבי בחלקות
12   לעמכה ויעצורו משקה דעת מצמאים ולצמאם ישקום חומץ למע(ן)[122] הבט אל
13   תעותם להתהולל במועדיה[ם][123] להתפש במצודותם כי אתה אל תנאץ כל מחשבת
14   בליעל ועצתכה היא תקום ומחשבת לבכה תכון לנצח והמה נעלמים זמות בליעל
15   יחשובו וידרשוכה בלב ולב ולא נכונו באמתכה שורש פורה רוש ולענה במחשבותם
16   ועם שרירות לבם יתורו וידרשוכה בגלולים ומכשול עוונם שמו לנגד פניהם ויבאו
17   לדורשכה מפי נביאי כזב מפותי תעות והם [ב]ל[ו]ע[ג] שפה ולשון אחרת ידברו לעמך
18   להולל ברמיה כול מעשיהם כי לא בחרו בדרך[124] לב]כה ולא האזינו לדברכה כי
19   אמרו
         לחזון דעת לא נכון ולדרך לבכה לא היאה כי אתה אל תענה להם לשופטם
20   בגבורת[כ]ה כ[גלוליהם וכרוב פשעיהם למען יתפשו במחשבותם אשר נזורו מבריתכה
21   ותכרת במ[שפ]ט כול אנשי מרמה וחוזי תעות לא ימצאו עוד כי אין הולל בכול מעשיך
22   ולא רמיה [ב]מזמת לבכה ואשר כנפשכה יעמודו לפניכה לעד והולכי בדרך לבכה
23   יכונו לנצח [וא]ני בתומכי בכה אתעודדה ואקומה על מנאצי וידי על כול בוזי כיא
24   לא יחשבונו[ע]ד הגבירכה בי ותופע לי בכוחכה לאורתום ולא תחתה בבושת פני
25   כול הנדרש[ים] לי הנועדים[חד] לבריתכה וישומעוני ההולכים בדרך לבכה ויערוכו
         לכה
26   בסוד קודשים ותוצא לנצח משפט ולמישרים אמת ולא תתעם ביד חלכאים
27   כזומם למו ותתן מוראם על עמכה ומפץ לכול עמי הארצות להכרית במשפט כול
28   עוברי פיכה ובי האירותה פני רבים ותגבר עד לאין מספר כי הודעתני ברזי
29   פלאכה ובסוד פלאכה הגברתה עמדי והפלא לנגד רבים בעבור כבודכה ולהודיע

---

[115] Schuller, "Hodayot," 197–198.
[116] Schuller, "Hodayot," 225.
[117] Schuller, "Hodayot," 224.
[118] Licht, *The Thanksgiving Scroll*, 91, reconstructs as [בוקר | עד עבר]ומ.
[119] See close reading for basis of this reconstruction.
[120] Most scholars follow Licht in emending thus. Sukenik transcribes as נמאסו. See Licht, *The Thanksgiving Scroll*, 92; Sukenik, *The Dead Sea Scrolls*, pl. 38.
[121] Erased letters.
[122] Most scholars emend thus. See Holm-Nielsen, *Hodayot*, 82. n. 83.
[123] The suffix ם, in non-final form, has been added later, probably by the second scribe.
[124] Restored from frg. 43.

30 לכול החיים גבורותיכה מי בשר כזאת ומה יצר חמר להגדיל פלאות והוא בעוון
31 מרחם ועד שבה באשמת מעל ואני ידעתי כי ל׳׳א לאנוש צדקה ול׳׳א לבן אדם תום
32 דרך לאל עליון כול מעשי צדקה ודרך אנוש ל׳׳א תכון כי אם ברוח יצר אל לו
33 להתם דרך לבני אדם למען ידעו כול מעשיו בכוח גבורתו ורוב רחמיו על כול בני
34 רצונו ואני רעד ורתת אחזוני וכול גׄרׄמׄיׄ ירועו וימס לבבי כדונג מ{ן|ל}פני אש וילכו ברכי
35 כמים מוגרים במורד כי זכרתי אשמותי עם מעל אבותי בקום רשעים על בריתך
36 וחלכאים על ᵈברכה ואני אמרתי בפשעי נעזבתי מבריתכה ובזוכרי כוח ידכה עם
37 המון רחמיכה התעודדתי ואקומה ורוחי החזיקה במעמד לפני נגע כי נשען[תי]
38 בחסדיכה והמון רחמיכה כי תכפר עוון ולטה[ר]אנוש מאשמה בצדקתכה
39 ול׳׳א לאדם [ ] [. .] עשיתה כי אתה בראתה צדיק ורשע [ ]
40 ואני[¹²⁵]אתחזקה בבריתכה עד[ ]
41 [ ]יכה כי אמת אתה וצדק כול[ ]מעשיכה
1 [ ]
2 [ ]
3 ליום עם חד. [ ]
4 סליחותיכה והמון [רחמיכה]
5 ובדעתי אלה נחמ[תי]. .[ ]
6 על פי רצונכה ובי[ד]כה משפט כולם vacat [ ]

3.2. *Translation*

IA (6) *Blank* I thank you, O Lord,
For you have enlightened my face according to your COVENANT[126]
and [... ...] (7) [with all my heart] I seek you.[127]
and like a sure dawn, with [perf]ect light[128] you have shone for me.

IB1 *But they*, your people[129] [...]
(8) [for the wor]ds they made smooth for them
and spokesmen of deceit caused them to err;
and they are brought down without understanding
for [they carry out] (9) in foolishness their deeds.
For I have been rejected[130] by them
nor do they esteem me when you exert your might through me.

---

[125] Douglas, "Power and Praise," 101, reads ואני, but the letters are only partly visible.
[126] Following de Vries. Holm-Nielsen translates instrumentally "with Thy covenant;" Mansoor and Douglas translate "for Thy covenant." See De Vries "The Syntax of Tenses," 392; Holm-Nielsen, *Hodayot*, 80. n. 2; Mansoor, *The Thanksgiving Hymns*, 122 n. 5; Douglas, "Power and Praise," 101.
[127] Mansoor considers this an "imperfect po'el pattern"; Holm Nielsen notes that it is an "otherwise unknown po'el with intensive meaning," or a scribal error. See Mansoor, *The Thanksgiving Hymns*, 122 n. 6; Holm-Nielsen, *Hodayot*, 80 n. 4.
[128] Meaning uncertain; cf. line 24 and 1QH^a X 27 [II 25]. See comments in Holm-Nielsen, *Hodayot*, 80 n. 6 and Mansoor, *The Thanksgiving Hymns*, 122 n. 8.
[129] This could also mean "with you." See Holm-Nielsen, *Hodayot*, 81 n. 7.
[130] Emended reading by most scholars. See Holm-Nielsen, *Hodayot*, 81 n. 12 and Mansoor, *The Thanksgiving Hymns*, 123 n. 7.

For one drives me[131] from my land (10) like a bird from its nest
and all my friends and my relatives have been driven away from me
and they esteem me like a broken vessel.

IB2 *But they* (are) spokesmen of (11) falsehood and seers of deceit
they have plotted against me Belial[132]
to exchange your torah which you engraved on my heart
for smooth things (12) for your people.
And they withhold the drink of knowledge from the thirsty ones
and for their thirst they give them to drink vinegar
in order to gaze upon (13) their error[133]
to act foolishly in their feasts
to be caught in their nets.

IB3 For *you*, O God, scorn every plan of (14) Belial
but your counsel is that which stands up
and the plan of your heart is sure[134] for evermore.

IC1 *But they* (are) hypocrites, the plans of Belial (15) they plot
and they seek you with a divided heart
nor do they stand sure in your truth
a root producing poison and bitterness (is) in their plans.
(16) And with stubbornness of their hearts they spy out
and they seek you among idols;
and the stumbling-block of their iniquity they have placed in front of their faces
and they go (17) to seek you from the mouth of prophets of falsehood
deluded by error[135]

IC2 *And they*, [with] stam[mer]ing lips and another tongue,
they speak to your people
(18) to make foolish with deceit all their deeds.

---

[131] I have translated using the generalised third person pronoun "one" to indicate that this is a singular verb although the context suggests a plural one. Holm-Nielsen and most scholars translate as a plural, assuming a defective plural or taking it collectively. Douglas however translates it as singular "he has banished me," interpreting it as referring to a particular historical person. See Holm-Nielsen, *Hodayot*, 81 n. 14; Douglas, "Power and Praise," 101 n. 14.

[132] Most translate as "worthlessness" or similar, taking the word as the object of the verb; a few take it as the collective subject. See Holm-Nielsen, *Hodayot*, 81 n. 17.

[133] This word תעות, which occurs also in lines 17 and 21, does not appear in the MT. Holm-Nielsen thinks it is equivalent to תועה in Isa 32:6. See Holm-Nielsen, *Hodayot*, 82 n. 24.

[134] Or "established;" for consistency with the opening stanza I have translated this verb as "be sure," "stand sure" etc. throughout.

[135] See note on this word in line 13 above.

100 CHAPTER THREE

> For they have not chosen the way of [your heart]
> nor have they listened to your words.
> For they said (19) of the vision of knowledge "It is not sure"
> and of the way of your heart "It is not that."

IC3 For *you*, O God, will answer to them
to judge them (20) with your might
[according to] their idols and according to the abundance of their transgressions
so that they are caught in their plans, who separate themselves from your COVENANT.
(21) And you will cut off in ju[dge]ment all men of deceit
and seers of error[136] will be found no longer.
For there is no foolishness in all your deeds
(22) nor deceit [in] the intentions of your heart.
And they who (are) as your soul will stand before your face forever;
and they who walk in the way of your heart (23) shall stand sure evermore.

ID1 [*And*] *I*, when I hold fast to you, I stand upright
and I rise up against them that scorn me
and my hands against all them that despise me.
For (24) they do not esteem [me altho]ugh you exerted your might through me
and you shine for me in your strength to a perfect light.

ID2 And you have not daubed in shame the faces of (25) all those sought by me,
those met together for your COVENANT;
and they listen to me, those who walk in the way of your heart
and they array themselves before you (26) in the council of the holy ones
and you bring forth for evermore[137] their judgement
and for their uprightness truth.

ID3 Nor do you cause them to err by the hand of scoundrels
(27) when they have plotted against them.
And you put their fear upon your people
and a smashing to all the peoples of the lands
to cut off through judgement all (28) transgressors of your command.[138]

---

[136] See note on this word in line 13 above.

[137] I have translated as "for evermore" for consistency with the other occurrences in this poem. Holm-Nielsen, *Hodayot*, 84 n. 58, has "And thou bringest their justice forth to victory." Newsom, *The Self as Symbolic Space*, 314, has "You bring their cause to victory."

[138] Literally "your mouth."

ID4   And through me you have enlightened the face of many
and you are mighty beyond reckoning.[139]
For you have made known to me the mysteries of (29) your wonder
and in the council of your wonder you have made mighty my position;
and you have done wonders[140] in front of many on account of your glory
and to make known (30) to all the living your mighty acts.

IIA   What is flesh compared to this?
and what is a creature of clay to magnify wonders?
And he is in iniquity (31) from the womb
and unto old age in guilt of unfaithfulness.

IIB1   *And I,* I know that not to a man righteousness
nor to a son of Adam perfection of (32) way.
To God Most High (belong) all deeds of righteousness
and the way of a man is not sure
except by the spirit (which) God formed for him
(33) to perfect the way for the sons of Adam[141]
So that all his works may know the strength of his might
and the abundance of his compassion upon all the sons of (34) his delight.

IIB2   *But I,* fear and trembling have seized me
and all my bones have broken
and my heart has melted like wax before the fire
and my knees go (35) like water poured down a slope.
For I have remembered my guilts with the unfaithfulness of my fathers
when the wicked rose up against your COVENANT
(36) and scoundrels against your word.

IIB3   *And I,* I said "In my transgression I have been forsaken from your COVENANT"[142]
But when I remembered the strength of your hand
With (37) the multitude of your compassions
I stood upright and I rose up
and my spirit held fast in position before affliction.
For [I] trusted (38) in your kindness and the multitude of your compassions.

---

[139] Literally "unto without number."

[140] Following Mansoor, *The Thanksgiving Hymns*, 128 n. 5, I emend to והפלאת.

[141] Here I have translated as "sons of Adam," rather than "humans," in order to show the parallelism with "sons of his delight."

[142] It is unclear where the reported speech begins. Holm-Nielsen translates as "I said in my sin, 'I am deserted by Thy covenant.'" citing Ps 31:22. See Holm-Nielsen, *Hodayot*, 78 n. 92.

> For you atone for iniquity and puri[fy]¹⁴³ a man from guilt by your righteousness.
> (39) And not for Adam [... ...] you have done
> For you, you created the righteous and the wicked [...]
> [... ...] (40) [... ... ...]

IIB4 [*And I*], I will hold fast in your COVENANT until [...]
> [... ... ...] (41) [... ... ...]
> [... ... ...] your [... ...]
> for truth you (are) and righteousness (are) all [your deeds]
> [...] (1) [... ... ...].
> [... ... ...]
> [... ... ...]
> (2) [... ... ...]
> [... ... ...]
> [... ... ...]

IIC? [...] (3) to the day with [... ... ...]
> [... ... ...]
> [... ... ...]
> [... the abundance of] (4) your forgiveness
> and the multitude of [your compassion ... ...]
> [... ... ...]
> [... ... ...]
> (5) and when I knew these things [I] gained comfort [...]
> [... ... ...]
> [... ... ...]
> [... ... ...] (6) in accordance with your will
> and in your ha[nd] (is) the judgement of them all.   *Blank*

3.3. *Analysis of Structure*

I. Introduction and Complaint Against Enemies	XII 6–30a [IV 5–29a]
A. Introductory Stanza (COVENANT)	XII 6–7b
B. The Speaker and his Enemies, part 1	XII 7c–14b
1. Misled people (exile)	*and they*
2. False teachers (drink of knowledge withheld)	*and they*
3. Vindication	*for you*
C. The Speaker and his Enemies, part 2	XII 14c–23a
1. Idolatrous people (seek)	*and they*
2. False prophets (vision of knowledge withheld)	*and they*
3. Vindication (COVENANT)	*for you*

---

¹⁴³ As noted by Holm-Nielsen, *Hodayot*, 86 n. 96, the ו in front of an infinitive makes this difficult to translate.

D. Climactic Conclusion	XII 23b–30a
1. Those who esteem me not	*And I*, they
2. Those who walk in the way of your heart (COVENANT)	you, they
3. The false teachers	you, they
4. The speaker	you, *I*
II. Prayer of Confession and Commitment	XII 30b–XIII 6 [IV 29b–V 4]
A. Introductory Stanza (rhetorical questions)	XII 30b–31a
B. The Speaker and his God	XII 31b–XIII ?
1. Acknowledgment of God's righteousness	*and I*
2. Confession (COVENANT)	*and I*
3. Remembrance of God's compassion (COVENANT)	*and I*
4. Renewal of Commitment (COVENANT)	*and I*
C. Conclusion (?)	XIII ?–6

This long poem has no blank spaces, but the use of independent pronouns is a marked feature which assists in the demarcation of stanzas. Licht indicated that the body of the poem falls into three main sections.[144] Initially I followed this division, but have since decided that the poem naturally falls into two main parts according to content, each with an introductory stanza.[145] Section I features the use of the independent pronoun *they* (המה) referring to the speaker's enemies. Section II features the independent pronoun *I* (אני). I have emphasised these independent pronouns in the translation and in the structural table.

Section I begins with an introductory stanza IA followed by two matching sub-sections IB and IC; each of these can be divided into stanzas on the basis of the independent pronouns *they* and *you*. It concludes with a climactic sub-section ID beginning with the independent pronoun *I*; this has no obvious stanza markers, but I have divided it by content into four stanzas. Section II consists of a short introductory stanza, IIA, containing rhetorical questions followed by the body of the text, IIB. This can be subdivided into four sub-sections beginning with the personal pronoun *and I*. The final part of this composition is too damaged to say anything definite. However, judging by length alone, I surmise that there may have been a final sub-section IIC which balanced sub-section ID.

There are differences in style and vocabulary between section II and the previous section; in fact, the first section would work well as a complete composition.[146] In particular, three key words/phrases

---

[144] Licht, *The Thanksgiving Scroll*, 90–98.

[145] Accordingly, in this revised version of my thesis I now place the climactic conclusion to part I as sub-section ID and not as a separate section.

[146] Tanzer considered the final section(s) to be a later addition, judging it different in

which occur in the introductory stanza IA recur, in reverse order, in sub-section ID; these are *you have enlightened my face/the faces of* (האירותה פני), *according to your covenant* (לבריתכה), and *for perfect light to me* (לאורתום הופעתה לי). Another key phrase which occurs with slight variation in both IB and ID1 is *they do not esteem me when you exert your might through me* (לא יחשבוני בהגברכה בי).

The first section is unified by a number of other keywords/themes. Those keywords which characterise the speaker/God are *be sure* ([כון]), *be/make might(y)* (גבר), *way of your heart* (דרך לבכה). Those which characterise the opposition are *error/lead astray* (תעה), *deceit* (רמיה), *falsehood* (כזב), *folly/act foolishly* (הולל), *Belial* (בליעל). The verbs *seek* (דרש), *esteem/plan* (חשב), *plot/plan* (זמם) are used of both groups.[147]

Although section I could stand alone, the manuscript has no break before section II and the four *and I* stanzas of section II appear designed to balance the four *and they* stanzas in Section I.[148] The keyword YOUR COVENANT appears three times in section I and three times in section II. I have emphasised this in the translation. The composition as it appears in 1QH^a, whatever its history, was clearly meant to be read as one poem.

---

style from the first two sections and containing material adapted from the Hymns of the Community. Douglas carefully describes the arguments for and against this view, and although undecided, treats the final section separately for the purposes of his analysis concerning authorship. His arguments for the unity of the composition are (i) the word *covenant* occurs three times in each part and the word *scoundrels* occurs once in each. (ii) the second part has the motifs of the melting heart and of self quotation in common with other Teacher Hymns. His arguments against unity are (i) apart from the two mentioned none of the other theme words occur in the second part. (ii) the motif of incongruity (rhetorical question) appears to be a redactional tendency not evident in the main block of Teacher Hymns identified by Douglas. (iii) there are several parallels between lines 30 to 39 and the Community Hymns. See Tanzer, "The Sages at Qumran," 112, 115; Douglas, "Power and Praise," 107–112.

[147] Douglas, "Power and Praise," 109, classifies the theme words as your covenant (בריתכה), seek (דרש), establish/stand firm (כון), error/(lead a)stray (תעה), deceit/falsehood (כזב,רמיה), folly/act foolishly (הולל), (to) plan/plot/esteem (חשב), might (גבר), (plots of) Belial, path of your heart (דרך לבכה).

[148] Douglas considers that the independent pronouns form a "pyramid" arrangement, with the climactic section at the apex. I am not convinced of this as my analysis suggests a final conclusion balancing the climax of the first half. Newsom merely notes that the pronouns המה and אתה introduce the strophes in the first part and that אני introduces some strophes in the second part. She considers that the poem is "not highly structured at the poetic level." See Douglas, "Power and Praise," 104–105; Newsom, *The Self as Symbolic Space*, 312–318.

3.4. *Close Reading*

As previously mentioned, although the composition as it now stands is obviously meant to be read as one long poem, section I could also stand as a complete composition. As this is such a long poem I will therefore divide my discussion of it into two. Section I contrasts the speaker and his enemies. Section II appears to contrast the speaker and his God.

3.4.1. *The Speaker and his Enemies*

The composition has a typical opening stanza beginning with the formula אודכה אדוני, followed by an opening line beginning with כיא.[149] The phrase *you have enlightened my face according to your covenant*, while not a verbal parallel, may be a subtle typological allusion.[150] On the occasion of the giving of the Torah to Moses the skin of Moses' face was said to radiate.[151] The only other place in the Hebrew Bible where light and covenant are linked is Isa 42:6.[152]

Part of the next poetic line is missing but it ends with the phrase *I seek you*. I suggest the restoration [... *with all my heart*] *I seek you* in contrast to the seeking with a divided heart mentioned in IC1.[153] The phrase *like a sure dawn* (כשחר נכון) in the final line of IA is a marker to Hos 6:3.[154]

---

[149] After examining 21 opening lines Kittel observed that "it can be stated with some assurance that a single opening pattern marks the psalms in columns 2–9." (I.e. columns X–XVII in Stegemann's reconstruction.) She described this pattern as an opening formula followed by כי, followed by a second person perfect verb, followed by some designation of a first person object. See Kittel, *The Hymns of Qumran*, 155–158.

[150] The phrase "you have enlightened my face" also occurs in 1QH^a XI 4 [III 3] but the surrounding text is too damaged to draw any conclusions about its context.

[151] "Moses came down from Mount Sinai. As he came down from the mountain with the two tablets of the testimony in his hand, Moses did not know that the skin of his face shone (קרן) because he had been talking with God." (Exod 34:29.) Brownlee notes this possible allusion, as does de Vries. See W.H. Brownlee, *The Meaning of the Qumrân Scrolls for the Bible: with Special Attention to the Book of Isaiah* (New York: OUP, 1964), 140; S.J. De Vries "The Syntax of Tenses and Interpretation in the Hodayoth" *RevQ* 5 (1964): 396.

[152] "I have given you as a covenant to the people, a light to the nations." (Isa 42:6, cf. Ps 19:8, Eccl 8:1.) Holm-Nielsen also notes that "the expression is probably thought of in analogy with the shining of God's countenance, cf. Num 6:25, Ps 31:17, 67:2, et al." The priestly benediction was evidently important to the community, e.g. 1QS II 2. See Holm-Nielsen, *Hodayot*, 80 n. 1.

[153] Sonne restores [and I found thee because] I searched for thee [with all my heart] (ומ[צאתיכה כיא בכל לבי] אדורשכה) on the basis of Jer 29:13. See Isaiah Sonne, "A Hymn against Heretics in the Newly Discovered Scrolls," *HUCA* 23 (1950): 287.

[154] "Let us know, let us press on to know the LORD; his appearing is *as sure as the dawn*; he will come to us like the showers, like the spring rains that water the earth." (Hos 6.3).

The line continues *with perfect light you have shone for me* (לאורתם הופעתה לי). This verb (יפע) occurs only eight times in the Hebrew Bible, four of which are in the context of God revealing himself.[155]

The word translated as perfect light (אורתום) is peculiar to the Qumran literature[156] and is thought by commentators to be a combination of the words light (אור) and perfection (תם). This in turn may refer to the Urim (אורים) and Thummim (תמים) of the priestly breastplate, which seem to have been connected with knowing God's will.[157] Fletcher-Louis further argues that the significance of the Urim and Thummim is evident at several other places throughout the poem and that there is also an influence from the Aaronic blessing in Num 6:25. He therefore concludes that the speaker is certainly a priest.[158] While not giving equal weight to all of the arguments of Fletcher-Louis, I agree that the cumulative effect of the language points to the speaker being a leader, quite possibly a priest.

To summarise, the introductory stanza uses light as a metaphor for God's revelation of himself and his covenant to the speaker. The parallel with Moses in Exodus and possible priestly language suggest that the speaker sees himself as a teacher/lawgiver. There may even be a veiled reference to the Teacher of Righteousness contained in the allusion to Hosea. Hos 6:3 is an exhortation to know the Lord whose coming is as sure as the dawn and is also like rain (יורה). The verb translated as to rain (ירה) can also mean to teach.[159] Thus the theme of

---

[155] "The LORD came from Sinai, and dawned from Seir upon us; *he shone forth* (הופיע) from Mount Paran (Deut 33:2); Out of Zion, the perfection of beauty, God *shines forth*." (Ps 50:2); "You who are enthroned upon the cherubim, shine forth before Ephraim and Benjamin and Manasseh." (Ps 80:1); "O LORD, you God of vengeance, you God of vengeance, shine forth!" (Ps 94:1); see also Job 3:4, 10:3, 10:22, 37:15. The verb occurs in 1QH\u1d43 XII 7, 24 [IV 6, 23], XIII 34 [V 32], XV 6, 27 [VII 3, 24], XVII 26, 31 [IX 26, 31], XIX 29 [XI 26], XXIII 7 [XVIII 6]. cf. CD XX 25–26, 1QM I 16.

[156] 1QH\u1d43 XII 7, 24 [IV 6, 23], XXI 15 [XVIII 29], 4Q392 1 5, 4Q403 1 I 45, 1 II 1, 4Q404 5 4. (Abegg, et al., *The Dead Sea Scrolls Concordance, Volume 1*, 19).

[157] These obscure objects are mentioned in Exod 28:30, Lev 8:8, Num 27:21, Deut 33:8, 1 Sam 28:6, Ezra 2:63, Neh 7:65. Sukenik suggested that this word is meant as a singular form of אורים ותומים. Sukenik, מגילות גנוזות סקירה שנייה, 43, cited in Mansoor, *The Thanksgiving Hymns*, 122, n. 8.

[158] Crispin H.T. Fletcher-Louis, *All the Glory of Adam: Liturgical Anthropology in the Dead Sea Scrolls* (STDJ 42; Leiden: Brill, 2002), 237–243. He cites the use of *judgement* and *truth* in line 26 [25] and the root תום used twice in lines 31–32 [30–31], as well as the repetition of *perfect light* in line 24 [23]. He also points to the similarity of the phrase in line 28 [27], *enlightened the face of the many*, with language describing the High Priest in 1QSb IV 7.

[159] There is a possible play on words in the phrase Teacher of Righteousness (מרה

the poem is declared to be interpretation of Torah, or as Newsom puts it "the issue of truth."[160]

This interpretation of the introduction is borne out by the rest of the section. Matching sub-sections IB and IC are an indictment of the people who have rejected the speaker and his teaching, and of the false teachers and prophets respectively. Stanza IB1 introduces the plight of the people, who have been *caused to err* by *spokesmen of deceit* (ומליצי רמיה). I have used the neutral translation spokesman, but Holm-Nielsen suggests that the phrase מליצי חידות in 1QpHab VIII 6 shows that it "indicates one who has a special insight into things which are not generally obvious."[161] מליץ is used several times in the *Hodayot*, both of those who speak truth and those who speak lies.[162] Douglas translates it as mediator and considers that the term referred to a recognised role, a teacher of God's Law, exercised by a scribe or a priest.[163] Using this plausible interpretation, it would seem that the speaker's opponents were rival teachers of the Law. However, Newsom's caution against identifying these literary constructs with actual persons or groups is an apt one.[164]

The word *deceit* (רמיה) and words derived from the root "to err" (תעה) occur five times each in this section of the poem. The parallel words *falsehood* (כזב) and *be foolish/foolishness* (הולל) occur twice and four times respectively.[165] The reference to making *smooth* (החליקו), when taken with the *smooth things* (הלקות) in IB2, may be an allusion to Isa 30:10.[166]

צדק), whose only close biblical equivalents occur in Joel 2:23 (המורה לצדקה) and Hos 10:12 (צדק ירה), both referring to rain. Cf. 1QpHab I 13, II 2, V 10, VII 4, VIII 3, IX 9, XI 5; 1QpMic 8 10 6; 4QpPs[b] 1 4; CD I 11, 20:32, etc. See Abegg, et al., *The Dead Sea Scrolls Concordance, Volume 1*, 433–434; W.H. Brownlee, "Messianic Motifs of Qumran and the New Testament" *NTS* 3 (1956–1957): 13.

[160] Newsom, *The Self as Symbolic Space*, 318.
[161] Holm-Nielsen, *Hodayot*, 35, n. 29.
[162] 1QH[a] X 15, 16, 33 [II 13, 14, 31]; XII 8, 10 [IV 7, 9]; XIV 16 [VI 13]; XXIII 12 [XVIII 11]; 2 I 6; 4Q427 7 II 18. The only other scrolls references to this root are 1QpHab VIII 6; 1QH[a] X 13 [II 11]; 4Q171 1–2 I 19; 4Q184 1 2; 4Q368 3 7; 4Q374 7 2; 4Q418 100 1; 4Q426 8 4; 4Q468 I 1; 5Q10 1 2. See Abegg, et al., *The Dead Sea Scrolls Concordance, Volume 1*, 417.
[163] Douglas, "Power and Praise," 258–264, supports his arguments by detailed analysis of biblical usage, usage in 1QH[a], *Ben Sira* 10:2, and 4Q374 7 2.
[164] Newsom, *The Self as Symbolic Space*, 319.
[165] I follow Holm-Nielsen in translating הולל as foolishness, (m. sg.) corresponding to הוללות in Ecclesiastes, a poel past participle without מ, from הלל. He comments further, "it is used especially of the ungodly, cf. Ps 5:6, 73:3, 75:5, and it occurs several times in the Hodayot in this sense." See Holm-Nielsen, *Hodayot*, 49 n. 17.
[166] "For they are a rebellious people, faithless children, children who will not hear the instruction of the LORD; who say to the seers, 'Do not see'; and to the prophets, 'Do

The result is that *they are brought down without understanding* (וילבטו בלא
בינה). This is a marker to Hos 4:14;[167] the context in Hosea, where the
Lord holds the priests and prophets culpable for the people's lack of
knowledge, is strikingly similar. This theme of knowledge or lack of it
(foolishness) continues throughout the composition.[168] In particular it is
picked up in IB2 and IC2 where lack of the *drink of knowledge* and *vision
of knowledge* respectively are linked to foolishness.

The second verse of IB1 describes the speaker's rejection by the
people. In translation it appears similar to Isa 53:3 but the Hebrew
vocabulary is different apart from the use of the commonly occurring
verb *esteem* (חשב). The speaker's rejection is in stark contrast to the
acceptance of the false prophets just described. The key phrase *when
you exert your might through me* (בהגבירכה בי) emphasises, also in contrast,
the validity of the speaker's teaching. This key phrase is repeated with
slight variation in IIA.

In the third verse there is an isolated change from the plural to
singular in referring to the speaker's adversaries. Most translators treat
this as a plural. However, Douglas sees this as a reference to the
Teacher's adversary, the Wicked Priest.[169] The expression *like a bird from
its nest* (כצפור מקנה) is best considered as the use of biblical imagery
rather than as an allusion.[170] But it introduces the motif of exile, which
may be linked to the allusions to Ezekiel which occur in sub-section IC.
It is more tempting to see an allusion to Ps 31:11–12 [12–13][171] in the last

---

not prophesy to us what is right; speak to us smooth things, prophesy illusions, leave the
way, turn aside from the path, let us hear no more about the Holy One of Israel'." (Isa
30:9–11).

[167] "thus a people without understanding comes to ruin (ועם לא־יבין ילבט)." (Hos
4:14); cf. 1QH^a X 21 [II 19].

[168] Newsom insightfully observes that in this poem the opposite of knowledge is not
mere ignorance but is wilful and related to moral character. She contrasts this with
the representation of knowledge in Ezra-Nehemiah, where ignorance is countered by
teaching and persuasion. See Newsom, *The Self as Symbolic Space*, 322–323.

[169] Douglas, "Power and Praise," 101 n. 14.

[170] Prov 27:8; Isa 16:2; Ps 11:1. Holm-Nielsen comments "Various interpreters have
found in the expression ... a reference to the author ... being banished or fleeing under
the persecution of the Jerusalem priesthood. However, since similar expressions come
in other Old Testament psalms as traditional material for portrayals of misery, it is
without justification to attach the expression to a concrete circumstance when there is
nothing in the context which would directly suggest it." See Holm-Nielsen, *Hodayot*, 81
n. 14, 307.

[171] "I am the scorn of all my adversaries, a horror to my neighbors, an object of
dread to *my acquaintances*; those who see me in the street flee *from me*. I have passed out
of mind like one who is dead; I have become *like a broken vessel*." (Ps 31:11–12).

two lines of this verse. The phrases *all my friends and my relatives have been driven away from me* (וכול רעי ומודעי נדחו ממני) and *like a broken vessel* (לכלי אובד) use nearly identical vocabulary to this psalm. Although these are both common biblical images their juxtaposition constitutes a probable marker.

Stanza 1B2 begins with another occurrence of the independent pronoun *they*. There are several connections with the previous stanza as well as some new elements. *Spokesmen of deceit*, found in the previous stanza, is elaborated to *spokesmen of falsehood and seers of deceit* (מליצי כזב וחוזי רמיה). The introduction of *seers* points to the transition from teaching to prophecy which is soon to follow. The word *seers* is linked with *smooth things* (חלקות) as in Isa 30:10. The reference to smooth things picks up on the words made smooth referred to in 1B1. These flatteries are contrasted with the torah engraved on the speaker's heart in a possible passing reference to Deut 6:6.[172] Another new element is the idea that, just as the adversaries in Ps 31:13 [14], *they have plotted* (זממו) against the speaker. The plotting is linked to the word *Belial*, whether as the collective subject of the verb or as the object (*worthlessness*), is unclear.

I suggest that the introduction of the word *Belial*, together with the use of the phrase *to exchange* (להמיר), constitutes a marker to Jer 2:11.[173] In this verse the phrase "something that does not profit" (בלוא יועיל) is a word play on the name of the god Baal. The word play also occurs in Jer 2:8[174] in which the priests, "those who handle the Torah," are accused along with the prophets "who prophesy by Baal." The reference to plotting in connection with Belial will be picked up later in the poem (1B3 and 1C1) in further allusions to Jeremiah.

The next verse introduces the motif of drinking, with the words *they withhold the drink of knowledge from the thirsty ones* (ויעצורו משקה דעת מצמאים).

---

[172] "Keep these words that I am commanding you today *in your heart* (על־לבבך). *Recite them* to your children (ושננתם לבניך)." (Deut 6:6–7) This verb (שנן) in the HB usually means to sharpen, but here means to inculcate. Cf. "But this is *the covenant* that I will make with the house of Israel after those days, says the LORD: I will put *my law* within them, and I will write it *on their hearts*; and I will be their God, and they shall be my people." (Jer 31:33).

[173] "Has a nation changed its gods, even though they are no gods? But my people have changed their glory for something that does not profit (ועמי המיר כבודו בלוא יועיל)." (Jer 2:11). Two similar verbs meaning to change (מור, ימר) occur in one and nine other verses respectively in the HB. A similar context occurs only in Ps 106:20 and Hos 4:7.

[174] "The priests did not say, 'Where is the LORD?' Those who handle the law did not know me; the rulers transgressed against me; the prophets prophesied by Baal, and went after things that do not profit." (Jer 2:8).

This is a probable allusion to Isa 32:6, where lying leaders and their followers are contrasted with noble ones. Although the markers are not exact the contextual link is good. This is followed by *and for their thirst they give them vinegar to drink* (ולצמאם ישקום חומץ), a very clear allusion to Ps 69:21 [22] in which the psalmist calls upon God for deliverance from his enemies.[175]

The phrase *drink of knowledge* indicates that drinking is being interpreted metaphorically. The positive effects of this drink are contrasted with the negative effects of the intoxicating *vinegar* supplied by the false teachers. The use of drinking as a metaphor for studying/obtaining knowledge seems to have been a common one, found certainly in rabbinic literature.[176] In Qumran literature it is found in the *Damascus Document* in an interpretation of Num 21:18:

> The well is the law. And those who dug it are the converts of Israel, who left the land of Judah and lived in the land of Damascus ... and the staff is the interpreter of the law ... (CD VI 4–7).[177]

The next three lines all begin with the preposition ל and the first two of them contain a clear allusion to Hab 2:15.[178] The marker to Hab 2:15, *in order to gaze upon ... their feasts*, contains the textual variant in their feasts (במועדיהם)[179] where the MT reads on their nakedness (על־מעוריהם). This same textual variant is found in 1QpHab XI 3, which suggests either that both used the same variant text[180] or that one text is dependent on the other.[181] However it should also be noted that here the

---

[175] "For fools speak folly, and their minds plot iniquity: to practice ungodliness, to utter *error* concerning the LORD, to leave the craving of the hungry unsatisfied, and to deprive *the thirsty of drink*." (Isa 32:6); "They gave me poison for food, and *for my thirst they gave me vinegar to drink*." (Ps 69:21).

[176] Mansoor, *The Thanksgiving Hymns*, 124 n. 3, cites *Aboth* 4:4: את שותה בצמא והוה דבריהם. See also my comments in §2.6.2 of chapter four on water as a metaphor for Torah.

[177] García Martínez and Tigchelaar, *The Dead Sea Scrolls Study Edition*, 559.

[178] "Alas for you who make your neighbors drink, pouring out your wrath until they are drunk, *in order to gaze on their nakedness!*" (Hab 2:15).

[179] Note the second scribe has added the suffix מ but not in its final form.

[180] Lim has suggested that the pesherist may have used more than one version of Habakkuk, including perhaps a Greek version of Habakkuk found at Nahal Hever (8HevXIIgr). See T.H. Lim, "The Qumran Scrolls, Multilingualism, and Biblical Interpretation" in *Religion in he Dead Sea Scrolls* (eds. J.J. Collins and R.A. Kugler; Grand Rapids: Eerdmans, 2000), 70–72.

[181] Holm-Nielsen suggests that the 1QH[a] passage is dependent on the pesher, but Davies convincingly argues the opposite. See Holm-Nielsen, *Hodayot*, 82 n. 25; Davies, *Behind the Essenes*, 93–96.

festival observance of the speaker's opponents are in view, whereas 1QpHab interprets Hab 2:15 as referring to the festival observance of the Teacher of Righteousness.[182] Commentators speculate that this is a reference either to incorrect conduct in the temple or to use of a different calendar.[183]

Holm-Nielsen has suggested that the interpolation of the words *their error, to act foolishly* (תעותם להתהול) into this allusion are due to the influence of Isa 28:7, and Jer 25:16 respectively.[184] The former evokes Isaiah's description of drunken priests and prophets and points forward to the allusion to Isa 28:11 in stanza IC2. The context of the latter evokes the metaphor of the cup of God's wrath; this metaphor is also employed in Hab 2:16. As the poem unfolds it will become increasingly clear why the speaker considers his opponents to be objects of God's wrath. As noted by Newsom, their error is not viewed in this poem as mere ignorance but as wilful perversion.[185] The term Belial has been introduced earlier in this stanza; it is possible, therefore, that the final phrase of this verse, *to be caught in their nets*, could be an allusion to the three nets of Belial. These are identified in CD IV 10–19 as fornication, wealth, and defilement of the temple. I discuss this pesher of Isa 24:17 in §3.5.1 of chapter five.

IB3, the final stanza of this sub-section, is addressed to God and incorporates two conflated gnomic allusions which reinforce the idea that despite the worthless plots (i.e. of Belial) of the speaker's enemies, which have just been described, it is God's purposes which will ultimately prevail. The speaker's enemies are thus now clearly identified with God's enemies. The phrase, *but it is your counsel that stands up* (ועצתכה היא תקום), is almost identical to Prov 19:21, where the contrast is with the many plans of man's heart. The phrase *plan of your heart* (ומחשבת לבכה) is a probable marker to Ps 33:11.[186] Thus, *every plan of Belial* (כל

---

[182] As noted by Holm-Nielsen in the above reference.

[183] Holm-Nielsen, *Hodayot*, 82 n. 25.

[184] "These also reel with wine and *stagger* (תעו) with strong drink; the priest and the prophet reel with strong drink, they are confused with wine, they *stagger* with strong drink; they err in vision, they stumble in giving judgement." (Isa 28:7); "They shall drink and stagger and *go out of their minds* (והתהללו) because of the sword that I am sending among them." (Jer 25:16, cf. 51:7). See Holm-Nielsen, *Hodayot*, 82 n. 25.

[185] Newsom, *The Self as Symbolic Space*, 322–323.

[186] עצה and מחשבה occur seven times in parallel in the HB, twice in Psalm 33. Only in two of these are the context and meaning similar. "The *counsel* of the LORD stands forever, *the thoughts of his heart* to all generations." (Ps 33:11); "The human mind may devise many *plans*, but it is the *purpose* of the LORD that will be established." (Prov 19:21).

מחשבת בליעל), which *you* (God) *scorn* (תנאץ), is contrasted with *the plan of your* (God's) *heart* (מחשבת לבכה) which *stands sure for evermore* (תכון לנצח). The plan of your heart is equivalent to the phrase *intentions of your heart* (מזמת לבכה) in matching stanza IC3. While the phrase *plan of Belial* is not a biblical one, a similar contrast between the plans of God and the plans of the false prophets of Baal is found in Jer 23:20, 27. This will be discussed further in §3.5.1 of this chapter.

The beginning of sub-section IC returns to consideration of the people, as in IB1. The theme is that of seeking with the wrong motivation and from the wrong sources.[187] The phrase *plans of Belial* provides a catchword link with the previous stanza. The first verse describes the people as *hypocrites* (נעלמים),[188] with *a divided heart*; this latter is a common expression but in Ps 12:2 it is used in parallel to *smooth lips* and so may be another link to the *smooth things* motif. This is made more likely by the fact that the root חלק is used with the meaning *smooth/flattery* in only a few places in the Hebrew Bible.[189]

Then follows a complex allusion to Deut 29:17–20 and Ezek 14:3, 4, and 7. The clear markers to Deuteronomy are the phrases *root producing poison and bitterness* (שורש פורה רוש ולענה), *stubbornness of their hearts* (שרירות לבם), and *idols* (גלולים). The reference to *idols* leads easily into an allusion to Ezekiel that *they place the stumbling block of their iniquity in front of their faces* (ומכשול עוונם שמו לנגד פניהם).[190] The reference to *prophets of falsehood deluded by error* (נביאי כזב מפותי תעות) evokes the repeated references in Ezek 13 to the lies of false prophets.

---

[187] Newsom, *The Self as Symbolic Space*, 323, aptly calls this seeking out of false spiritual sources a "doubled doubleness" of heart.

[188] The only use of the word נעלמים in the HB is Ps 26:4. In this biblical psalm the speaker contrasts his own blameless conduct with that of the wicked. The context is thus similar to this hodayah. However there is no other marker or indication of evoked connotations. I therefore take this as the idiomatic use of a biblical word possibly adopted by the sectarians as a technical term for their enemies. cf. 1QH^a XI 29 [III 28], XV 37 [VII 34].

[189] Cf. Ps 12:2; Isa 30:10; Prov 6:4; Prov 7:21; Job 17:5.

[190] "You have seen their detestable things, *the filthy idols* (גלליהם) of wood and stone, of silver and gold, that were among them. It may be that there is among you a man or woman, or a family or tribe, whose heart is already turning away from the LORD our God to serve the gods of those nations. It may be that there is among you *a root sprouting poisonous and bitter growth* (שרש פרה ראש ולענה). All who hear the words of this oath and bless themselves, thinking in their hearts, 'We are safe even though we go our own *stubborn ways* (בשררות לבי)' (thus bringing disaster on moist and dry alike)." (Deut 29:17–19 [16–18]); "Mortal, these men have taken their *idols* (גלוליהם) into their hearts, *and placed their iniquity as a stumbling block before them* (ומכשול עוונם נתנו נכח פניהם)." (Ezek 14:3).

IC2 begins with an allusion to Isa 28:11.[191] The context in Isaiah is one of God's judgement on drunken priests and prophets. This verse, which probably referred to God's instrument of judgement being foreigners, is here interpreted as the misleading teaching of the false prophets. The image of drunken priests corresponds to the drinking motif in IB2, which also alludes to Isa 28. The next two verses accuse the false prophets not only of rejecting God's *way* and *words* themselves but of denying their validity altogether. The *vision of knowledge* is effectively withheld from the people just as the *drink of knowledge* was in IB2. Commentators have not noted any allusions in these verses but there are similarities of style to Ezekiel in the use of reported speech.[192]

Also in these verses the key phrase *the way of your heart* (דרך לבכה) is introduced. The phrase occurs twice in IC2, and again in IC3 and IIB. It is an allusion to Isa 57:17, which at first sight appears to bear no relation to the original context. However Kister has argued that the expression, which occurs also in CD I 11, may be understood by means of an implicit underlying pesher.[193] I will discuss this further in my consideration of the allusions in this passage (see §3.5.1).

IC3, beginning *For you O Lord*, matches the beginning of IB3. There are several lines describing the coming judgement of God upon the false prophets. The phrase *intentions of your heart* marks an allusion to Jer 23:20.[194] This verse, which has already been subtly alluded to in IB3, is part of a longer passage denouncing false prophets. Thus there are many connotations which are likely to be picked up by an ideal reader (see §3.5.1).

The final lines of affirmation echo the last line of IB3 while subtly changing the focus from God's plans to those who walk in God's plans. This is the first explicit mention of the speaker's own followers. It neatly sets up the theme of the next sub-section, ID, which is the vindication of the speaker and his followers and the judgement of the false teachers and their followers. Newsom describes these two groups of actors as

---

[191] "Truly, with stammering lip and with alien tongue he will speak to this people." (Isa 28:11).

[192] Cf. "Yet your people say, 'The way of the LORD is not just'." (Ezek 33:17).

[193] M. Kister, "Biblical Phrases and Hidden Biblical Interpretations and Pesharim," in *The Dead Sea Scrolls. Forty Years of Research* (ed. D. Dimant and U. Rappaport; Jerusalem: Magnes Press, 1992), 27–39.

[194] "The anger of the LORD will not turn back until he has executed and accomplished *the intents of his mind* (מזמות לבו)." (Jer 23.20) In the HB the phrase occurs only here and in the almost identical verse in Jer 30:24.

"mirror images" of each other. By means of a semiotic square she elaborates upon this symmetry, and how it provides ideological closure for the sectarians.[195]

Newsom's analysis focuses upon how the poem resolves the conflict between the speaker's possession of the truth and the rejection of that truth by God's people. She argues that this resolution requires two additional sets of characters. The lying teachers provide the explanation for why God's people have rejected the truth. The speaker's followers, "the many," provide the necessary recognition of the truth. The threat to this scheme is represented by betrayal and disaffection amongst the speaker's followers. Newsom calls this poem "the map of truth" because, she argues, it maps out for his followers the role of their leader and themselves in relation to the truth; it thus reinforces and confirms the sectarian ideology. Thus Newsom calls the recitation of this hodayah "an act of leadership."[196]

The four short stanzas of ID quicken the pace of the poem and act as a climax to section I. They contain many echoes of phrases found earlier in section I. ID1 expresses the vindication of the speaker against his adversaries. *I stand upright and I rise up* may be a marker to Ps 20:8, which is the only biblical reference where these two verbs are combined.[197] If so, then there is probably an unspoken assumption that, as in the Psalm, "they will collapse and fall." In this case, *they* refers to those that *esteem me not*. This echoes IB1, but the additional *those that despise me* gives a stronger marker to Isa 53:3. The words *you reveal to me … for a perfect light* echo the introductory stanza of the poem.

ID2 expresses the vindication of the speaker's followers, *all those sought by me* and who *have listened to me*. This is in contrast to those in IC1 who *seek you among idols* and in IC2 have not *listened to your words*. They are also described as *those who walk in the way of your heart*, in contrast to those in IC2 who *have chosen not the way of your heart*. They are *met together for your covenant* (הנועדים יחד לבריתכה) and *have arrayed themselves before you in the council of the holy ones* (ויערוכו לכה בסוד קודשים).

The latter two expressions may be technical phrases referring to the sectarian community, as both יחד (which has been inserted above

---

[195] Newsom cites Fredric Jameson as having developed this device for mapping the closure of an ideological system. See Newsom, *The Self as Symbolic Space*, 320–322; Fredric Jameson, *The Political Unconscious: Narrative as a Socially Symbolic Act* (NY: Cornell University Press, 1981), 166–169, 254–257.
[196] Newsom, *The Self as Symbolic Space*, 318–325.
[197] "They will collapse and fall, but we shall rise and stand upright." (Ps 20:8).

the line), and סוד are used in 1QS for the community.[198] Ps 89:7 uses the phrase *council of the holy ones* referring to the heavenly council. In view of the theme of false prophets there may also be an implied comparison with Jeremiah's accusation that the false prophets had never stood in God's council, as true prophets did.[199] Ezek 13:9 (see the allusion referred to below) states that "the lying prophets will not be in the *council of my people*," perhaps echoing the verses from Jeremiah. Leslie Allen comments "those who had wrongly claimed this prophetic credential would lose their membership of the סוד at the lower level of the community of faith."[200]

The vindication of the speaker's followers is expressed negatively by the phrase *you have not daubed in shame the faces*. This phrase employs a common image of shame-faced-ness[201] but the verb *daub* (טוח) appears mainly in Ezekiel used of false prophets.[202] Holm-Nielsen notes all the above references and concludes that since similar references to Ezekiel are found in CD VIII 12 and XIX 25 this may be an indirect allusion to Ezek 13:10.[203] Ezekiel likened the misleading message of the false prophets to daubing in whitewash an unsafe wall. This poem turns the metaphor back to front. When his followers are vindicated it will be not they but their enemies who are daubed in shame. This vindication is also expressed positively as *you bring forth for evermore their judgement and for their uprightness truth*. Holm-Nielsen considers this might be a combination of Isa 42:3 and Hab 1:4.[204] However, the phrases are too general and the context not specific enough to warrant considering this an allusion.

---

[198] e.g. 1QS II 24–25.

[199] "For who has stood in *the council* of the LORD so as to see and to hear his word? Who has given heed to his word so as to proclaim it?" (Jer 23:18); "But if they had stood in my *council*, then they would have proclaimed my words to my people, and they would have turned them from their evil way, and from the evil of their doings." (Jer 23:22).

[200] Leslie C. Allen, *Ezekiel 20–48*, (Word Biblical Commentary 29; Dallas: Word Books, 1998).

[201] See Jer 7:19; Ezra 9:7; 2 Chr 32:21; Dan 9:7, 8; as the subject of verb כסה (cover) in Ps 44:16. cf. 1QH[a] XIII 37 [V 35]; XVII 20, 22 [IX 20, 22].

[202] Of 12 occurrences in the HB, 7 are in Ezek, e.g. Ezek 13:10ff; 22:28.

[203] "But the builders of the wall have not understood all these things, nor those who daub with whitewash." (CD VIII 12) "When the people build a wall, these prophets smear whitewash on it." (Ezek 13:10.). See Holm-Nielsen, *Hodayot*, 84 n. 53.

[204] "He will faithfully bring forth justice (לאמת יוציא משפט)." (Isa 42:3); "So the law becomes slack and justice never prevails (ולא־יצא לנצח משפט). The wicked surround the righteous—therefore judgement comes forth perverted." (Hab 1.4). See Holm-Nielsen, *Hodayot*, 88.

ID3 also expresses the vindication negatively and positively. Negatively, his followers are *not caused to err by the hand of scoundrels*. Positively they have become a cause of *fear, smashing,* and *judgement* to *all those who transgress God's commands*. There are a number of distinctive words in this stanza, which could be markers to specific verses, but the contextual links appear weak at best.²⁰⁵

ID4 matches ID1 in its description of the vindication by God of the speaker. It echoes the enlightenment language of ID1. This language also refers back to that of IA and IB1, thus rounding off this half of the poem. The threefold repetition of the roots *might(y)* (גבר) and *wonder* (פלא) has a crescendo effect ensuring that this part of the poem ends on a loudly triumphant note. The final verse concerns revelation to the speaker and through him *to all the living*. This last phrase is an echo of Ps 145:12, but there is not enough similarity of context to constitute an allusion.

3.4.2. *The Speaker and his God*

Section II has an introductory stanza posing rhetorical questions followed by four stanzas beginning with *and I*; this is in contrast with and balances the introductory stanza and fourfold *and they* of section I. The final lines of the composition are damaged but the available space allows for the possibility that there may be a concluding sub-section IIC balancing concluding sub-section ID.

This new section is linked to the previous one by use of the catchword *wonder* which also occurred three times at the end of sub-section ID. However the tone of this section is very different from the triumphalistic climax of the previous one. This raises the possibility that the identity of the implied speaker has changed, perhaps from the leader of the group to one or more of its members. However, a similar abrupt change of tone to expressions of unworthiness is evident elsewhere in the *Hodayot*. It is often marked by the use of rhetorical questions. This phenomenon has been noted by several commentators.²⁰⁶ For Newsom in particular this is a key feature of the Community

---

²⁰⁵ Scoundrels (חלכאים) occurs in the HB only in Ps 10, but the context and meaning is different. Smashing (מפץ) is found in the HB only in Ezek 9:2. and Jer 51:20, both in the context of judgement. The phrase transgressors of your commands (עוברי פיכה) most closely matches Num 14:41.

²⁰⁶ Douglas calls it the "motif of incongruity." Newsom calls it the "masochistic sublime." See Douglas, "Power and Praise," 110; Newsom, *The Self as Symbolic Space*, 172–173, 220–221.

Hymns. She sees this section of the poem as the self-presentation of the leader as one who exemplifies this attitude.

IIA acts as an introduction to the change of theme, which concerns the *iniquity, guilt* and *unfaithfulness* of humanity. Each of these words is picked up in sub-section IIB. The all-encompassing phrase, *from the womb and unto old age*, echoes biblical language such as that found in Ps 51:5 [7].

IIB is in the style of a prayer of confession and commitment. This is a common form, appearing both within and outside the Hebrew Bible.[207] It begins with an acknowledgment that God is in the right (IIB1), continues with a confession of guilt (IIB2) and a remembering of God's mercy (IIB3), followed by a renewal of commitment (IIB4).

The theme of stanza IIB1 is that to God alone belongs *righteousness* (צדקה). This has echoes of Jer 10:23 but on closer analysis the whole of IIB1 is very close to 1QH^a VII 25b–27a [XV 12b–14a], discussed earlier in this chapter. The latter composition contains a more certain allusion to Jer 10:23. This suggests that the direction of influence is from the composition (or the tradition it represents) in column VII [XV] to this composition in column XII [IV].

In stanzas IIB2 and IIB3 the speaker uses the verb *remember*. By contrast with God's *righteousness* the speaker has *remembered* his own *guilt* (אשמה), *iniquity* (עוון), and *transgression* (פשע). In the Hebrew Bible it is usually God, not the people, who remembers their sins. This language therefore evokes Ezekiel's promise of the renewed covenant. In response to God's forgiveness the people will remember their ways and be ashamed. (Ezek 16:60–63, 20:43, 36:31).

In common with similar prayers of penitence, the speaker also identifies himself with the *unfaithfulness* (מעל) *of my fathers*. In this he is obeying the instruction in Lev 26:40.[208] This causes him to be overcome. He describes this using common biblical imagery of distress *(fear and trembling, broken bones, melted heart, weak knees.)* The juxtaposition of *like wax before the fire* and *like water poured down a slope* is a marker to the theophany of judgement in Mic 1:4. The connotation is that the speaker is physically overwhelmed by fear of God's awesome judgement for his sins.

---

[207] Ezra 9:6–15; Neh 1:5–11; 9:5–38; Bar 1:15–3:8; 1QS I 22–II 1; 4QWords of the Luminaries. See also Isa 59:12–15; 64:4–11; Jer 14:7–9, 19–22; Pss 51, 106; Prayer of Manasseh.

[208] "But if they confess their iniquity and the iniquity of *their fathers*, in that they committed *unfaithfulness* against me … … then will I remember my covenant." (Lev 26:40) Cf. Ezra 9:4, 10:6. Dan 9:7, Ezek 20:27–44.

This is contrasted in stanza IIB3 where he has *remembered* God's *compassion* (רחמים) and *stood upright* (התעודד), *rose up* (קום) and *held fast* (החזיק), echoing the verbs of IIA. The language is similar to that of biblical prayers for deliverance[209] but is not specific enough for a certain allusion. The phrase *the strength of your hand* (כח ידכה) is also too common an idea to constitute a marker to a specific verse. It would however almost certainly bring to mind the archetypal act of deliverance from Egypt.[210] Isa 63:15 is the only biblical reference to *the multitude of your compassions*, a phrase which is twice repeated here and probably again in XIII 4 [V 2]. This passage in Isaiah is a plea for God to turn back to his rebellious people and grant them repentance. It therefore serves as a shorthand allusion reinforcing the theme of penitence.

Stanza IIB4 is badly damaged but appears to be a pledge of commitment that *I will hold fast in your covenant*. This combination of the verb to *hold fast* (חזק) and *covenant* occurs only in Isa 56:4, 6, where the promise of the covenant is extended to outsiders who keep its laws, specifically the Sabbath. Because of the damage to most of this stanza one can only speculate as to which of these connotations is being evoked here, Sabbath observance or inclusivity!

Judging by the available space, there are probably one or more stanzas following this one. I conjecture that there was a short concluding sub-section matching the climactic conclusion of section I. The composition probably ends in line XIII 6 [V 4] where *in your hand is the judgement of them all* appears to be followed by a blank space.

3.5. *Allusions*

The main allusions have been noted in the close reading of the text. I will now discuss the biblical passages which seem of particular significance. These include passages from Deuteronomy, Isaiah, Jeremiah, Ezekiel, Hosea and Psalms. I will once again divide my discussion into two parts.

---

[209] e.g. Ps 31:22, 20:8.

[210] The phrase "with a mighty hand" (ביד חזקה) is frequently used in references to the Exodus from Egypt, e.g. Deut 4:34, 5:15. The noun, כוח seems to be preferred to use of חזק as a noun or adjective in the *Hodayot*. In Ex 32:11 it is used in parallel with the phrase "with a mighty hand." See Abegg, et al., *The Dead Sea Scrolls Concordance, Volume I*, 257, 342.

3.5.1. *Correct and Incorrect Interpretation of Torah*[211]

There are two clues to the main biblical underpinning of the first part of this poem. Firstly, as already noted, the introductory stanza clearly alludes to Moses, whose *face* was *enlightened* after receiving the *covenant* at Sinai when God *shone* for him (Exod 34.) This theme is repeated in ID1 and ID4. Secondly, the keywords which occur more frequently in this poem than in any other hodayah are *covenant*, *way*, *seek*, and *heart*. In addition, this is one of only three hodayot which use the word *Torah*.[212] These all point to a Deuteronomistic, covenantal context.

Douglas believes that the first part of the poem "is patterned on the pericope concerning the 'Prophet like Moses' in Deut 18: 9–22. This paragraph contrasts legitimate and illicit means of prophecy or divination."[213] Douglas argues that the speaker sees himself as the promised Prophet like Moses in contrast to his opponents who are the false prophets mentioned in the passage. The speaker may well have regarded himself as the Prophet like Moses but Douglas fails to show any convincing markers which would serve to establish an allusion. The one verbal parallel he uses is the injunction to *listen* to the prophet. He also seeks to argue that the use of the verb *seek* in this poem can be connected with the biblical passage's condemnation of divination. Both of these are very general, weak points of connection.

There are undoubtedly allusions to Deuteronomy. As well as the afore-mentioned allusion to Moses in the opening stanza, there is a firm allusion to Deut 29:1–30:20 in sub-section IC. This allusion to the account of the covenant renewal in Moab reinforces the strong covenantal theme of the poem. The specific markers in IC1 are shown below in italics. Other significant words are shown in capitals.

> Nor is it with you only that I make this sworn COVENANT, but with him who is not here with us this day as well as with him who stands here,

---

[211] I chose this heading before reading Newsom's chapter on the centrality of Torah in the discourses of Second Temple Judaism. Her discussion admirably sets the theme of this hodayah in its context. See Newsom, *The Self as Symbolic Space*, 23–75.

[212] In 1QH^a *covenant* occurs 26 times, 6 times in this poem, 3 times in 1QH^a XV [VII]; *way* occurs 25 times, 8 times in this poem, and three times in 1QH^a VII [XV]; *seek* occurs 10 times, 5 times in this poem and 3 in 1QH^a X [II]; the remaining occurrences of these words in 1QH^a are well spread out. *Heart* (לבב/לב) occurs 54 times, the largest clusters being in this poem (8 times), and 1QH^a XIII [V], XV [VII] and XXI [XVIII] (5 times each). *Torah* occurs in 1QH^a XII 11 [IV 10], XIII 13 [V 11], XIV 13 [VI 10]. See Abegg, et al., *The Dead Sea Scrolls Concordance, Volume 1*, 158, 197, 199, 398, 759.

[213] Douglas, "Power and Praise," 293–295.

with us this day before the LORD our God. You know how we dwelt in the land of Egypt, and how we came through the midst of the nations through which you passed; and you have seen their detestable things, *their idols* of wood and stone, of silver and gold, which were among them. Beware lest there be among you a man or woman or family or tribe, whose HEART turns away this day from the LORD our God to go and serve the gods of those nations; lest there be among you *a root bearing poisonous and bitter fruit*, one who, when he hears the words of this sworn (covenant), blesses himself IN HIS HEART, saying, "I shall be safe, though I WALK in *the stubbornness of my heart.*" This would lead to the sweeping away of MOIST AND DRY alike. (Deut 29:14–19 [13–18] RSV)

There is an implicit dualism in the covenant renewal speech attributed to Moses, because not everyone will remain faithful to the covenant. It "predicts" the turning away from the covenant and subsequent exile, with a promise of restoration for those who return to the Lord. The speaker in this poem aligns himself and his followers with those who have returned to the covenant, and his enemies with those who are under the covenantal curses.

Unsurprisingly then, the majority of the other allusions in this poem are drawn from prophetic books that stress the covenantal theme.[214] Just as the speaker sees himself as a successor to Moses, so he views those teachers who oppose him as false prophets leading the people astray from their covenant with God to the worship of false Gods. Three of the main passages alluded to, from Hosea, Jeremiah and Ezekiel, may be considered structural allusions because of the overall parallels between them and this poem. In addition some shorthand notation allusions to Isaiah are used which can only be fully understood by a reader familiar with the source passages.

Hos 4:1–6:3 is an indictment of Israel, particularly its priests and prophets because of whom "my people are destroyed for lack of *knowledge*" (4:6) and "*brought down without understanding*" (4:14); it ends with a plea to return to the Lord whose "appearing is *as sure as the dawn.*" Allusions to the latter two verses set the scene at the beginning of the poem, in IB1 and IA respectively. In IB2 *the drink of knowledge* and in IC2 *the vision of knowledge* are withheld from the people. By alluding to this passage, which identifies a lack of knowledge and understanding as

---

[214] The majority of references to the word *covenant* are in the Pentateuch, the Deuteronomistic histories (Joshua, Judges, Kings, Samuel), and Chronicles. There are also 24 mentions in Jeremiah, 21 in Psalms, 18 in Ezekiel, 12 in Isaiah, 7 in Daniel, 6 in Malachi, 5 in Hosea, and 5 in Ezra-Nehemiah.

the consequence of the false prophets and priests, the poem reinforces the speaker's self-identification as an enlightened teacher. Hos 4:6 also equates lack of knowledge with forgetting God's Torah. Finally, as mentioned in the close reading, the allusion to Hos 6:3 may contain an implicit reference to the title Teacher of Righteousness.

Jer 23:9–40 is another passage which condemns false priests and prophets. In verse 26 we read that these prophets prophesy lies (שקר) and *deceit* (תרמה)[215] and thus, in verse 32, *cause* the people *to err* (ויתעו). As mentioned in the close reading, these latter two key words feature throughout section I. The phrase *intentions of your heart* in IC3 comes from Jer 23:20. The contrasting *plans of Belial* in IB2, IB3 and IC1 may be based upon verse 27: "They plan (החשבים) to make my people forget my name … … just as their ancestors forgot my name for Baal." Verse 32 also contains the phrase "they do not profit" (לא־יועילו), Jeremiah's word play on the name Baal.[216] There is also a reference to *poison* and *bitterness* and *stubborn hearts* which provides a link with Deut 29.[217]

Ezek 13:1–14:11 is the other passage which is alluded to structurally. It is part of a larger section concerning prophecy beginning in Ezek 12:21. Ezekiel also alludes to Jeremiah. Just as Ezekiel appeals to an earlier authority so the speaker in this poem claims to be the true inheritor of Moses and the prophets.[218] In IC1 the allusion to Ezekiel is closely linked with the allusion to Deut 29:17–20. Both biblical passages use the word *idol* (גלול), which in the Hebrew Bible occurs thirty-nine times

---

[215] cf. Jer 8:5, 14:14; Ps 119:118.

[216] cf. Jer 2:11 alluded to in IB2. "But my people have changed their glory for something that does not profit (בלוא יועיל)."

[217] "Therefore thus says the LORD of hosts concerning the prophets: I am going to make them eat *wormwood*, and give them *poisoned* water to drink; for from the prophets of Jerusalem ungodliness has spread throughout the land. Thus says the LORD of hosts: Do not listen to the words of the prophets who prophesy to you; they are deluding you. They speak visions of their own minds, not from the mouth of the LORD. They keep saying to those who despise the word of the LORD, 'It shall be well with you'; and to *all who stubbornly follow their own stubborn hearts*, they say, 'No calamity shall come upon you'." (Jer 23:15–17; cf. Jer 9:12–16).

[218] For example Ezek 13:3, נביאי מלבם, echoes Jer 23:16, חזון לבם. For other examples see the commentary by Allen. "The prophet's case was reinforced by reference to two earlier types of religious authority. First Ezekiel echoed Jeremiah's attacks on false prophets and so claimed to stand in the same, now vindicated, tradition. Jeremiah himself, at an earlier stage of history, had professed to stand in an established tradition of antiestablishment prophets (Jer 28:7–9). Second, Ezekiel found firm warrant for his opposition to religious compromise in the case laws of Lev. 20 (Ezek 14:7–8). A similar double recourse to the Torah and to prophetic revelation appears in another unit later in the book, chap. 22." See Allen, *Ezekiel 1–19*, 209.

in Ezekiel and only nine times outside it. The markers to these passages found in this poem are indicated by the emphasised phrases below.

> Son of man, these men have taken their *idols* into their hearts, and *set the stumbling block of their iniquity before their faces*; should I let myself *be sought* at all by them? (Ezek 14:3 RSV amended)

> Therefore thus says the Lord God: Because you have uttered delusions and seen *lies*, therefore behold, I am against you, says the Lord GOD. My hand will be against *the prophets* who see delusive visions and who give *lying* divinations; they shall not be in the council of my people, nor be enrolled in the register of the house of Israel, nor shall they enter the land of Israel; and you shall know that I am the Lord GOD. Because, yea, because they have CAUSED MY PEOPLE TO ERR, saying, 'Peace,' when there is no peace; and because, when the people build a wall, these prophets DAUB IT with whitewash; (Ezek 13:8–11 RSV amended)

Several allusions to Isaiah provide metaphorical expressions to describe the conduct of the speaker's opponents and of his followers. IB1 and IB2 evoke the indictment in Isa 30:8–14 of "a rebellious people who say to the seers, 'Prophesy not to us what is right; speak to us *smooth things.*'" The expressions "seekers of smooth things" and "builders of the wall" also occur in the *Damascus Document*.[219] Some see these as referring to the Pharisees. Schiffman, for example, argues that there is a word-play between smooth things (חלקות) and halakhot (הלכות) meaning laws. He links the second phrase with an instruction in the Mishnah to "build a fence around the Torah."[220] On the basis of her analysis of the social discourse, Newsom counsels caution in identifying a particular group.[221] My analysis shows that a number of scriptures have been called into service to symbolically characterise opponents of the group. There is sufficient exegetical impetus for the selection of these passages without resorting to possibly anachronistic links with specific groups. I thus agree with Newsom.

Isa 28:1–13 is an oracle against drunken priests and prophets which underlies the two stanzas concerned with drink, IB2 and IC2.

---

[219] For seekers of smooth things see CD I 18; 1QH^a X, 34 [II 15, 32]; 4Q163 23 II 10; 4QpNah 3–4 I 2, 7; 4QpNah 3–4 II 2, 4; 4QpNah 3–4 III 3, 7; 4Q266 2 I 21. For builders of the wall see CD IV 19, 8:12, 18, 19:25, 31.

[220] Lawrence H. Schiffmann, *Reclaiming the Dead Sea Scrolls: The History of Judaism, the Background of Christianity, the Lost Library of Qumran* (The Anchor Bible Reference Library; New York: Doubleday, 1995), 249–252.

[221] Newsom, *The Self as Symbolic Space*, 308–309.

> These also reel with wine and *stagger* (תעו) with strong drink; the priest and the prophet reel with strong drink, they are confused with wine, *they stagger* (תעו) with strong drink; they err in vision, they stumble in giving judgement … … Nay, but by men of *strange lips and with an alien tongue* the LORD will speak to this people. (Isa 28:7, 11 RSV)[222]

Isa 57:14–21 is the odd one out among the passages which underlie this part of the poem, in that it is not a condemnation of false prophets but a promise of restoration. The key phrase *the way of your heart*, which occurs four times in this poem, is derived from the reading of Isa 57:17 found in 1QIsa^a. The phrase cannot be derived from the MT, as the following translation shows:

> Because of the iniquity of his covetousness I was angry,
> I smote him, I hid my face and was angry;
> but he went on backsliding in the way of his own heart.
> I have seen his ways, but I will heal him;
> I will lead him and requite him with comfort,
> creating for his mourners the fruit of the lips. (Isa 57:17–18 RSV)

In the MT וילך שובב בדרך לבו (but he went on backsliding in the way of *his* own heart) makes the following verse read as a non-sequitur. However, 1QIsa^a has the variant reading בדרך לבי (in the way of my heart). This can then be interpreted as "but he, the backslider, went in the way of *my* heart," giving it a meaning opposite to that of the MT. Verse 18 may then be understood as a response to this change of heart. That this is the interpretation underlying this allusion is clear from the *Damascus Document*.

> For when they were unfaithful in forsaking him, he hid his face … and they realised their iniquity … and God appraised their deeds, because they sought him with an undivided heart, and raised up for them a Teacher of Righteousness, in order to direct them in the path of his heart. (CD I 3–11)[223]

Kister has outlined a plausible pesher on Isa 57:14–21.[224] He observes that in the sectarian texts the community is described as those who prepare the way[225] and walk in the way of his heart.[226] They are the

---

[222] Other possible allusions to Isaiah include Isa 53:3 in IB1 and IIA, Isa 32:6 in IB2, Isa 42:3 in IIB, Isa 63:15 in IIIB3, Isa 56:4–6 in IIIB4. These were referred to in the close reading.
[223] García Martínez and Tigchelaar, *The Dead Sea Scrolls Study Edition*, 551.
[224] Kister, "Biblical Phrases," 27–39.
[225] 1QS VIII 13, IX 19–20, alluding to Isa 40:3.
[226] 1QH^a XII 18, 19, 22, 25 [IV 17, 18, 21, 24], XIV 10, 24 [VI 7, 21].

contrite ones (נדכאים) and the mourners (אבלים)²²⁷ and God revives their spirit.²²⁸ Their opponents are described as being like the tossing sea.²²⁹ All these phrases could be taken from Isa 57:14–21, although some are more certainly allusions than others.

> And it shall be said, "Build up, build up, *prepare the way*, remove every obstruction from my people's way." For thus says the high and lofty One who inhabits eternity, whose name is Holy: "I dwell in the high and holy place, and also with him who is of a contrite and humble spirit, *to revive the spirit* of the humble, and to revive the heart of *the contrite*. For I will not contend for ever, nor will I always be angry; for from me proceeds the spirit, and I have made the breath of life. Because of the iniquity of his covetousness I was angry, I smote him, I hid my face and was angry; but he, the backslider, *went in the way of my heart*. I have seen his ways, but I will heal him; I will lead him and requite him with comfort, creating for his *mourners* the fruit of the lips. Peace, peace, to the far and to the near, says the LORD; and I will heal him. *But the wicked are like the tossing sea; for it cannot rest, and its waters toss up mire and dirt.* There is no peace, says my God, for the wicked." (Isa 57:14–21 RSV, amended)

3.5.2. *A Prayer of Confession and Commitment*

As already stated, section II may best be understood in terms of a prayer of confession and commitment. A key to the model for the prayer here may be given in the use of the phrase *guilt of unfaithfulness* (אשמת מעל) in the very first stanza. It is not a biblical phrase, but the two words occur in close proximity in the prayer found in Ezra 9:1–10:6. *Unfaithfulness* (of the exiles) occurs in Ezra 9:2, 4 and 10:6, *guilt and iniquities* in 9:6, 7, 13, and *guilt* alone in 9:15.

After the introductory stanza, the prayer begins in IIB1 with an acknowledgement that God is right. This may contain an allusion to Jer 10:23, but I think it more likely that the wording here is a summary of the wording and exegesis found in other hodayot. I discuss this in §3.6.2 of this chapter.

Stanzas IIB2 and IIB3 contain confession and reliance on God's mercy respectively. They are linked by the common theme of remembering. In stanza IIB1 the speaker says *I have remembered my guilts with the unfaithfulness of my fathers*. This may be an allusion to Lev 26:40, "But if they confess their iniquity and the iniquity of their ancestors, in that they committed unfaithfulness against me." But in Leviticus the

---

[227] 1QHª XXIII 16 [XVIII 15].
[228] 1QHª XVI 37 [VIII 36].
[229] 1QHª X 14–15 [II 12–13], and possibly XVI 16 [VIII 15] and XI 33 [III 32].

reference is to confession. In the Hebrew Bible it is usually God who remembers sins. Ezek 16:59–63, 20:27–44, 36:16–37 are the only places where the people remember their sins. In Ezek 20:27–44 God refers back to *the unfaithfulness of the fathers* (v. 27) and promises that he will gather the exiles, renewing the covenant in the wilderness (v. 36) and that they will remember their wickedness and loathe themselves (v. 43, cf. 36:31). Furthermore God says that he will do this, not for their sake but for his own holy name (36:22).

IIB3 uses biblical language associated with God's deliverance, as discussed in the close reading. But the most clearly identifiable marker in this stanza is the repeated phrase from Isa 63:15, *the multitude of your compassions*. In sub-section IIC the phrase recurs in parallel with *the abundance of your forgiveness*. In IIB1 the related phrase *abundance of his compassion* occurs, emphasising that this is a major theme of this part of the poem. *Multitude of your compassions* appears to be derived from "The multitude of your bowels and your compassion" in Isa 63:15, which is in the context of a prayer of communal penitence, appealing for God's mercy. The prayers in Neh 9:6–37 and Dan 9:4–19 both use a similar phrase "your abundant compassion" (רחמיך הרבים).[230] These two prayers are also the only places in the Hebrew Bible where the plural noun *forgiveness* (סליחות) is used.[231]

Not enough of stanza IIB4 and the following stanzas is preserved to say anything more than was mentioned in the close reading. To summarise, this prayer of confession contains probable allusions to similar prayers in Isa 63:7–64:12, Ezra 9:1–10:6, Neh 9:1–37, and Dan 9:1–19. The prayers in Ezra and Nehemiah are in the context of covenant renewal, as are the other probable allusions to Ezek 16:59–63, 20:27–44, 36:16–37.

3.6. *Intertexts*

As with the close reading, I will divide the consideration of intertexts into two parts. Section I has similarities with other hodayot and with the *Damascus Document*, and the *Pesher to Habakkuk*. Section II has similarities with Community Hymns, but also with a number of other Teacher Hymns containing a distinctive phrase.

---

[230] Neh 9:19, 27, 28, 31; Dan 9:18. cf. 2 Sam 24:14; 1 Chr 21:13; Ps 119:156; Isa 63:7. There are no other occurrences of this phrase in the HB.
[231] Neh 9:17; Dan 9:9. The singular occurs once, in Ps 130:4.

3.6.1. *Spokesmen of Error and Plots of Belial*

Tanzer classified this composition as one of three "admonitions not to be seduced away from the psalmist," a sub category of compositions with "limited wisdom" content. The other two are 1QH[a] X 5–21 [II 3–19] and XIII 22–XV 8 [V 20–VII 5].[232] Newsom chose these three poems for her analysis of the Hodayot of the leader. She also considers that 1QH[a] XII 6–XIII 6 [IV 5–V 4] and 1QH[a] X 5–21 [II 3–19] are closely related, briefly noting some of the similar phrases.[233] In her analysis of the former Newsom concentrates on rival discourses, calling the poem a "map of truth." In her analysis of the latter Newsom concentrates on the rival groups, calling the poem a "map of the social world" with the leader at the centre. She argues that both communities are related to God through the speaker. The speaker's followers are God's followers and the speaker's enemies are God's enemies. I agree with Newsom that these poems have similarities; much of what Newsom says about one poem could also apply to the other.[234]

The final lines of the composition in 1QH[a] X 5–21 [II 3–19] are dualistic in outlook, describing the speaker examining people, and thus distinguishing between those who love truth and those who oppose them. It has a number of phrases in common with this composition. These are *spokesmen of error, seekers of smooth things, men of deceit*, and *plots of Belial*. It also uses the phrases *a people without understanding to be brought down*, alluding to Hos 4:14, and *lip and another tongue*, alluding to Isa 28:11. These correspond to similar allusions in this poem, in IB1 and IC2 respectively.

Douglas notes that these are the only two occurrences of לבט and ולשון אחרת in the Dead Sea scrolls. He considers that two separate authors would not make such similar use of these two biblical passages.[235] Douglas also notes that *they have exchanged them* (וימירום) uses a root which occurs only four times in the scrolls, including once each in these two compositions. He considers that a possible allusion to Jer 2:11 is contained in these two and in 1QH[a] X 38 [II 36].[236]

---

[232] Tanzer, "The Sages at Qumran," 106–116.
[233] Newsom, *The Self as Symbolic Space*, 311.
[234] Newsom, *The Self as Symbolic Space*, 300–325.
[235] Douglas, "Power and Praise," 116.
[236] The four references are 1QH[a] VI 31 [XIV 20], X 21 [II 19], X 38 [II 36], XII 11 [IV 10]. The root occurs 14 times in the HB. (Douglas, "Power and Praise," 117).

Douglas observes that "spokesmen of" (מליצי) is used in the *Hodayot* negatively in five places, three of which occur in these poems.[237] In the Hebrew Bible and elsewhere in the scrolls it is used only in a positive sense.[238] Belial occurs only eleven times in the *Hodayot*,[239] and in conjunction with plots/plans it occurs only in these two compositions. Douglas suggests that 1QH^a XII 6–30 [IV 5–29] is an expanded and more explicit version of X 5–21 [II 3–19] probably written by the same author.[240] I am in agreement with Douglas that this large number of significant similarities points to a literary relationship between these two poems. However, there are also differences between these poems, and most of the similarities can be linked to the use of allusions. Therefore, I would not rule out as an explanation the existence of an exegetical tradition linking these verses.

The other composition in Tanzer's subcategory is 1QH^a XIII 22–XV 8 [V 20–VII 5].[241] Line 22b begins *and they* followed by a description of those who have deserted the speaker's group. It is this common *Sitz im Leben* of desertion from the group which Tanzer postulates for her subcategory. This third composition in Tanzer's group has fewer links of vocabulary with column XII; the most noteworthy are two occurrences of *the way of your heart* in XIV 10, 24 [VI 7, 21], and one of *multitude of your compassions* in XIV 12 [VI 9]. There are also several uses of the word *Belial*. Because of its links with so many of the other hodayot I believe Tanzer's third poem to be a special case. I discuss this more fully in §2.6.1 of chapter four.

There are also links between the poem being considered here and the *Damascus Document*. CD I 1–2:1 is divided into two sections by blank spaces. The first section, lines 1–11a, describes the origins of the movement. CD I 11 contains the phrase *the way of his heart*. The second section describes those outside the movement, and includes the phrase *smooth things*. As I have already noted, phrases similar to both of these

---

[237] 1QH^a X 16, 33 [II 14, 31], XII 8, 10 [IV 7, 9], XIV 16 [VI 13]. See Douglas, "Power and Praise," 117.

[238] 1QH^a X 15 [II 13], XIV 16 [VI 13], XXIII 12 [XVIII 11], 2 I 6, XXVI 37/7 11]; 4Q368 3 7; 4Q374 7 2; 4QpPs^a I 27. See Douglas, "Power and Praise," 117.

[239] 1QH^a X 19, 25 [II 17, 23], XI 29, 30, 33 [III 28, 29, 32]; XII 11, 14 [IV 10, 13], XIII 28, 41 [V 26, 39], XIV 24 [VI 21], XV 4 [VII 3].

[240] Douglas, "Power and Praise," 118.

[241] This poem is divided by Douglas into three shorter pieces: (a) XIII:22–XIV:6b+XV:3 7; (b) XIV:6d–22a; (c) XIV:22b–39. It is composition (b) which corresponds to Tanzer's category "material adapted from the Hymns of the Community." See Douglas, "Power and Praise," 194, Tanzer, "The Sages at Qumran," 111–112.

occur more than once in the poem under consideration. Moreover, both are markers to scriptural allusions (Isa 57:17 and Isa 30:11).

Campbell detects many other allusions to the prophetic books in CD I 1–2:1; he deems Isa 30, Jer 25–27, Ezek 7–11 and Hos 4–5, 10–11 to be particularly significant.[242] Among allusions to the Pentateuch, he considers Deut 28–32 (and Lev 26) to be significant. Thus there is a close correlation between the passages underlying both the poem analysed in this chapter and CD I 1–2:1. Other links with the *Damascus Document* include the emphasis on covenant and the use of water as a metaphor for the teaching of the law (cf. CD V 4–7). In §3.7 I will comment on the significance of the links with the *Damascus Document*.

Along with CD I 1–2:1, the *Pesher to Habakkuk* is often used in discussions about the history of the sectarian community and in particular the Teacher of Righteousness. One of the oft-quoted arguments for the Teacher of Righteousness being the author of the Teacher Hymns is the correspondence between 1QH[a] XII 9–15 [IV 8–14] and 1QpHab XI 2ff. The latter reads as follows:

2 היים לרב הוי משקה רעיהו מספח 3 חמתו אף שכר למען הבט אל מועדיהם
4 פשרו על הכוהן הרשע אשר 5 רדף אחר מורה הצדק לבלעו בכעס 6 חמתו אבית
גלותו ובקץ מועד מנוחת 7 יום הכפורים הופיע אליהם לבלעם 8 ולכשילם ביום צום
שבת מנוחתם שבעתה

> Woe to anyone making his companion drunk, spilling out (3) his anger, or even making him drunk to look at their festivals! (4) *Blank* Its interpretation concerns the Wicked Priest who (5) pursued the Teacher of Righteousness to swallow him up with the heat (6) of his anger in the place of his exile. In festival time, during the rest (7) of the day of Atonement, he appeared to them, to swallow them up (8) and make them stumble on the day of fasting, the Sabbath of their rest. (1QpHab XI 2–8)[243]

An alternative view of the relationship between these two texts has been argued by Davies. He considered that because the pesher derived from the quotation of Hab 2:15, any information not obviously derived from this text could be assumed to have another source. He detected three such allusions, namely to "exile," "to make them stumble," and "to swallow them up."[244] The allusion to exile obviously corresponds to the phrase "they have banished me like a bird from the nest" in

---

[242] Jonathan G. Campbell, *The use of Scripture in the Damascus Document 1–8, 19–20* (BZAW 228; Berlin: de Gruyter, 1995), 51–67.
[243] García Martínez and Tigchelaar, *The Dead Sea Scrolls Study Edition*, 18–21.
[244] Davies, *Behind the Essenes*, 93–96.

1QHª XII 9–10 [IV 8–9]. "To make them stumble" he connected to a combination of the idea of drunkenness from Hab 2.15 and of leading astray in 1QHª. "To swallow them up" (לבלעם) he connected to the "devilish scheming" (בליעל) of the enemies in 1QHª.

Davies also noted that 1QHª XII and 1QpHab XI both quote Hab 2.5 using "their feasts" (מועדיהם) instead of "their nakedness" (מעוריהם). In his opinion, while they could both have referred to the same defective text, it is possible that one composition influenced the other. Davies then went on to consider various similarities of language between the two documents. He noted a change from the general in 1QHª to the particular in 1QpHab. Specifically he noted that plural references tend to become singular ones and that general descriptions of enemies become sobriquets for particular groups. He concluded that the direction of influence was from the *Hodayot* to the *Pesher to Habakkuk*. I find Davies arguments persuasive. At the very least they show that there is a need for caution in making historical assumptions on the basis of these similarities. In §3.7 I will comment on this further.

3.6.2. *What is Flesh?*

Douglas has already noted the parallels between the second part of this poem and the Community Hymns.²⁴⁵ In particular section II has parallels with 1QHª VII 21–VIII ? [XV 8–25], discussed in the first part of this chapter, and with 1QS XI. These are indicated below.

ואני ידעתי בבינתך כיא לא ביד בשר […]	ואני ידעתי כי לוא לאנוש צדקה
And I, I know by your understanding that not by the hand of flesh [… …] 1QHª VII 25 [XV 12]	And I, I know that not to a man righteousness 1QHª XII 31 [IV 30]
ולא ל[אדם דרכו ולא יוכל אנוש להכין צעדו	ודרך אנוש לא תכון
[and not for] a human (26) his way nor can a man direct his steps. 1QHª VII 25–26	and the way of a man is not sure 1QHª XII 32
	כיא לאדם דרכו ואנוש לוא יכין צעדו
	For not to a human his way and a person cannot direct his steps 1QS XI 10 cf. 1QS III 9–10

---

²⁴⁵ Douglas, "Power and Praise," 110–111.

כי אם ברוח יצר אל לו	ואדעה בידך יצר כול רוח
except by the spirit (which) God formed for him 1QH^a XII 32 [IV 31]	But I know that by your hand (is) the formation of every spirit 1QH^a VII 26 [XV 13]
מה ישיב חמר ויוצר יד	
What will the clay reply and the formation of hand 1QS XI 22	
כי אתה בראתה צדיק ורשע	רק אתה [ברא]תה צדיק ... ורשעים בראתה
For you, you created the righteous and the wicked 1QH^a XII 39 [IV 38]	Only you, you [created] the righteous one ... But the wicked you created 1QH^a VII 27, 30
בהמון רחמיכה	בהמון רחמיך
the multitude of your compassions 1QH^a XII 37, 38 [IV 36, 37]	in the multitude of your compassions 1QH^a VII 29 [XV 16]
מי בשר כזאת	ומה אף הוא בשר
What (is) flesh compared to this? 1QH^a XII 30 [IV 29]	And what then itself (is) flesh 1QH^a VII 34 [XV 21]
ואני לאדם רשעה ולסוד בשר	
And I belong to wicked humanity and to the council of flesh 1QS XI 9	
ובי[ד][[כה משפט כולם	ובידך משפט כולם
and in your ha[nd] (is) the judgement of them all. 1QH^a XIII 6 [V 4]	and in your hand is the judgement of them all 1QH^a VIII 11 [frg. 13 4]
בידו משפטי כול	
In his hand is the judgement of all 1QS X 16–17. cf. 1QS III 16–17	

In most instances the phrases in 1QH^a VII 21–VIII ? [XV 8–25] seem much more clearly related to the underlying biblical allusions. In particular there seems to be an exegetical link between Jer 10:23, Zech 12:1 and Job 12:10; markers to these verses introduce and close the poetic unit. I surmise therefore that the direction of influence is either from that poem to one or both of the other two, or more probably, that all three are based on the same underlying exegetical tradition. In the latter case, the first poem is an exposition of the tradition whereas the other two poems merely allude to it.

The three uses of the phrase *multitude of your compassions* in 1QH^a XII 6–XIII 6 [IV 5–V 4] prompts the question whether this phrase can be traced to the same tradition. The occurrence in 1QH^a XIV 12 [VI 9] is probably a special case (see §2.6.1 in chapter four.) There are two occurrences in the poem discussed in chapter four, which fit well into the context of compassion and the underlying use of Isaiah. I will leave discussion of these until §§2.5.3 and 2.6.3 in chapter four. This leaves the occurrences in 1QH^a XV 33, 38 [VII 30, 35] and XVIII 23 [X 21].

The first of these occurrences is in the short poem in 1QH^a XV 29–36 [VII 26–33]. There are no obvious links with either of the poems discussed in this chapter, but there may be links with the poem in chapter four (see §2.6.3 of that chapter). There are however reasons to suspect some influence for the occurrence in 1QH^a XV 38 [VII 35], which also survives in 4Q428 10 2. 1QH^a XV 37–XVI 4 [VII 34–VIII 3], as reconstructed by Schuller and Puech,[246] has several other similarities to section II of the poem just analysed. It uses the phrase *guilt of unfaithfulness* (1QH^a XII 31 [IV 30], cf. 1QH^a XIX 14 [XI 11], 1QS IX 4) and stages of life terminology (1QH^a XII 31 [IV 30], cf. 1QH^a XVII 30 [IX 30]; 4Q507 1 2.)[247] It also appears to allude to Jer 10:23 (see discussion in §2.6.2 of this chapter.) Moreover, it uses the phrase *way of your heart*, which occurs in section I of this poem (see discussion in §3.6.1 above.)

Finally, the phrase in 1QH^a XVIII 23 [X 21] is followed by words which also have similarities to the poems analysed in this chapter.

ה[מון רחמיכה ולסליחותיכה אקוה כי אתה יצרתה ר[וח ...]ונכה הכינותני ולא
נתתה משעני על בצע ובהון[... ל]בי ויצר בשר לא שמתה לי מעוז

> ... Mu]ltitude of your compassion and in your forgiveness (24) I hope. For you, you have formed the spi[rit ...] you have destined me You have not placed (25) my support in robbery, nor in wealth [...] my [hea]rt, and the formation of flesh you have not placed for my defence.

I have already noted the similarities of context between section II of this poem and Isa 63:15–64:12, namely both are prayers of penitence.

---

[246] This composition has been restored by both Schuller and Puech using 4Q428 and 1QH^b. See Schuller, "A Thanksgiving Hymn from 4QHodayot^b," 527–541; Schuller, "Hodayot," 141–144; Puech, "Restauration d'un texte hymnique," 543–558.

[247] Schuller, "Hodayot," 143; cf. Ps 22:9–10.

I suggest that there are two or three exegetical clusters which have been combined in these poems. The predestination cluster concerns the distinction between the righteous and the wicked. There may be associated clusters concerned with repentance, right conduct and the forgiveness and compassion of God. The ideas are associated as follows. Those *destined* for destruction are the *wicked* who persist in their *iniquity* and *guilt of unfaithfulness*. Those *destined* for *compassion* are the *righteous* who have repented and *walk in the way of* (God's) *heart*.

3.7. *Observations and Comments*

In my introduction to this poem I quoted the opinion of Douglas that it is important because of its significance for understanding the authorship of the Teacher Hymns. I agree that this poem is important, but for different reasons. The strong dualism of this poem offers possible insights into the way that the sectarians defined themselves and their leader(s) in contrast with their opponents. The scriptural allusions indicate some of the passages which served to reinforce that group identity. It is clear that the implied speaker is a leader of the community. However, I agree with Holm-Nielsen that the strong use of scripture militates against the possibility of identifying autobiographical information in this poem.[248]

The exile motif in IB1 may be explained sufficiently as use of stereotyped language for distress or persecution. However, in view of the allusion in IC1 to the covenant renewal ceremony (Deut 29), it could be explained further as an identification with the exiled people of God. Moses' covenant renewal speech predicts the exile and restoration for those who return to the LORD (Deut 30:2). Undoubtedly the reader of the poem is meant to identify with this latter group.

The clear Mosaic motif sits well with the theme of covenant renewal. The implied speaker, as a leader of this renewed covenant community, sees himself in the tradition of faithful teachers and prophets going back to Moses. In particular he draws upon the message of Hosea, Jeremiah, Ezekiel and Isaiah. He applies their indictments of false

---

[248] Holm-Nielsen, *Hodayot*, 307, comments: "Various interpreters have found in the expression, 'they have expelled me from my country like a bird from its nest,' a reference to the author (in other words, the Teacher of Righteousness) being banished ... ... One could just as well force XV 5 [VII 2] and XVI 34 [VIII 33] to signify that the author was so unfortunate as to fall and break his arm, or to have been subjected to torture!"

priests and prophets to his own opponents. The people have been punished because they listened to and were led astray by *spokesmen of falsehood and seers of deceit*. The key to renewal is *knowledge* as imparted by the speaker and his group.

It is significant that the poem equates law and prophecy, priests and prophets, as do the evoked texts from Jeremiah and Ezekiel. The priests are spokesmen who are meant to dispense the *drink of knowledge*. The prophets are seers who are meant to convey the *vision of knowledge*. Just as correct interpretation of Torah can be derived from prophetic as well as Pentateuchal writings, the leaders of this community see themselves in the tradition of both priests and prophets.

Douglas has noted literary dependence between this poem and two others, 1QH^a VII 21–VIII ? [XV 8–25] and X 5–21 [II 3–19]. He views this as evidence for the same author. But there are also similarities with passages in the *Rule of the Community* and the *Damascus Document*. Many of these similarities can be linked to scriptural allusions. I suggest that particular scriptural passages and related exegesis became prominent in the sectarian self-understanding; this exegetical tradition and vocabulary would naturally be drawn upon by sectarian writers. There is therefore no need to assume, for instance, that because CD I 1–2:1 and this poem both refer to *the way of his heart* and *smooth things* that they were written by the same author. It is sufficient to note that both passages are concerned with the group's self-understanding.

Similar comments may be made concerning the *Pesher to Habakkuk*. Davies has made a case for a literary connection with the *Hodayot*. He has also argued that the direction of influence is from the *Hodayot* to the *Pesher to Habakkuk*. His case is strongest in regard to this poem. However, it is also possible that in some cases the influence is indirect. The *Hodayot* may attest to exegetical traditions which have also influenced other sectarian texts. The identification of common exegetical traditions is an area for development, as more Dead Sea texts are analysed for their use of scriptural allusions.

This poem is also notable for being, in the words of Tanzer, a hybrid poem. That is, the first part exhibits the characteristics of a Teacher Hymn, while section II appears more like a Community Hymn. The poem as it now stands is a unity. As well as the structural unity described already, the penitential theme of section II fits in well with the idea of covenant renewal present in section I. I agree with Douglas that this questions the assumption that Teacher and Community Hymns were written by different authors. But unlike Douglas, I think it shows up the futility of seeking to identify the author(s) of poems which probably have a long history of community use and reuse.

Finally, although Deuteronomy and Isaiah are obviously evoked by this poem, their use has often been noted in discussions of the use of the Bible at Qumran. Therefore it is worth noting that it is Hosea, Jeremiah and Ezekiel which provide the key structural allusions in this poem.

CHAPTER FOUR

A POEM IN THREE MOVEMENTS

1. Introduction

As mentioned in chapter one, Kittel recognised that her detailed study was limited to mainly shorter poems and that the style and technique of longer poems might be different.[1] It remains the case that most studies have been of short poems or of sections of longer poems. I have therefore endeavoured to select poems of varying lengths for this study. Three of the five poems in this study are fairly short, each one covering about half of a manuscript column. The second composition analysed in chapter three is longer, filling one column of the manuscript. In this chapter I have considered one very long poem in its entirety.

2. Sustained Artistry
1QH^a XVI 5–XVII 36 [VIII 4–IX 36]

This poem extends over almost two columns of the manuscript. It is possibly the longest and most complex of the poems in 1QH^a.[2] Douglas has noted that length alone sets such a composition apart from the biblical psalms and brings it closer to that of a wisdom composition.[3] However Tanzer considered it to be a hybrid composition in which

---

[1] Kittel, *The Hymns of Qumran*, 155.
[2] Because of the problem of lacunae there are differences of opinion among commentators over the delimitation of some compositions.
[3] Douglas estimates that the poems in 1QH^a XIII 22–XV 8 [V 20–VII 5] and XVI 5–XVII 36 [VIII 4–IX 36] are equivalent to approximately 107 and 111 poetic lines of biblical psalms. He further notes that "In the Psalter there are only three psalms over 50 lines: Ps 78 (72 lines), Ps 89 (53 lines), and Ps 119 (176 lines). According to the headings, the genre of Psalms 78 and 89 is that of the maskil (wisdom composition?). Psalm 119 is certainly a poetic wisdom discourse." See Douglas, "Power and Praise," 205 nn. 114, 115.

the wisdom elements are limited to a Community Hymn segment in XVII 14–36 [IX 14–36].⁴

The poem also warrants study because of its content. In an early study of this composition, Wallenstein stated that it contains "two well-developed ideas of paramount importance."⁵ These ideas are of the "everlasting branch" and the "joy in tribulation." It is the first of these concepts, that of garden and gardener, which has elicited the most interest from later commentators. Beyond a recognition that the imagery is to some extent allegorical there is no consensus on its interpretation. Charlesworth has offered an autobiographical interpretation and Davila a mystical one.⁶

Douglas has considered the whole poem. His interpretive premise, that it reflects the experience of a single individual, does provide a link between the sections. But, as the recent study by Newsom has argued, this is not the only way of reading the Teacher Hymns. I therefore consider that how the content of this poem may be understood in its entirety remains very much an open question.⁷

2.1. *Delimitation and Text*⁸

This composition can be found on Sukenik plates 42 and 43. Sukenik numbered it as VIII 4–IX 36 but Stegemann and Puech have reassigned it as XVI 5–XVII 36. The beginning of the composition is indicated by a blank space at the end of the previous line and the first two letters of the opening formula אודכה אדוני. The end of the composition is less certain. Line 37 of column XVII is clearly blank, although the opening formula of the next poem is not preserved.

---

⁴ Tanzer, "The Sages at Qumran," 118–122.
⁵ M. Wallenstein, *The Nezer and the Submission in Suffering Hymn From the Dead Sea Scrolls: Reconstructed, Vocalised and Translated with Critical Notes* (Istanbul: Nederlands Historisch-Archaeologisch Instituut in het Nabije Oosten, 1957).
⁶ e.g. J.H. Charlesworth, "An Allegorical and Autobiographical Poem by the Moreh HaS-Sedeq (1QH 8:4–11)," in *Sha'arei Talmon: Studies in the Bible, Qumran and the Ancient Near East presented to Shemaryahu Talmon* (ed. M. Fishbane and E. Tov; Winona Lake: Eisenbrauns, 1992), 295–307; J.R. Davila, "The Hodayot Hymnist and the Four who Entered Paradise," *RevQ* 17 (1996): 457–478.
⁷ Douglas, "Power and Praise," 144–170; Newsom, The Self as Symbolic Space, 287–300.
⁸ Unless otherwise stated references in this section are to Sukenik, *The Dead Sea Scrolls*; Stegemann, "The Material Reconstruction of 1QHodayot," 280; Puech, "Quelques aspects," 41–43.

A POEM IN THREE MOVEMENTS

Some scholars treat this long composition as two, as it is just possible that an introductory formula was contained in the missing lines at the bottom of column XVI and the start of column XVII.[9] However, as my analysis of the literary structure will show, the content of the beginning of column XVII is connected on literary grounds to that of the end of column XVI.

Only one corresponding Cave 4 fragment has been identified, consisting of only a few letters. This is 4QpapH[f] 13 1–2,[10] which overlaps with 1QH[a] XVI 9–10 [VIII 8–9]. Two partially preserved lines from 1QH[b] 2 1–2 (1Q35)[11] overlap with 1QH[a] XVI 13–14 [VIII 12–13].

1QH[a] XVI 5–41 [VIII 4–40]

5 או[ד]כה אדוני כי נ[ת]תני במקור נוזלים ביבשה ומבוע מים בארץ ציה ו[מ]שקי
6 גן [בערבה ..][12] מטע ברוש ותדהר עם תאשור יחד לכבודכה [13] עצי
7 חיים במעין רז מחובאים בתוך כול עצי מים והיו להפריח נצר למטעת עולם
8 להשריש טרם יפריחו ושורשיהם ליוב[ל] ישלחו ויפתח למים חיים וגזעו
9 ויהי למקור עולם ובנצר עליו ירעו כול [חי]ת יער ומרמס גזעו לכל עוברי
10 דרך ודליתו לכל עוף כנף וירמו עליו כול ע[צי] מים כי במטעתם יתגשגשו
11 ואל יובל לא ישלחו שורש ומפריח נצר ק[ו]דש למטעת אמת סותר בלוא
12 נחשב ובלא נודע חותם רזו   vacat   ואתה[א]ל שכתה בעד פריו ברז גבורי כוח
13 ורוחות קודש ולהט אש מתהפכת בל י[בוא זר ב]מעין[14] חיים ועם עצי עולם
14 לא ישתה מי קודש בל יונבב פריו עם [   ] [ע שחקים כי ראה בלא הכיר
15 ויחשוב בלא האמין למקור חיים ויתן י[   ].[ח[15] עולם ואני הייתי ל[ב]זא[י]ן.}הרות[16]

---

[9] Douglas notes that Licht, Jeremias, Becker, Kuhn, Dupont-Sommer, and Delcor treat it as two compositions; Holm-Nielsen, Morawe, Wallenstein, Carmignac, Tanzer, Puech, Douglas treat it as a single composition. See Douglas, "Power and Praise," 153–154 nn. 74, 75.

[10] Schuller, "Hodayot," 227.

[11] Milik, J.T., "35. Recueil de cantiques d'action de grâces (1QH)," in *Qumran Cave 1* (ed. D. Barthélemy and J.T. Milik; DJD 1; Oxford: Clarendon, 1955), 136–138.

[12] I follow Holm-Nielsen in restoring [בערבה] on the basis of Isa 51:3. There are two or three faintly visible letters at the end of the lacuna which possibly read ש.ה. Douglas follows Puech who, on the basis of "traces de toutes les lettres" restores ואגם מים בשדה. See Holm-Nielsen, *Hodayot*, 148 n. 2; Douglas, "Power and Praise," 144 n. 48; Puech, *Croyance*, 339 n. 21.

[13] This is a slightly longer than normal space between words.

[14] Puech, *Croyance*, 340 n. 25, restores thus from 1Q35 2 1.

[15] Licht reads י.[דו בפ[רה; Puech reads יב[ול] פרה. See Licht, *Thanksgiving Scroll*, 135; Puech, *Croyance*, 340 n. 27.

[16] Wallenstein explains "The first copyist made it run together with its preceding word. A later hand, however, apparently realising the absurdity of this combination, attempted to erase the nun and added one dot above it and another below it to indicate elision and superimposed a nun of his own (note its shape which differs from that of other nuns in the MS.) meant to be drawn to הרות." See Wallenstein, *The Nezer*, 22 n. 70.

16 שוטפים כי גרשו עלי רפשם   *vacat*
17 ואתה אלי שמתה בפי כיורה גשם לכול [ ] ומבוע מים חיים ולא יכזב לפתוח
18 הש. ים[17] לא ימישו ויהיו לנחל שוטף ע[ל [18] מים ולימים לאין ח[קר]
19 פיתאום יביעו מחובאים בסתר [ ] ויהיו למי מ[בול לכול עץ[19]
20 לח ויבש מצולה לכול היה וע[צי מים יצללו כ]עופרת[20] במים אדירי[ם]
21 ..... [21] אש ו'בשו ומטע פרי [ ]. ר[22] עולם לעדן כבוד ופר[ן] [23]
22 ובידי פתחתה מקורם עם מ[23]פלגי[ו]ם לפנות על קו נכון ומטע
23 עציהם על משקלת השמש לא[ ]נו לפארת כבוד בהניפי יד לעזוק
24 פלגיו יכו שרשיו בצור חלמיש ו[ ]. בארץ גזעם ובעת חום יעצור
25 מעוז ואם אשיב יד יהיה כערע[ר בערבה ו]גזעו כחרלים במלחה ופלגיו
26 יעל קוץ ודרדר לשמיר ושית י[היה ועצי]שפתו יהפכו כעצי באושים לפני
27 חום יבול עליו ולא נפתח עם מ' עי[ן ואני][24] מגור עם חוליים ומ[וד]ע לב[25]
28 בנגיעים ואהיה כאיש נעזב ביגונ[ים ו][26] אין מעוז לי כי פרח נגעי
29 למרורים וכאיב אנוש לאין עצור [ ] ונפשי ה[ ]מה עלי כיורדי שאול ועם
30 מתים יחפש רוחי כי הגיעו לשחת ח[יי בתוכי] תתעטף נפשי יומם ולילה
31 לאין מנוח ויפרח כאש בוער עצור בע[צמי] עד ימימה תואכל של(ה)בתה[27]
32 להתם כוח לקצים ולכלות בשר עד מועדים ויתעופפו [עלי][28] משברים
33 ונפשי עלי תשתוחח לכלה כי נשבת מעוזי מגויתי וינגר כמים לבי וימס
34 כדונג בשרי ומעוז מותני היה לבהלה ותשבר זרועי מקניה [ואי]ן להניף יד
35 [ורג]לי נלכדה בכבל וילכו כמים ברכי ואין לשלוח פעם ולא מצעד לקול רגלי

---

[17] There is disagreement about how to restore the unclear letter. Although a מ would fit the sense, there is doubt about whether it fits with the letter traces. See Holm-Nielsen, *Hodayot*, 153 n. 34, Douglas, "Power and Praise," 144 n. 53.

[18] Puech, *Croyance*, 341 n. 31, reads ע[ל פ]ל[ג]י.

[19] Thus Licht; Puech has מר[יבה לכול עץ]. See Licht, *Thanksgiving Scroll*, 136; Puech, *Croyance*, 341 n. 32.

[20] Thus Licht, *Thanksgiving Scroll*, 136.

[21] These letters are indistinct. Puech, *Croyance*, 341 n. 34, reads בשביבי.

[22] Puech, *Croyance*, 341 n. 35, reads [י]תן והיה במ[קור.

[23] Puech, *Croyance*, 341 n. 36, reads ופא[רת עד].

[24] I agree with García Martínez and Tigchelaar in reading [... עי]ן מ', where the י has been added above the line. I also think that there is space within the lacuna for the word ואני, possibly preceded by a small *vacat*. Licht has [עם מע]ן גזעו ואני; Puech reads עם מטר מל[קוש יבו]א. See García Martínez and Tigchelaar, *The Dead Sea Scrolls Study Edition*, 182; Licht, *The Thanksgiving Scroll*, 138; Puech, *Croyance*, 342 n. 42.

[25] Puech, *Croyance*, 342 n. 43, has ומ[ג]ע לו.

[26] Douglas and Puech read ביגון [ובאנח]ה but the letter before the lacuna appears to be נ, not a final ן. I therefore follow García Martínez and Tigchelaar. See Douglas, "Power and Praise," 146; Puech, *Croyance*, 342 n. 44; García Martínez and Tigchelaar, *The Dead Sea Scrolls Study Edition*, 182.

[27] I emend thus, assuming that there is a missing letter, following Holm-Nielsen, *Hodayot*, 157 n. 65.

[28] There are traces of letters which some read thus. It is, in any case, a reasonable reconstruction. See Holm-Nielsen, *Hodayot*, 157 n. 68; Mansoor, *The Thanksgiving Hymns*, 157 n. 7.

A POEM IN THREE MOVEMENTS

36 .... [²⁹] . רותקו בזקי מכשול ולשון הגברתה בפ[י]ן בלא נאספה ואין להדים³⁰
37 קול[לשו]ן למודי[ם]³¹ לחיות רוח כושלים ולעות לעאף דבר נאלם כול שפתי
38 מפ.. [ ] בזקי משפט ל.. לבי ....] [... במרורי [ ] לבב ...רים ממשל
39 [ ] [...]. [ ]. התבל...
40 [ ] נאלמו כאין
41 [ ] אנוש לא[

1QHᵃ XVII 1–36 /IX 1–36/

1 [ ] [..אפ [ ]
2 [ ] [ע[ ] תנום בלילה ..] [
3 [ ] לאין רחמים באף יעורר קנאה ולכלה [...אפפוני]
4 משברי מות ושאול על יצועי ערשי בקינה תשא [ ] בקול אנחה
5 עיני כעש בכבשן ודמעתי כנחלי מים כלו למנוח עיני ו[ ]י עמד לי
6 מרחוק וחיי מצד ואני משאה [א]ו[למשו]ראה³² וממכאוב לנגע ומחבלים
7 למשברים תשוחח נפשי בנפלאותיכה ולא הזנחתני בחסדיכה מקץ
8 לקץ תשת[ע]שע³³ נפשי בהמון רחמיכה ואשיבה למבלעי דבר
9 ולמשתוחחי בי תוכחת וארשיעה דיני ומשפטכה אצדיק כי ידעתי
10 באמתכה ואבחרה במשפטי ובנוגעי רציתי כי יחלתי לחסדיכה ותתן
11 תחנה בפי עבדכה ולא גערתה חיי ושלומי לא הזנחתה ולא עזבתה
12 תקותי ולפני נגע העמדתה רוחי³⁴ כי אתה יסדתה רוחי ותדע מזמתי
13 ובצקותי נחמתני ובסליחות אשתעשע ואנחמה על פשע ראשון
14 ואדעה כ[י]ן יש מקוה ב[ח]סדיכה ותוחלה ברוב כוחכה כי לא יצדק
15 כול במ[שפ]טכה ולא יז[כה ב]רי`בכה אנוש מאנוש יצדק וגבר[מרעה]ו
16 ישכיל ובשר מיצר [חמר] יכבד ורוח מרוח תגבר וכגב[ורת]כה אין
17 בכוח ולכבודכה אין [חקר ו]לחכמתכה אין מדה ולאמ[ונתכה אין]
18 ולכול הנעזב ממנה [ ] *vacat* ואני בכה הצ[די]
19 עמדי ולא ה. [ ] [³⁵
20 וכזומם לי ת[ ] ואם לבושת פנים ..] [..

---

[29] I judge these letters too indistinct for a certain reading. Douglas, following Puech, reads בחזוק זרועי. See Douglas, "Power and Praise," 146 n. 61; Puech, *Croyance*, 342 n. 47.

[30] Thus García Martínez and Tigchelaar, Sukenik does not transcribe the middle letter. Licht, followed by most, has להרים. See García Martínez and Tigchelaar, *The Dead Sea Scrolls Study Edition*, 182; Licht, *The Thanksgiving Scroll*, 139.

[31] Thus Wallenstein; Sukenik has two untranscribed letters; Licht has [פי] (Wallenstein, *The Nezer*, 5; Licht, *The Thanksgiving Scroll*, 139).

[32] The א has clearly been erased by dots above and below. The ו has one dot above it, which may indicate an erasure.

[33] The text inexplicably has a blank space in the middle of this word, where one would expect an ע.

[34] There is a slightly larger than usual space between these two words, but it is too small to be considered a *vacat*.

[35] Puech, *Croyance*, 344 n. 66, reads ולא התן ב[אנשו ריבי. Both Licht and Puech offer restorations for most of the following lacunae. However, because of the extent of the damage to these lines, I have decided to include only the few most certain ones.

140 CHAPTER FOUR

21 לי ואתה בר[חמיכה   ולא י]תגבר³⁶ צרי עלי למכשול ל. [   ]
22 אנשי מלחמ[תי   בו]שת פנים וכלמה לנרגני בי   vacat
23 כי אתה אלי 'מ[   ]   תריב ריבי כי ברז חכמתכה הוכחתה בי
24 ותחבא אמת לקץ [ל]מועדו ותהי תוכחתכה לי לשמחה וששון
25 ונגיעי למרפא ע[ולם ו   ]נצח ובו צרי לי לכליל כבוד וכשלוני לגבורת
26 עולם כי בש[   ] ובכבודכה הופיע אורי כי מאור מחושך
27 האירותה ל[י   מח]ץ מכתי ולמכשולי גבורת פלא ורחוב
28 עולם בצרת נפש[י כי אתה אלי]³⁷ מנוסי משגבי סלע עוזי ומצודתי בכה
29 אחסיה מכול מ[   ] לי לפלט עד עולם   vacat   כי אתה מאבי
30 ידעתני ומרחם [   ]אמי גמלתה עלי ומשדי ה'רותי רחמיך
31 עלי ובחיק אומנתי[   ]ה ומנעורי הופעתה לי בשכל משפטכה
32 ובאמת נכון סמכתני וברוח קודשכה תשעשעני ועד היום [   ]...חל. י
33 ותוכחת צדקכה עם .. ותי ומשמר שלומכה לפלט נפשי ועם מצעדי
34 רוב סליחות והמון [רח]מים בהשפטכה בי ועד שיבה אתה תכלכלני כיא
35 אבי לא ידעני ואמי עליכה עזבתני כי אתה אב לכול [בנ]י אמתכה ותגל
36 עליהם כמרחמת על עולה וכאומן בחיק תכלכל לכול מעש[י]כה   vacat
37   vacat

2.2. *Translation*

Meshalim

IA1   (5) I th[ank you, O Lord,
       for] you have [pl]aced me by³⁸ a wellspring of streams on the dry-ground
       and a spring of water in the dry land
       and an [ir]rigation³⁹ of (6) a garden [in the desert].
       [... ...] a *planting* of juniper and pine
       with box together for your glory.

IA2a   Trees of (7) life by a well of mystery,
       hidden-things in the midst of all the trees of the water.
IA2b   And they shall be for the sprouting of a shoot,
       for a *planting*⁴⁰ of eternity
       (8) to take root before they sprout.

---

³⁶ Following Licht, Thanksgiving Scroll, 146.
³⁷ Following Licht, Thanksgiving Scroll, 148.
³⁸ Or "as." See discussion in §2.4.1.
³⁹ משקי = משקה can also be translated as "irrigator" but this translation is preferable because of the parallelism. See Wallenstein, *The Nezer*, 17 n. 6.
⁴⁰ There appears to have been a change from the masculine form of the noun in line 6 above to a feminine form. However, the meaning is the same. See Wallenstein, *The Nezer*, 18 n. 19.

IA2c	And their roots to the water-sou[rce] they stretch out
	and opens itself to the water of life, its *stump*[11]
	(9) and it comes to an eternal wellspring.[12]
IA2d	And on the shoot of its leaves[13] graze all the [anim]als of the forest
	and its *stump* (is) a treading-place for all passers (10) by
	and its branches for all winged birds.
IA2c'	But all the tr[ees] of the water exalt themselves over it,
	for in their *planting* they are magnified
	(11) though unto the water-source they do not stretch out a root.
IA2b'	And the sprout of the h[o]ly shoot for a *planting* of truth
IA2a'	(is) concealed in the not (12) being noticed[14]
	and in the not being known sealed (is) its mystery. *Blank*
IB1	But You, O G[od], you have put a fence around its fruit
	with the mystery of powerful heroes (13) and holy spirits
	and the flame of the fire turning-about,
	That no [stranger may enter] the wellspring of life
	nor with the eternal trees (14) drink the waters of holiness
	nor produce its fruit with [...] of the clouds.
	For he sees, but does not perceive
	(15) and notices[15] but does not believe in the wellspring of life
	and he gives eternal [... ...].
	But I, I had become the [mo]ckery of the overflowing torrents
	(16) for they threw their mire over me. *Blank*
IB2	(17) But you, my God, have put (words) in my mouth
	as showers of rain for all [...]
	and a spring of water of life.
	And it will not fail to open (18) the hea[ve]ns,[16]
	they will not cease.
	And they shall become an overflowing river
	o[ver ... ...] water
	and to seas without l[imit.]
	(19) Suddenly they shall swell from hidden-places in concealment
	[... ... ...]

---

[11] וגזעו or יגזעו in the MS, which most scholars emend to גזעו or גיזעו. Williams emends to גוזעו. Wallenstein retains the reading and rejects the following conjunction as dittographic. He then translates מקור as "stem" giving "its stem becoming an everlasting stem." See Williams, "Parallelism," 457; Wallenstein, *The Nezer*, 19 n. 29.

[12] Literally "And it shall become an eternal wellspring" but I have followed Williams who justifies his translation by analogy with Ezek 31:7 (כי־היה שרשו אל־מים רבים), and by the parallelism and context. See Williams, "Parallelism," 457.

[13] Or "And upon its shoot."

[14] Elsewhere I have translated this root as "esteem."

[15] Elsewhere I have translated this root as "esteem."

[16] Disputed reading; the context implies some source of water.

142 CHAPTER FOUR

>
> And they shall become waters of the fl[ood for every tree] (20) green and dry]
> a lake for every animal.
> And [… … … … … … … as] lead in mighty waters.
> [… …] (21) [… …] fire and they shall dry up.
> And the *planting* of fruit [… … … … … … … …] eternity
> to Eden of glory and frui[t … … … … …].

IC1   (22) And by my hand you have opened[47] their wellspring
with [its] channels [… … …] to face[48] according to a sure measuring-line;
and the *planting* of (23) their trees according to the plumb-line of the sun.
[… … … … … … … … …] for foliage of glory.

IC2   In my lifting of (my) hand to hoe (24) its ditches
strike-down its roots into the flinty stone
and [… … … … …] into the earth their *stump*.
And in the time of heat it retains (25) its strength.

IC3   But if I withdraw (my) hand
it will become like a bus[h in the desert]
[and] its *stump* as nettles in a salt-waste.
And its ditches (26) will produce thorns and thistles
briars and weeds [it will become].
And [the trees of] its banks will turn into trees of stinking-things,
before (27) the heat its leaves will wither
and it is not opened with water of a we[ll].

Lament

IIA1   [And I] (my) dwelling[49] is with sicknesses
and my heart is ac[quaint]ed (28) with afflictions;
and I am like a man forsaken in grief[s and …]
I have no strength.[50]

IIA2a   For my affliction has broken forth (29) to bitterness
and an incurable pain to no restraint […].

---

[47] I have translated "opened" for consistency. An alternative translation is "dug."

[48] Holm-Nielsen, *Hodayot*, 155 n. 44, notes that it is impossible to decide whether this is the infinitive of פנה or the plural of פנה meaning "corners."

[49] Following Holm-Nielsen; Mansoor translates as "[and I] am cast down." Possibly a play on words is intended. Wallenstein has "[on every side] terror," cf. Jer 6:25 etc. See Holm-Nielsen, *Hodayot*, 156 n. 56; Mansoor, *The Thanksgiving Hymns*, 156; Wallenstein, *The Nezer*, 4, 13.

[50] This could be translated as "refuge" but the context implies "strength." There may be a word play.

IIA2b1	[My soul gr]oans within me like those that descend to *Sheol*
	and with (30) the dead is hidden[51] my spirit;
	for has drawn near to the pit [my li]fe
IIA2b4	[and within me] fainted my soul day and night (31) without *rest*.
IIA3a	And it breaks-forth as a burning fire shut-up in [my] b[ones]
	unto the seas consumes its flame.
IIA3b	(32) To end strength for times
	and to destroy flesh unto appointed-times.
IIA3c	And *breakers* fly-about [against me][52]
	(33) and my soul within me is bowed-down to *destruction*.
IIA4a	For my strength has ceased from my body
	and my heart is poured out like water
	and my flesh melts (34) like wax
	and the strength of my loins has become a terror.
IIA4b	And broken is my arm from its socket
	[and it is not possib]le to lift my hand.
IIA4c	(35) [And] my [foot] is caught in shackles
	and my knees go like water
	and it is not possible to stretch-out a pace
	and there is no step to the sound of my feet
	(36) [… … …] are bound by the chains of stumbling.
IIB1	But (my) tongue you have strengthened in [my] mouth without being drawn back[53]
	and it is not possible to silence[54] (37) the sound of [the tong]ue of the learned
	To give life to the spirit of those who stumble,
	and to succour the weary (with) a word.
IIB2	Silent are all lips (38) [… …] because of the chains of judgement
	[…] my heart [… … …] in the bitter things of […]
	[…] heart […] dominion (39) [… …]
	[… … … … … … … … … … … …]
	[… … … … … … … … … … … …]
	[… … … … … … … … …] the world […]
	(40) [… … … … … … … … … … … …]

---

[51] Translating as pual impf. as in Prov 28:12; or translate as qal impf. "searches" as in Ps 77:6 [7].

[52] See Holm-Nielsen, *Hodayot*, 157 n. 68, for a discussion of the uncertainties of translating this line.

[53] Following Mansoor, but the translation is uncertain. See Mansoor, *The Thanksgiving Hymns*, 157; Holm-Nielsen, *Hodayot*, 157 n. 81.

[54] Mansoor and Holm-Nielsen have "to raise." See Mansoor, *The Thanksgiving Hymns*, 157; Holm-Nielsen, *Hodayot*, 144.

144 CHAPTER FOUR

        [... ... ...]
        [... ... ...] they are silenced as nothing

IIC1   (41) [... ... ...]
        [... ... ...]
        [... ...] mortal not [...]
        (1) [... ... ...]
        [... ... ...]
        [... ... ...]
        (2) [... ... ...]
        [...] sleep in the night [... ...]
        [... ... ...] (3) [... ...] without compassion

IIC2? in anger he awakens jealousy
        and to *destruction* [... ... ...]
        [surround me] (4) the *breakers* of death
        and *Sheol* upon my bed
        my couch in lamentation shall shall take up
        [... ...] in the sound of sighing
        (5) my eyes like a moth[55] in a furnace
        and my tears like streams of water
        fail for *rest* my eyes.
        And my [...] stands to me (6) from a distance
        and my life on one side.

Psalm of Confidence

IIIA1 And I, from devastation to desolation,
        and from pain to affliction,
        and from cords (7) to breakers;[56]
        my soul ponders your wonders.

IIIA2a And you have not put me aside in your mercy[57] for ever (8) more;[58]
        my soul *delights* in *the multitude of your compassions.*
IIIA2b And I answer to my destroyers a word
        (9) and to the enviers of me correction.
IIIA2c And I will declare unrighteous my accusation[59]
        but thy judgement I will declare righteous.

---

[55] Or "grief" or "like smoke;" see Holm-Nielsen, *Hodayot*, 160 n. 89; Williams, "Parallelism," 487.

[56] Or "from pangs to throes;" see my discussion in §2.3.1 of chapter five on the word play in 1QH^a XI 6–19 [III 5–18].

[57] The noun is plural here and in lines 10 and 14; cf. Ps 17:7; Ps 106:7.

[58] Literally "from one time to another;" this phrase could end this poetic line or start the next one.

[59] Some translators read "his" instead of "my;" the noun itself could be translated as "judgement."

IIIA2d For I have known (10) your truth
and I accept my judgement;
and in my affliction I have *delighted*
for I wait for your mercy.

IIIA3a And you set (11) a prayer in the mouth of your servant
and you have not threatened my life
and my peace you have not put aside
nor have you forsaken (12) my hope
and in the face of affliction you have upheld my spirit.
IIIA3b For you, you have established my spirit
and you know my intentions.
IIIA3c (13) And in my adversities you have comforted me
and in forgiveness[60] *I delight*
and I find comfort on account of past transgression.
IIIA3d (14) And I know th[at] there is hope in your [me]rcy
and expectation in the abundance of your strength.

IIIB1 For none is justified (15) in your ju[dgeme]nt
nor [is innocent in] your law-court.
Person from person may gain right;
and a man [than] his [neighbour] (16) may be wiser;
and flesh than a creature of [clay] be more honoured;
and spirit than spirit may be mightier.
But like your mig[ht] there is no (17) strength,
and for your glory there is no [limit]
[and] for your wisdom there is no measure
and for your fait[hfulness there is no …]
(18) And for everyone who has been forsaken from it […]   *Blank*

IIIB2 But I, in you [… … … …] (19) my stand
And not [… … … … … … …]
[… … … … … … … … … …]
[… … … … … … … … … …]
(20) and as they plot against me you [… … …]
And if for shame of face [… … … …]
[… … …] (21) for me
And you, [in your compassions …]
[And] my adversary will [not] be strong against me
For a stumbling [… … … …] (22) those that war [against me]
[… … … … sha]me of face
and disgrace to the slanderers against me.   *Blank*

---

[60] The noun is in the plural; cf. Neh 9:17; Dan 9:9. The singular occurs once, in Ps 130:4.

IIIB3   (23) For you, my God, [... ...]
        [... ...] you plead my cause
        for in the mystery of your wisdom you have corrected me.
        (24) And you hide the truth for the time [...] for its appointed time.
        And your correction became for me joy and gladness,
        (25) and my affliction for et[ernal] healing [and] everlasting [...],
        and the derision of my adversary for me a crown of glory,
        and my weakness (for) (26) eternal might.

IIIC1   For [... ... ...]
        and by your glory was revealed my light;
        For light from darkness (27) you have caused to shine for [me].
        [... ... ... the inju]ry of my wound
        and for my stumbling a wonderful might,
        (28) and an eternal expanse for the constriction of [my] soul.
        [For you, my God] (are) my refuge, my stronghold,
        the rock of my strength, and my fortress;
        in you (29) I take refuge from all [... ...]
        [...] to me for deliverance for ever.   *Blank*

IIIC2   For you, from my father (30) you have known me
        and from the womb [... ... ...]
        [... ...] my mother you have dealt bountifully towards me
        and from the breasts of her that conceived me your compassion (31) upon me
        And in the embrace of my nurse [... ... ...]

IIIC3   And from my youth you have revealed yourself to me in the insight of your judgement
        (32) and in the sure truth you have sustained me
        and by your holy spirit you *delight* me.
        And unto this day [... ... ...]
        (33) and your righteous correction (is) with [...]
        and the guarding of your peace to deliver my soul
        and with my steps (34) the abundance of forgiveness
        and *the multitude of [compas]sions* in your judging of me
        and unto old age you yourself nourish me

IIIC4   For (35) my father has not know me
        and my mother unto you has forsaken me.
        For you (are) a father to all [son]s of your truth
        and you rejoice (36) over them as motherly compassion upon her infant
        and as a nurse in the embrace, you nourish all your works.   *Blank*

2.3. Analysis of Structure

I. Meshalim[61]   XVI 5–27 [VIII 4–26]
   A. A *Planting* of Trees by Water in the Dry Land   XVI 5–12
      1. Introductory stanza (Isa 41:17–19)
      2. The hidden sprouting of the holy shoot
         a. well of mystery
         b. sprouting of shoot, *planting*
         c. roots stretch out to the water source (Jer 17:8)
         d. shoot from the *stump* (Isa 11:1)
         c'. roots stretch out to the water source (Jer 17:8)
         b'. sprouting of shoot, *planting*
         a'. sealed mystery
   B. Fruit of Eden and Water of Life   XVI 12–21
      1. Access denied: a fence around its fruit
      2. Access restored: *planting* of fruit … for eternity
   C. The Hand of the Gardener   XVI 22–27
      1. By my hand … the *planting* of their trees
      2. When I lift my hand … their *stump* takes root
      3. If I withdraw my hand … its *stump* as nettles in a salt waste

II. Lament[62]   XVI 27–XVII 6 [VIII 26–IX 6]
   A. Afflictions and No Strength   XVI 27–36
      1. Introductory stanza (Isa 53:1–4)
      2. My afflictions—incurable pain and death
         a. my affliction has broken forth.
         b1. my soul groans, *Sheol*
         b4. my soul fainted … without *rest*
      3. My afflictions—fire and destruction
         a. it breaks forth
         b. to end strength
         c. *breakers*, my soul is bowed down to *destruction*
      4. No strength
         a. my bodily strength has ceased
         b. my arm is broken, not possible to lift my hand
         c. my feet are bound, not possible to stretch out a pace
   B. Tongue of the Learned and Silenced Lips   XVI 36–XVII ?
      1. The tongue of the learned (Isa 50:4)
      2. But silent are all lips
   C. Sleeplessness and Lamentation   XVII ?–6
      1. ?
      2. ? to *destruction*, *breakers* of death, *Sheol*, my eyes fail for *rest*

---

[61] Structural keywords: *planting* (Isa 61:3), *stump* (Isa 11:1).
[62] Structural keywords: *Sheol, breakers, destruction, rest*, etc. (Ps 88).

III. Psalm of Confidence[63]　　　　　　　　　　　　　XVII 6–36 [IX 6–36]
　　A. God is Merciful　　　　　　　　　　　　　　　　XVII 6–14
　　　　1. Introductory (transitional) stanza
　　　　2. And you (legal language)
　　　　　　a. your mercy, the *multitude of your compassions*
　　　　　　b/c. correction, judgement
　　　　　　d. I wait for your mercy
　　　　3. And you (nurture language)
　　　　　　a. my peace, my hope
　　　　　　b/c. you know me, you have comforted me
　　　　　　d. there is hope in your mercy
　　B. God is the Judge (legal)　　　　　　　　　　　　　XVII 14–26
　　　　1. None is justified in your judgement (wisdom, glory, might)
　　　　2. But I (take my stand) in you (shame of face to those against me)
　　　　3. You, O God, plead my cause (wisdom, glory, might)
　　C. God is a Compassionate Parent (nurture)　　　　　XVII 26–36
　　　　1. By your glory was my light revealed (refuge and deliverance)
　　　　2. From my father you have known me (mother, embrace of nurse)
　　　　3. From my youth you have revealed yourself (*delight* deliver)
　　　　　　(the *multitude of compassions*, your judging, you nourish)
　　　　4. My father does not know me, my mother has forsaken me
　　　　　　(as a nurse in the embrace you nourish)

There are a few blank spaces within this poem at the end of stanzas IA2, IB1, IIIB1, IIIB2, and IIIC1. Because their significance is unclear and they are few in number I have not included them in the structural analysis. The composition may be clearly divided on the basis of keywords into three major sections. In the translation and structural table I have emphasised these main structural keywords. Section I has a garden theme, and begins and ends with reference to the *stump* and the *planting*. The central section is a lament which begins and ends with reference to *breakers, destruction, Sheol, rest*, and other associated words. Section III has the twin theme of God's (legal) advocacy and nurturing; it begins and ends with use of the verb *delight*, and the phrase *multitude of compassions*.

The division into sub-sections is not quite as clear, partly due to lacunae in the text. However keywords are also used as structural devices throughout the poem. I have divided each section into three sub-sections on the basis of these keywords along with other poetic devices, and also by content. Each of the first sub-sections, labelled A, begins with a short introductory/transitional stanza. These are linked by one or more catchwords to the following stanzas, but otherwise stand out-

---

[63] Structural keyword: *delight* (Ps 94:19), *multitude of compassions* (Isa 63:15).

side the keyword structuring of the sub-section. Each of these three introductory stanzas can, in effect, be viewed as introducing the whole section rather than just the first sub-section in which I have placed it.

Thus IA1 introduces Section I and contains the keyword *planting*. IA2 is chiastically structured beginning and ending with keywords *mystery*, *shoot*, and *planting*. IB and IC employ the keywords *fruit* and *hand* respectively. The introductory stanza of sub-section II is linked to the rest of the sub-section by the catchwords *afflictions* and *strength*. The keywords in the rest of sub-section IIA, are *breaks-forth* and *strength*. IIB employs the keywords *tongue* and *silence*. The lacunae make the structure of IIC harder to discern but it seems to be based upon key-themes characterised by the words *sleep/bed* and *eyes/tears* respectively. The transitional stanza IIIA1 is linked by several catchwords to the previous sub-section but in its final phrase echoes the style and sentiments of the following stanza. In the rest of sub-section IIIA the key phrase is *your mercy* and in IIIB the keywords are *might*, *wisdom*, and *glory*. In IIIC two stanzas featuring the keywords *reveal* and *deliver* alternate with two stanzas featuring the *compassion* of *father* and *mother* and the *embrace* of *a nurse*.

Keywords are also used in other hodayot. For example, in chapter three I noted the use of keywords as a unifying/thematic factor throughout a poem and as catchwords linking sections of a poem together. But in this poem they seem to be the main structural technique.[64] I believe that the recognition of this use of keywords is decisive in deciding the structural divisions of this poem. This division of the text also gives a fairly balanced structure in terms of word/line count.[65] As well as their delimiting function, keywords serve to emphasise the themes of particular units. Many of the words used in this way do not seem to bear a direct relation to the use of allusions. However, the keywords marking the three main sections are linked to specific allusions, as indicated in the table above.

---

[64] Watson describes a similar use of keywords in the poetry of the HB. He uses the terminology "envelope figure" for the framing of a poem or stanza by repeated elements. The repeated element can be a complete line (e.g. Ps 118:1, 29), partial line, phrase (e.g. Ps 150:1, 6), word (e.g. "wicked" in Ps 1:1, 6), or root (e.g. "answer" in Ps 20:1[2], 9[10]). He links this with the more general use of keywords. He identifies three functions. The main one is to express the principal theme of a poem; secondly they can serve to indicate the structure of a poem, and finally as catchwords linking separate verses or stanzas. See W.G.E. Watson, *Classical Hebrew Poetry*, 283–295.

[65] The counting of manuscript lines gives a very rough indication of balance. Section I = 23 lines approx (8+10+6); II = 20 lines approx (9+6+5); III = 30 lines approx (8+15+7).

As far as I am aware the only other significant analysis of the structure of this poem is that undertaken by Douglas. He divides the composition into five sections calling this a "pentateuchal structure," which has "rich symbolic overtones in Jewish tradition, being the number of the Books of Moses." However, beyond using this to legitimate his structural analysis, he does not offer any reason why the use of this number might be particularly significant here.[66] My second two sections broadly coincide with those of Douglas. I also broadly agree with Douglas' division of the first part of the poem into three meshalim.[67] Where I differ with him is that I see these not as three major sections but as subsections of section I. This gives three sections of roughly comparable length and clearly identifiable themes. In my opinion, the number five has no role in this composition.

2.4. *Close Reading*

The poem consists of three quite distinct sections each of which can stand alone and be read separately. I will treat each section separately first, and leave discussion of their relationship until later.

2.4.1. *The Secret Garden Tended by the Speaker*

The composition begins with an introductory stanza introduced by the (reconstructed) formula אודכה אדוני. The particle כי introduces a triplet of descriptions of water in the desert, reminiscent of several passages in Isaiah.[68] The phrase *irrigation of a garden* (משקי גן) recalls the description of Eden in Genesis.[69] It functions as a pointer allusion to the development of the Eden theme in IB.

---

[66] Douglas, "Power and Praise," 144–172.

[67] I have placed MS lines 12b–16 [11b–15] in the second mashal, because of the Eden theme and keyword *fruit*. Douglas notes both of these but places the stanza at the end of the first mashal. See Douglas, "Power and Praise," 155–156.

[68] Similar water vocabulary and imagery is found in Isa 44:3 (*streams* on the *dry-ground*), 41:18 (*dry land* into founts of water), 35:7, and 49:10 (*springs of water*). The first two satisfy criteria 1b, 2a and 1c, 2a respectively.

[69] "And the LORD God planted *a garden* in Eden, in the east; and there he put the man whom he had formed. Out of the ground the LORD God made to grow every tree that is pleasant to the sight and good for food, the tree of life also in the midst of the garden, and the tree of the knowledge of good and evil. A river flows out of Eden *to water the garden*." (Gen 2:8–10); "Lot looked about him, and saw that the plain of the Jordan was *well watered* (משקה) everywhere like *the garden* of the LORD." (Gen 13:10). Only these two verses use the root שקה in connection with a garden. The latter verse satisfies allusions criteria 1b, 2a.

The phrase *you have placed me by* (... נתתני ב) occurs in the first line and is understood by ellipsis in the following two. Whether one translates the preposition as "by"[70] or "as"[71] is crucial to the interpretation of the poem. The latter option would mean that the speaker refers to himself as the source of water. Charlesworth is among the minority who favour this translation, but his arguments seem coloured by his determination to interpret the poem as allegorical and autobiographical. If however one translates the preposition as "by" then the speaker may be referring to himself as the gardener mentioned later in the section. Alternatively the speaker includes himself metaphorically as one of the trees described in the next stanza.

The final couplet[72] of this stanza contains an unmistakable allusion to the *juniper, pine, and box together*[73] of Isaiah. The main allusion is almost certainly a shorthand notation for the creation and Exodus imagery of Isa 41:19; but there is a supplementary pointer allusion to Isa 60:13. This would encourage the reader to interpret some of the garden imagery which follows in light of traditions which use the garden metaphor for the temple.[74] As Isa 60:13 begins and ends with *glory*

---

[70] Translated as "by" or "at" by Wallenstein (citing Ezek 32:23), Holm-Nielsen, Mansoor, and Douglas. See Wallenstein, *The Nezer*, 11, 17; Holm-Nielsen, *Hodayot*, 142; Mansoor, *The Thanksgiving Hymns*, 153; Douglas, "Power and Praise," 149.

[71] Translated "as" by Charlesworth; he explains it as "an example of the rare so-called beth essentiae." However, he admits that his translation is prompted by his allegorical and autobiographical interpretation of the poem. Puech has "tu as fait de moi une source de flots." Daise agrees with Charlesworth and also notes that a pronominal accusative object with a preposition is never found in the Bible. See Charlesworth, "An Allegorical and Autobiographical Poem," 296 n. 4; Puech, *Croyance*, 339; M.A. Daise, "Biblical Creation Motifs in the Qumran Hodayot," in *The Dead Sea Scrolls: Fifty Years after Their Discovery. Proceedings of the Jerusalem Congress, July 20–25, 1997*, (ed. L.H. Schiffman, E. Tov, and J.C. VanderKam; Jerusalem: Israel Exploration Society in cooperation with the Shrine of the Book, Israel Museum, 2000), 302, 304.

[72] I was unsure in which stanza to place this line, but have placed it in the introductory stanza so as not to disturb the chiasm of the next stanza. Wallenstein, Puech, and Douglas also place it in the first stanza. See Wallenstein, *The Nezer*, 11, 17; Puech, *Croyance*, 339; Douglas, "Power and Praise," 149.

[73] The allusion criteria are 1d and 2a. This distinctive phrase occurs only in Isa 41:19 and 60:13. The nouns *pine* (תדהר) and *box* (תאשור) occur in the Hebrew Bible only in these two verses. In the Dead Sea corpus they are found only here. Possibly the use of the term יחד in this passage led to its becoming a technical term for the community in other sectarian literature. Charlesworth comments on this possibility. See Abegg, et al., *The Dead Sea Scrolls Concordance, Volume 1*, 754, 755; Charlesworth, "An Allegorical and Autobiographical Poem," 297 n. 9.

[74] In Isa 41:19 *juniper* (ברוש) is probably in parallel with *cedar* (ארז) (cf. 1 Kings 5:10 [5:24]). The trees of Lebanon, particularly the cedar, were considered of the highest

(כבוד ... אכבד), so these trees are also *a planting ... ... for your glory* (מטע ... לכבודכה). The keyword *planting* (מטע) is a marker to Isa 60:21 and 61:3 inviting the reader to interpret the trees as a metaphor for God's righteous people.[75] In §2.5.1 I will further discuss this metaphorical combination of community, sanctuary, and garden.

Thus, in the introductory stanza, the poem alerts us to the main theme of section I, which is based upon Isaiah's use of Eden imagery for his vision of restoration for the exiles. This is explicitly expressed in Isa 51:3, "For the LORD will comfort Zion; he will comfort all her waste places, and will make her wilderness like Eden, her desert like the garden of the LORD."

Stanza IA2 is a chiastic description of the garden introduced in the first stanza.[76] It begins (a) and ends (a') with the key word *mystery* (רז) and the theme of hidden-ness. These *trees of life* (עצי חיים) are planted *in the midst of* (בתוך) *all the trees of the water* (כול עצי מים), just as in Gen 2:9 the tree of life (עץ החיים) is planted in the midst of (בתוך) the garden, a garden containing all kinds of trees (כול־עץ). The specific phrase "all the trees of the water" is found only in Ezek 31:14 in a chapter which seems to be a description of the mythical garden of God, a conflation of Eden and Lebanon.[77] As the poem proceeds it will become clear that

---

quality and associated with temples and palaces. Isa 60:13 specifically refers to the sanctuary. Examples of similar traditions include *Jub.* 3, which interprets Eden as the sanctuary. Brooke observes that in the Dead Sea scrolls, as well as in later Jewish exegetical tradition, the vineyard imagery of Isa 5 seems to have been interpreted as applying to the temple and Eden. See G.J. Brooke "4Q500 1 and the Use of Scripture in the Parable of the Vineyard," *DSD* 2 (1995): 268–294.

[75] "Your people shall all be righteous; they shall possess the land forever. They are the shoot that I *planted* (נצר מטעי), the work of my hands, so that I might be glorified (להתפאר)." (Isa 60:21); "They will be called oaks of righteousness, the *planting* (מטע) of the LORD, to display his glory (להתפאר)." (Isa 61:3). There are only 6 occurrences of *planting* in the HB. The similarity of context and proximity to other allusions point to these passages. See also comments below on IA2b. Cf. *Pss. Sol.* XIV 3: "The garden of the Lord, the trees of life are his holy ones. Their planting is rooted for ever." This translation is taken from S.P. Brock "The Psalms of Solomon" in *The Apocryphal Old Testament*, (ed. H.F.D. Sparks; Oxford: Clarendon, 1984), 673.

[76] Holm-Nielsen, *Hodayot*, 165, considers the principal background to be Ps 80:9–15.

[77] Nielsen points out that two thirds of the approx 70 biblical references to Lebanon are figurative with connotations of a fertile and beautiful place. She cites Fritz Stolz regarding a tradition concerning a garden of God in Lebanon which was separate from the Eden tradition. She argues that Ezek 31 "is helping either to create or to strengthen an already-existing connexion between the ideas about Eden and the ideas about Lebanon." See Kirsten Nielsen *There is Hope for a Tree: The Tree as Metaphor in Isaiah* (JSOTSup 65; Sheffield: Sheffield Academic Press, 1989), 126–128.

the trees of life continue the metaphor for God's righteous ones, and that the trees of the water are contrasted with them. There will also be further connotations drawn from the mythical imagery of Ezek 31.

In IA2b the poet returns to Isaiah as he introduces the significant keyword *shoot* (נצר) in an unmistakable allusion to Isa 60:21.[78] The shoot is *for a planting of eternity* (למטעת עולם); this phrase corresponds to the planting of the LORD in Isa 60:21 and Isa 61:3, "of eternity" serving as a circumlocution for "of the LORD."[79] The combination of allusion and keywords indicate that this is a structural allusion inviting multiple comparisons between the two texts.

In a double allusion to Jer 17:8,[80] the trees of life are described as *stretching out their roots to the water-source*, (IA2c), whereas the trees of the water do not so stretch out their roots (IA2c'). The Jeremiah verse is part of a wisdom poem contrasting the tree which flourishes, because it has a good source of water, with the tree in the desert. These are a metaphor for the person who "trusts in the LORD" in contrast to the one "whose heart turns away from the LORD." This allusion thus serves as a shorthand notation confirming that the two sets of trees stand for two types of people. Although the sense of IA2b and c is a little unclear, I interpret it as indicating that the glory of the trees of life is not yet apparent as they draw nourishment and strength from the water of life in preparation for the future sprouting of the shoot. This is contrasted with the misleading but unsustainable exaltation of the trees of the water in IA2c'. This theme of non-recognition will be expressed explicitly at the end of this section.

Beginning with the three parallel descriptions in the introductory stanza, water is very important in this poem. The phrases *water of life*

---

[78] The combination of *planting* and *shoot* is a clear marker to this verse, occurring nowhere else in the HB. The allusion satisfies criteria 1b, 2a. The word *shoot* occurs only 4 times in the HB, in Isa 11:1, 14:19, 60:21, Dan 11:7; Isa 11:1 and 60:21 have a similar positive eschatological context to this poem. The context of the other two references is clearly dissimilar.

[79] "Your people shall all be righteous; they shall possess the land forever. They are *the shoot that I planted*, the work of my hands, so that I might be glorified." (Isa 60:21); "They will be called oaks of righteousness, *the planting of the LORD*, to display his glory." (Isa 61:3). Note that in Isa 60:21 1QIsa[a] has מטעי יהוה "plantings of the LORD" where MT has Q מטעי "my planting," K מטעו "his planting." *Planting* occurs only six times in the HB, in Isa 60:21, 61:3; Ezek 17:7, 31:4, 34:29; Mic 1:6.

[80] The term *water-source* (יובל) occurs only here in the HB. Wallenstein notes a possible further allusion to Job 29:19, "my roots spread out (פתוח) to the waters," in the next line which begins "and it opens itself (ויפתח)." See Wallenstein, *The Nezer*, n. 27.

and *wellspring of life* are each used twice. The first phrase could be translated as "living water" and simply mean water which is flowing, not still. However, we also have the *trees of life*, and the word "life" is twice parallel to "eternal" and once to "holiness." The phrase *eternal trees* is also used, probably as a synonym for *trees of life*. Thus in most cases, if not all, the word "life" connotes a divine quality. In wisdom literature similar terms are used for wisdom and/or teaching/torah.[81] This connotation is confirmed later in the poem, in stanza IB2, when the speaker likens the words that God has given him to a *spring of living water*.

The *stump* (גזע) is now introduced in parallel to the *roots* (שורשים) from which the *shoot* (נצר) shall *sprout* (פרח). This combination of keywords brings to mind Isa 11:1. Although the imagery of a shoot sprouting from a fallen stump may have been a commonplace idea, the word translated here as stump occurs only three times in the Hebrew Bible. In view of the many other allusions to Isaiah an allusion to Isa 11:1 is probable.[82] If this is the case we are invited to interpret the stump as the remnant of Israel and the shoot as its messianic leader. However the messianic figure may also be interpreted as a group of people as in Isa 60:21, where the shoot refers to the righteous people of God, not to an individual.

The importance of the shoot-stump combination is emphasised by its position at the midpoint of this chiastic construction. The description of the animals and birds feeding on the stump of the felled tree appears to use a combination of vocabulary from Ezek 31:12–13 (cf. v. 6) and Ps 80:12–13 [13–14] (cf. Dan 4:9 [12]).[83] In both passages the present

---

[81] *Tree of life* in Prov 3:18, 11:30, 13:12, 15:4; *fountain/water of life* in Jer 2:13, 17:13; Prov. 10:11, 13:14, 14:27, 16:22; Ps 36:9. cf. *wells of salvation* in Isa 12:3; cf. also 1QH^a XIII 27–28 [V 25–26]: "And on account of their guilt you have concealed the *well of understanding* and the foundation of truth."

[82] "A shoot (חטר) shall come out from the *stump* (מגזע) of Jesse, and a *branch* (ונצר) shall *grow out* of his *roots* (משרשיו יפרה)." (Isa 11:1); Job 14:7–9 gives a good description of the imagery: "For there is hope for a tree, if it is cut down, that it will sprout again, and that its shoots (וינקתו) will not cease. Though its root grows old in the earth, and its stump (גזעו) dies in the ground, yet at the scent of water it will bud and put forth branches like a young plant." The only other biblical occurrence of גזע is Isa 40:24, where the context is dissimilar.

[83] "On the mountains and in all the valleys *its branches* (דליותיו) have fallen, and its boughs lie broken in all the watercourses of the land; and all the peoples of the earth went away from its shade and left it. On its fallen trunk settle *all the birds* (כל־עוף) of the air, and among its boughs lodge all the wild *animals* (כול חית השדה)." (Ezek 31:12–13); "Why then have you broken down its walls, so that *all who pass along the way* (כל־עברי)

fallen state of the tree is contrasted with its former glory. Although the context of the latter passage is relevant, the markers are weak and it is debatable whether it should be considered an allusion. However, the vocabulary and image of the fallen tree is part of this stanza's structural allusion to the description of the cosmic tree in Ezek 31 (see above).

Verse 1A2c' has already been discussed along with its counterpart 1A2c. The image of the trees which proudly tower over the stump is drawn from Ezek 31 and thus the inference is that these proud trees are also destined to be cut down. While it is clear from the correspondence of vocabulary that the remaining lines correspond with 1A2a and 1A2b, it is not entirely clear how to arrange them.[84] There is the repetition of the sprouting shoot, which is now described as *holy*, in a possible allusion to the holy seed of Isa 6:15. The *planting of truth* corresponds to the *planting of eternity*.

In 1A2a' the poem returns to the paradisiacal image of the secret garden of delight with its sealed well. This evokes well-known positive imagery.[85] The chiastic parallelism of the final two lines echoes a paradoxical rhetorical device of Isaiah. The garden is in fact in plain view; its hidden-ness is a result of a lack of perception.[86] *In the not being esteemed* (בלוא נחשב) and *in the not being known* (ובלא נודע) may be deliberate echoes of Isa 53:1–3. A similar thought is expressed in 1B1, *For he sees but does not perceive*, (כי ראה בלא הכיר) *esteems but does not believe* (ויחשוב בלא האמין). Douglas calls this the motif of non-recognition[87] and notes other occurrences of it in the *Hodayot*.

(דרך) pluck its fruit? The boar from *the forest* (מיער) ravages it (יכרסמנה), and all that move in the field *feed* on it (ירענה)." (Ps 80:12–13). Note that "ravages it" is from a different root but is spelt similarly to the word translated "treading place" (מרמס). Some play on words or a confusion of the two words is possible. The use of מרמס may be an anticipation of the later allusion to Isa 5, where it occurs in verse 5.

[84] As Williams notes there is considerable disagreement over the syntactical arrangement of these lines. I follow his arrangement which gives comparable line lengths and good parallelism. It also fits the context. See Williams, "Parallelism," 465.

[85] The metaphor of a sealed well of water flowing from Lebanon is used in Song 4:8–15, though in a different context. Nielsen considers that both Gen 3 and Song 4 reflect a widely-used positive imagery which originates in the Canaanite holy grove. See Nielsen, *There is Hope for a Tree*, 81, 128.

[86] This motif is combined with the concept of something sealed in Isa 29:10–12 "The vision of all this has become for you like the words of a sealed document. If it is given to those who can read, with the command, 'Read this,' they say, 'We cannot, for it is sealed.' And if it is given to those who cannot read, saying, 'Read this,' they say, 'We cannot read.'" cf. Isa 6:9, 43:8, 44:18; Jer 5:21.

[87] Douglas, "Praise and Power," 157.

As well as the use of the motif of non-recognition, stanza IB1 is also linked to IA2 by the repetition of the catchword *mystery*. This stanza has a small blank space at the beginning and a longer one at the end. The significance of these is unclear. The sub-section IB begins and ends with the use of the keyword *fruit* and with a reference to *Eden*. At the beginning of IB1 the Eden reference is implied by the use of an exclusion-from-paradise motif alluding to the *flame turning about* of Gen 3:24. The cherubim in the Genesis verse are here referred to as *powerful heroes* and *holy spirits* (cf. Ps 103:20; 104:4). At the end of IB there is an explicit mention of *Eden*, one of the few surviving occurrences of this word in the scrolls.[88] The effect is to emphasise that access to the garden is restricted to all but the members of the chosen group.

The change to the first person in the final verse of IB1 serves as a transition from the description of the exclusion from the garden in IB1 to the description in IB2 of the speaker. In contrast to the life giving water the wicked are seen as a raging torrent threatening to engulf the speaker. This first person parenthesis is a gnomic allusion using the language of Isaiah;[89] it points forward to the lament of section II and leads into the theme of the next stanza. The rest of the manuscript line has been left blank, possibly to highlight this verse as significant. The use of the word *overflowing* (שוטפים) to describe the *torrents* provides a catchword linking to the next stanza, IB2.

IB2 continues the watery theme introduced in stanza IA. The instruction of the speaker is seen as life giving water. This is a common wisdom motif. The phrase *as showers of rain* (כיורה גשם) combines two roots which occur together only in Hos 6:3 and Joel 2:23.[90] The words are used of rain metaphorically in the first reference and literally in

---

[88] The others are 4Q216 VI 3; 4Q265 7 12, 14; 4Q504 8 6; 1QH^a XIV 19 [VI 16]; 4Q428 8 4; 4Q484 7 1. References with the meaning delight occur in 1QS X 15; 1QH^a V 34 [XIII 17], XVIII 32 [X 30], [5 7]; 4Q256 XX 3; 4Q258 X 3; 4Q418 138 3; 4Q418^a 25 2; 4Q433^a 2 3; 4Q577 8 1; 11Q14 1 II 11. There is an indeterminate reference in PAM 43.691 13 1. See Abegg, et al., *The Dead Sea Scrolls Concordance, Volume 1*, 546.

[89] The phrase *for a mockery of the torrents* (לבזאי נהרות) could be derived from a variant reading of Isa 18: 2, 7. MT reads אשר בזאו נהרים, usually translated as "whose land the rivers divide." 1QIsa^a reads אשר בזאי נהרות. *They threw their mire over me* is a marker to Isa 57:20, "But the wicked are like the tossing sea that cannot keep still; its waters *toss up mire* and mud." Holm-Nielsen notes other possible allusions in 1QH^a X 14 [II 12] and XI 33 [III 32] and observes that possibly "it was a traditional picture among the community for the elect's position in a world of ungodliness." See Wallenstein, *The Nezer*, 22 n. 69; Holm-Nielsen, *Hodayot*, 152 nn. 29, 30.

[90] "He shall come unto us as the rain (כגשם), as the latter and former rain (יורה) unto the earth." (Hos 6:3 KJV); "for he has given the early rain for your vindication

the second. Their common context is that of eschatological blessing. The verb can also mean "to teach" (cf. Isa 30:20; Job 36:22; Prov 5:13) and so leads to rain being used metaphorically here for teaching.[91] It is promised that these rains *will not cease*. The rest of IB2 is unclear because of the lacunae. After the picture of life-giving rain we appear to have a picture of water rising from the earth.[92] Holm Nielsen has noted another possible double meaning referring to either water or words.[93] These waters will be beneficial for every tree[94] and every animal. The phrase *lead in mighty waters* (cf. Exod 15:10) and the mention of *fire* could indicate that the next verse gives a contrasting picture of judgement, but it is too incomplete to be certain.[95] IB ends with a repeated reference to key terms *planting*, *fruit* and *Eden*, but this verse too is poorly preserved.

In sub-section IC the use of the keyword *hand*, points to the gardening activities of the speaker. In IC1 we hear how he dug the irrigation channels and laid out the garden. Although these verses are poorly preserved the terms *measuring-line* and *plumb-line*[96] indicate a precision not evident in the more natural descriptions of the rest of the

---

(את־המורה לצדקה), he has poured down for you abundant rain (גשם), the early and the later rain, as before." (Joel 2:23).

[91] The possible play on words based on Joel 2:23, with the title Teacher of Righteousness is noted by Holm-Nielsen (cf. discussion in §3.4.1 of chapter three). This possible exegetical link gives a double allusion, applying criteria 1d and 2c. However the allusion could be solely to Hos 6:3, where the context is metaphorical and associated with knowledge (criteria 1c, 2a, b). See Holm-Nielsen, *Hodayot*, 153 n. 32.

[92] The phrase *they shall become an overflowing river* (והיו לנחל שוטף) echoes Jer 47:2, "Thus says the LORD: See, waters are rising out of the north and shall become an overflowing torrent (והיו לנחל שוטף); they shall overflow the land and all that fills it, the city and those who live in it." Because the biblical picture is of judgement and the picture here seems to be positive, I tentatively classify this as the use of biblical language rather than an allusion. However, it is not possible to be certain of the context here because of the lacunae.

[93] The first meaning of יביעו מחובאים is "they shall swell from hidden places," referring to water. The second meaning, indicated by the Hiphil of נבע, is "they shall bring forth hidden things," referring to words. See Holm-Nielsen, *Hodayot*, 154 n. 37.

[94] cf. Ezek 20:47 [21:3]; this is probably also use of biblical language rather than an allusion.

[95] Douglas, "Power and Praise," 159, interprets the whole stanza as referring to judgement, "a second flood and a second 'Red Sea' that … drowns the group's adversaries." See also the similar eschatological imagery of 1QH[a] XI 20–37 [III 19–36]; I discuss this poem in chapter five.

[96] These terms are found in parallel in Isa 28:17, indicating that there is probably a poetic parallelism intended here. There is not sufficient similarity of context to indicate an allusion.

section. The reference to the sun may also indicate that some importance was attached to the direction of planting. It is in Ezek 40–47 that we find a preoccupation with measuring in the context of a vision of a restored temple. Ezekiel emphasises the fact that the temple faced east, the direction of the rising sun.

This allusion points back to the trees in the desert described in the opening stanza, and forward to further allusions to the temple, including in IC3 a clearly marked allusion to Ezek 47:1–12. This biblical passage describes a river flowing east from the restored temple towards the Dead Sea; this river had all kinds of tree on its banks. Leslie Allen comments, "The climax in the narrative, as in the ensuing explanation (v 12), comes with the discovery of an oasis of trees growing in the barren Wilderness of Judah between Jerusalem and the Dead Sea. Do they find an echo in Second Isaiah's trees in the desert (Isa 41:19; cf. 35:1–2)?"[97]

In IC2 the keyword *stump*, which was found in IA2, makes its reappearance.[98] There is a contrast between the fate of the stump in IC2 and that in IC3, which mirrors the contrast between the trees of life and the trees of the water in IA2. In IC2 the nurturing hand of the gardener sustains the trees[99] even in a time of *heat*. But in IC3 we are warned that if the gardener removes his care then the garden reverts to *a bush in the desert ... a salt-waste*. This contrast echoes the language used in Jer 17:5–8[100] contrasting the one who trusts in human resources and the one who trusts in the LORD. This passage has already been alluded to in IA2c and c'.

The similarity to the gardener motif in Isa 5:1–7 is no coincidence.[101] The allusion is confirmed by the distinctive vocabulary. The verb to *hoe* (עזק) is found only in Isa 5:2 and the word here translated as *stinking* (באושים) is translated as wild-grapes in Isa 5:4. The phrase *briars and weeds* (שמיר ושית) is peculiar to Isaiah, occurring in Isa 5:6 and six other passages.[102] In Isaiah it is the LORD who is the gardener. Here it is

---

[97] Leslie C. Allen, *Word Biblical Commentary, Volume 29: Ezekiel 20–48* (Dallas, Texas: Word Books, 1998).

[98] For similar language about rooting see Hos 14:6; Isa 40:24. I consider these as use of biblical language but not allusion; however the unexpected use of the plural here (their stump) may be an echo of Isa 40:24.

[99] The use of the catch word "strength" provides a link to section II.

[100] Cf. the language in Zeph 2:9; Hos 10:8; Isa 7:23.

[101] Cf. Isa 27:2–13; Ps 80:8–15; Jer 2:21.

[102] Isa 5:6, 7:23, 24, 25, 9:18, 10:17, 27:4. The phrase "thorns and thistles" is found in Gen 3:18; Isa 32:13; Hos 10:8. All of these verses have connotations of judgement, but

the speaker. However the phrase "*by my hand you ...*" and the further references to his hand indicate that the speaker regards himself as the agent of God. Finally in this section, the reference to the trees on *its banks* whose *leaves wither* is in clear contrast with the trees in Ezek 47:12.[103] It also echoes the wisdom motif of the righteous man, the wording here closer to Ps 1:3 than to Jer 17:8.

Stylistically section I is unified and symmetrically organised by the use of keywords. However, there is also a definite progression from emphasis on the garden itself as the creation of God to an emphasis on the speaker as the one who nourishes and nurtures the garden. In the second section this emphasis on the speaker is sustained.

2.4.2. *The Afflicted Teacher*

There is an abrupt change of tone in line XVI 27b [VIII 26b] leading most commentators[104] to treat this as the start of a separate section, which I have numbered as section II. This section is however linked to the previous one by its use of Isa 53:3–4 and by the catchword *strength* (מעוז). This word can also mean "refuge" or "stronghold" and its use here may be a word play subtly pointing forward to the theme of God as refuge in IIIC1. In this section the speaker feels forsaken by God, with no refuge. IIA1 is based on the first few verses of Isa 53, picking up on the earlier use of the motif of non-recognition.[105] There is a clear coincidence of theme and the words (or related words) *sicknesses* (חליים), *acquainted with* (מודע ב), *afflictions* (נגיעים), *pain* (כאב) occur in both passages.[106]

This short opening stanza is followed by three stanzas which elaborate on its themes. Stanzas IIA2 and IIA3 pick up on the *afflictions*; stanza IIA4 elaborates on the theme of *no strength* (אין מעוז). Matching stanzas IIA2 and IIA3 each begin with a line using the verb to *break*

---

the Genesis verse is also in the context of exclusion from Eden. In absence of a clear exegetical link this phrase is better classed as use of biblical language.

[103] This combination of words marks an allusion to Ezek 47:12, using criteria 1b, 2a.

[104] See for example, Wallenstein, *The Nezer*, 4, 13; Douglas, "Power and Praise," 150, 154.

[105] Another possible link with the theme of section I may be the reference in Isa 53:2 to "a root out of a dry ground" (וכשרש מארץ ציה).

[106] "He was despised and rejected by others; a man of suffering (איש מכאבות) and acquainted (וידוע) with infirmity (חלי); and as one from whom others hide their faces he was despised, and we held him of no account. Surely he has borne our infirmities (חלינו) and carried our diseases (ומכאבינו); yet we accounted him stricken (נגוע), struck down by God, and afflicted." (Isa 53:3–4).

forth (פרח) and end with a phrase using the word *soul* (נפש). There may be a contrast intended with the positive connotation of the verb פרח translated as "to sprout" in section I.

The first couplet of IIA2 repeats the catchword *affliction* in parallel to *an incurable pain* (כאיב אנוש). Holm-Nielsen's suggestion that the allusion to Isa 53:3–4 is continued by a word play on אֱנוֹשׁ/אָנוּשׁ (*incurable/man*) is a plausible one. He also suggests an allusion to Isa 17:11, which I reject because there is insufficient contextual linkage.[107] Jer 15:18 or Jer 30:15 are equally likely to come to mind when reading this phrase.[108] Jer 15:18 is also a lament and balances another allusion to a lament of Jeremiah in IIA3 (see below). The next four lines are a complex interweaving of lament components familiar from the biblical psalms, particularly Psalms 42, 77, and 88.[109] The first two lines exhibit chiastic parallelism; the phrase *like those that descend to Sheol* is in parallel with *and with the dead*, and *my soul* is in parallel with *my spirit*. The second and third lines also contain parallel elements; *with the dead* is in parallel with *to the pit*, and *my spirit* is in parallel with *my life*. *And within me fainted my soul*, in the fourth line, is in parallel with *my soul groans within me*, in the first line.

The first couplet in IIA3 introduces the theme of fire with an allusion to Jer 20:9.[110] The immediate context in Jeremiah is of the Lord's message burning within the prophet, although the wider context is of persecution. There may be a pointer here to the speaking theme which follows in IIB. The middle couplet has a more general, even eschatological, tone. The poem returns to a more personal reference in the final line, *my soul within me is bowed down*, alluding to Ps 42:5, 6, 11 [6, 7, 12].[111]

---

[107] Holm-Nielsen, *Hodayot*, 167 n. 26, 156 n. 56; Carmignac, "Les citations de l'ancien testament," 363.

[108] "Why is my *pain* unceasing, my wound *incurable*, refusing to be healed?" (Jer 15:18); "Why do you cry out over your hurt? Your *pain* is *incurable*." (Jer 30:15). The conjunction of terms occurs only in these verses and Isa 17:11. Jeremiah uses the word *incurable* 5 times, compared with 4 isolated instances in other books.

[109] Why are you cast down, O *my soul*, and why are you *disquieted within me*? (נפשי ותהמי עלי)" (Ps 42:5 [6]); "I think of God, and I moan; I meditate, and *my spirit faints*." (Ps 77:3 [4]); "I commune with my heart in the night; I meditate and *search my spirit*. (ויחפש רוחי)" (Ps 77:6 [7]); "For my soul is full of troubles, and *my life draws near to Sheol*. I am counted among those who go down to the Pit; I am like those who have no help, like those *forsaken among the dead* (במתים חפשי), like the slain that lie in the grave." (Ps 88:3–5 [4–6]).

[110] "His word in my heart is like a fire, a fire shut up in my bones" (Jer 20:9).

[111] The mention of *breakers* may also be an allusion to Ps 42:7 [8] and/or Ps 88:7 [8].

IIA4 elaborates on the theme of no strength introduced in the opening stanza, IIA1. The first four lines have an ABBA structure; they describe general bodily weakness. The fourth line parallels the second with its mention of weakened *strength*, with *body* and *loins* being parallel terms. The middle couplet combines two familiar biblical images in a novel way. Here instead of the melting heart we have melting flesh, whereas the heart is poured out like water.[112] The next couplet uses a combination of words which bring to mind the suffering of another righteous person. In Job 31:21–22, Job protests that if he has *lifted a hand*[113] against the fatherless (אם־הניפותי על־יתום ידי) then may his *arm* be *broken from its socket* (ואזרעי מקנה תשבר). This latter word, though common in the Hebrew Bible, only means bone-socket in this passage.

The exact structure of the remaining five poetic lines is harder to decide on, partly because of the illegibility of the first part of the last line. The *shackles* in which the speaker's *feet* are *caught* appear to be paired with *chains* in the last line. The middle three lines all refer to legs/feet. One would expect therefore the last line to refer to feet. The relevant words are badly damaged but most commentators read them as referring to *arms*. However because of the preceding lines I am inclined to agree with Wallenstein's restoration, *all my steps are bound* (וכול מצעדי רותקו).[114] The phrase *my knees go like water*[115] is similar to one found only in Ezek 7:17 and 21:7 [12]. The latter verse also states that every *heart* will *melt*, every *hand* go limp and every spirit become faint. It is possible to consider this stanza of the poem may be modelled on Ezek 21:7 [12] which pronounces judgement upon Jerusalem.[116]

IIB1 continues the bodily theme by reference to the *mouth* and the *tongue* of the speaker. This is a return to the theme of the speaker as teacher, introduced in section IB2. The main allusion is to Isa 50:4 "The LORD God has given me the *tongue of a teacher*, that I may know how to *sustain the weary with a word*." Each of these phrases from Isaiah

---

[112] "The hearts of the people melted and turned to water." (Josh 7:5); "I am poured out like water, and all my bones are out of joint; my heart is like wax; it is melted within my breast." (Ps 22:14 [15]); cf. 1QH^a XII 34–35 [IV 33–34], the second poem considered in chapter three.

[113] Note also the contrast with the speaker's lifting of his hand in IC2.

[114] Wallenstein, *Nezer*, 5, 29 n. 168.

[115] cf. 1QH^a XII 34–35 [IV 33–34].

[116] "And when they say to you, 'Why do you moan?' you shall say, 'Because of the news that has come. Every heart will melt and all hands will be feeble, every spirit will faint and all knees will turn to water. See, it comes and it will be fulfilled,' says the LORD God." (Ezek 21:7).

is contained in the second line of two couplets. Because of the damage to these lines it is not possible to be certain of the reading. I take these couplets to mean that unlike the rest of his body the speaker's tongue is not restrained. Others have read it in a more negative sense.[117] The reference to reviving *those who stumble*[118] is a further link to the previous stanza where the speaker himself was caused to stumble because of his chains.

Chains is repeated in the next stanza, IIB2, and the phrase *silent are all lips* continues the theme of speaking. The silent lips may belong to the speaker's opponents in contrast to his own speech. However, due to the lacunae it is not possible to say much more about these lines. Somewhere within this damaged section there appears to be a change back to the theme of death and affliction but it is unclear where this final sub-section starts.

As with section I the end of the section is marked by the repetition of certain keywords; in this case they are *destruction* (כלה),[119] *breakers of death* (משברי מות),[120] *Sheol*, and *rest* (מנוח). Yet another physical aspect is focussed upon, namely the *eyes*, as the speaker languishes in *lamentation* upon his *bed*. The poem certainly employs biblical language[121] in this description of lamentation. It would undoubtedly bring to mind certain passages in Psalms and Lamentations but there is insufficient evidence of specific allusion.

The section concludes by echoing the theme of nearness to death found at the beginning of the section. "My [soul] stands to me from a distance, and my life on one side." Alternatively, Wallenstein sees here an allusion to Ps 38:11 [12] and translates as "My [friend] stands far off, and my kinsman is aloof." This would echo the idea of being forsaken found in the opening stanza.[122]

---

[117] E.g. Douglas, "Power and Praise," 150, reads "Though you continually made mighty the tongue in my mouth, there is (now) no (ability) to lift up the voice ..."

[118] It has also been suggested that Isa 57:15 "*to revive the spirit* of the lowly" is a possible influence but this is a common biblical use of language. Kister, "Biblical Phrases," 27–39, has linked this phrase to a possible pesher. I discuss this in 3.5.1 of chapter three.

[119] Preceded by a possible allusion here to Isa 42:13 "he awakens jealousy."

[120] For this phrase see 2 Sam 22:5 and 1QH^a XI 8–9 [III 7–8]. I discuss this poem in chapter five.

[121] Cf. Job 17:7,13; Ps 6:7–8; 22:2; 31:10; 102:6; Lam 1:2, 3; 2:11, 18.

[122] Wallenstein, *The Nezer*, 14, 32 n. 211, justifies the translation of חיי as "kinsman" by reference to an Arabic word and to 1 Sam 18:18.

2.4.3. *God the Compassionate Judge and Parent*

In section III the speaker declares his faith in God's mercy, compassion and right judgement. This enables him to answer his opponents. The section begins with a triplet featuring the prepositions מ and ל. Holm-Nielsen describes this construction as a "rhetorical superlative."[123] The threefold repetition of word pairs builds up an intensity of feeling which requires completion and resolution in the final line of the stanza.

It is difficult to decide whether to place this stanza at the end of Section II or the beginning of Section III. As it begins with an independent pronoun most commentators place it at the start of this section. However, the theme of *pain* and *affliction*[124] echoes precisely that of section II. After some equivocation, I view this triplet as part of an opening stanza, picking up the theme from section II but, with the line *my soul ponders your wonders*, moving it on from lament to confidence.[125] There are echoes of biblical thanksgiving psalms in this phrase, but no specifically identifiable allusion.[126]

In IIIA2 the line *my soul delights in the multitude of your compassions* (תשתעשע נפשי בהמון רחמיכה) matches the final line of the introductory stanza.[127] It combines markers to Ps 94:19, "your comforts delight my soul" (תנחומיך ישעשעו נפשי) and Isa 63:15, "the yearning of your heart and your compassion" (המון מעיך ורחמיך). This conflation equates "your compassions" with "your comforts," ensuring that in the rest of the poem the use of one recalls the other. The expression *you have not put me aside for evermore* negates language commonly found in psalms of lament.[128] The closest equivalents to the entire sentiment and vocabulary of this couplet are probably Ps 77:7–12 [8–13] and Lam 3:31–32.

---

[123] Holm-Nielsen, *Hodayot*, 160 n. 92.

[124] Each of these word pairs is rare in the HB. For the second pair see Isa 53:4, already alluded to in IIA1; for the third pair see 2 Sam 22:5–6, alluded to in IIC2. For the first word pair see Zeph 1:15; Job 30:3, 38:27, there is no corresponding allusion but this may be hidden in the lacunae. See also, 1QH^a XIII 32 [V 30]; 1QH^a XI 8–12 [III 7–11]; 1QH^a XXII 23 [frg. 4 4]; 4QH^a (4Q427) 2 2.

[125] Licht and Puech place it at the start of a new stanza. Douglas places it at the end of a section, but includes the following line as the conclusion of the verse. See Licht, *Thanksgiving Scroll*, 143; Puech, *Croyance*, 343; Douglas, "Power and Praise," 151.

[126] cf. Ps. 105:2=1 Chr 16:9; Ps 119:27; 145:5.

[127] Williams, "Parallelism," 493, arranges these lines as a triplet, based on the parallelism, especially between the first and third lines.

[128] cf. 1 Chr 28:9; Ps 44:23, 74:1, 77:7; Lam 3:31. Various Hebrew terms are used to express the idea of forever. So it is no surprise that this poem uses another variant.

The key phrase *in your mercy* (בחסדיכה) is central to this verse and is repeated in the closing verse of this sub-section.

The next two couplets introduce the speaker's opponents whose *accusation* he is able to *answer* because of his trust in God's mercy. The vocabulary is that of the law court. The next verse, IIIA2d, continues the legal theme. It is an ABBA pattern with the two outer and two inner lines in parallel. The final line of this verse repeats the key word *your mercy*. The verb "to wait" (יחל) introduces the theme of the next stanza, which is hope in God.

The theme of hope (תקוה) is taken up in the first verse of stanza IIIA3, which has five lines. The matching outer lines describe God's positive actions to the speaker; they enclose a triplet of lines expressing God's favour in negative phrases. The middle phrase, *my peace you have not put aside*, echoes the verb of IIIA2a. The words are a negation of similar words in Lam 3:17, with possible echoes of the expressions of hope found in this chapter of Lamentations. The theme is continued in three more verses. The first line of the next couplet, *For you, you have established my spirit*, expresses the same thought of the previous line and develops it to imply God's knowledge of the speaker.

This is followed by a triplet on being *comforted* and taking *delight* in forgiveness, which echoes the allusion to Ps 94:19 found in the opening triplet of this section. Both of these Hebrew roots have associations with motherly nurture,[129] a theme which will be picked up in IIIC. Verse IIIA3d repeats the key phrase *in your mercy* to round off this sub-section. In addition to this neat inclusio, as noted above, this final stanza subtly echoes the ideas and phrases of the opening verse of IIIA2. Unlike many biblical psalms which appeal to God for vindication, the speaker here seems to acknowledge his own unworthiness but nonetheless hopes in God's mercy.[130]

Sub-section IIIB returns to the legal language of IIIA2. Unworthiness is the theme of the opening stanza. The first couplet sets the scene as the *judgement* (משפט) and *law-court* (ריב) of God, before whom *none*

---

[129] "that you may nurse and be satisfied from her consoling breast (משד תנחמיה)" (Isa 66:11); "and you shall nurse and be carried on her arm, and dandled (תשעשעו) on her knees" (Isa 66:12).

[130] *I know that there is hope* occurs in 1QH^a XI 21 [III 20] (see discussion in §3.5.1 of chapter five) and XIV 9 [VI 6] in a similar context of turning from sin. See also XXII 10 [frg. 1 7]. Kuhn identifies this phrase as a formula used to introduce soteriological confessions in Community Hymns. The phrase occurs in the HB in Ezra 10:2. See Holm-Nielsen, *Hodayot*, 67 n. 5, 112 n. 9; Kuhn, *Enderwartung*, 34, 179.

is justified (לא יצדק). This is followed by four lines featuring the use of the comparative particle מן. They express that it is possible to judge between humans as to who is more *righteous* (צדק), *wise* (שכל), *honoured* (כבד), or *mighty* (גבר). These keywords are echoed in slightly different form in the next verse.[131] Characterised by the use of the particle אין, it states that no such comparison with God is possible. The final line of stanza IIIB1 is incomplete but probably echoes the sentiment of the first couplet.

Stanza IIIB2 is set off by a short blank space at each end; it is poorly preserved but appears to be concerned with the disgrace (כלמה) due to the speaker's adversaries. The key phrase, *for shame of face* (לבושת פנים), occurs twice.[132] Together with the phrase *those that war [against me]* (אנשי מלחמה), these mark an allusion to Isa 41:11–12. In this biblical court scene Israel is promised God's help against those who strive against him (אנשי ריבך).[133] Stanza IIIB3 continues the court scene as the speaker realises that *You, my God ... plead my cause* (תריב ריבי).[134] The next couplet is damaged but seems to imply that God's vindication of the speaker is hidden until the right time. The final lines use the preposition ל to contrast the speaker's condition before and after his vindication. The keywords from IIIB1, wisdom, glory and might, are repeated.

In sub-section IIIC the speaker leaves the court scene, returning to the language of refuge and nurture. I have divided this sub-section into two matching halves of two stanzas each. IIIC1 corresponds with IIIC3 and IIIC2 with IIIC4. In stanza IIIC1, the initial triplet repeats the catch word *glory*, by which *was revealed* my light. In both Ps 80:1 and Ps 94:1 God is exhorted to shine forth and vindicate the psalmist. The verb reveal/shine (יפע), which is repeated in matching stanza IIIC3, indicates a theophany and occurs only eight times in the Hebrew Bible, including Moses' encounter on Sinai.[135] There are, however,

---

[131] Probably the four nouns of the later verse correspond to the four verbs of the former. The corresponding term to *gain right* is lost in a lacuna. The corresponding term to *be wiser* is *wisdom* (חכמה) from a different root but with equivalent meaning. *Glory* (כבוד) corresponds to *be honoured* and *might* (גבורה) to *be mightier*.

[132] Cf. Ezek 7:18; Jer 7:19; Ezra 9:7; 2 Chr 32:21; Dan 9:7, 8; Ps 44:16.

[133] "Yes, all who are incensed against you shall be *ashamed and disgraced*; those who strive against you shall be as nothing and shall perish. You shall seek those who contend with you, but you shall not find them; *those who war against you* shall be as nothing at all." (Isa 41:11–12).

[134] cf. Mic 7:8–10; Ps 43:1; 119:154.

[135] Deut 33:2; Ps 50:2, 80:1, 94:1 + 4 refs in Job. See the discussion in chapter three on

insufficient grounds for regarding this as a Mosaic motif, as Douglas claims.[136]

The following verse picks up another key word, *might*, from the previous sub-section. It describes how God has reversed the speaker's fortunes. A shorthand allusion links this to God's promise to Jerusalem in Isa 30:18–26 that "the *light* of the sun will be sevenfold ... in the day that the LORD healeth *the stroke of their wound*." (Isa 30:26 KJV). The final line of the verse contains the phrases *expanse* and *constriction of soul* which are clear markers to Ps 31:7–8 [8–9].[137] This shorthand allusion not only has connotations of deliverance but recalls the descriptions of distress in the previous section. The stanza ends with a cluster of images of God as *refuge*, *stronghold*, *rock*, and *fortress* and *deliverance*. Such images are found particularly in the Psalms.[138]

These ideas of God's deliverance are repeated in stanza IIIC3. In this stanza the speaker declares God's support and deliverance from *youth*, *unto this day*, and *unto old age*. The key phrase from the beginning of the section, *multitude of your compassions*, is repeated here. Other words from IIIA which are repeated are *correction*, *delight*, *peace*, and *forgiveness*.

Matching stanzas IIIC2 and IIIC4 contain images of parental nurturing. The first stanza tells how God's care has been with the speaker *from the womb*. The introduction of this biblical language[139] and a possible allusion to Isa 46:3–4[140] connects this stanza with IIIC3, and paves the way for the use of the parental metaphor applied to God in IIIC4.

In this final stanza, the reference to being *forsaken* by *father* and *mother* may indicate a gnomic allusion to Ps 27:10. The combination *compassion* and *nursing-child* (עולה) uniquely mark Isa 49:15, "Can a woman forget her nursing child, or show no compassion for the child of her womb? Even these may forget, yet I will not forget you." Clear use of mother-

---

1QHᵃ XII 7, 24 [IV 6, 23]. This verb is also used in 1QHᵃ XIII 34 [V 32], XV 6, 27 {VII 3, 24}, XIX 29 [XI 26], XXIII 7 [XVIII 6] as well as in other scrolls.

[136] Douglas, "Power and Praise," 166.

[137] "I will exult and rejoice in your steadfast love, because you have seen *my affliction* (בְּצָרוֹת נַפְשִׁי); you have taken heed of my adversities, and have not delivered me into the hand of the enemy; you have set my feet *in a broad place* (בַמֶּרְחָב)." (Ps 31:7–8 [8–9]).

[138] Ps 18:2[3]; 62:2[3]; 144:2.

[139] Ps 22:9–10[10–11]; 71:5–6; 139:13.

[140] "Listen to me, O house of Jacob, all the remnant of the house of Israel, who have been borne by me from your birth, carried from the womb; even to your old age I am he, even when you turn gray I will carry you. I have made, and I will bear; I will carry and will save." (Isa 46:2–3).

ing imagery for God is rare in the Hebrew Bible.[111] And so the poem turns to Naomi and her grandson to fill out the image. The combination of words found in the concluding lines of stanzas IIIC2, 3 and 4 provide a unique marker to Ruth 4:15–16. These are *embrace* (חיק) of a *nurse* (אמון) with the words *nourish* (לכלכל) and *old-age* (שיבה).[142]

2.5. *Allusions*

The main influence upon this poem appears to be Isaiah. One could consider it as a meditation upon various themes/motifs which occur in Isaiah 40–66.[143] Section I elaborates upon the themes of the trees/planting of the Lord, water in the desert, the tree(s) of life in the garden of God (primeval and eschatological), and the messianic/remnant motif of the shoot/branch. Section II takes up the motif of the suffering servant. Section III concentrates on the themes of compassion and hope, with the particular motifs of the law-court and of the parent.

While the sections can be read as free-standing compositions, and may even have existed as such, the reader needs to make sense of them as they appear together here. I suggest that one way of reading this poem is to regard the sections as representing successive stages that the speaker and his community believed themselves to be destined to go through. While expressed in terms of the experiences of an individual

---

[111] In Isa 66:7–13 Zion is likened to a mother ending with the declaration: "Rejoice with Jerusalem, and be glad for her, all you who love her; rejoice with her in joy, all you who mourn over her—that you may nurse and be satisfied from her consoling breast; that you may drink deeply with delight from her glorious bosom. For thus says the LORD: I will extend prosperity to her like a river, and the wealth of the nations like an overflowing stream; and you shall nurse and be carried on her arm, and dandled on her knees. As a mother comforts her child, so I will comfort you; you shall be comforted in Jerusalem." (Isa 66:10–13; cf. Num 11:12.) God as father is found in Isa 63:15–16, 64:8; Jer 3:4, 19; etc.

[142] "'He shall be to you a restorer of life *and a nourisher* (ולכלכל) of your *old age* (את־שיבתך); for your daughter-in-law who loves you, who is more to you than seven sons, has borne him.' Then Naomi took the child and laid him *in her bosom* (בחיקה), and became his *nurse* (לאמנת)." (Ruth 4:15–16).

[143] Wise has suggested that it is the version of Isaiah found in 1QIsa[a] that lies behind the *Hodayot*. He argues that the *Hodayot* reflects variants found in this scroll in at least ten instances. The variants he cites are found in Isa 40:13, 57:17, 54:17, 59:5, 57:20, 17:11, 60:21, 18:2, 7, 30:12, 40:11, 41:29. It seems likely that this version of Isaiah underlies at least some of the Isaiah allusions in the *Hodayot*, but I consider that Wise probably goes too far in seeking to link this scroll directly with the Teacher of Righteousness himself. See Michael O. Wise, *The First Messiah: Investigating the Savior before Jesus* (New York: HarperSanFrancisco, 1999), 91–95, 291 n. 14.

leader of the community, the experiences of the speaker can also be seen as representative of the experiences of each individual member.

The hope expressed in Isaiah 40–66 is that God has not completely forsaken his people but that after exile will come restoration. This hope is reinterpreted in eschatological terms by the community which produced this poetry. They saw themselves as that part of the exiled people of God who would be restored. They interpreted the wilderness passages in Isaiah as referring to their community which had gone into the wilderness to prepare the way.[144] This is the theme of section I.

However the new age would not come without suffering. The community saw their own sufferings as part of the cosmic battle between good and evil. They expected that in the last days things would get worse before they got better. Section II interprets the suffering servant passages of Isaiah in light of this expectation. Whereas the sufferings of the wicked would culminate in destruction, the sufferings of the righteous would result in vindication. Section III picks up the legal language of Isaiah, with its idea that the judgement of God will not last for ever because God is also merciful and cares for Israel as a parent correcting a child.

2.5.1. *Preparation*

As already explained, the introductory phrase *a planting of juniper and pine with box together for your glory* alludes to Isa 41:19 and 60:13, conflated with 60:21 and 61:3. This constitutes a structural allusion to Isa 41:17–20 and 60:13–61:3 which contain all the key ideas of the section. Isa 41:17–20 contains the key themes of water and trees, a garden in the desert. It also refers to *seeing* and *knowing together*. Isa 60:13–61:3 contains the key words of *planting, glory, shoot*. It also links the trees metaphor to the sanctuary (Isa 60:13) and to God's people (Isa 60:21, 61:3). This encourages the reader to simultaneously interpret the planting metaphor as the community of God's righteous people, the garden of the LORD, and the temple sanctuary.[145] We thus have in this section a complex interweaving of exegetical motifs and traditions.

---

[144] "As it is written: In the desert, prepare the way of ****, straighten in the steppe a roadway for our God. This is the study of the law" (1QS VIII 14) in García Martínez, and Tigchelaar, *The Dead Sea Scrolls Study Edition*, 89.

[145] cf. Brooke's comments on another Qumran text. "4Q500 1 thus seems to stand at a highly potent metaphorical interchange. In just a few words there are hints of the vineyard which is the chosen people of God, there are hints that the vineyard was associated with Jerusalem, and with the sanctuary in particular. And the traditions about

Further key allusions to Gen 2:8–10, 3:22–24; Ezek 31:1–18; and Jer 17:5–8 act as shorthand notation to fill out the imagery. The myth of the garden of God, which is linked both with Eden and Lebanon, is the main idea in the Genesis and Ezekiel passages. Both of these passages also contain ideas of judgement. In Genesis mankind is judged and excluded from the garden. In Ezek 31 the towering tree was cut down. But there is hope. The shoot of God's planting (Isa 60:21) is linked exegetically to the shoot which will grow from the stump in Isa 11:1.

In Jer 17:5–8 we have a wisdom motif in which the righteous are likened to trees with a reliable water supply in contrast to the parched trees which represent the wicked (cf. Ps 1:3, 92:12, Prov 11:28, 30). This poem connects the former with *the trees of life*, and the latter with *the trees of the water* which although they are exalted have not tapped into the hidden source of water. The motif of the water of life, which is the source of sustenance for the trees, is implicit in most of the biblical passages considered but its exegesis owes most to the wisdom tradition, where it refers firstly to wisdom and later to Torah (e.g. Sir 24). This exegesis becomes explicit in IB2 when the speaker states that God has put words in his mouth as showers of rain and a spring of water of life.[146]

The sequence of thought in IB2 is difficult to ascertain because of a number of lacunae. However it appears to emphasise the fruit of Eden, which is protected and watered by God. This may be an allusion to the tradition that just as Adam and Eve had been excluded from Eden lest they eat of the tree of life, that access to the tree will be restored in the new age (cf. 1 Enoch 24:4–25:5, 4 Ezra 8:52).

In IC an allusion to Isa 5:1–7 acts as a shorthand notation filling out the metaphor of the gardener. From this allusion we know that the speaker is the agent of God, the real gardener, and that Israel is the

---

the sanctuary link it with two theological perspectives, one in which the earthly mirrors the heavenly, the other an *Urzeit-Endzeit* typology which invokes the eschatological sanctuary's being described in terms of the garden of Eden. Through other closely related Qumran texts these ideological motifs are variously reinforced or expanded." See Brooke, "4Q500 1 and the Use of Scripture," 279.

[146] Cf. "He disclosed these matters to them and they dug a well of plentiful water" (CD III 16); "And he raised from Aaron men of knowledge and from Israel wise men, and made them listen. And they dug the well … … … The well is the law." (CD VI 4). This translation from García Martínez, and Tigchelaar, *The Dead Sea Scrolls Study Edition*, 555, 559.

garden. The water imagery is continued in an allusion to Ezek 47:1–12. This acts as a shorthand notation confirming the temple connotations already implicit in the poem. Ezek 47:1–12 explicitly refers to the temple, but in Jewish exegesis Isa 5:1–7 was also interpreted in this way. Baumgarten notes that in *Targum Jonathan* the watchtower and winepress are interpreted as the sanctuary and the altar respectively. In *t. Sukkah* 3:15 the channels under the altar are also referred to. Baumgarten links this to the tradition found in the Mishnah that the sacrificial fluids which flowed into these channels were "a source of fructification for the gardens of the area." He traces this tradition to the water issuing from the temple in Ezek 47.[147]

A reader familiar with this tradition would therefore associate the allusions to Isa 5:1–7 and Ezek 47:1–12 with the temple. The wellspring with its channels would be associated with the altar. Thus the well-being of God's people, his planting, is seen to depend not only upon the right teaching alluded to in IB2, but also on the maintenance of correct sacrificial worship in the temple. Isa 5:1–7 laments God's judgement upon his people and the temple. Ezek 47:1–12 looks forward to a restored temple. This poem and its speaker appear to dwell in the tension between.

To summarise, the allusions in this section of the poem amount to far more than the artistic use of biblical language. There is a complex web of exegetical assumption underlying their use. The prophetic visions of a restored paradise and a restored temple, the messianic hope, and the concept of Israel as the planting of the LORD are here linked to the wisdom motif of the blessedness of the righteous person. The speaker's community is seen as the fulfillment of this prophetic vision. They are the righteous people of God who study and keep the law and from which will emerge the messianic community. As a metaphorical (?) temple, they represent the true worship of God.

Evidence for this exegesis can be found in other contemporary literature, some of which has been found at Qumran,[148] as well as in clearly sectarian works such as the *Rule of the Community* and the *Damascus Document*. Two quotes from these latter texts illustrate the point.

---

[147] Joseph M. Baumgarten, "4Q500 and the Ancient Conception of the Lord's Vineyard," *JJS* 40 (1989): 2–3.

[148] For a discussion of some of these texts see Shozo Fujita, "The Metaphor of Plant in Jewish Literature of the Intertestamental Period" *JSJ* 7 (1976): 40–44.

When these things exist in Israel the Community council shall be founded on truth, *Blank* to be an everlasting plantation, a holy house for Israel and the foundation of the holy of holies for Aaron, true witnesses for the judgement and chosen by the will (of God) to atone for the land and to render the wicked their retribution. (1QS VIII 4–6)[149]

For when they were unfaithful in forsaking him, he hid his face from Israel and from his sanctuary and delivered them up to the sword. But when he remembered the covenant with the forefathers, he saved a remnant for Israel and did not deliver them up to destruction ... he visited them and caused to sprout from Israel and from Aaron a shoot of the planting, in order to possess his land and to become fat with the good things of his soil. (CD I 3–8)[150]

2.5.2. *Testing*

Section II uses a recognisably biblical vocabulary of suffering and lament as well as alluding to a number of passages which describe suffering. The introductory stanza IIA1 signals a structural allusion to Isa 53:2–4. IIB1 contains a clear allusion to Isa 50:4–9; this is probably another structural allusion, but the lacunae preclude certainty. The two passages are linked by the common theme of the suffering of a righteous person. The former passage may already have been alluded to in section I and may be linked to that section by an underlying "root/shoot" exegesis.

This section has similarities to the biblical psalms of lament. Psalms 42, 77 and 88 in particular seem to be the source of allusions of the shorthand notation type. As well as providing suitable language, allusions to laments of Jeremiah and of Job confirm to the reader that the suffering of a righteous individual is the subject. The allusion to Ezek 21:7 has connotations of the suffering of righteous and wicked, and of judgement against the Jerusalem sanctuary. It is probable that other allusions are lost in the lacunae.

Some of the key words in this section also function as allusion markers. *Pain* and *affliction* are markers to Isa 53:2–4; they occur in the opening stanzas and in the transitional stanza at the beginning of the next section. *Sheol/dead* which demarcate the section are also markers to Ps 88:3–5 [4–6]. *Breakers* also occurs near the beginning and end of the section. This word occurs in only five places in the Hebrew Bible and there may be an underlying exegetical link between Ps 42:7 [8], 88:7

---

[149] García Martínez, and Tigchelaar, *The Dead Sea Scrolls Study Edition*, 89.
[150] García Martínez, and Tigchelaar, *The Dead Sea Scrolls Study Edition*, 551.

[8], and 2 Sam 22:5, all psalms describing distress.[151] There is probably another link made via the phrase *incurable pain*. These two words occur together in Jer 15:18 and by word play in Isa 53:3, both in the context of undeserved suffering. The link between Jer 20:9 and Isa 50:4 seems to be the prophet who suffers because of speaking God's words. There appears to be a development on the theme of *silence*, but this part of the poem is too damaged to be certain. The lacunae in this section preclude any other observations.

2.5.3. *Vindication*
Section III has two major themes with associated vocabulary. These are the theme of vindication using legal terminology and the theme and language of compassionate nurturing. Both of these themes are scattered throughout the book of Isaiah.[152]

The nurturing theme is introduced in IIIA2a by the line *my soul delights in the multitude of your compassions*. This allusion to Ps 94:19 and Isa 63:15 points forward to the unfolding of the parental theme. The key words from Ps 94:19, *delight* and *comfort*, both suggest motherly nurture. Isa 63:15 is followed by an appeal to the fatherhood of God. A closer look at Ps 94:12–23 reveals that its main theme is God's advocacy for the righteous against those who condemn them. Verse 14 states that "the Lord will not forsake his people; he will not abandon his heritage." The passage beginning with Isa 63:15 is a prayer of penitence which, in Isa 63:17, calls upon God to act on behalf of "the tribes that are your heritage" and "your holy people."

There are a number of compositions in the *Hodayot* which use the phrase *multitude of compassions*. In chapter three I noted its use in the context of a prayer of penitence, a context very similar to the context of the evoked scriptural text. I also noted that the aforementioned poem is one of several that use the phrase in the context of God's predestined vindication of the righteous and judgement upon the wicked. This poem's association of Ps 94:12–23 with Isa 63:15–64:12 could be a clue to possible elements of an exegesis linking these themes of penitence and vindication. If so, then this poem has taken an existing exegetical link and developed it in a novel way.

---

[151] The other two occurrences are in Jonah 2:3 [4] and Ps 93:4. For the related word "mouth of the womb" see 2 Kings 19:3=Isa 37:3; Hos 13:13.
[152] For legal terminology see for example Isa 1:18; 3:13; 41:1ff; 43:26; 50:7; 51:22.

Another key phrase of sub-section IIIA is *in your mercy* (בחסדיכה). The reference to God's mercy (cf. Lam 3:22, 32), and the language of waiting (יחל cf. Lam 3:21, 24) and hope (תוחלת/מקוה/תקוה cf. Lam 3:18, 21, 24, 29) combined with allusions to Lam 3:17, 31 indicate that a structural allusion to Lam 3:21–66 underlies IIIA. Lam 3:58–59 appeals to God for vindication from one who accepts his suffering as from the LORD. It has similarities of imagery to Isa 50:7–9, one of the evoked passages in section II.

The keywords of sub-section IIIB are *wisdom, might, glory* which belong to God, and thus to the speaker, whereas *shame of face* and *disgrace* are the lot of his adversaries. The legal language of judgement (משפט), pleading (ריב), justice (צדך), correction (תוכחה), and affliction (נגיע) is also evident as it was in IIIA2. The most clearly identifiable allusion is to Isa 41:11–12. This suggests a structural allusion to the court scene of Isa 41:1–29 in which God calls the nations to witness his vindication of Israel. Part of this biblical passage, Isa 41:17–20, was one of the main evoked passages of section I.

Sub-section IIIC has as its main keyword *compassion* and its main theme is the nurturing parenthood of God. This picks up on the phrase which demarcates the entire section, *multitude of compassions*. As mentioned above, this is a marker to Isa 63:15. In IIIA2a it was conflated with an allusion to Ps 94:19 which also evoked *delight* and *comfort*, words associated with motherly nurture (cf. Isa 66:11–13). This parenting metaphor is now filled out by allusions to Isa 46:3–4, 49:13–15, 63:15–16 and Ruth 4:15–16. Holm-Nielsen notes that this is the only known use of Ruth in the *Hodayot*.[153] It is difficult to see any connotations from the story of Naomi and her grandchild apart from the use of mothering language. Possibly the restoration of Naomi's heritage (נחלה cf. Ruth 4:10; Ps 94:14; Isa 63:17) was seen as analogous to the restoration by God of his people. Naomi's son, borne for her by Ruth, was an ancestor of Jesse and David. This gives a further link via Isa 11:1 to the shoot-stump motif of the first section.

---

[153] Holm-Nielsen, *Hodayot*, 169.

2.6. *Intertexts*

In my introduction to this poem I quoted Wallenstein regarding the two "well-developed ideas" of the "everlasting branch" and the "joy in tribulation." I will consider the first of those ideas in §2.6.2, and the second in §2.6.3. But firstly I wish to compare this very long poem with another very long poem from the *Hodayot*.

2.6.1. *Another Long Hodayah and its Sequel*

There are a number of reasons for comparing this poem with the hodayah found in 1QH^a XIII 22–XV 8 [V 20–VII 5].[154] Firstly, as I have already commented in the introduction to this chapter, the poem in columns XIII [V] and XIV [VI] and the poem in columns XVI [VIII] and XVII [IX] are, as far as is known, the two longest compositions in 1QH^a. There may be, as Stegemann appears to think, two or more long poems within 1QH^a XX 7–XXV 33, but the lacunae make the division of poems within this part of the scroll difficult to ascertain.[155] This would still in any case make these the two longest poems in the hypothetical book of Teacher Hymns. Secondly, they both make use of similar imagery. Thirdly, they both contain long laments which have several coincidences of distinctive biblical language (see below). In addition, there are a number of similarities with the poem in 1QH^a XV 9–28 [VII 6–25], which Holm-Nielsen has noted "almost gives the impression of being a continuation" of the previous poem.[156]

One would expect that for a long poem to be comprehensible to a reader a clear structure is very important. I have argued that the poem found in XVI 5–XVII 36 [VIII 4–IX 36] is very well structured as three clear sections of comparable length. While not having analysed this other long poem in detail, my first impression is that it has a much less obvious structure. This view is supported by the lack of agreement by those who have analysed its structure.

Newsom also notes that the poem "does not have a strongly marked formal structure." She does, however, discern an alternation of top-

---

[154] This hodayah has already been discussed briefly in §3.6.1 of chapter three as an intertext of the second poem.
[155] Stegemann, "The Number of Psalms in 1QHodayot^a," 204 n. 47, 219, 229. See also Schuller, "Hodayot," 86, n. 17; Puech, "Quelques aspects," 53.
[156] Holm-Nielsen, *Hodayot*, 137.

ics which she labels A¹, B¹ etc. These "strophes" are of very disparate length, as noted by Newsom herself. Her division reflects her interest in the rhetorical shape of the composition rather than any formal divisions. She considers that topic A concerns the "antagonism of the speaker's associates" and topic B is that of "divine assistance." The final description of distress XV 4–8 [VII 1–5], which Newsom labels A⁵, is not followed by a corresponding B strophe. Newsom comments that this unexpected ending for a prayer of thanks is the most noticeable feature of the poem's structure. She describes this lack of a final affirmation of God's help as an "empty space" which invites the hearers to provide community support for the speaker in the spirit of the preceding B strophes.[157]

Douglas has, by contrast, identified this problematic ending as properly belonging with the first part of the composition XIII 22–XIV 6b [V 20–VI 3b], which he labels as composition 22a. He classes this as a lament. He discerns two other main sections, XIV 6d–22a [VI 3d–19a] and XIV 22b–39 [VI 19b–36], which he calls compositions 22b and 22c respectively. He considers that these are eschatological discourses. Although arguing for the unity of the composition, he suggests that either it was composed as four discourses in an ABBA structure,[158] or that composition 22a was redacted by the original author to include the eschatological material.[159] His divisions coincide well with Tanzer's observation that XIV 9–22 [VI 6–19] is a distinct section within the poem.[160]

I consider that the structural analysis of Douglas is more plausible than that of Newsom. Her identification of the first two B strophes is not convincing. They each consist of only one or two poetic lines and do not break the flow of the lament. She herself comments that the reference to divine assistance is only fleeting and that the text is more concerned with describing the conflict. However, her remaining two B strophes are more substantial. Her third B strophe corresponds with Douglas' composition 22b. The strophes that she labels A¹ and B¹ correspond with Douglas' composition 22c. However, her main argument

---

[157] Newsom, *The Self as Symbolic Space*, 331–342.
[158] I.e. lament part 1 (XIII 22–XIV 6b), eschatological discourse 1 (XIV 6d–22a), eschatological discourse 2 (XIV 22b–39), lament part 2 (XV 4–8).
[159] Douglas, "Power and Praise," 194–195.
[160] Tanzer, "The Sages at Qumran," 106–116.

depends upon the latter two B strophes giving a positive description of community life in contrast to the betrayal depicted in the A strophes. Therefore her analysis of the poem's overall effect still remains plausible. Her explanation of why the poem ends on such a negative note is particularly intriguing. In summary, I consider that, while the two analyses I have described are illuminating, there is still more work to be done on the structure of this poem.

This poem employs many images and metaphors one after the other with no apparent linkage between them. This is in contrast to the poem just analysed which employs one underlying image/theme for each main section; i.e. garden imagery in section I, bodily suffering in section II, nurturing imagery in section III. However, the two poems have distinctive images in common. They both make use of the image of a hidden well.¹⁶¹ They both make quite extensive use of shoot/eternal planting imagery.¹⁶²

They both also contain long laments and expressions of confidence which have strong similarities. The use of bodily images in laments is common, but both of these poems employ this imagery in a sustained and extensive manner. There are some particular linguistic similarities, also noted by Douglas. These are as follow:

- The phrase כאיב אנוש (incurable pain) occurs once in the HB (Isa 17:11; cf. Jer 15:18, 30:15),¹⁶³ and in the Dead Sea texts only in 1QHᵃ XIII 30 [V 28]; XVI 29 [VIII 28], 4Q429 2 11.
- The word pair שאה ומשואה (ruin and destruction) occurs in the HB only in Zeph 1:15, Job 30:3, 38:27 and in the Dead Sea texts only in 1QHᵃ XIII 32 [V 30] and XVII 6 [IX 6].
- קנה usually means "reed" in the HB and only in Job 31:22 is it used for a bone. It occurs with this meaning in the Dead Sea

---

¹⁶¹ "Trees of life by a well of mystery; hidden things in the midst of all the trees of water." (1QHᵃ XVI 7 [VIII 6]); "And the mystery you have hidden in me ... ... you have concealed the well of insight." (1QHᵃ XIII 27–28 [V 25–26]). This has been noted by both Holm-Nielsen and Douglas. Douglas calls it the motif of hidden revelation. See Holm-Nielsen, *Hodayot*, 107 n. 29; Douglas, "Power and Praise," 156.

¹⁶² e.g. "And they shall be for the sprouting of a shoot for a planting of eternity ... ... and the sprout of the holy shoot for a planting of truth ..." (1QHᵃ XVI 7–12 [VIII 6–11]); "their root will sprout like a flower of the field for ever to make a shoot grow in the branches of the everlasting plantation ... ..." (1QHᵃ XIV 21–23 [VII 18–20]). Douglas, "Power and Praise," 197, also notes similarities of imagery.

¹⁶³ See my observations in §§ 2.4.2 and 2.5.2 on the possible marker to Jer 15:8 or Jer 30:15.

texts only in 1QH͏ͣ XV 5 [VII 2] and XVI 34 [VIII 33] (the only other occurrences are in 1Q16 9–10 3; 4Q266 16a 3; 11Q19 IX 9; 11Q21 2 2).[164]

Douglas also notes that both these poems employ the language of the lawsuit, as does the poem in 1QH͏ͣ XV 9–28 [VII 6–25].[165] To these observations I would add the following phrases. *To end strength* (להתם כוח) occurs in 1QH͏ͣ XVI 32 [VIII 31], and XIII 31, 38 [V 29, 36]. *I know that there is hope* (ואדעה כי יש מקוה) occurs in 1QH͏ͣ XVII 14 [IX 14] and XIV 9 [VI 6]. *I will take comfort* (ואנחמה) occurs in 1QH͏ͣ XVII 13 [IX 13] and XIV 10 [VI 7]. *Multitude of compassions* (המון רחמים) occurs in 1QH͏ͣ XVII 8, 34 [IX 8, 34] and XIV 12 [VI 9]. *(Abundance of) forgiveness* (רוב סליחות) occurs in 1QH͏ͣ XVII 13, 34 [IX 13, 34] and XIV 12 [VI 9].

Douglas argues that the two compositions also have sufficient distinctiveness to make it unlikely that one "served as a pattern for the other." He prefers to suppose that the similarities are due to them both having the same author.[166] One possibly very significant factor to which I believe Douglas has not given sufficient weight is the very large number of similarities that 1QH͏ͣ XIII 22–XV 8 [V 20–VII 5] appears to have with other compositions in 1QH͏ͣ. When one takes these into account in total, the distinctiveness of this poem appears very small. In this study alone, I have observed similarities with all the other compositions analysed.

There are also a number of striking similarities with the psalm of confidence in 1QH͏ͣ XV 9–28 [VII 6–25], which I have dubbed a sequel to the previous long hodayah. As in IIB of this poem, in XV 13–14 [VII 10–11] God makes *my tongue as your disciples'* (לשוני כלמודיך) (cf. Isa 50:4) and *lips of deceit shall be silenced* (תאלמנה שפתי שקר). In XV 21–22 [VII 18–19] there is a reference to a *planting* and a *shoot* (cf. Isa 60:21), giving a link to IA of this poem. Similarly to IIIB2, in XV 25 [VII 22]

---

[161] See Douglas, "Power and Praise," 160–162; Abegg, et al., *The Dead Sea Scrolls Concordance, Volume 1*, 334, 490, 656. Douglas notes two other similarities which are rare in the scrolls and the HB, as follows: The pairing יגון (grief) and אנחה (sighing) occurs in XVI 28 [VIII 27] and XIII 36 [V 34]. This depends upon a reconstruction by Douglas. The noun מרור (bitterness) occurs in XVI 29, 38 [VIII 28, 37] and XIII 34, 36 [V 32, 34]. I consider that this may be an echo of Lam 3:15.

[165] In particular he notes that the term ריבי (my lawsuit) occurs in the Dead Sea texts only in these three compositions. But see also 4Q511 48–49+51 7, where it is probably a plural noun. See Douglas, "Power and Praise," 164–165; Abegg, et al., *The Dead Sea Scrolls Concordance, Volume 1*, 684.

[166] Douglas does however allow the possibility that XIV 6–39 is a pseudepigraphic addition to the poem. Douglas, "Power and Praise," 162, 206.

there is a reference to *those that war against me* (אנשי מלחמה) and *those that strive against me* (בעלי רבי) (cf. Isa 41:11–12). But most striking of all are the coincidence of imagery with section IIIC of this poem. In XV 23–25 [VII 20–22] the speaker describes himself as a *father* and *nurse* to members of his community. They are *like a suckli[ng at its mother's breast]* (כיונ[ק שדי אמו]) and *like the delight* (כשעשע) of *an infant in the embrace of its nurse* (עוליל בחיק אומניו) (cf. Isa 49:15, 66:10–13; Num 1:9; Ruth 4:15–16). In XV 27–28 [VII 24–25] the speaker declares that *I shine with sevenfold light* (הופעתי בא[ור] שבעתים) (cf. Isa 30:26).

Finally, the short poem in 1QH\u1d43 XV 29–36 [VII 26–33] contains law court language and the phrase *multitude of your compassions*. It would require further analysis to substantiate, but I provisionally hypothesise that 1QH\u1d43 XIII 22–XV 8 [V 20–VII 5], while an individual poem in its own right, has been constructed as a pastiche of ideas and images drawn from a number of other compositions. The following two poems, 1QH\u1d43 XV 9–28 [VII 6–25] and 29–36 [26–33] may also be sequels. As psalms of confidence perhaps they are meant to counteract the negative ending of the preceding long poem. Thus, while I agree with Douglas that there is a literary dependence between this poem and several others,[167] I consider that there are strong indications that the dependence is from those other poems to this one.

2.6.2. Garden Imagery

The interrelated imageries of plant, garden, and life-giving water are common biblical ones which have been utilised and developed widely in Jewish literature of the late Second Temple period. For ease of discussion I will discuss each of these images separately, bearing in mind that in this poem and elsewhere they are closely intertwined.

Fujita observes that the metaphor of God's people having been planted in the land appears in the Deuteronomistic source (2 Sam 7:10; cf. Ps 80) and is particularly strong in Jeremiah.[168] Israel is described as a vine (Jer 2:21) or a green olive tree (Jer 11:16–17) which God had planted, but which would be removed. However the destruction is not complete, as the remnant are promised that God will once again plant them in the land (Jer 24:6, 31:27–28, 32:41).

---

[167] Douglas notes this dependence specifically several times. See Douglas, "Power and Praise," 130, 135, 162, 198–204.
[168] Fujita, "The Metaphor of Plant," 30.

In Ezekiel and Isaiah the metaphor is also used negatively of judgement (e.g. Ezek 15:1–8; Isa 5:1–7, 10:33–34) and positively of promised restoration (Isa 60:21, 61:3). As well as the nation as a whole, the image can refer to the royal line as representative of the nation (Ezek 17:1–24, 19:10–14; Isa 11:1).

In *Jubilees*, the phrases "upright plant" and "plant of righteousness" are used of God's covenant people, the chosen line of descendants of Abraham (*Jub.* 1:16, 7:34, 16:26, 21:24, 36:6) who will possess the land in contrast with those who are "uprooted" because of sin (e.g. *Jub.* 22:20.) In *Jub* 16:26 one particular descendant is singled out as the "holy seed." The phrase is used similarly in 1 Enoch, where the plant of righteousness is also described as an eternal plant, and is used in a clearly eschatological context (1 Enoch 10:16, 93:1, 2, 14, cf. 84:6).

Either or both of these compositions has probably influenced the use of the term in 1QS VIII 5, XI 8, CD I 7, 4Q418 81+81a 13 and the already mentioned two long hodayot in 1QH^a.[169] In the *Damascus Document* the term "shoot of the planting" appears to be a designation for the pre-cursor to the community being addressed. In the *Rule of the Community* "eternal plantation" appears to refer to the community itself.

It is but a short step by association from the idea of God's chosen people as an eternal plant to the idea of the garden of God, particularly in light of the eschatological hope, already evident in Isaiah, of a return to paradisiacal conditions. Thus we read in *Pss Sol.* 14:3 "The garden of the Lord, the trees of life, are his holy ones. Their planting is rooted for ever."[170]

A number of texts use the motifs of the garden of God and the tree of life.[171] David Aune notes that there were two primary tree of life traditions which eventually merged. These were "eschatological access to the tree of life in the heavenly paradise, clearly a metaphor for the

---

[169] Abegg lists 23 references for מטע and מטעת of which only these obviously use the word in a similar context. See Abegg, et al., *The Dead Sea Scrolls Concordance, Volume 1*, 442.

[170] cf. "And I said, Blessed, O Lord, are those who have been planted in thy ground, and those who have a place in thy paradise, and grow up in the growth of thy trees" (*Odes Sol.* 11:18). See Brock "The Psalms of Solomon," 673; J.A. Emerton, "The Odes of Solomon," in *The Apocryphal Old Testament.* (ed. H.F.D. Sparks; Oxford: Clarendon, 1984), 702.

[171] *1 Enoch* 25–32; *T. Levi* 18:11.

enjoyment of eternal life" and "the tree(s) of life as a metaphor for the elect community."[172] It appears to be the latter which is particularly prominent in this poem, although there is probably also an eschatological element in the partly damaged section which uses the motif of expulsion from Eden.

As already noted in the close reading, there is also a wisdom tradition which likens the wise, righteous person to a tree planted by the water. Wisdom herself is also likened to a tree by Ben Sira, and then identified with the Torah of Moses; this is in turn likened to an overflowing river. Ben Sira as a teacher of wisdom sees himself as a rivulet bearing water from Wisdom's stream to water his own garden and beyond. This has similarities to the way that the speaker refers to himself in IB2 of the hodayah. There is also a passing reference to a "shining like dawn" motif; this is similar to the motif in the opening stanza of the second hodayah considered in chapter three. The significance of these similarities is to make the claims of the speaker in these hodayot appear less extravagant than some commentators have suggested. Perhaps the author(s) of these poems was, like Ben Sira himself, neither more nor less than a humble wisdom teacher, occasionally carried away by his own rhetoric. The similarities make the last part of Ben Sira's poem worth quoting in full:

> As for me, I was like a canal from a river,
> like a water channel into a garden.
> I said, "I will water my garden
> and drench my flower-beds."
> And lo, my canal became a river,
> and my river a sea.
> I will again make instruction shine forth like the dawn,
> and I will make it clear from far away.
> I will again pour out teaching like prophecy,
> and leave it to all future generations. (Sir. 24:30–33)

Thus Ben Sira takes us on to the third distinct but related metaphor, life-giving water. The use of this metaphor is prolific in the Hebrew Bible, and this hodayah alludes to many such passages. As we have seen God's provision and restoration is likened to streams in the desert and the one who trusts in God is likened to a tree planted by waters. The Temple sanctuary, where God is particularly present, is also associated

---

[172] David Aune, *Revelation 1–5*, (Word Biblical Commmentary 52a; Dallas: Word Books, 1998).

with life giving water. However, the identification of Torah with water appears to be a relatively late development. Within the Hebrew Bible, William P. Brown attributes to the author of Psalm 1 the unique use of water imagery in this way:

> The manner in which the water metaphor is deployed in Psalm 1 indicates innovative usage. Departing from its traditional association with the temple, water imagery, redirected by the poet, indicates the written and spoken words of *tôrâ*. *Tôrâ* replaces the temple as the sustaining and guiding force for the psalmist. *Tôrâ* becomes the object of deepest desire for those who thirst for God's sanctuary presence. By identifying *tôrâ* with flowing channels, the poet imbues such imagery with unmistakable didactic nuance. The individual is "instructed" as the tree is nourished by water. Authoritative instruction is thereby identified as the psalmist's sole source of sustenance.[173]

Thus, while there is no evidence of direct influence from either Psalm 1 or Ben Sira, the hodayah appears to reflect an emerging tradition. This metaphorical usage also appears in the *Damascus Document*, where in a pesher on Num 21:18 we are told that "The well is Torah."[174]

2.6.3. *Suffering and Vindication*

Sections II and III of this poem describe the suffering and vindication of a righteous person and appears to have been patterned in part on Isa 50:4–9 and Isa 52:13–53:12. Nickelsburg has identified this theme in late Second Temple literature, for example the Wisdom of Solomon. He traces its development from biblical wisdom tales such as Joseph (Gen 37ff), via the influence of the Isaiah servant passages to Dan 12:1–3. He also identifies the related judgement scene form in, for example, 1 Enoch 94–104; he likewise traces the development of this form via the influence of passages in Isaiah.[175] The ideas in this hodayah can be understood in the context of these developing concepts and forms. However, I am not aware of any Second Temple texts with any close resemblance to sections II and III of this hodayah.

Section II is an example of the common genre of lament, and it thus has many similarities with biblical compositions which employ this genre. These were discussed in §§2.4.2 and 2.5.2. Section III is very distinctive. Both legal and nurturing language are used of God

---

[173] W.P. Brown, *Seeing the Psalms*, (Louisville: Westminster John Knox Press, 2002), 131.
[174] "The well that the leaders sank, that the nobles of the people dug, with the scepter, with the staff." (Num 21:18; cf. CD III 16, VI 3–7).
[175] Nickelsburg, *Resurrection, Immortality, and Eternal Life*, 170–176.

elsewhere, but the interweaving of them in this way is unusual. Only in Isaiah, the main inspiration for this composition, do we find anything comparable. I have not been able to find any other Second Temple texts which elaborate upon these themes in this distinctive way. The use of mothering language for God also sets this poem apart.

2.7. *Observations and Comments*

The most immediately apparent characteristic of this poem is its length. Some commentators have questioned its unity because it is less obvious exactly how the seemingly different topics are linked. Holm-Nielsen has already observed that the poem has three distinct themes. In his words these are "a description of the salvation which God has provided within the community, followed by a portrayal of misery, and concluded with a developed declaration of confidence in God."[176]

By detailed analysis of the keywords I have shown that the poem is not only divided into three sections by theme, but that there is a clear structure based upon the use of keywords. I have also shown that the poem makes use of a variety of genres and poetic devices. Each of the themes is developed in an appropriate biblical style, namely mashal, lament and psalm of confidence. While the overall biblical basis for the poem appears to be Isaiah, the poem alludes to supplementary biblical passages typical of the style of each section. The poem, then, is an impressive piece of sustained artistry. As we shall see in the following chapter, there are other poems in the collection which rival it in terms of intricacy and allusion. However none of these is of such an ambitious length.

In §2.6.1 I have briefly considered another poem of comparable length which also has several similarities of language and style with this poem. The analysis of Douglas and Tanzer indicates that this poem may also consist of three sections. Although I expect that if subjected to a similar analysis this poem too would yield up its structuring principles, my initial impression is that it is not as intricate or as allusive as the one which I have studied in detail. One factor which leads me to say this is that none of the images used by the poem is sustained. Instead, it piles up one image after another. Most of these images seem to occur in greater detail in other poems. I have proposed that the pos-

---

[176] Holm-Nielsen, *Hodayot*, 170.

sibility that this other long poem may be a pastiche warrants further consideration.

To return to the poem which is the main subject of this chapter, the second most obvious feature is its use of Isaiah. This was also noted by Holm-Nielsen. He suggested that the allusions were predominately from "the servant" passages in Isaiah. I would widen this to the whole of Isaiah 40–66. The particularly dominant passages, in approximate order of main use are Isa 41:17–19, 60:13–61:3, 53:1–4, 50:4–9, 49:13–15, 63:15–16. Ezekiel, Jeremiah and Psalms are also prominent.

Many have seen this poem as autobiographical, although Holm-Nielsen early observed that the extensive use of scriptural allusion argues against supposing that the poet's own experience is being described. In §2.5 I have suggested that the poem is more exegetical than autobiographical, in that it reflects how the community interpreted its identity in light of scripture. While, as demonstrated by the various pesher material in other documents, the sectarians utilized a wide selection of scriptures for this exegesis, the broad brush strokes of their self-understanding may well have been drawn from Isaiah. I have summarised this in terms of preparation, testing, and vindication.

CHAPTER FIVE

TWO ESCHATOLOGICAL POEMS

1. *Introduction*

In this chapter I shall consider two adjacent poems, each with an eschatological theme. Although at first sight there appears to be no other reason for considering these two compositions together, my analysis will show that they do in fact have much else in common.

2. *Three Images of Distress*
1QH^a XI 6–19 [III 5–18]

There was considerable early interest in this poem sparked by its supposed messianic content. One of the first and most enthusiastic advocates of a messianic interpretation was Dupont-Sommer.[1] He speculated that there was an underlying "myth concerning the Mother of the Messiah" developed from Isa 7:14 and Mic 5:2 and also appearing in Rev 12.[2] The strongest advocates of a non-messianic reading were Silberman and Hinson.[3]

The poem is also very complex and employs strong word play which defies translation. Those commentators who have tried to fathom its structure include Silberman, Hinson, Thiering, Frechette and Newsom.[4] Their very lack of agreement testifies to the poem's complexity.

---

[1] A. Dupont-Sommer, "La mère du Messie et la mère de l'Aspic dans un hymne de Qoumrân," *RHR* 147 (1955): 174–188.
[2] Dupont-Sommer, *The Essene Writings From Qumran*, 208 n. 1.
[3] Lou H. Silberman, "Language and Structure in the Hodayot (1QH3)," *JBL* 75 (1956): 96–106; Glenn Hinson, "Hodayoth, III, 6–18: In What Sense Messianic?" *RevQ* 2 (1959–1960): 183–204.
[4] Silberman, "Language and Structure in the Hodayot"; Hinson, "Hodayoth, III, 6–18"; Thiering, "The Poetic Forms of the Hodayot;" Frechette, "Chiasm;" Newsom, *The Self as Symbolic Space*, 240–253.

Finally, and of particular interest to this study, the poem was reckoned by Holm-Nielsen to contain the greatest number of biblical allusions of all the poems in the *Hodayot*.[5]

2.1. *Delimitation and Text*[6]

This composition can be found on Sukenik plate 37. Sukenik numbered it as III 5–18 but Stegemann and Puech have reassigned it as XI 6–19. The damage to the first few lines of the column and the last few of the preceding one make it difficult to pinpoint accurately the start of this composition. Lines 1–3 of the column are extremely damaged; the damage to the beginning and end of lines 4–6 leaves room to restore a blank space and/or opening formula on any one of them.

Stegemann and Douglas reconstruct the opening formula in line 6,[7] and I have followed them on the grounds that beginning in any of the preceding lines would give an uncharacteristically long opening stanza. The end of the composition is clearly indicated by a blank space in line 19 and the opening formula of the next composition in line 20.

Parts of this poem are preserved in the Cave 4 manuscripts. There are some significant variations, which are noted in the footnotes to the Hebrew text and the translation. 1QH^a XI 12–14 overlaps with 4QH^b 4 1–2. 1QH^a XI 14–19 overlaps with 4QpapH^f 5 1–7.[8]

---

[5] Holm-Nielsen, *Hodayot*, 61.

[6] Unless otherwise stated, references in this section are to: Sukenik, *The Dead Sea Scrolls*; Stegemann, "The Material Reconstruction of 1QHodayot," 280; Puech, "Quelques aspects," 41–43.

[7] Note that Douglas has line 7 where I, following Stegemann, have line 6. Newsom, who uses Sukenik's line numbers throughout, starts the composition in line 4 [3]. See Douglas, "Power and Praise," 172 n. 83; Newsom, *The Self as Symbolic Space*, 242–245; Stegemann, "The Number of Psalms in 1QHodayot^a," 203.

[8] Schuller, "Hodayot," 135–156, 219–220.

1QH^a XI 6–19 [III 5–18]

6 [ ] vacat   אודכה אדוני כיא אמ[ת] פיכה ותצילוני[10] מ[כל איבי]ומ[שאול][11]
7 [הוש]עתה[12] נפש[י] [ ] יחשובוני וישימו נפש[י] ב[מ]צולות ים כאוניה[13]
8 וכעיר מבצר מלפנ[י] אויביה ו[]אהיה[14] בצוקה כמו אשת לדה מבכריה כיא נהפכו ציריה
9 וחבל נמרץ על משבריה להחיל בכור הריה כיא באו בנים עד משברי מות
10 והרית גבר הצרה בחבליה כיא במשברי מות תמליט זכר ובחבלי שאול יגיח
11 מכור הריה פלא יועץ עם גבורתו ויפלט גבר ממשברים בהריתו החישו כול
12 משברים וחבלי מרץ במולדיהם ופלצות להורותם ובמולדיו יהפכו כול צירים
13 בכור הריה והרית אפעה לחבל נמרץ ומשברי שחת לכול מעשי פלצות וירועו
14 אושי קיר כאוניה על פני מים ויהמו שחקים בקול המון ויושבי עפר
15 כיורדי ימים נבעתים מהמון מים וחכמיה[ם][15] למו כמלחים במצולות כי תתבלע
16 כול חכמתם[16] בהמות ימים ברתוח תהומות על נבוכי מים ויתרגשו[17] לרום גלים
17 ומשברי מים בהמון קולם ובהתרגשם יפתחו ש[אול][ ][.] [ ] כו[ל] חצי שחת
18 עם מצעדם[18] לתהום ישמיעו קולם ויפתחו[19] שערי [עולם תחת][20] מעשי אפעה
19 ויסגרו דלתי שחת בעד הרית עול ובריחי עולם בעד כול רוחי אפעה   vacat

2.2. Translation

I   (6) [*Blank*   I thank you, O Lord, for truth] (is) your mouth
and you have delivered me from[all my enemies]
and from[Sheol] (7) you have [sav]ed [my] soul.

---

[9] For this reconstruction see Stegemann "The Number of Psalms in 1QHodayot^a," 203.

[10] Most scholars read thus although Sukenik has ותצו לנו.

[11] For justification of this reconstruction see §2.5 of this chapter.

[12] I follow Licht and Holm-Nielsen who reconstruct thus on the basis of meaning although no trace of letters is evident in the remains of the preceding lacuna. See Licht, *Thanksgiving Scroll*, 78; Holm-Nielsen, *Hodayot*, 52 n. 6.

[13] Most recent scholars read thus although Sukenik has באוניה. See Holm-Nielsen, *Hodayot*, 52 n. 8.

[14] Most commentators follow this reconstruction by Licht. See Licht, *Thanksgiving Scroll*, 79.

[15] Sukenik transcribes the supralinear addition as כו. But ם is also possible and makes better sense. See Malachi Martin, *The Scribal Character of the Dead Sea Scrolls*, vol. 2 (Louvain: Université de Louvain, Institut Orientaliste, 1958), 477.

[16] 4Q432 has the different orthography חוכמתמה. See Schuller, "Hodayot," 219.

[17] 4Q432 omits the ו at the beginning of this word. See Schuller, "Hodayot," 219.

[18] 4Q432 may have a space here or a slightly expanded text. See Schuller, "Hodayot," 219.

[19] 4Q432 has ו[יפחת]ו. See Schuller, "Hodayot," 219.

[20] This restoration suggested by Schuller. The restoration of שאול לכול] followed by Douglas and Newsom is contradicted by 4Q432. See Schuller, "Hodayot," 219; Douglas, "Power and Praise," 173; Newsom, *The Self as Symbolic Space*, 245.

IIA [... ... ...] they esteem me
and they set [my] soul like a ship[21] in the [d]epths of the sea
(8) and like a city fortified from before [her enemies].
I am in distress like a woman giving birth for the first time.[22]

IIB1a For her PANGS HAVE COME SUDDENLY upon her,
(9) and AGONISING PAIN upon her *cervix*[23]
to bring to birth the FIRSTBORN of the *mother*.[24]
IIB1b For children have come up to the *throes* of death
(10) and the *mother* of a boy is distressed in her pains.
IIB1c For in the *throes* of death she gives birth to a son,
and in the pains of Sheol bursts forth (11) from the crucible of the
mother a wonderful counsellor with his might,
and a boy is delivered from the *throes*.

IIB2a In his *mother* come quickly all (12) the *throes*
and PAINS OF AGONY[25] in their birth
and TERROR to their *mothers*;
IIB2(b) and in his birth all PANGS COME SUDDENLY
IIB2(b) (13) IN THE CRUCIBLE[26] of the *mother*
IIB2c And the *mother* of VANITY for AGONISING PAIN
and the *throes* of the pit for all WORKS of TERROR.

IIC1a (14) And the foundations of the wall shake like a ship upon the surface
of the WATERS
and the clouds roar with a SOUND of TUMULT
IIC1b And those who dwell in dust (are) (15) like those who go down to the
seas
they are terrified from the TUMULT of the WATERS
IIC1c And her[27] wise men for them like sailors in the depths
for swallowed up (is) (16) all their wisdom in the TUMULT of the seas.

---

[21] Holm-Nielsen, *Hodayot*, 52 n. 8, translates as "in affliction" following Sukenik's transcription.

[22] I follow Holm-Nielsen in reading as a hiphil participle. See Holm-Nielsen, *Hodayot*, 52 n. 10; Mansoor, *Thanksgiving Hymns*, 112 n. 7.

[23] Literally the "breaking forth" (of the baby); i.e. the mouth of the womb. This translation is less cumbersome, though possibly anachronistic.

[24] Literally "pregnant-one" but this gives a cumbersome translation.

[25] I have kept more difficult reading; some scholars emend to "agonising pain" as in lines 9 and 13.

[26] A double meaning is probably intended; "in the crucible" can be translated "the firstborn."

[27] Or translate as "their" reading supralinear addition as final ם.

IIC2a In the seething of the deeps over the springs of the WATERS
       (and)[28] they rage forth to the heights of the waves
       (17) and the *breakers* of the WATERS in the TUMULT of their SOUND
IIC2b And in their raging forth they open Sh[eo]l
       [... ... al]l the arrows of the pit
       (18) with their going[29] to the deep they make heard their SOUND
IIC2c And the [eternal] gates open[30] [under] WORKS of VANITY
       (19) and the doors of the pit shut behind the *mother* of wickedness
       And eternal bolts behind all the spirits of VANITY.   Blank

2.3. *Analysis of structure*

I. Introductory Stanza	XI 6 [III 5]
II. Main Body of Poem	XI 7–19 [III 6–18]
A. Three Metaphors—ship, city, childbirth	XI 7–8a
B. Childbirth	XI 8b–13c
1. The birth of a boy (each verse begins with "for.")	
a. her PANGS; PAIN upon her *cervix*; FIRSTBORN	INCLUSIO 1
b. up to the *throes* (of death)	
c. in the *throes* of death ... a boy delivered from the *throes*	
2. The agony of childbirth	
a. all the *throes*, PAINS and TERROR of childbirth	INCLUSIO 2
b. PANGS in-the-crucible/FIRSTBORN	INCLUSIO 1
c. PAIN and TERROR; *throes* of the pit	INCLUSIO 2
mother of VANITY; WORKS (of terror)	INCLUSIO 3
C. Ship and City	XI 13d–19
1. The city and its inhabitants are like a ship in the depths of the sea	
a. like a ship upon the WATERS ... SOUND of TUMULT	
b. like those who go down to the seas ... TUMULT of the WATERS	
c. like sailors in the depths ... TUMULT of the seas	
2. The surging waters of the deep and the gates of Sheol	
a. *breakers* of the WATERS in the TUMULT of their SOUND	
b. Sheol opened; arrows of the pit make their SOUND	
c. WORKS of VANITY; doors shut behind the *mother* of wickedness and spirits of VANITY	INCLUSIO 3

Although the first few lines are badly damaged it is probable that the poem begins with an opening stanza using the introductory formula אודכה אדוני followed by a declaration of God's deliverance. In this case, but not in all the poems, I have judged the short opening stanza to be

---

[28] The prefix "and" is missing in 4Q432. See Schuller, "Hodayot," 219.
[29] Douglas and Williams translate this phrase as "dog their steps." See Douglas, "Power and Praise," 174; Williams, "Parallelism," 181.
4Q432 has a space or slightly expanded text. See Schuller, "Hodayot," 219.
[30] Or "break;" for comments on the meaning of this verb see Schuller, "Hodayot," 220.

separate from the main body of the poem; it seems to be included more for the sake of conformity to the basic form than for any reason integral to the poem's structure.

Another distinct possibility would be to have one rather long introductory stanza ending in line 8. However, I have judged that the main body of the poem begins in line 7, in a poetic line which ends with the phrase *they esteem me*. The next three lines introduce metaphors for the speaker's distress, namely *a ship in the depths of the sea, a fortified city* and *a woman giving birth for the first time*. Some commentators[31] place the line introducing the third metaphor at the start of the next stanza; this has the effect of emphasising its importance over the other two metaphors. As I explain in the close reading, I consider that this emphasis on the third metaphor is mistaken and that all three metaphors are interwoven throughout the poem.

The poem is so dense and intricate that, although there have been several attempts to analyse its structure, there has been little agreement. Thiering,[32] and more recently, Frechette[33] have looked to chiasm as the main structural device. The weakness of this approach is its dependence on the repetition of words or phrases and neglect of context and meaning. This particular poem contains an abundance of word play and repetition into which it is possible to read a number of plausible structures.

Both Silberman and Hinson[34] are keen to play down the supposed messianic context and so have analysed the use of the three metaphors in some detail. By concentrating more on content they divide the poem into two main parts. The first part is based on the metaphor of childbirth and the second on the interwoven city and sea metaphors. I have followed Hinson's division in broad outline, but have tried also to pay attention to other more stylistic factors.

Therefore, on the basis of the use of the metaphors and a moderate attention to repetition of phrases I have divided the main body of the poem as follows. There is a short sub-section, IIA, which introduces the metaphors and two main sub-sections, IIB and IIC, which elaborate them in reverse order to their introduction.

---

[31] e.g. Dupont-Sommer, "Le Livre des Hymnes," 36; Douglas, "Power and Praise," 173.
[32] Thiering, "The Poetic Forms of the Hodayot," 189–209.
[33] Frechette, "Chiasm," 71–102.
[34] Silberman, "Language and Structure," 106; Hinson, "Hodayoth, III, 6–18," 199–200.

Sub-section IIB elaborates upon the metaphor of childbirth. It begins and ends with the two phrases PANGS COME SUDDENLY and IN-THE-CRUCIBLE/FIRSTBORN OF THE *mother*[35] forming an inclusio. This first inclusio does not encompass IIB2c, which is a transitional couplet. I have placed it in stanza IIB2 partly because it would disturb the pattern of the following stanza. But it also matches the vocabulary of IIB2a (PAIN, TERROR, *throes*); although this symmetry may not strictly speaking merit the term, I have shown it as inclusio 2 in the structural table. Alternatively one could see the phrase AGONISING PAIN as forming an inclusio with the identical phrase in IIB1a. Verse IIB2c is transitional because it also matches the vocabulary at the end of sub-section IIC (MOTHER, VANITY, WORKS); this is the third inclusio shown in the structural table.

Most commentators have noted the contrast between the *mother of a boy* in IIB1b and the *mother of vanity/wickedness* in IIB2c and IIC2c. Dupont-Sommer[36] described the poem as a diptych portraying two women, the mother of the Messiah and the mother of Belial, signifying the congregations of the just and the wicked respectively. Newsom likewise states that "the whole symbolic economy of this poem is organised around the comparison and contrast of the two female figures."[37] She argues that the poem addresses the sectarian's problem of identity. This arises, she argues, because in the sectarian worldview there is no clear distinction between the righteous and the wicked, depending as it does upon God's choice. In her view the poem is an attempt to account for the "difference between the self and the other." She suggests that symbolically the mother of the boy represents the speaker with the gift of God's insight hidden within; the mother of the viper represents the enemy.[38]

I disagree with this extremely dualistic interpretation of the poem. There is undoubtedly a comparison, but the mother is not the major metaphor in IIC. Sub-section IIC elaborates the ship and city metaphors. As observed by Silberman, "The city's inhabitants יושבי עפר and the ship's sailors יורדי ימים are equally helpless and equally doomed."[39]

---

[35] The word translated "in the crucible" can also mean "firstborn."
[36] Douglas also highlights this distinction. See Dupont Sommer, *The Essene Writings from Qumran*, 207–208; "La mère du Messie et la mère l'Aspic," 174–188; Douglas, "Power and Praise," 174–175.
[37] Newsom, *The Self as Symbolic Space*, 251.
[38] Newsom, *The Self as Symbolic Space*, 241, 251–252.
[39] Silberman, "Language and Structure," 98.

I would prefer to portray the contrast as between fruitful suffering, such as that of a mother giving birth, and unfruitful suffering which ends in destruction. The term *mother of vanity* serves this contrast rather than drives it.

The two main sub-sections are arranged symmetrically. IIB1 and IIC2 refer to particular events with positive outcome (i.e. the birth of a child, and the defeat of chaos respectively). IIB2 and IIC1 present a general and negative picture of the distress of childbirth and the terror of the natural elements on land and sea.

Based on the above analysis of the poetic structure, a tentative interpretation is that the speaker sees his own distress in terms of the sufferings which will precede the messianic age. For his enemies, who are associated with the forces of chaos, there will be a negative outcome; but the sufferings of the speaker will lead to his participation in the birth of a new age.

2.3.1. *Repetitions and Wordplays*

There are a number of key-words or phrases which are repeated throughout the poem. Some of these involve word play. *Throes/breakers/cervix* (משברי) occurs 7 times; *mother* (pregnant-one) (הריה) also occurs 7 times plus once in the plural. These occur in both sections, and serve to unify the poem. The word pain (חבל) can also mean a rope of cords; it occurs 5 times always in parallel with throes, three of the occurrences being qualified by the word agonizing/agony (נמרץ/מרץ).

The poem plays on the similarity between the two related words cervix (מַשְׁבֵּר) and breakers (מִשְׁבָּרִם). The first occurrence is the singular word cervix with a pronominal suffix. This form resembles the plural construct of breakers, used figuratively in the next five occurrences and here translated as throes. The final occurrence is non-figurative, translated as breakers. In this poem then throes/breakers/cervix and pain refer primarily to childbirth, with a secondary allusive reference to the breakers of death and the cords of Sheol.

Another problematic word group is *firstborn/in the crucible/from the crucible* (מכור/בכור). The birth metaphor at first leads one to translate בכור as the noun firstborn. However, the unmistakable reading[40]

---

[40] The two letters are easily confused, but most commentators believe them to be clearly distinguishable here. This does not of course rule out the possibility of a copyist's error. Chamberlain originally emended מ to ב, but later changed his mind. Silberman emends to read *firstborn* in all three instances, contesting Chamberlain's argument

מכור poses problems for this. Another solution is to read some or all of the three occurrences as the noun crucible prefixed by a preposition. This noun is used metaphorically in the scrolls, usually of suffering, but in two instances it seems to pertain to conception and childbirth.[11]

The term vanity (אפעה) occurs three times, once in parallel with the term terror (פלצות) in couplet IIB2c and twice in parallel with the term wickedness (עול) in stanza IIC2. It has been variously translated as "asp/viper,"[12] "vanity/nought,"[13] or "groaning."[14] Most translators[15] opt for either "vanity/nought" or "asp/viper" but Frechette ingeniously translates it as "venomous vanity."[16] All three meanings are possible in the context and the poem probably plays upon the ambiguity. The sense behind all the meanings is that the product of this pregnancy is worthless and wicked.[17]

---

that *crucible* has been understood in rabbinic writings as metaphorical for the female pudenda. See John V. Chamberlain, "Another Qumran Thanksgiving Psalm," *JNES* 14 (1955): 32–41; "Further Elucidation of a Messianic Thanksgiving Psalm from Qumran," *JNES* 14 (1955): 181–182; Silberman, "Language and Structure," 101–103.

[11] The 9 occurrences of כור in the HB are all figurative. In the scrolls, apart from 1QM V 11, there are 8 other references which seem to be figurative. Most refer to testing or suffering. However, two references may support the use of crucible in a birth context. In 4Q416 2 III 17 (= 4Q418 9+9a–c 18) parents are described as being "the crucible of your conception (כור הוריכה)." 1QapGen ar VI 1 reads "and in the crucible of her who was pregnant with me I burst forth for truth (ובכור הורתי יעית לקושט)." See Abegg, et al., *The Dead Sea Scrolls Concordance, Volume 1*, 369; Garcia Martinez and Tigchelaar, *The Dead Sea Scrolls Study Edition*, 30, 852.

[12] Cf. Job 20:16; Isa 30:6, 59:5.

[13] Cf. Isa 41:24; 1QH X 30 [II 28].

[14] Cf. Isa 42:14, meaning "I groan" from the verb פעה.

[15] Dupont-Sommer and Chamberlain translate as "asp/viper;" Mansoor translates as "nought;" Holm-Nielsen has "wickedness;" Douglas has "wickedness" and "worthless;" Silberman has "groans." For a discussion of these alternatives see E.-M. Laperrousaz, "La mère du Messie et la mère de l'aspic dans les hymnes de Qumran: Quelques remarques sur la structure de '1QH' III, 1–18," in *Mélanges d'histoire des religions offerts à H.-C. Puech* (ed. P. Levy and E. Wolff; Paris: Presses Universitaires de France, 1974), 176–178. See also Dupont-Sommer, "La mère du Messie," 174–188; Chamberlain, "Another Qumran Thanksgiving Psalm," 32–41; Mansoor, *The Thanksgiving Hymns*, 114; Holm-Nielsen, *Hodayot*, 60 nn. 25, 42; Silberman, "Language and Structure," 104.

[16] Frechette, "Chiasm," 99–100.

[17] Douglas, "Power and Praise," 174 n. 88, 176, helpfully compares this to the biblical play on the meaning of the name Belial, as worthlessness. He also notes that in the only other occurrence of the term in the Dead Sea corpus (אפעה ושוא in 1QH^a X 30–31 [II 28–29], cf. Isa 59:5) it is used in conjunction with another term with the connotation of nought.

2.4. Close Reading

The first few lines of the column are poorly preserved but it seems likely that the opening stanza expressed thanks for deliverance from enemies. I discuss the reconstruction of this stanza in §§ 2.3 and 2.5 below. In line 7 there is a change to the third person plural which indicates that we are no longer in the opening stanza, but beginning the main body of the poem. The first line of IIA is partially missing. The second and third poetic lines contain the metaphors of ship and city set in parallel, with one verb doing double duty for both lines. This is an early indication that these two metaphors will be closely linked in this poem. The stanza either ends with a single emphatic line or the verse has an ABBA structure with the last line balancing the first.

The last line of stanza IIA introduces the third metaphor of the poem, that of childbirth. The image of childbirth is widely used in the Hebrew Bible as a metaphor for suffering, particularly in Jeremiah. The phrases *like a woman giving birth* (כמו אשת לדה) and (one bringing forth) *for the first time* (מבכריה) are markers to Jer 13:21 and 4:31 respectively. In these verses Jeremiah likens the sufferings of Jerusalem to labour pains, those of the first time mother being particularly severe.

Stanza IIB1 is marked by the strategic use of the particle כיא. It is also marked by a change from the first to the third person. In elaboration of the initial simple statement I am *in distress* (בצוקה), the poem makes use of a wide repertoire from the overlapping vocabulary of distress and childbirth; i.e. *pangs* (צירים), *agonising pain* (וחבל נמרץ), *throes* (משברים), *to bring to birth* (להחיל), (she) *is distressed* (הצרה).

Each of the three verses represents a stage in the birth process from the initial onset of labour (perfect verb), through the presentation of the child at the mouth of the womb (perfect verb), climaxing in the safe delivery of the child (imperfect verb).[48] The word *cervix/throes* (משברי) plays a key role in the progressive feel of the stanza; it appears in each verse, each time in a closer position to the initial particle כיא, mirroring the approach of the child to the mouth of the womb.

---

[48] Frechette notes this progression and, following Brown and citing Muilenburg, translates the particle כיא as 'when'. See Frechette, "Chiasm," 79; Schuyler Brown, "Deliverance from the Crucible: Some Further Reflexions on 1QH III. 1–18," *NTS* 14 (1967–1968): 255–256; James Muilenburg "The Linguistic and Rhetorical Usages of the Particle כי in the Old Testament," *HUCA* 32 (1961): 146.

Each of the three verses also contains at least one scriptural allusion which relates to childbirth and/or distress. The first, *her pangs came suddenly* is to 1 Sam 4:19 (cf. Dan 10:16). There the labour pains of Eli's daughter-in-law are brought on by her grief at the death of her relatives and the loss of the Ark of God. The dying mother names her son אי־כבוד, "the glory has departed." Thus with one short phrase the poem elicits dark thoughts of the danger and pain of childbirth, defeat by one's enemies, and the judgement of God.

The second allusion is a conflation of Isa 37:3 (=2 Kgs 19:3) and 2 Sam 22:5 (cf. Ps 18:5). In Isa 37:3 the phrase about childbirth is being used metaphorically of distress, just as it is in this poem.[49] But instead of the despair of the previous allusion, there is a request for God's deliverance. The final word of the clause, משבר, has been changed to *throes of death* (משברי מות). This phrase is taken from David's psalm of praise for deliverance from his enemies. Newsom has noted the tension between the surface description of distress in this middle verse and the connotations of deliverance introduced by the allusions. Not until the third verse will the tension be resolved. She comments that at this stage "danger and promise co-exist ... as they do for the pregnant woman."[50]

The allusion to 2 Sam 22:5–6 is elaborated in the third verse by the repetition of the phrase *throes/breakers of death* in parallel with the phrase *pains/cords of Sheol*. In 2 Samuel it is the second meaning of each word (breakers and cords) which are clearly meant,[51] whereas the context of our poem primarily requires the meanings of throes and pains. By this skilful word-play the poem manages to link two metaphors for anguish; the pain of childbirth is likened to the engulfing chaos and entrapping snares of the realm of death. This second metaphor, introduced here, will be picked up later in the poem.

The first line of this verse contains another allusion. *She gives birth to a son* is a marker to Isa 66:7.[52] Unlike most biblical references, this one uses the metaphor of childbirth in a positive way to express hope for Jerusalem. The theme of hope is continued in the phrase, *a wonderful*

---

[49] "This day is a day of distress, of rebuke, and of disgrace; *for children have come to the birth*, and there is no strength to bring them forth." (Isa 37:3).

[50] Newsom, *The Self as Symbolic Space*. 249.

[51] "For *the waves of death* encompassed me, the torrents of perdition assailed me; *the cords of Sheol* entangled me, the snares of death confronted me." (2 Sam 22:5–6).

[52] "Before her pain came upon her *she delivered a son* (בטרם יבוא חבל לה והמליטה זכר)." Isa 66:7 is the only occurrence in the HB of this verb and noun together.

counsellor with his might, which alludes to Isa 9:6, a promise of the birth of a Davidic king to end the people's distress. In order to retain the parallelism it is necessary to assume that the second line of IIB1c is longer than average. This is fitting, as the climax of this stanza, and of the whole sub-section IIB, undoubtedly occurs here as the child is finally born. Kittel has noted the use of such "double lines" at strategic points.[53]

The final line, *and a boy is delivered from the throes*, is in chiastic parallelism to the first line of this verse. The short line following the unusually long one brings a sense of completion; this is reinforced by the line ending in the longer plural non-construct form משברים in contrast to its previous three occurrences. This line is ambiguous. It could also refer to a man's deliverance from distress.[54] Thus in a final word play we are reminded that this vivid depiction of birth is in fact a metaphor for distress and deliverance.

After the denouement of this first metaphorical narrative stanza, IIB2 prepares the way for the metaphorical narrative of the second part of the poem. The emphasis shifts from *distress* to *terror*.

In IIB2a the verb in the first line does duty for the next two lines which contain parallel phrases for distress. The next line could end this verse or begin the next verse, IIB2b. The parallels between the first and fourth line are *in his mother/in his birth, come quickly/come suddenly, all throes/all pangs*. Whereas the first and fourth lines refer to his mother and his birth, the second and third lines have the comparable plural phrases *in their birth* and *to their mothers*. Combined with the use of the word "all" in the outer lines this suggests a move from the particular birth of the first three verses to a more general consideration of childbirth. It also mirrors the plural word "children" in the allusion of verse IIB1b.

It is extremely difficult to know what to do with the line *in the crucible of the mother* (בכור הריה), which could also be translated as "the firstborn of the mother." As I have translated it, this phrase completes the sense of the previous line. However, Frechette noted that taken with the first two words of the next line this phrase forms a central four word chiasm אפעה והריה הריה בכור. While not agreeing with Frechette's overall chiastic structural analysis, I agree that these lines are pivotal,

---

[53] Kittel, *The Hymns of Qumran*, 42, 92.
[54] The more usual meaning of this verb in the HB is to escape (qal), or rescue (piel). Of the 25 occurrences only Job 21:10 is in a birth context.

linking the two major sub-sections. I suggest that this final phrase of IIB2b is a deliberately ambiguous, double-duty line. With the meaning "in the crucible of the mother" it completes the previous line, giving the location of the pangs; with the meaning "the firstborn of the mother" it starts the next line, and is equated with *vanity*, the child of this second mother.

Newsom has also noted the difficult ambiguity of these lines. She argues that at first the reader is led to identify with the mother in this stanza, assuming that it refers to the mother of the boy described in the previous stanza. Then with the introduction of the mother of vanity, the reader is confronted with the possible error of his initial identification. While agreeing with her description of the deliberate confusion forced upon the reader, I am not convinced by her argument that the poem is primarily about the problem of identity. As I argued earlier, I consider that most commentators place undue emphasis on the contrasting mother figures.

Each line of IIB2c contains two phrases linked by the preposition ל. Based on previous parallelism, *agonising pains* probably corresponds to the phrase *breakers of the pit* in the next line and therefore *the mother of vanity* corresponds to *all the works of terror*.[55] This type of chiastic parallelism about a preposition Kittel calls "reversal of object."[56] The couplet is transitional, linking the pain of childbirth to the destruction of the pit. It forms an inclusio with the opening lines of IIB2 and with the closing lines of IIC2. In contrast with the *mother of a boy* (הרית גבר) in IIB1b we now encounter the *mother of vanity* (הרית אפעה). Vanity could also be translated as viper. The conjunction of pregnancy and viper is most likely to call to mind Isa 59:4–5 which also combines the metaphors of childbirth and viper in a graphic description of the wickedness of God's people.[57]

Like sub-section IIB, sub-section IIC also consists of two stanzas. As in the former sub-section, the first stanza elaborates a metaphor in three verses, this time of ship and city. In the first the particle כיא was strategic; here it is the prefix כ. However, the major correspondence of stanzas is in reverse order. Stanza IIC1 corresponds with IIB2 in

---

[55] But note that in the previous verse *terror* is in parallel to *agonising pains*.
[56] Kittel, *The Hymns of Qumran*, 68–69.
[57] "... *conceiving* mischief and begetting iniquity. They hatch adders' eggs, and weave the spider's web; whoever eats their eggs dies, and the crushed egg hatches out *a viper*." (Isa 59:4–5).

presenting a general picture of terror. Stanza IIC2 corresponds with IIB1 in presenting a narrative sequence with a definite outcome.

Stanza IIC1 consists of three couplets. In the first line of each couplet a phrase recalling the metaphor of the fortified city is linked by the prefix *like* (כ) to a phrase recalling the ship metaphor. The second line of each couplet contains the keyword *tumult/roaring* (המון/המות). In particular the phrase *sound of tumult* (קול המון) in IIC1a consists of two catchwords which are repeated in stanza IIC2.

The first, middle two, and last lines end in the words *waters* (מים) or *seas* (ימים) creating a pattern, possibly a rhyming effect. If, as favoured by Williams,[58] one places the line beginning *in the seething of the deeps* at the end of this stanza then the effect is completed by yet another occurrence of waters.[59] However, I believe there are better reasons for placing it as the first line of the next stanza (see below). The catch words "waters," "seas," "sound" and "tumult" in partial combinations are evocative of a number of biblical passages.[60] In particular Jer 10:13 (cf. Jer 51:16, Isa 33:3) suggests that the "tumult of the waters (המון מים) in the heavens" is the voice (קול) of God himself.[61]

As noted by Silberman,[62] this stanza interweaves the metaphors of the ship and the city. It describes the terror and helplessness of land-dwellers and seafarers alike at the power of the elements. This combination of motifs is found in a non-metaphorical sense in Psalm 107. The use of the phrases *those who go down to the seas* (יורדי ימים) and *swallowed up is all their wisdom* (תתבלע כול חכמתם) echo verses 23 and 27 respectively of this Psalm. The phrase *her wise men* refers back to the feminine city. I agree with Douglas[63] that it is desirable not to read this as "their wise men" despite the scribal correction. The reader is thus reminded of the biblical prophets' use of feminine imagery for the city of Jerusalem alluded to at the very beginning of the poem. Indeed all three metaphors, woman, ship and city, are feminine in gender.

---

[58] Williams, "Parallelism," 177–179.

[59] Perhaps the uncertainty over where to place this line is reflected in the possible scribal variation between 1QH[a] and 4Q432. The former appears to have a ו before the following verb whereas the latter does not. See Schuller, "Hodayot," 220.

[60] e.g. Jer 10:13, 51:16; 1 Sam 4:14; 1 Kgs 18:41; Isa 13:4, 17:12, 33:3.

[61] cf. 11Q5 XXVI; in 1QH X 18, 29 [II 16, 27] the phrase is applied to the noise of the wicked.

[62] Silberman, "Language and Structure," 98.

[63] Douglas, "Power and Praise," 173 n. 86.

Stanza IIC2 consists of three triplets; the first two begin with a temporal clause introduced by ב and an infinitive construct, and end with *their sound* (קולם). The phrase *tumult of their sound* at the end of IIC2a reverses the use of these catchwords in IIC1a. There is a mix of the vocabularies of sea and city as in the previous stanza. The sea was a powerful image of threat and danger because of its association with the primeval forces of chaos. In ancient Near Eastern creation myths God is depicted as subduing the monster of the deep. There are widespread echoes of this myth in the Hebrew Bible, particularly in poetic passages. Thus the image of peril at sea naturally leads into images of Sheol in this stanza. These images had already been introduced in IIB1 in connection with childbirth.

Much of the vocabulary and imagery is similar to that used in the creation account in Job 38. The reference to the *springs of the waters* (נבוכי מים) echoes Job 38:16. In Job 38:8–10 the sea is described as being shut up by God with *bolts* (בריחים) and *doors* (דלתים); in Job 38:17 it is linked with the forces of chaos and the *gates of death* (שערי־מות). Similar imagery is also found in Jonah 2. The imagery undoubtedly evokes Job 38 and possibly Jonah 2. However, I am tentative about identifying this as an allusion to a particular scripture passage. I suspect that the majority of the connotations will derive from the underlying traditional myth rather than from the biblical passages which utilise it.

As noted by Frechette, the use of ב in a temporal sense makes this stanza a progressive narrative in much the same way as the use of כיא in stanza IIB1. In IIC2a we encounter the waters boiling up from the deeps in huge waves. The verse has an ABA structure with the outer lines in chiastic parallelism. The phrase *springs of the waters* is parallel to *breakers of the waters* and the two clauses beginning with the preposition *in* (ב) are also in parallel. As mentioned above, I believe this analysis makes better sense than placing the *seething of the deeps* as the last line of the previous stanza.

The narrative moves on in IIC2b as the raging waters *open Sheol*, there possibly being a causal link with the preceding verse, as well as a temporal one. Once Sheol has been opened the arrows of the pit can be dispatched to where they belong. As Hinson observes, in light of the next line of the verse "the 'hellish arrows' might be interpreted as entering Sheol, rather than departing from it."[64] The arrows, a

---

[64] Hinson, "Hodayoth, III, 6–18," 196.

common image, here stand for all the weapons and onslaughts of wickedness. The raging waters also return to the deep from whence they emerged.

Finally, in IIC2c *the doors of the pit shut behind the mother of wickedness* and *the works/spirits of vanity* are similarly confined by *eternal bolts*. Hinson again puts it well, "Behind the evil forces the gates are slammed shut, and the forces that had cast their fury against the Psalmist are restrained."[65] However, I disagree slightly with Hinson's emphasis. The deliverance of the speaker was indeed the starting point of this poem, and never entirely disappears from view. But the eschatological theme, already predominating in IIB, has by now taken centre stage. The speaker has changed his perspective on deliverance from his personal distress by placing it within a cosmic framework.

2.5. *Allusions*

The theme of the poem is undoubtedly deliverance from distress and I suggest that there is an overall structural allusion to David's psalm of thanksgiving for deliverance, found in 2 Sam 22:2–20. My reasons for identifying this allusion are the poem's unexpected introduction of the phrase *throes/breakers of death*[66] into a description of childbirth. The term, which is a clear marker to 2 Sam 22:5, appears twice in stanza IIB1. The poem's use of throes/breakers/birth as a unifying term strengthens this possibility. A further indication that 2 Sam 22:2–20 may be the main inspiration for this poem is that in both poems the psalmist's deliverance from his enemies has been given a cosmic dimension.[67] (See the discussion below on stanza IIC2.) By its use of the term "breakers," the poem in 2 Sam 22:2–20 has already associated the psalmist's distress with imagery of the sea. The few biblical passages which use this term,

---

[65] Hinson, "Hodayoth, III, 6–18," 198.

[66] This phrase occurs in the HB only in 2 Sam 22:5. In Psalm 18, which is nearly identical, the equivalent phrase is *the cords of death*.

[67] As expressed by Craigie, commenting on Psalm 18, "The simple theme may be expressed as follows: the psalmist, in mortal danger, cries for help, and God appears to deliver him from danger. But in the amplification, the whole theme has been given cosmic dimension; this cosmic dimension has been achieved by the utilization of language which is rooted in Near Eastern mythology, but which has been transformed to express the Lord's deliverance of his human servant" Peter C. Craigie, *Psalms 1–50* (Word Biblical Commentary 19; Waco: Word Books, 1983), 173.

or the related term "cervix," may have been exegetically linked.⁶⁸ The link with Isa 37:3 is clearly made in IIB1b. The other two metaphors can both be derived from this verse, which uses the metaphor of childbirth in the context of a besieged Jerusalem. Thus all of the metaphors used by the poem are implicit in the conflation of Isa 37:3 and 2 Sam 22:5.

I conjecture that the introductory stanza may have contained the thanksgiving "you delivered me from [all my enemies] and from [Sheol] you have [sav]ed [my] soul" in echo of 2 Sam 22.1.⁶⁹ In stanza IIA the three images of distress are introduced as similes. The poem fills out the metaphor of childbirth by shorthand allusions to Jer 13:21 and Jer 4:31. Both of these texts use childbirth as a metaphor for the distress of Jerusalem, daughter Zion. The speaker's distress is thus closely associated with the distress of Jerusalem.⁷⁰ The poem then goes on to elaborate upon these three images of distress as extended metaphors, introducing new layers of meaning.

Apart from the allusion to 2 Sam 22:5–6, IIB contains shorthand allusions to 1 Sam 4:19, Isa 37:3, 66:7, 9:6 and 59:4–5 respectively. All the adopted passages are associated in some way with childbirth, but also bring in other connotations for the ideal reader. In IIB1a the connotation of judgement, present in the allusions to Jeremiah, is continued by an allusion to 1 Sam 4:19. In the adopted passage the birth pangs of Eli's daughter in law are brought on by news of death and defeat by enemies, and the loss of the ark of God.⁷¹ This temporary departure of the glory of the LORD from his sanctuary possibly may have been seen by a reader in the Second Temple period as a precursor of the exile of Jeremiah's time.⁷²

---

⁶⁸ Ps 42:7, 88:7, 93:4; Jonah 2:3[4] are the only other passages in the HB which use *breakers*. *Cervix* occurs only in 2 Kgs 19:3 = Isa 37:3; Hos 13:13.

⁶⁹ Cf. 2 Sam 22:18, 49.

⁷⁰ Cf. Jer 4:6: "let us flee to the fortified cities."

⁷¹ Frechette sees three contextual parallels between this poem and 1 Sam 4:19–22. These are defeat by one's opponents, the onset of distress (real and metaphorical labour pains), and closeness to death. He also identifies one contextual contrast; God's glory is absent in the biblical passage whereas the imminent eschatological demonstration of God's glory is expected in this poem. Frechette, "Chiasm, Reversal and Biblical Reference," 95–97.

⁷² Klein comments "The glory of Yahweh had again departed from Israel in 587, as Ezekiel made clear (10:18). However sad and shocking its departure was, it did not necessarily bring a condition without promise. Why not? When the ark had been captured in the days of the judges, it had provided an opportunity for a most dramatic display of Yahweh's glory—in the eyes of one of the nations. Is the deuteronomistic

Isa 37:3 is itself a metaphorical use of childbirth, in what appears to be a proverb quoted by Hezekiah. It is part of an account of impending judgement on Jerusalem which is averted after prayer to God "for the remnant that is left." This may well have resonated with a member of a community which saw itself as such a remnant. Frechette notes, as I have done above, the contextual link of a fortified city besieged by enemies. But he also goes on to draw parallels between the position of the poem's author regarding his enemies and the context of Isa 37:3. In particular he draws a parallel between "the blasphemous theological charge made by the Assyrian Rabshekah" and "the similar stance taken by the Qumran community's opponents."[73] While this is an appealing thought, I believe it makes too many assumptions about the historical situation of the poem's author and his community.

Frechette makes another very interesting observation about the omission of the final clause from the "quotation" of Isa 37:3. The complete quotation reads "children have come to the birth, and there is no strength to bring them forth." He argues that the omission of the phrase "there is no strength ..." would invite the reader to conclude that in this poem's context the strength was not lacking and that the subsequent allusion to Isa 9:5 would imply that the required strength (*his might*) indeed came from God. Part of Frechette's purpose is to support his contention that the *wonderful counsellor* is to be understood as the agent of the birth rather than as the child who is delivered. I believe that his argument betrays a misunderstanding of the difference between quotation and allusion. In allusion a sufficiently clear marker to the alluded text is all that is required to bring to mind the whole passage and its context. The nature of allusion is that the marker has a double referent; in most cases this militates against the inclusion of a complete quotation, which would disturb the flow of the text in which the allusion marker is embedded.

If it can be established by other means that the wonderful counsellor with his might is indeed God, the agent of birth, then the contrast

---

historian hinting that history might repeat itself? Other exilic writers did expect the glory of Yahweh to manifest itself in the future as much as in the past. Think only of the glory of Yahweh and the priestly tabernacle (Exod 40:34–35; Lev 9:23–24), the return of the glory of Yahweh to Ezekiel's reconstructed temple (43:1–5), or Second Isaiah's account of the new Exodus that makes the old forgettable (Isa 43:18–21)." Ralph W. Klein, *1 Samuel* (Word Biblical Commentary 10; Dallas: Word Books, 1998), 45.

[73] Frechette, "Chiasm," 98–99.

between the lack of strength in the adopted passage and God's might in this poem would indeed be strongly evident. However, all the attempts to read it in this way appear, in my view, to be cumbersome and contrived.[74] Frechette himself admits that his view is a minority one and his argument is based not on linguistic grounds but on his theological and literary interpretation of the poem.[75]

On literary grounds, *the wonderful counsellor* is parallel to *son* and *boy* in the other two lines of IIB1c. The long central line of this verse is the climax of the stanza, moving from pain to joy as, with one last push, the child emerges. The context of Isa 9:6 is the promise of a descendant to reign in David's line. Isa 66:7 is part of a longer passage in which the future restored Jerusalem is likened to a mother giving birth to many children. Both of these references therefore look forward to the restoration of Jerusalem, its king and its people. After pain there will be joy.

Thus, one interpretation of this poem is that the individual speaker's distress caused by his enemies is set in the context of Jerusalem's distress at the hand of her enemies. As God delivered David from his enemies, so he has delivered the speaker. So also he has promised to deliver David's city (2 Sam 22:50–51). This interpretation allows a messianic connotation of the allusion to Isa 9:6 but does not give it central importance.

In sub-section IIC the metaphors of the city and sea will come to the fore. But just as the city and sea metaphors are present in muted form in sub-section IIB so in IIC the childbirth metaphor is present, though in a lower key. In transitional verse IIB2c, by means of an allusion to Isa 59:5,[76] childbirth is transformed from a metaphor for distress into a metaphor for those who conceive wickedness. Unlike the righteous remnant whose distress ends in deliverance by God, the wicked

---

[74] This is a key point of interpretation in the discussion about the messianic significance of this allusion. Chamberlain changed his mind on this very point, originally reading "a Wonderful Counsellor in his might delivers a man from the birth canal of his pregnant one." He later changed this to "there bursts forth from the womb of her who is pregnant a Wonderful Counsellor with his might and a man is delivered from the birth canal." Holm-Nielsen and Mansoor have a similar reading to this latter one. Holm-Nielsen gives a detailed summary of the arguments. See Chamberlain, "Another Qumran Thanksgiving Psalm," 34; "Further Elucidation," 181; Holm-Nielsen, *Hodayot*, 56 nn. 18–20; Mansoor, *Thanksgiving Hymns*, 114.

[75] Frechette, "Chiasm," 88–94.

[76] "They hatch adders' eggs, and weave the spider's web; whoever eats their eggs dies, and the crushed egg hatches out a viper." (Isa 59:5).

are destined for the pit. The structural allusions to David's psalm of thanksgiving have already prepared the reader for the cosmic dimension which unfolds in part IIC of the poem. 2 Sam 22:8–16 describes a theophany; God appears in the storm to deliver the psalmist. The earth shakes, the voice of God thunders from the clouds, and the sea parts to lay bare the foundations of the world.

A similar scene unfolds in sub-section IIC of this poem. However, for its description the poem draws on the language of another passage which describes God's power over nature. The phrase *tumult of the waters* is a marker to Jer 10:13, "when he utters his voice there is a tumult of waters in the heavens" (לקול תתו המון מים בשמים). The keywords tumult, sound/voice and waters in various combinations feature prominently throughout this sub-section of the poem. Although God is not mentioned by name the allusion makes it clear that the poem is indeed describing a theophany.[77] There are two remaining allusions. In stanza IIC1 the entwined city and sea metaphors are elaborated by clear allusions to Psalm 107. In stanza IIC2 the language echoes traditional imagery found in Job 38.

Psalm 107 describes God's deliverance from various kinds of distress with the refrain "Then they cried to the LORD in their trouble, and he delivered them from their distress." Whatever its original context, this psalm seems to have been adapted to refer to return from exile. "He turns rivers into a desert, springs of water into thirsty ground," and "He turns a desert into pools of water, a parched land into springs of water" echo words from Isaiah's promise of restoration.[78] The implication of Psalm 107 is that although God brings distress on those who rebel against him, those that repent and call upon him are delivered. Because of this allusion I am reluctant to interpret stanza IIC1 of the poem as referring to God's judgement on the speaker's enemies. I think that at

---

[77] Frechette notes the "general reference to the biblical motif of God's voice in the storm," citing several passages but omitting any reference to Jer 10:13. He cites 1 Sam 2:10; Ps 18:14; Job 37:4–5; Ps 29:3; Ex 15:1–18; Isa 17:12–13; Ps 46:3–4. However he is on shaky ground in seeing a specific allusion to Ps 46:2–4. He states that the imagery is similar while admitting that much of the vocabulary is different. As already stated, I think that a stronger case can be made for the influence of 2 Sam 22:2–20. Frechette, "Chiasm," 100–101.

[78] Verse 33 probably alludes to Isa 50:2 and verse 35 to Isa 41:18. It is possibly significant that Psalm 107 is preserved in the Dead Sea scrolls only in 4QPs^f which is a collection of Psalms with a possible eschatological emphasis. See Patrick W. Skehan, Eugene Ulrich, and Peter W. Flint, "Psalms" in *Qumran Cave 4.XI: Psalms to Chronicles*. (ed. E.C. Ulrich et al.; DJD 16; Oxford: Clarendon, 2000.), 85–106.

most it can be interpreted as a more general description of the distress that God justly (in the speaker's view) visits upon all humans, and from which in his mercy he delivers some.

In stanza IIC2 the cosmic dimension, associated with the sea in Near Eastern myth, comes to the fore in a description of the final destiny of all wickedness. The vocabulary and imagery echoes that of Job 38 in particular. Job 36:22–39:40 is a magnificent celebration of God the creator's control over the natural world. It is obviously then the place for any poet to turn when seeking inspiration upon this theme. However the lack of contextual link makes me inclined to classify the similarities as use of biblical language rather than allusion. Similar imagery is found in Jonah 2 and here the context has some similarities due to the preceding metaphor of the ship on the sea. However the poem has by now moved on from this metaphor to a more cosmic dimension. So once again I am disinclined to attribute a specific allusion.

I am also less certain that this final poetic imagery is primarily metaphorical. The biblical allusions have served their purpose in establishing the power of God over nature and enemies alike, and his promise of deliverance to his chosen remnant who call upon him. The poem now ends in an eschatological projection of these themes which echo biblical language and imagery but also possibly reflect an extra-biblical and ongoing mythological world-view. In effect the poem uses a fourth metaphor for the speaker's distress, that of the eschatological tribulation. However, in the view of Collins, although the poem is not meant as a prophecy "it is inadequate to say it is 'only a simile.'" The pattern that the speaker sees in his own distress and deliverance is a pattern he expects to be repeated on a larger scale.[79]

2.6. *Intertexts*

The primary intertext for this poem is the one which immediately follows it in 1QH^a XI 20–37 [III 19–36]. For further discussion of this relationship see §3.7 below. Also, the poem 1QH^a XIII 22–XV 8 [V 20–VII 5] uses all three metaphors of distress. The woman in labour occurs in XIII 32 [V 30] and the combined ship and fortified city in

---

[79] See John J. Collins, "Patterns of Eschatology at Qumran," in *Traditions in Transformation, Turning Points in Biblical Faith* (ed. B. Halpern and J.D. Levenson; Winona Lake: Eisenbrauns, 1981), 365–370.

XIV 25–28 [VI 22–25] and XV 7 [VII 4]. I discuss this poem in §2.6.1 of chapter four. Douglas comments that the word ship (אוניה) is never used in the Hebrew Bible as a metaphor for suffering and that in the Dead Sea corpus it occurs only in these two poems.[80] I would modify that observation slightly by noticing that the metaphors for distress of childbirth and storm at sea are briefly employed together in Ps 48:6–7 [7–8].

Collins notes that "birth imagery is found in an eschatological context in the New Testament and the Jewish apocalypses." (E.g. Rev 12, 4 Ezra 4:42, 1 *En.* 62:4–5.) But he does not consider that these provide any close parallel to this poem. Collins also notes that "birth imagery is very common in all sorts of contexts and is not necessarily eschatological."[81] I have already noted that the sea and city imagery echoes ideas from ancient Near Eastern creation myths. I will return to this topic in §3.5.2.

2.7. *Observations and Comments*

The disappearance of the first person after the introductory stanza sets this poem apart. There are two narrative sequences, called meshalim by Douglas;[82] this genre occurs also in the second poem discussed in this chapter and in the poem discussed in chapter four. It does not however appear to be a common feature of the *Hodayot* collections. Another distinctive feature of this poem is the extensive word play. This short but intricate poem illustrates that the compositions in the 1QH[a] collection are far from uniform either in their subject matter or in their poetic techniques.

The eschatological imagery progressively takes over, but this is still primarily a poem about the distress of an individual. However, although it is usually classed as a Teacher Hymn there is nothing to single out the speaker as a particular individual. I do not find convincing the arguments of those, such as Douglas, who see in this poem claims by the speaker to be the "progenitor of the remnant community."[83] The speaker could be any member of the community.

---

[80] Douglas, "Power and Praise," 176; Abegg, et al., *The Dead Sea Scrolls Concordance, Volume 1*, 16.
[81] Collins, "Patterns of Eschatology," 369.
[82] Douglas, "Power and Praise," 174–175.
[83] Douglas, "Power and Praise," 177.

However, this poem displays none of the self-doubt evident in most of the Community Hymns. The viewpoint is that of an omniscient third-person narrator. The short poem is very skilfully constructed for maximum use of the language. There is extravagant use of word-play and other poetic devices. The use of allusion displays a mastery of scripture. All of these factors contribute to the confidence exuded by this poem. For these reasons I am not convinced by Newsom's arguments that the poem is primarily about identity. She makes a strong case that many of the poems address problems of identity and community. However, I consider that her desire to fit this poem into that general model may have influenced her interpretation.[84] This clever, artistic and intriguing poem defies categorization!

I will now go on to argue that the poem which follows this one in 1QH[a] utilises the same underlying model. I will therefore reserve my other comments on this poem until §3.7.

3. *From the Depths to the Heights*
1QH[a] XI 20–37 [III 19–36]

This poem is of interest firstly because commentators are undecided on how to classify it. Holm-Nielsen and Morawe classified it as a thanksgiving psalm,[85] but Jeremias, Becker and Kuhn classified it as a Community Hymn.[86] Tanzer classified both this and the preceding poem as Teacher Hymns, but suggested that the apocalyptic material may have been added by an editor.[87] More recently both Puech and Douglas have tentatively classified this poem as a Teacher Hymn on the grounds of its vocabulary.[88] However the most recent study by Newsom includes this and the preceding poem in a discussion of Community Hymns.[89]

---

[84] Newsom, *The Self as Symbolic Space*, 191–346. Newsom deals with this poem in pages 240–253.
[85] See my discussion in §5.3 of chapter one on the various terms used for classification of the compositions.
[86] As summarised in Michael C. Douglas, "The Teacher Hymn Hypothesis Revisited: New Data for an Old Crux," *DSD* 6 (1999): 239–266, 245.
[87] Tanzer, "The Sages at Qumran," 126.
[88] Douglas, "Power and Praise," 184–190; Puech, *Croyance*, 366. Douglas thinks it possible that this is a "pseudo-Teacher Hymn," written to imitate their style.
[89] Newsom, *The Self as Symbolic Space*, 253–261.

Another main area of interest is the poem's description of communion with heavenly beings. This aspect of the hymn has been discussed by Frennesson, who regards it as an example of "liturgical communion with angels."[90] Puech included this poem in his study of beliefs about immortality in the Dead Sea texts. Finally, the description of eschatological judgement and destruction marks this poem out for special interest. Both Puech and Kittel have commented on this aspect of the poem.[91]

3.1. *Delimitation and Text*

This composition can be found on Sukenik plate 37. Sukenik numbered it as III 19–36 but Stegemann and Puech have reassigned it as XI 20–37.[92] The poem is clearly delimited and well preserved. The beginning is marked by a blank space at the end of line 19 and a clearly indented opening formula in line 20. Likewise the end is marked by a space at the end of line 37 and by the opening formula of the next hymn in line 38. Parts of this poem are also preserved in the Cave 4 manuscripts. 1QH^a XI 27–32 overlaps with 4QH^b 5 1–7 and 4QpapH^f 6 1–6.[93] The latter manuscript contains the variant reading וקו (for וקץ in 1QH^a XI 29). In 1QH^a XI 30 על has been inserted above the line whereas in 4QpapH^f it is an integral part of the text.

1QH^a XI 20–37 [III 19–36]

20 vacat   אודכה אדוני כי פדיתה נפשי משחת ומשאול אבדון
21 העליתני לרום עולם ואתהלכה במישור לאין חקר ואדעה כיא יש מקוה לאשר
22 יצרתה מעפר לסוד עולם ורוח נעוה טהרתה מפשע רב להתיצב במעמד עם
23 צבא קדושים ולבוא ביחד עם עדת בני שמים ותפל לאיש גורל עולם עם רוחות
24 דעת להלל שמכה ביחד ר[נ]ה ולספר נפלאותיכה לנגד כול מעשיכה ואני יצר
25 החמר מה אני מגבל במים ולמי נחשבתי ומה כוח לי כיא התיצבתי בגבול רשעה
26 ועם חלכאים בגורל ותגור נפש אביון עם מהומות רבה והוות מדהבה עם מצעדי
27 בהפתח כל פחי שחת ויפרשו כול מצודות רשעה ומכמרת חלכאים על פני מים

---

[90] Björn Frennesson, *"In a Common Rejoicing": Liturgical Communion with Angels in Qumran* (Studia Semitica Upsaliensia 14; Uppsala: Acta Universitasis Upsaliensis, 1999), 47–50.
[91] Kittel, *The Hymns of Qumran*, 33–98; Puech, *Croyance*, 366–373.
[92] Sukenik, *The Dead Sea Scrolls*; Stegemann, "The Material Reconstruction of 1QHodayot," 280; Puech, "Quelques aspects," 41–43.
[93] Schuller, "Hodayot," 136–137, 220–221.

28 בהתעופף כול חצי שחת לאין השב ויורו[94] לאין תקוה בנפול קו על משפט וגורל אף
29 על נעזבים ומתך חמה על נעלמים וקץ[95] חרון לכול בליעל וחבלי מות אפפו לאין
  פלט
30 וילכו נחלי בליעל על כול אגפי רום כאש[96] אוכלת בכול שנאביהם להתם כול עץ לח
31 ויבש מפלגיהם ותשוט בשביבי להוב עד אפס כול שיתיהם[97] באושי חמר תאכל
32 וברקוע יבשה יסודי הרים לשרפה ושורשי חלמיש נחלי זפת ותאוכל עד תהום
33 רבה ויבקעו לאבדון נחלי בליעל ויהמו מחשבי תהום בהמון גורשי ר[פ]ש וארץ
34 תצרח על ההווה הנהיה בתבל וכול מחשביה ירועו ויתהוללו כול אשר עליה
35 ויתמוגגו בהווה ג[דו]לה כיא ירעם אל בהמון כוחו ויהם זבול קודשו באמת
36 כבודו וצבא השמים יתנו [ב]קולם [ו]יתמוגגו וירעדו אושי עולם ומלחמת גבורי
37 שמים תשוט בתבל ולא תש[ו]ב ע[ד][98] כלה ונחרצה לעד ואפס כמוה   vacat
38   vacat

3.2. Translation

I   (20) *Blank*   I thank you, O Lord, for you have ransomed my soul from the pit
         and from Sheol of Abaddon (21) you have raised me to an eternal height
         And I walk about on a plain without limit.

IIA1a   And I know that there is hope
         for him whom (22) you formed from dust
         for an eternal council.

IIA1b   And a perverted spirit you purified from great sin
         TO TAKE HIS STAND in position with (23) the army of holy ones
         and to enter in community with the congregation of the sons of heaven.

IIA1c   And you cast for a man an eternal *lot* with the spirits of (24) knowledge
         to praise your name in the community of re[joic]ing
         and to recount your wonders in front of all your works.

IIA2a   But I (am) a creature of (25) clay;
         what (am) I, kneaded with water?
         And for whom am I reckoned?
         and what strength have I?

---

[94] Thus Puech; Sukenik reads ויפרו. Sukenik, *The Dead Sea Scrolls*, pl. 37; Puech, *Croyance*, 367 n. 180.

[95] 4QpapH[f] has variant וקו. See Schuller, "Hodayot," 220–221.

[96] Puech, *Croyance*, 367 n. 181, reads באש.

[97] Thus Douglas, following Licht; Sukenik has שותיהם. See Douglas, "Power and Praise," 181 n. 93.

[98] Sukenik transcription shows no lacuna but has a note that the letters are missing on the plate. Sukenik, *The Dead Sea Scrolls*, pl. 37.

IIA2b	For I TAKE MY STAND in the territory of evil
	(26) and with SCOUNDRELS[99] in *lot*.
IIA2c	And sojourns the soul of the poor one with the tumults of the great
	and the disasters of arrogance[100] (are) with my footsteps.

IIA3a	(27) In the opening of all the snares of the pit
	and (as) all the nets of EVIL are spread out
	and the fishing net of the SCOUNDRELS (is) upon the face of the waters.
IIA3b	(28) In the flying forth of all the arrows of the pit without respite[101]
	and (as) they are shot out[102] without hope.
IIA3c	In the falling of the measuring line upon judgement
	and the *lot* of anger (29) upon the forsaken ones
	and the outpouring of fury upon the hypocrites
	and the time of wrath for all of Belial
	and (as) the cords of death surround without escape.

IIB1a	(30) Then go THE TORRENTS OF BELIAL over all the high banks[103]
	like a fire consuming all their watering places[104]
	to destroy every tree, green (31) and dry, from their channels;
	and it travels in flames of lightning until *no more* (are) all their canals.[105]
IIB1b	The foundations of clay it consumes
	(32) and the expanse of the dry land;
	the bases of the mountains for burning
	and the roots of flint for torrents of pitch.
IIB1c	And it consumes unto the (33) great deep
	and the TORRENTS OF BELIAL break into Abaddon.

---

[99] Meaning uncertain. חלכאים appears in the HB only in Ps 10:10 (cf. 1QH[a] XII 26, §3.2 of this thesis).

[100] Meaning uncertain. מדהבה appears in HB only in Is 14:4 where it is often emended to מרהבה and translated as arrogance. The latter is also the reading in 1QIsa[a].

[101] Literally "without return," but this meaning makes better sense in the context. Holm-Nielsen translates as "without cease." He observes that if the expression meant "without return" it would be attached to the verb, and also that the translation should take into account that the expression is in parallel with "without hope." See Holm-Nielsen, *Hodayot*, 70 n. 29.

[102] The transcription and meaning are both uncertain. Here I follow Williams for the two reasons he gives; i.e. the plate appears to show a ו or a י rather than a פ; also this verb is more applicable to the subject "arrows." See Williams, "Parallelism," 201.

[103] Holm-Nielsen, *Hodayot*, 71 n. 38, translates thus, following rabbinic usage; the noun appears only in Ezekiel in the HB meaning "army."

[104] The meaning is uncertain. This translation assumes a scribal error, reading שואביהם instead of שנאביהם but no satisfactory solution has been suggested. See Holm-Nielsen, *Hodayot*, 71 n. 40.

[105] I follow Douglas, "Power and Praise," 181 n. 93.

IIB2a And the schemers of the deep roar in the tumult of the casting up
       of[106] the mud
       and the earth (34) cries out over the disaster which comes on the
       WORLD
       and all its schemers[107] scream
IIB2b and all who (are) upon it become mad
       (35) and they are DISSOLVED in the g[rea]t disaster.

IIB3a For God thunders in the tumult of his strength
       and his holy dwelling roars in the truth (36) of his glory
       and the army of heaven utter their voice
       [and] the eternal foundations are DISSOLVED and tremble.
IIB3b And the war of the mighty ones of (37) heaven travels in the WORLD
       nor does it re[turn un]til complete,
       and (it is) determined forever
       and (there are) *no more* like it.   *Blank*

3.3. *Analysis of structure*

I. Introductory Stanza   XI 20–21 [III 19–20]
II. Main Body of Poem.   XI 21c–37 [III 20–36]
   A. From the Heights to the Depths   XI 21c–29
      1. Hope that a man may TAKE HIS STAND with the army of heaven
         a. formed for an eternal council
         b. purified from sin
         c. an eternal *lot* ... in the community of rejoicing
      2. But I TAKE MY STAND in the territory of EVIL
         a. what am I?
         b. with SCOUNDRELS in *lot*
         c. disasters are with my footsteps
      3. When all the weapons of the pit come upon those of Belial
         a. snares of the pit, nets of EVIL and SCOUNDRELS
         b. arrows of the pit
         c. the *lot* of anger
   B. From the Depths to the Heights   XI 30–37
      1. The TORRENTS OF BELIAL (their canals are *no more*)
         a. go over all the high banks like a consuming fire
         b. consume down to the foundations
         c. consume to the deep and break into Abaddon.

---

[106] Or "them that cast up." See Holm-Nielsen, *Hodayot*, 72 n. 50.
[107] Meaning uncertain. I follow Holm-Nielsen in translating as a Piel participle of the verb חשב. Qimron lists this as a word not attested in BH or MH, possibly meaning "depth." Holm-Nielsen, *Hodayot*, 72 n. 49; Elisha Qimron, *The Hebrew of the Dead Sea Scrolls* (HSS 29; Atlanta: Scholars Press, 1986), 110.

    2. Disaster comes on the WORLD, the earth cries out
    3. God thunders and the army of heaven utter their voice
       b. war of the mighty ones travels in the WORLD ... *no more* like it

The poem has a typical opening stanza. The content of the main body of the poem clearly falls into two parts. The first part is concerned with the position of the speaker and his community and the second is a description of eschatological events. Following Kittel, I make the division after stanza IIA3. I agree with her that this stanza is a transitional one but that placing it in the first section gives a better balance of length between the two sections.[108] This division also means that an allusion to Ps 18:4 both ends sub-section IIA and begins sub-section IIB (see discussion below).

An even stronger case for this arrangement is made when one notices the symmetry of the poem. The stanzas are arranged in a chiasm. The poem starts with the heavenly army, progressing down through the earth and the pit in sub-section IIA. In sub-section IIB the direction is reversed as destruction bursts forth from the pit, consumes the earth and ends with the war of the heavenly beings. This division is also emphasised by the use of keywords. In the first half of the poem the poet solidly TAKES HIS STAND in the heavenly and the earthly realm, whereas in contrast the WORLD is DISSOLVED in the second half. Newsom cites Lohfink in likening the poem's techniques to those of modern film-making. She suggests that the "shifting scenes" and "manipulation of perspective" work to form the "reader's subjectivity."[109]

IIA is unified by the theme word *lot*, which occurs once in each stanza. IIA1 is linked to IIA2 by the repetition of the verb TO TAKE ONE'S STAND (התיצב). IIA2 is linked to IIA3 by the repetition of the parallel terms EVIL (רשעה) and SCOUNDRELS (חלכאים). Douglas has also noted that words for hope (מקוה, תקוה) appear near the beginning and end of this section. The two allusions to Ps 18:4 and the repetition of Belial link IIB to IIA.

---

[108] Kittel labels this stanza C. She observes that the vocabulary of this stanza is closer to that of the opening stanza, although thematically it is closer to what follows it. She conjectures that its size and difference from the preceding stanza suggest that it should be regarded as an independent unit, saying: "Stanzas D and E balance stanzas A, B, and C rather exactly in weight. As it now stands, the poem is intended as a single composition." Kittel, *The Hymns of Qumran*, 70–71, 74–76.

[109] Norbert Lohfink, *Lobesänge der Armen*. (SBS 143. Stuttgart: Katholisches Bibelwerk, 1990), 96; Newsom, *The Self as Symbolic Space*, 258.

IIB contains no personal references and is a description of cataclysmic eschatological events. It is bounded by the phrase *no-more* (אפס), which occurs in the first and last verses of the sub-section. Stanza IIB1 begins and ends with the phrase TORRENTS OF BELIAL, forming an inclusio. It is balanced in length by stanzas IIB2 and IIB3. IIB2 is linked to IIB1 by the repetition of *deep* (תחום). IIB2 and IIB3 could be regarded as one stanza. They are unified by the repetition of several key phrases. These include *roar(s)* (יהם), *in the tumult of* (בהמון), *they are dissolved* (יתמוגגו) and *in the world* (בתבל).

3.4. *Close Reading*

The poem has an introductory stanza which at face value appears to be thanking God for deliverance from deadly peril in the manner of some biblical psalms.[110] However it could also be interpreted as describing the speaker's elevation to the presence of God. In keeping with the multi-valent nature of poetic literature it is not necessary for the reader to choose between these meanings.[111] For example, *I walk about on a plain* (ואתהלכה במישור) could also be interpreted figuratively as *I walk in uprightness*. It probably has this double meaning in Ps 26:11–12, the context of which is preparation for entering the temple.[112] This allusion is a pointer to the theme of heavenly worship in the next stanza.

The first two lines of the stanza exhibit a chiastic parallelism; *from the pit* corresponds with *from Sheol of Abaddon*,[113] and *you have ransomed my*

---

[110] "I will extol you, O LORD, for you have drawn me up, and did not let my foes rejoice over me.
O LORD my God, I cried to you for help, and you have healed me. O LORD, you brought up my soul from Sheol, restored me to life from among those gone down to the Pit." (Ps 30:1–3; cf. Ps 16:10, 49:15; 103:4; Job 33:28; Isa 38:17).

[111] However this is exactly what some commentators seek to do. See for example the discussion by Laurin. By contrast, Penner's comparison of Kuhn's "realized eschatology" and Puech's "future interpretation" takes account of "the associative nature of poetry and the ambiguity it produces." (R.B. Laurin, "The Question of Immortality in the Qumran 'Hodayot,'" *JSS* 3 (1958): 344–355; K. Penner, "Realized or Future Salvation in the Hodayot," *JBS* 5 (2002): 45).

[112] "But as for me, *I walk* (אלך) in my integrity; *redeem me* (פדני), and be gracious to me. My foot stands *on level ground* (במישר); in the great congregation I will bless the LORD." (Ps 26:11–12); Fletcher-Louis sees here an allusion to the ideal priest in Mal 2:6, who "*walked* (הלך) with me in integrity and *uprightness* (במישר), and he turned many from iniquity." See Crispin H.T. Fletcher-Louis, *All the Glory of Adam: Liturgical Anthropology in the Dead Sea Scrolls* (STDJ 42; Leiden: Brill, 2002), 108–112. I discuss this further in §3.5.

[113] The phrase *Sheol of Abaddon* does not occur in the HB, but the two terms appear in association in Job 26:6; Prov 15:11, 27:20. As the phrase *from Sheol of Abaddon* is parallel

soul corresponds with *you have raised me*. The phrases *I thank you Lord* and *to an eternal height*, though not semantically or grammatically parallel, balance each other.[114] The latter phrase is also paralleled by another quasi-geographical phrase in the final single line of the stanza.[115] The phrase *eternal height* is not found in the Hebrew Bible but Mansoor notes that it "appears twice in the Jewish daily morning service, as the seat of His divine majesty, where his angels attend on him."[116] This supports the interpretation of this as referring to the heavenly realm. It may be that the term *Abaddon* is used here in conjunction with *Sheol* to signify that the very lowest region of the pit is in mind. Thus in this opening stanza we have the two extremities of height and depth.

The beginning of stanza IIA1 is marked by a change from the first person object *me* to the third person *him*. This stanza is linked to the introductory stanza by means of double repetition of the catchword *eternal*. It consists of three verses of the form ABB. The second two verses, as observed by Kittel, are of the form independent clause (action) plus two infinitive clauses (results of action).[117] The first verse, though not containing infinitives, seems to imitate their structure by the use of two lines beginning with the preposition ל.[118] Each of the three verses express confidence that God places individuals in relation to the heavenly realm, expressed as *eternal council* (סוד עולם),[119] *army of holy ones*, *congregation of the sons of heaven* (עדת בני שמים), *spirits of knowledge* (רוחות

---

to the phrase *from the pit* there may be some play being made with the distinctive phrase in Isa 38:17, "From the pit of destruction (משחת בלי)."

[114] In this case the introductory formula is integral to the first poetic line. This appears to vary between compositions.

[115] *Plain* and *height* are both geographical terms. *Eternal* and *without limit* both have the sense of stretching on for ever and both are also used to describe the attributes of God, e.g. Isa 40:28.

[116] Mansoor, *The Thanksgiving Hymns*, 116 n. 6.

[117] Kittel, *The Hymns of Qumran*, 62–63.

[118] Williams analyses the parallelism of this verse thus. Kittel however places this as the last line of the opening stanza. Although this gives a rather long line, Kittel notes that the opening stanza often does end in such a line. She also argues that *an eternal council* is parallel to *an eternal height*. The arguments are finely balanced, as shown by the disagreement amongst commentators. Wallenstein and Puech favour Kittel's arrangement whilst Douglas is similar to Williams. See Williams, "Parallelism," 182–183; Kittel, *The Hymns of Qumran*, 60, 65; Meir Wallenstein, *Hymns from the Judean Scrolls* (Manchester: The University Press, 1950), 15; Puech, *Croyance*, 366; Douglas, "Power and Praise," 181.

[119] Mansoor, *The Thanksgiving Hymns*, 117 n. 2, translates as *eternal foundation*. The reader who notices this secondary meaning is prepared for the emphasis on foundations which occurs in IIB.

דעת) and *community of rejoicing* (יחד רנה).[120] The first three of these evoke descriptions of the heavenly court found in several biblical psalms.[121]

The phrases *for him who you formed from dust* (לאשר יצרתה מעפר), *and a perverted spirit* (ורוח נעוה), and *for a man* (לאיש), in each verse respectively, indicate the individual's lowly origin. The action of God on his behalf is progressively described as destining the individual for, making him fit for, and placing him in communion with the heavenly realm. The individual progresses from having *hope*, to being enabled *to take his stand/to enter* in the community, and finally *to praise your name* and *to recount your wonders*. The latter phrase is a marker to Ps 26:7, matching the allusion to this psalm in the last line of the opening stanza.[122] *There is hope* may be an allusion to Ezra 10:2, with connotations of repentance. Fletcher-Louis has also argued that the term hope (מקוה) has here a double meaning; in view of the reference to purification in the next verse it could also refer to a pool for ritual immersion. Fletcher-Louis is of the view that the entire stanza has a cultic context.[123]

In stanza IIA2 there is a change from the second person singular to the first person. The speaker contrasts his own status with that described in IIA1. He emphasises his lowly status by means of rhetorical questions, a technique used elsewhere in the *Hodayot*.[124] As noted by Kittel, in the first couplet the two halves of the phrase *a creature of clay, kneaded with water* are placed in parallel.[125] Newsom, in keeping with

---

[120] This term יחד may not be used in the technical sense that it has in other scrolls. It occurs in 1QH^a VI 30 [XIV 19], VII 18 [frg. 10 7], XI 23, 24 [III 22, 23], XIX 17 [XI 14], XXVI 15 [frg.] as the phrase ביהד Frennesson translates it here as "in a common rejoicing." Douglas argues that "the concept of 'communion with angels' preceded the institutional founding of the Yahad and was itself the source of the name Yahad." See also my note on "together" (יחד) in §2.4.1 of chapter four. Frennesson, "*In a Common Rejoicing*," 48 n. 24; Douglas, "Power and Praise," 181 n. 94.

[121] "Let the heavens praise your wonders, O LORD, your faithfulness in the assembly of the holy ones (בקהל קדשים). For who in the skies can be compared to the LORD? Who among the heavenly beings (בבני אלים) is like the LORD, a God feared in the council of the holy ones (בסוד־קדשים), great and awesome above all that are around him?" (Ps 89: 5–7 [6–8]; cf. Ps 29:1, 82:1, 6).

[122] Although the verb ספר occurs with נפלאותיכה elsewhere in the HB, only in this verse is the infinitive construct used.

[123] Fletcher-Louis, *All the Glory of Adam*, 108–112.

[124] 1QH^a V 31–32 [XIII 14–15], VII 34 [XV 21], IX 25–28 [I 23–26], XI 25 [III 24], XII 30 [IV 29], XV 35 [VII 32], XVIII 5–14 [X 3–12], XIX 6 [XI 3], XX 30–36 [XII 27–33], XXI 5 [XVIII 19], XXII 14 [frg. 1 12], XXVII 10 [frg?], [2 I 4, 2 I 7, 3 12, 4 10–11, 10 3]; 1QS XI 20–22.

[125] Kittel, *The Hymns of Qumran*, 60–61; cf. 1QH^a IX 23 [I 21].

her overall thesis describes this as "the language of self-loathing."[126] In view of the confident tone of the previous stanza, I think that this is too negative an interpretation of the speaker's passing use of a familiar idiom. I read this as the speaker objectively describing his present status, rather than subjectively wallowing in guilt.

Likewise the speaker describes his present position, contrasting it with that of stanza IIA1. He reinforces the contrast by repeating two key terms from that stanza, *I take my stand … in lot*. The words the speaker uses to describe his position, *the territory of evil* and with *scoundrels* (הלכאים), are markers to Mal 1:4 and Ps 10:10 respectively. Both these scriptural passages are about the wicked. Douglas observes that in Mal 1:4 *the territory of evil* (גבול רשעה) is a unique expression referring to Edom, Israel's arch-enemy, whereas "territory of Israel" occurs ten times in biblical texts. He comments that "in this terse comment, the author inverts Israel and Edom."[127]

This shorthand allusion is thus very effective in emphasising the extent of Israel's wickedness. In my view, the problem which the poem addresses is the continued existence and flourishing of the wicked. This is in contrast to Newsom's view that the poem is about identity. In the opening stanzas the speaker has clearly stated his confidence in his identity as one whom God has delivered and placed in communion with angels. What exercises him is not confusion between his own status and that of the wicked, but why God still allows the wicked to continue. This is, as I will discuss briefly in my conclusions, a manifestation of the tension between a realized and a future eschatology.

IIA2 ends with two lines in chiastic parallelism which summarise the speaker's precarious position. Kittel calls this type of construction "reversal of object" and notes that it is a subtle way of representing the entanglement of good and evil.[128] In the biblical Psalms, *poor-one* (אביון) can refer to the LORD's servant; this is probably the thought behind the speaker's self-description.[129] *Arrogance* (מדהבה) is a biblical hapax which marks a shorthand allusion to Isa 14:4. This adopted passage is a taunt song against a wicked king who thinks to ascend to heaven like a god but is brought down to Sheol. This fills out the contrast with the exalted

---

[126] Newsom, *The Self as Symbolic Space*, 258.
[127] Douglas, "Power and Praise," 185.
[128] Kittel, *The Hymns of Qumran*, 68–70.
[129] This is the sense of the term in the pesher on Psalm 37 in 4Q171.

position of the previous stanzas and leads into the judgement theme which follows.[130]

As noted by Kittel, the three verses of stanza IIA3 all begin with the preposition ב + infinitive construct. This is normally followed by a verb which continues the action. A non-literal translation of this construction would be of the form "when ... then."[131] The three verses are also unified by four repetitions of *all* (כול), four of *upon* (על) and three of *without* (לאין). This stanza is a transitional one linking the speaker's plight in stanza IIA2 with the eschatological imagery of section IIB. The first verse focuses upon the imagery of the *snares of the pit* (פחי שחת), found elsewhere in the scrolls corpus.[132] The parallel terms *evil* (רשעה) and *scoundrels* (חלכאים) provide a link to the previous stanza. The second image is of *the arrows of the pit* (חצי שחת), an image already encountered in the previous poem in this column.[133] The final verse picks up on the keyword *lot* (גורל) used in stanzas IIA1 and IIA2. In the previous stanza *the lot* represents the present position of the scoundrels and the speaker. Here it represents the destiny of the scoundrels, in contrast with the *eternal lot* (destiny) described in IIA1.

The structure of this final verse is complex. The final line is in semantic parallelism to the first line. Both imply *judgement* and use the related imagery of a *measuring-line* and *cords*. The three central lines employ the parallel terms *anger*, *fury* and *wrath*. Line one is parallel to line two in that the verb of line one is implied in line two (ellipsis). The idea of a measuring line and of casting lots are semantically parallel,[134] but line two subtly changes the use of the preposition *upon* to characterise the recipients of the judgement. This enables it to be in parallel to lines three and four, which also characterise the recipients.[135] Finally, as noted by Kittel, the five phrases *the measuring-line*, *the lot of*

---

[130] The two parallel phrases *the tumults of the great* (מהומות רבה) and *the disasters of arrogance* (והוות מדהבה) have caused some difficulty for translators. Kittel's suggestion is creative. She suggests that the feminine singular terms, *great* and *arrogant*, which appear to be in a construct relationship to the nouns *tumults* and *disasters*, represent the splitting of a stereotypical compound noun epithet for Belial, the great raging (arrogant) one. Kittel, *The Hymns of Qumran*, 69.

[131] Kittel, *The Hymns of Qumran*, 63.

[132] See §3.5 for a possible underlying exegesis.

[133] 1QH^a XI 17 [III 16]; see also 1QH^a X 28 [II 26].

[134] cf. Isa 34:17.

[135] The phrases "forsaken ones," "hypocrites" and "all of Belial" seem to be idiomatic epithets for evil-doers. "Hypocrites" occurs in the HB only in Ps 26. See my note on this word in the close reading in §3.4 of chapter three.

*anger, the outpouring of fury, the time of wrath*¹³⁶ and *the cords of death* constitute a list structure.¹³⁷ This list helps to build to the climax of the stanza which is an allusion to Ps 18:4 [5].¹³⁸

In the second half of the poem the speaker has disappeared from view. Like the poem which precedes it in 1QHᵃ this sub-section is in the form of a narrative. Newsom perceptively reads the whole poem in terms of perspective. She describes this change from the personal perspective to that of narrator as going from "the worm's eye view" to the "bird's eye view."¹³⁹

Stanza IIB1 is linked to stanza IIA3 by repetition of *Belial* and by a further allusion to Ps 18:4 [5]. The main focus of this stanza is a description of the destructive power of *the torrents of Belial*, this phrase forming an inclusio delineating the stanza. The verses describe the progressive action of the torrents of Belial starting with *the banks* of the river, through *the expanse of the dry land*, down to *the bases of the mountains*, until finally it breaks into *the great deep/Abaddon*. This action is *like a consuming fire* and *flames of lightning*. The verb to consume (אכל) is used in each of the three verses. In the Hebrew Bible God's glory upon Sinai was like a consuming fire (Exod 24:16; Isa 30:27), and in various scriptures his judgement is described in terms of fire. In particular Ezek 20:47, Deut 32:22, Isa 34:9 and Amos 7:4 are evoked by the language of this stanza.¹⁴⁰ The implication is that the torrents of Belial are not independent but are the agent of God's judgement. I discuss this imagery in §3.5.2 of this chapter.

The general import of the first verse is clear despite difficulties about the precise translation of some words. The loose parallelism shows an ABAB structure for the verse. Lines one and three describe the torrent destroying all the trees upon its banks. Lines two and four describe the fiery nature of the torrent. Although initially the plural torrents are in view, by verses two and three feminine singular verbs are being used

---

¹³⁶ Douglas translates this phrase as 'the line of fury', presumably preferring the variant reading found in 4QpapHᶠ. This makes little difference to the analysis of verse structure. See Douglas, "Power and Praise," 182; Schuller, "Hodayot," 220–221.
¹³⁷ Kittel, *The Hymns of Qumran*, 63–64.
¹³⁸ "*The cords of death encompassed* me; *the torrents of Belial* assailed me." (Psalm 18:4 [5]).
¹³⁹ Newsom, *The Self as Symbolic Space*, 260.
¹⁴⁰ "it shall devour every green tree in you and every dry tree (ואכלה בך כל־עץ־לח וכל־עץ יבש)." (Ezek 20:47); "and shall be turned her *torrents* into *pitch* (ונהפכו נחליה לזפת)." (Isa 34:9); "the foundations of the mountains" (מוסדי הרים) and down to "the lowest Sheol (עד־שאול תחתית)." (Deut 32:22); "*devoured the great deep* (ותאכל את־תהום רבה)." (Amos 7:4).

referring to the fire. The second verse consists of two parallel couplets. The first couplet describes the consuming of *the foundations of clay* in synonymous parallelism to *the expanse of the dry land*, the verb doing double duty for both lines. In the second couplet the *burning* progresses down to *the bases of the mountains* in synonymous parallelism with the phrase *the roots of flint*.

The final verse consists of two lines in grammatical parallelism. The verb *it consumes* is parallel to *they break into*, the singular implied subject (fire) of the first line reverting to the explicit plural *torrents of Belial* in the second. *Unto the great deep* (עד תהום רבה) is parallel to *into Abaddon* (לאבדון). Thus the flow of the fiery torrent reaches the end of its journey culminating in its entry into Abaddon. This descent into Abaddon contrasts with the raising up from Abaddon in the opening stanza of the poem.

The next two stanzas present a scene of great noise and upheaval. IIB2 begins with three lines with consecutive verbs for making sound, namely *roar* (המה), *cry-out* (צרח) and *scream* (רוע). Catchword *the deep* (תהום) links it to the previous stanza. Having reached the extreme depth, the poem returns to survey the disaster from the vantage point of the *earth* and the inhabited *world*. The *cries* of the schemers of *the earth* are contrasted with the *roar* of the schemers of *the deep*. The context here seems to suggest that *the schemers* are conscious beings, but the word is unattested outside of certain songs and prayers found at Qumran.[141]

The final stanza also begins with three consecutive lines describing sound. As in the structurally evoked passage we have a theophany expressed in the standard imageries of storm and earthquake.[142] In particular, God *thunders* as in Ps 18:13. In this and similar biblical verses[143] it is usually God or the elements that *utter their voice*, but here in the hodayah it is *the army of heaven*. The location is *his holy dwelling*, which also *roars*. This evokes Jer 25:30, but the phrase translated as holy dwelling occurs only in Isa 63:15. In Joel 2:11 "the LORD *utters* his *voice* at the head of his army" and in Joel 3[4]:16 he "roars from Zion." The last climactic verse develops this motif from Joel of God's *mighty men* who wage *war* (Joel 2:7) on the day of the LORD. There has and never will be again anything *like it* (Joel 2:2 cf. Exod 11:6). The finality

---

[141] 4Q286 5 1; 4Q403 1 II 13, 14; 4Q405 23 II 10; 4Q427 7 II 23; 4Q428 21 5; 4Q504 1–2 VII 7; 4Q511 37 4. See Abegg, et al., *The Dead Sea Scrolls Concordance, Volume 1*, 440.

[142] Ps 18:6–18. cf. Ps 29:3–10, 77:17–20, 97:2–6.

[143] Cf. Ps 46:6, 68:33, 77:17; Jer 10:13, 25:30, 51:16, 55; Joel 2:11, 3[4]:16; Amos 1:2.

of this denouement is emphasised in three parallel phrases *complete, and determined, and no more*. The first two of these echo an expression of Isaiah which is reused by Daniel in the context of the final war.[144]

3.5. *Allusions*

This poem contains much biblical language but very few certain allusions. There are however two unmistakable markers to Ps 18:4 [5] at the very heart of the poem. These are *the cords of death surround* at the end of IIA3, and *the torrents of Belial* at the beginning and end of IIB1. Ps 18:1–19 is a royal thanksgiving psalm, another version of which can be found in 2 Sam 22:2–20. In the MT Ps 18:4 differs from 2 Sam 22:5 because it refers to *the cords of death* instead of *the breakers of death*.

Ps 18:1–19 describes God's deliverance of the speaker using the language of a theophany. This hodayah has several similarities of language and imagery with the biblical psalm. The introductory stanza speaks of the raising up of the speaker from the depths to a place of safety (cf. Ps 18:4–5, 16, 19). Sub-section IIB of the poem uses the imagery of a theophany, including the trembling of the foundations (cf. Ps 18:7), a consuming fire (cf. Ps 18:8) and the voice of God thundering from heaven (cf. Ps 18:13). These together indicate a structural allusion to Ps 18:1–19.

Newsom comments that this poem lacks thematic integration.[145] I suggest that the structural allusion to Ps 18:1–19 provides the missing key to the underlying theme of this poem. In addition, the poem uses a small number of specific shorthand allusions together with a considerable use of scriptural language and imagery. I will now discuss both of these aspects together.

3.5.1. *Raised to the Heights but Living in the Midst of Evil*

The first two stanzas seem to use more language from the Psalms, which I have noted in the close reading. The two most likely allusions are to Ps 26:7, 11–12. As mentioned in the close reading this psalm is in the context of preparing oneself for worship. This contextual link for two possible markers to the same psalm reinforces the likelihood that they are allusions.[146] The phrase *there is hope*, which begins IIA1, is found

---

[144] Dan 9:27; Isa 10:23, 28:22. cf. Rom 9:27–28.
[145] Newsom, *The Self as Symbolic Space*, 257.
[146] Fletcher-Louis has pointed out that Mal 2:6 also fits the first marker and is in a

in the Hebrew Bible only in Ezra 10:2. It is used there in the context of repentance, connotations of which lead well into the declaration that *you have purified a perverted spirit from great sin*. The other two clear uses of this phrase in 1QH^a are also associated with turning from sin.[147] This may be an instance of an allusion which has become almost an idiom.

Various terms are used for the beings of heaven. This language draws on biblical passages which describe the heavenly court and thus evokes the general scene. However no particular passage appears to be alluded to. The term *sons of heaven* is probably a circumlocution for "the sons of God."[148] In Psalm 89 this appears to be synonymous with the *congregation/assembly of the holy-ones*. "Holy ones" appears in *1 Enoch* as a term for heavenly beings. Sons of heaven and holy ones are also found in parallel in Wis 5:5. The term *spirit* is used in 1 Kgs 22:22 (2 Chr 18:20)[149] of a member of the *army of heaven* surrounding the throne of God. In *1 Enoch* 14 it is used for heavenly beings as opposed to humans who are "flesh." Thus the *spirits of knowledge* in IIA1c are probably to be understood as heavenly beings. However, in IIA1b it is clearly a human *spirit* that is meant.

In IIA2 various terms are also used for the wicked, including *the territory of evil* (גבול רשעה), and *scoundrels* (הלכאים). These are distinctive markers to Mal 1:4 and Ps 10:10 but they appear to add little except some elaboration on the character of the wicked. However Isa 14:4, marked by the hapax *arrogance* (מדהבה), reinforces the poem's main contrast between height and depth. It is a powerful poem containing graphic imagery of how God brings down the god-like aspirations of the wicked.

In IIA3 the only clear markers are to the already discussed Ps 10:10 and Ps 18:8. But there may be an underlying exegesis to the imagery of the *snares* (פחים), *nets* (מצודות) and *fishing nets* (מכמרת). In 4Q171 II 9–12a, a pesher on Ps 37:11, we find the term *snares of Belial* (פחי בליעל), from which the poor will be delivered; the wicked who plot against them will be destroyed by their own weapons. In CD IV 10–19 Belial will be set loose against Israel but will be caught in the three nets of Belial

---

cultic context. However there is no geographical connotation to this reference. Also in the few references to *plain* (מישור) in the scrolls, there are no obvious markers to this verse. There is at least one, 1QH^a X 31 [II 29] (possibly more), to Ps 26:12.

[147] 1QH^a XIV 9 [VI 6], XVII 14 [IX 14], cf. 1QH^a XXII 10 [1 7].

[148] Gen 6; Deut 32:8 (4QDeut^j); Job 1:6, 2:1, 38:7, Ps 29:1* 82:6, 89:6*; (* indicates the phrase "sons of the Elim").

[149] cf. Ps 104:4.

(שלושת מצודות בליעל), fornication, wealth, and defilement of the temple. This is a pesher on Isa 24:17.[150] There is continuity with the usage in the Hebrew Bible of hunting terms in connection with the threat from wicked enemies.[151] However the terms have been extended to apply to the particular threat posed by Belial.

The meaning of Belial in the Hebrew Bible seems to range from "worthless" to "rebellious." Thus, in Deut 14:13 "sons of Belial" refers to those who oppose God and worship false gods. Belial appears to be associated with the underworld in Ps 18:4 (2 Sam 22:5).[152] It is a small step from these references to the personification of Belial as a spiritual being opposed to God. This usage is attested in *Jubilees* and *Testament of Levi*.[153] This spiritual being opposed to God appears by several other names in the Dead Sea corpus, including Melchiresha, and the Angel/Prince of darkness.[154] Of particular interest here is the curse against Belial in 4Q286 in which he is also described as the Angel of the Pit and the Spirit of Abaddon.[155] This gives some justification for taking the terms Pit, Abaddon and Belial as almost synonymous in sectarian compositions, certainly when used as epithets.[156]

3.5.2. *Eschatological Destruction and Holy War*

IIB1 gives a graphic description of the overflowing of the torrents of Belial and their destructive flow down into Abaddon.[157] The description draws upon a cosmology similar to that found in chapters 17 and 18 of *1*

---

[150] For a detailed discussion of this pesher see Hans Kosmala, "The Three Nets of Belial," *ASTI* 4 (1965) 91–113.

[151] The phrase *nooses of the pit* (מוקשי שחת) occurs in 1QH^a X 23 [II 21] and *snares of the pit* (פחי שחת) in 1QH^a XI 27 [III 26]. The term *nooses of the pit* also occurs in 4Q428 frg. 13 (= 1QH^a XXI?), 4Q 228 1 I 8 and CD XIV 2 (=4Q267 9 V 5); cf. the term *nooses of death* in Ps 18:5.

[152] J.J. Collins comments "In most cases [in the HB], Belial appears to be an abstraction, roughly equivalent to evil. In Psalm 18:5 (=2 Sam 22:5), however, Belial is clearly associated with the netherworld ... The etymology of the name is uncertain, but the two most plausible explanations also point to the netherworld: *bᵉly yaʻal* = (the place from which) one does not go up; or a derivation from *blʻ*, to swallow, a verb often associated with Mot, Death, in Canaanite texts." See J.J. Collins, *Apocalypticism in the Dead Sea Scrolls*, 101.

[153] *Jub.* 1:20; *T. Levi* 19; cf. 1QS II 5; CD V 18–19.

[154] 4Q544 2 3; 4Q280 2 2.

[155] 4Q286 10 II 1–13 (cf. 7 II 5, 7).

[156] E.g. 'sons of the pit' (CD VI 15); 'men of the pit' (1QS IX 16, 22; X 19); 'you made Belial for the pit' (1QM XIII 11).

[157] Holm-Nielsen is unsure and gives an alternative explanation. "There may be the unusual concept here of 'the floods of Belial' breaking into the underworld, so that not

Enoch, including a river of fire.[158] There is no explicit mention of such a river of fire in the Hebrew Bible. But the poem cleverly inserts biblical language from various sources into the description. This pastiche of biblical passages brings with it connotations of God's fiery judgement, but is a minimal use of allusion. However the depiction of consuming fire would be certain to evoke the theophany at Sinai (Exod 24:16) and is also a component of the theophany in the structurally evoked passage in which "fire from his mouth consumed" (Ps 18:8 [9]).

This raises the question of the significance of the term Belial in the poem. Despite what was said above concerning the personification of Belial in some texts, it seems to be used here more as an epithet for the realms of evil and of the underworld. As mentioned in the close reading it appears that the torrents of Belial are mere instruments of God's judgement. There is only a slight hint of personification in the term *schemers of the deep* in stanza IIB2. In IIB2 we also have *the tumult of the casting-up-of the mud* of the deep. Holm-Nielsen sees here a reference to Isa 57:20, presumably because this is the only biblical occurrence of mud (רפש). He also thinks the context is similar to Ps 107:26 where the same verb *dissolve* (מוג) is used.[159] However I do not consider there is sufficient similarity of context, and would deem this merely use of biblical language.

The main allusions in this poem are not to individual biblical passages but rather to a whole complex of ideas about the universe. The poem takes for granted that these ideas are known to the reader. These ideas appear to be of two kinds. Those which were part of the common currency of ancient Near Eastern mythology; ideas which are nowhere explicitly spelled out in the Hebrew Bible but are often alluded to. Secondly there are ideas which probably derive from biblical exegesis, some of which is known to us from extra-biblical writings including those found at Qumran.

---

even the dead are spared the eschatological afflictions, but this is not necessarily the case. Lines 29 and 32 together may adversatively signify a totality: no one and nothing escapes the destruction, cf. Amos 9:1–4." See Holm-Nielsen, *Hodayot*, 72 n. 47.

[158] Nickelsburg comments on *1 En.* 17:5 thus: "The river of fire is Pyriphlegethon, often mentioned in connection with the underworld and journeys to it. A graphic description of this torrent in connection with the abyss (see vv 7–8), the realm of death, Belial, and eternal punishment occurs in 1QH^a 11(3): 28–36." George W.E. Nickelsburg, *1 Enoch 1: A Commentary on the Book of 1 Enoch, Chapters 1–36; 81–108* (Hermeneia; Minneapolis: Fortress Press, 2001), 283–284.

[159] Holm-Nielsen, *Hodayot*, 72 nn. 50, 74; 35 n. 26.

The cosmology underlying this poem appears to be a version of the "three-storey universe." Elements of this are alluded to in some biblical passages, although there is no consistent or systematic cosmogony or cosmology in the Hebrew Bible. It is also the cosmology of *1 Enoch*, the *Testament of Abraham* and the *Apocalypse of Ezra*. The earth was seen as resting upon the waters of the deep, supported by pillars. Under the earth was the deep (תהום) which contained Sheol, the place of the dead, also referred to as the pit (שחת). Sheol was seen as having gates and compartments, much like an earthly tomb. The deep itself rested upon a foundation of primeval mud.

In the Hebrew Bible Abaddon, meaning destruction, is sometimes used in combination with Sheol.[160] The development of a dualistic view of the universe seems to have been accompanied by a division of Sheol into separate compartments for the spirits of the good and evil.[161] In later usage Abaddon seems to have developed into the name of a distinct compartment within Sheol and/or the name of an angel associated with that region. This may explain the use of Sheol and Abaddon in a construct relationship in 1QH^a XI 20 [III 19] and 4QM^a (4Q491) 8–10 I 15. In 11Q11 IV 10 Abaddon is used in connection with the phrase "to the great deep and to the lowest [Sheol]" (לתהום רבה [ולשאול] התחתיה), and in 1QH^a XI 32–33 [III 31–32] and 4Q504 1–2 VII 8 it is used in combination with the phrase "unto the great deep" (עד תהום רבה). These terms are used in Deut 32:22, Job 31:12, Amos 7:4 in the context of fire consuming to the lowest region. They may reflect an existing association of the terms or may have been the basis for it.[162]

The *torrents of Belial*, although it is a biblical phrase, seem in our poem to be envisioned as a river of fire. A similar river is described in *1 En.* 17:5. Nickelsburg connects this with the following Greek cosmography.

> The earth is actually honeycombed with many rivers, which rise to the surface and then plunge beneath it—originating from and returning to the great chasm of Tartarus. Named among these are the four: Oceanus,

---

[160] Job 26:6, Prov 15:11, 27:20; cf. the remaining biblical reference to Abaddon in Job 28:22, 31:12; Ps 88:11.

[161] Cf. Luke 16:26.

[162] "For a fire is kindled by my anger, and burns to the depths of Sheol (עד־שאול תחתית); it devours the earth and its increase, and sets on fire the foundations of the mountains." (Deut 32:22); "For that would be a fire consuming down to Abaddon (כי אש היא עד־אבדון תאכל)." (Job 31:12); "The LORD God was calling for a shower of fire, and it devoured the great deep (את־תהום רבה) and was eating up the land." (Amos 7:4).

> Acheron, Pyriphlegethon, and the Stygian ... Pyriphlegethon, a boiling torrent of mud and water and fire, flows beneath the surface and makes its own lake, larger than the Mediterranean Sea ... these rivers, especially the Pyriphlegethon, are closely connected with the underworld and with post-mortem punishment.[163]

Above the earth was the expanse of heaven which was spread out rather like the roof of a building or tent. This also was sometimes described as resting upon pillars or foundations which could be mountains or winds.[164] Under the heavens moved the sun and moon and other heavenly bodies. Above this heavenly expanse were more waters, and above that the highest heaven, the dwelling of God and the angels. The final stanza of the poem takes us back to this heavenly realm. The image of the river of fire gives way to images of God the warrior. J. Jeremias categorises this as a theophany of Yahweh as warrior thus:

> In the OT we very often hear about a 'coming' of Yahweh which produces a reaction of terror. The description follows a fixed pattern: the first part refers to the 'going forth' or descent of Yahweh; the second refers to the resultant agitation of nature ... This pattern is documented in the oldest poetry of Israel (Judg. 5:4–5; cf. Deut 33:2), and was still in use in post-OT times (Ecclus 16:18–19; 43:16–17; Jth 16:15; Wisd. Sol. 5:21–23; Asmp. Moses 10:3–6; 1QH 3:32–36). It may encompass one or two verses (Amos 1:2) or extensive compositions (Ps. 18:7–15; Hab. 3:3–15; etc.) ... Within the older prophetic writings the direction of the pattern was completely changed: Yahweh's coming is now a future event which will bring judgement upon Israel (Mic 1:2–7; Amos 1:2)! In exilic and postexilic times the prophets often announced the coming of Yahweh as the warrior to free Israel (Isa 40:10–11; 42:13); to do battle against foreign nations (Isa 19:1; cf. Zech 9:14 and 14:3–4); and to fight against the wicked in Israel (Isa 59:15–19; 66:15–16; Mal 3:1–5). Finally, in the beginnings of Apocalyticism, the Warrior comes to bring judgement upon the world (Jer 25:30–31; Isa 26:21; 1QH 3:32ff. etc).[165]

---

[163] Nickelsburg, *1 Enoch 1*, 283.

[164] On *1 En.* 18:2 Nickelsburg comments "The cosmos is depicted as a building. The earth rests on a foundation with a cornerstone. The firmament is set on the ends of the earth (cf. v10), and its height is supported by the winds, which function as pillars. The 'foundations of the earth' are part of the well-known trappings of biblical cosmology (Ps 18:16 [15], 82:5; Prov 8:29; Isa 24:18, 40:21; Jer 31:37; Mic 6:2.) and are perhaps to be identified with the 'pillars of the earth' (1 Sam 2:8; Job 9:6; Ps 75:3[4]) ... For the whole context, cf. Ps 104:2–5, where cosmic imagery fluctuates between tent and house." Nickelsburg, *1 Enoch 1*, 284.

[165] J. Jeremias, "Theophany in the OT" in *The Interpreters Bible Dictionary, supplementary volume* (ed. G.A. Butterick; New York: Abingdon Press, 1962), 897–898.

It is the structural allusion to God the warrior portrayed in Ps 18:7–15 that sets the scene for this final stanza. As can be seen from the observations of Jeremias quoted above, this kind of language is ubiquitous in the scriptures. However, the description and some of the language is most likely to evoke Joel 2:1–11, 3[4]:9–16. The distinctive phrase *complete and determined* evokes the heavenly war scenario of Dan 9:27, which itself may well be alluding to Isa 10:23, 28:22.

3.6. *Intertexts*

The relationship of this poem to the one preceding it in 1QH^a will be discussed in §3.7. The poem in 1QH^a XIII 22–XV 8 [V 20–VII 5] also has similarities with this poem. The speaker uses the key phrase "I know that there is hope"[166] and describes his deliverance in terms of being purified and joining in community with the angels (XIV 9–16). He concludes with the eschatological triumph of God's armies (XIV 31–41). I discuss this poem in §2.6.1 of chapter four.

There are a number of other Dead Sea texts which employ language of communion with angels similar to that of stanza IIA1. These are discussed more fully by Frennesson in his PhD dissertation on the subject.[167] As previously discussed by Kuhn,[168] the most striking similarities occur in 1QH^a XIX 13–17 [XI 10–14]. I have emphasised these in the translation which follows.

> For the sake of your glory *you have purified* man *from sin*
> To make himself holy for you
> from all impure abominations and guilt of unfaithfulness
> To BE UNITED WITH THE SONS OF your truth and in the LOT *with* your *holy ones*
> To raise *from dust* the worms of the dead[169] *to an eternal council*
> And from *a perverted spirit* to your understanding
> *To take his stand in position* before you
> *with the* everlasting *army* and the [eternal] SPIRIT[s]
> To renew himself with every being
> and with the KNOWLEDGEABLE *in a community of rejoicing.*
> (1QH^a XIX 13–17 [XI 10–14])

---

[166] Found in the Dead Sea corpus only in 1QH^a XI 20 [III 19], XIV 9 [VI 6], XVII 14 [IX 14]. The significance of this phrase is discussed in §3.5.
[167] Frennesson, *In a Common Rejoicing.*
[168] Kuhn, *Enderwartung,* 80–85; see also Nickelsburg, *Resurrection,* 152–156.
[169] Or "of men."

4QH^a II 18–V 3 also has similarities of language to the first part of this poem.[170] It has excited much interest because its human(?) speaker appears to describe himself as exalted to heaven. For example, "he lifts up from the dust the poor-one ... with the Elim in the congregation of the community" (4QH^a II 8–9), and "how is [dust and clay] to be recko[ned] that he should recount these things continually, and take his stand in position [...] the sons of heaven" (4QH^a II 16c–18a). However, of equal interest is that, unlike most hodayot, it uses plural imperatives to praise and first person plural expressions; this invites speculation that 4QH^a II 18–V 3 was used liturgically.

Another feature of all these passages is their use of language found in 1QS concerning membership of the community. Their similarities may be explicable if both are alluding to liturgical formulae used at the covenant renewal ceremony described in 1QS I 16–II 12.[171] Frennesson, commenting on this poem, has drawn particular attention to the phrase *to stand in position* (להתיצב במעמד). He notes that in the Hebrew Bible the verb can be used of presenting oneself in the royal or heavenly court or in the temple, but also of withstanding an enemy. He suggests that this dual religious and military context is significant. In 1QS these words can be used of the community, and in 1QM of the earthly or heavenly army.[172] Certainly in this poem, the royal court appears to be mobilised as the royal army. A similar idea is evident in 1QM.

> For there is a multitude of holy ones in heaven and armies of angels in your holy dwelling to [praise] your [truth.] And the chosen of the holy people you have established for yourself among them. ... to muster the armies of your chosen ones according to its thousands and its myriads, together with your holy ones and with your angels ... (1QM XII 1–4)

I have already mentioned the similarities of this poem to *1 Enoch*. One finds a similar cosmology (*1 En.* 17:4–5, 23:1–24:1) and passages describing a theophany and judgement (*1 En.* 1:3c–9, 102:1–3). Although the

---

[170] 4QH^a II 18–V 3 is the most complete copy of a hymn partially preserved in 1QH^a, 4QH^b and 4QH^c. What appears to be another recension of this hymn appears in 4Q491 11 I 8–24. See Schuller, "Hodayot," 96–108, 158–159, 203–208; Eshel, "Self-Glorification Hymn," 421–432; M. Baillet, *Qumrân Grotte 4, III* (DJD7; Oxford: Clarendon, 1982), 12.

[171] Cf. also 1QS XI 7–8 "To those whom God has selected he has given them as *everlasting* possession; and he has given them an inheritance in *the lot of the holy ones*. He unites their *assembly* to *the sons of the heavens* in order (to form) the council of the *community* and a *foundation* of the building of holiness to be an everlasting plantation throughout all future ages."

[172] Frennesson, "*In a Common Rejoicing*," 47–50.

two texts share a similar apocalyptic worldview, there is no evidence of literary dependence between them. Rather, this poem and its intertexts attest a lively and continuing development of cosmological and eschatological ideas during this period.

3.7. *Observations and Comments*

As mentioned in my introduction the interest in this poem has centred around its classification and its theology. The theological controversy revolves around whether this poem attests belief in a realized or future eschatology. From my analysis the poem clearly falls into two parts. The first concerns the speaker's communion with the heavenly realm, while dwelling in the present evil age. The second concerns the eschatological judgement.

These scenarios, while mythic, are not merely metaphorical for deliverance from distress. Rather the poem invites the reader to participate in the heavenly realm and to identify with its final triumph. This experience transcends and transforms the individual's distress. Thus the eschatology is both realized and future. The poem has nothing directly to say about immortality or resurrection although, as noted by Kittel, its theology is compatible with such ideas.[173] However, this is a poem, not a theological treatise. Its use of allusion and imagery is designed to evoke an experience and reinforce a worldview. The reader who is sensitive to the genre is unlikely to want to press the imagery too far.

There has been considerable disagreement over the classification of this poem as Teacher or Community Hymn. There is nothing in the first part of the poem to distinguish the speaker from any other member of his community. Moreover IIA1 has a cultic feel and similarity of language with Community Hymns and with 1QS and 1QM. Also, as noted by Douglas, the second part of the poem "is distinguished by its cosmic perspective." By this time the individual has completely disappeared. After some discussion Douglas allows the possibility that this could be a "pseudo-Teacher Hymn."[174] I suggest that a far simpler solution is to recognize that the categories of Teacher and Community Hymn are inadequate. This poem has a more obviously distinctive style and content than some. But one objective of this study has been to

---

[173] Kittel, The Hymns of Qumran, 80.
[174] Douglas, "Power and Praise," 187–190.

demonstrate that if one looks beyond the "thanksgiving" format there is a great variety of style and subject matter in these poems.

However, I think it is more than coincidence that places this poem and the preceding one together in 1QH^a. They are both eschatological poems and both are based upon a structural allusion to different versions of the same biblical psalm. It is probably this allusion which gives both poems the same basic shape; i.e. the first part can loosely be associated with the distress of the speaker, but the second part launches into a description of the eschatological judgement. But the end result is two very distinctive poems, different from each other as well as from the other poems in the collection.

Their juxtaposition invites the reader to compare and contrast them. They make use of very different imagery and different allusions. The first poem uses extensive word play; the second employs infinitive clauses and lists. The first depends greatly upon allusion. The second is not so obviously allusive but draws upon biblical language and tradition in a more general way. In the first the main contrast is between the opposite outcomes of distress for the speaker and his enemies. In the second the contrast is between height and depth, between those who are joined to heaven and those who are "of Belial."

I suggest that these two poems are deliberate exercises of biblical interpretation and poetic artistry. Whether they are by the same author or different authors seems to be the wrong question. What they show is the importance of Ps 18:2–19 (=2 Sam 22:1–20) in the community which produced this poetry. They also indicate that the biblical psalm was interpreted by them in an eschatological context. We now know from the Cave 4 manuscripts that there were indeed differing collections of poetic compositions. One can almost imagine that many such meditations on this psalm were composed and that these two, whether by merit or accident, have been preserved.

That this is not such an imaginative flight of fancy is demonstrated by a recent article by Esther Chazon. Her purpose is to consider the biblical allusions in two poems. Chazon, quoting Schuller, says of the first of these, the *Tehillah of the Man of God* in 4Q381, that it "draws extensively upon a single biblical psalm," namely Psalm 18.[175] Chazon observes that the poem reworks Psalm 18 into a lament which petitions

---

[175] Esther Chazon, "The Use of the Bible as a Key to Meaning in Psalms from Qumran," in *Emanuel: Studies in Hebrew Bible, Septuagint and Dead Sea Scrolls in honor of Emanuel Tov* (ed. S.M. Paul et al.; VTSup 94; Leiden: Brill, 2003), 87; Eileen Schuller,

for deliverance and "commits God's tested ones to recite—evidently in the future—a prayer that is a reworked version of Psalm 18."[176] Although not necessarily composed by the sectarian community, this poem shows that Psalm 18 was viewed as a suitable "template" for the composition of new prayers and poems.

"381. 4QNon-Canonical Psalms B," in Qumran Cave 4.VI: Poetical and Liturgical Texts, Part 1 (DJD 11; ed. E. Eshel et al.; Oxford: Clarendon, 1998), 121–122.

[176] Chazon, "The Use of the Bible," 89.

CHAPTER SIX

CONCLUSIONS

1. *Introduction*

The primary aim of this study has been to establish a fresh approach to reading the *Hodayot*. Questions that previously have been asked of these compositions include who wrote them, what was their *Sitz im Leben*, and what theological assumptions do they contain? I have sought to ask a more basic question; namely, how would an informed reader interpret these poems and why?

The question itself betrays one basic premise of mine, that these are poems and that an ideal reader will read them according to certain poetic conventions. The title of this study has arisen from my other main premise, that the most obvious poetic device employed in the *Hodayot* is scriptural allusion. However, it is only one of many devices used. This recognition means that I have started my analysis not with the allusions but with the overall structure of each poem. I have sought to understand how the allusions function within the context of each composition as a whole.

In short, I have attempted to let the poems speak for themselves. However, one of the insights from the field of comparative literature is that any reader, ancient or modern, is always part of the equation. The readings thus produced are therefore uniquely my own. Others can and should produce alternative readings. It is not my contention that mine is the only possible interpretation. My more modest ambition has been to demonstrate that the method I have used can produce fresh insights and indicate new avenues of exploration. With that in mind I will now seek to summarise the observations that have arisen from this study.

2. *Diversity*

Firstly, even amongst the small sample of poems selected for this study, close analysis has revealed a considerable diversity of style and content. In some of the allusion markers, word plays and double meanings feature, especially in the first poem discussed in chapter five. In some cases two allusions are conflated so that their connotations are combined. There is a delightful example of the conflation of Isa 63:15 and Ps 94:19 in the poem in chapter four. All the poems use structural allusions and shorthand notations. Some also use pointer or gnomic allusions. Because of the way that the first poem in chapter three alters one's understanding of Jeremiah, I have judged it to be an example of a dialectical allusion.

Apart from the allusions, the most common poetic device is the repetition of key words or phrases. Both allusions and key words are employed in a variety of ways and combinations. Some, but not all, key words are also allusion markers. Some are repeated throughout in a unifying manner; others are used as catchwords. Keywords are the main structural device in the poem considered in chapter four. Differing forms of symmetry are also used including matching stanzas, chiasms and inclusios.

The poem in chapter four, 1QH^a XVI 5–XVII 36 [VIII 4–IX 36], illustrates the changes of genre between different sections of the same poem—meshalim, lament, declaration of confidence. There is often a close matching of style to content as a poem slows or quickens the pace, builds to a climax, etc. This is nowhere better illustrated than in 1QH^a XI 6–19 [III 5–18], the first poem discussed in chapter five. This displays a masterful use of keyword, allusion and line length to describe the progressive stages of the birth process. The climax is reached in the "final push" of the penultimate long line of the stanza; the following short anti-climactic line expresses relief at the successful outcome of a healthy baby boy.

This diversity highlights the inadequacy of the categories of Teacher and Community Hymns. For example, in chapter three we have a Community Hymn, 1QH^a VII 21–VIII ? [XV 8–25], which does not fit the stereotypical lack of allusions. Moreover it possibly contains material taken over from non-sectarian wisdom traditions. In chapter five we have two poems, 1QH^a XI 6–19 [III 5–18] and 1QH^a XI 20–37 [III 19–36], which also defy categorisation. They are not obviously oriented towards either the individual or the community. Instead they appear to be artistic interpretations of Psalm 18, on an eschatological theme. I have, not altogether fancifully, suggested that these are neither Teacher nor Community Hymns but representative examples of a sectarian "class exercise" in poetic interpretation.

The diversity in style and content also has implications for the *Sitz im Leben* of the *Hodayot*. The most complex poems, such as 1QH^a XI 6–19 [III 5–18], discussed in chapter five, are unlikely to have been used liturgically. But other poems, such as those in chapter three, appear to have liturgical elements. This reinforces the likelihood that 1QH^a is an anthology of compositions which had a variety of backgrounds before they were collected together.

3. *A Literary Tradition*

The above examples reinforce my growing conviction that the search for a core of poems written by an individual author is misguided. There are undoubtedly similarities as well as differences between the poems. However, I suggest that these are due to a variety of causes.

One possibility which I believe merits further study is that the long hodayah in 1QH^a XIII 22–XV 8 [V 20–VII 5] is a deliberate pastiche of motifs and imagery drawn from other poems in the collection (see §2.6.1 of chapter four). Possibly it was composed as the centrepiece to the so-called Teacher Book. If this is the case it would be evidence, not for a common authorship, but for conscious literary borrowing by an editor.

Another probable cause of similarities is a common exegetical tradition. Thus I have suggested, in §3.7 of chapter three, that coincidences of language in certain compositions are due to their common concern with group identity. One of the ways that the group legitimised its identity was by appeal to scripture. This would lead to a common stock of fundamental passages and associated exegesis by which the group defined itself. This is another area meriting further study. Other similarities, such as the use of plant imagery discussed in chapter four, or creation and destiny discussed in chapter three, have counterparts in non-sectarian literature. This suggests that some similarities are simply reflections of a wider non-sectarian literary heritage.

The extensive use of Isaiah and Psalms in the *Hodayot* has long been noted. This is confirmed by the detailed analyses in this study. However, the key role of the two prophets of the renewed covenant, Ezekiel and

Jeremiah, comes across more clearly as a result of this study. I argue in §2.6.2 of chapter three that Jer 10:23 is pivotal to an exegesis combining the ideas of predestination and the two ways. I suggest that Jeremiah is understood as an archetypal righteous person, perhaps even a Moses figure. This observation leads onto the question of authorship.

4. *The Implied Speaker*

The longer poems discussed in chapters three and four have both been considered, either in whole or in part, as undisputed Teacher Hymns. Does this study shed any light upon the identity of their author(s)? In both poems I have drawn attention to a possible veiled reference to the Teacher of Righteousness based on an allusion to Hos 6:3. This depends upon a word play on the double meaning "teach/rain" of the verb ירה. Both poems also use the verb "reveal/shine" (יפע) which occurs only eight times in the Hebrew Bible, including Moses' encounter on Sinai, and indicates a theophany.

I have suggested that these and other factors identify the implied speaker in these two poems as a leader and teacher, probably a priest. But the use of scriptural allusions and typology is ambiguous. It could be interpreted as a special claim to uniqueness. It could equally well indicate that the speaker identifies himself within a tradition of faithful teachers and prophets. He may be saying no more nor less than that, starting with Moses and including Hosea, Jeremiah, Ezekiel and Isaiah, in every generation God has raised up leaders to guide the faithful remnant. The reader would also place the Teacher of Righteousness in this succession. Moreover, any subsequent leader could also identify himself with the speaker of this poem. This latter observation is very much in line with the arguments of Carol Newsom.[1]

An additional distinction needs to be made between the implied speaker and the author of a poem. For example, the lowliest member of the community could have written such a poem as a tribute to his teacher. The "I" of the poem is not necessarily that of the author. The very proliferation of pseudepigraphic works during this period, some of which are attested amongst the Dead Sea scrolls, should make this point obvious. However, it is not often raised in the discussion.

---

[1] Newsom, *The Self as Symbolic Space*, 287–300.

5. Artistic Merit

Finally, and perhaps above all, I hope that my study has demonstrated that these poems may be read for their own sake. For a modern reader familiar with the biblical tradition the allusions still resonate. Some connotations may be lost but other newer ones may replace them. The same may be said of the imagery and other poetic devices. One need not be versed in the theological connotations of the imagery to appreciate a skilful evocation of the physical and emotional sensations of childbirth. One does not need to know who "they" were to appreciate the polemical power of a poem which characterises "them" as hypocritical, scheming liars and enemies of God!

At the beginning of this study I quoted the opinion of Furniss and Bath that "poetry achieves its emotional power by working the resources of the language to the limit." It is my opinion that these compositions are worthy examples of this effect. It is the multi-layered quality of this poetry which gives it such an enduring impact.

BIBLIOGRAPHY

Abegg, Martin, Jr., Peter Flint, and Eugene Ulrich. *The Dead Sea Scrolls Bible.* Edinburgh: T&T Clark, 1999.

Abegg, Martin G., Jr. with James E. Bowley and Edward M. Cook, in consultation with Emanuel Tov. *The Dead Sea Scrolls Concordance. Volume One: The Non-Biblical Texts from Qumran.* Leiden: Brill, 2003.

Allen, Leslie C. *Ezekiel 1–19.* Word Biblical Commentary 28. Dallas: Word Books, 1994.

———. *Ezekiel 20–48.* Word Biblical Commentary 29. Dallas: Word Books, 1998.

Alter, Robert. *The Art of Biblical Poetry.* Edinburgh: T&T Clark, 1990.

Aune, David E. *Revelation 1–5.* Word Biblical Commentary 52a. Dallas, Texas: Word Books, 1998.

Baillet, M. *Qumrân Grotte 4.III (4Q482–4Q520).* Discoveries in the Judaean Desert 7. Oxford: Clarendon, 1982.

Bakhtin, Mikhail M. *The Dialogic Imagination.* Translated by Caryl Emerson and Michael Holquist. Vol. 1, University of Texas Press Slavic Series. Austin, TX: University of Texas Press, 1981.

Bardtke, Hans. "Considérations sur les cantiques de Qumrân." *Revue biblique* 63 (1956): 220–233.

———. "Die Loblieder von Qumran." *Theologische Literaturzeitung* 81 (1956): 149–154, 589–604, 715–724, and 82 (1957): 2–19.

Barthes, Roland. "From Work to Text." Pages 155–164 in *Image-Music-Text.: Essays by Roland Barthes.* Selected and translated by S. Heath. London: Fontana, 1977.

Baumgarten, Joseph M. "4Q500 and the Ancient Conception of the Lord's Vineyard." *Journal of Jewish Studies* 40 (1989): 1–6.

Beal, Timothy K. "Glossary." Pages 21–24 in *Reading Between Texts: Intertextuality and the Hebrew Bible.* Edited by D.N. Fewell. Louisville, Ky.: Westminster John Knox Press, 1992.

Becker, Jürgen. *Das Heil Gottes: Heils-und Sündenbegriffe in den Qumrantexten und im Neuen Testament.* Studien zur Umwelt des Neuen Testaments 3. Göttingen: Vandenhoeck & Ruprecht, 1963.

Ben Porat, Ziva. "The Poetics of Literary Allusion." *PTL: A Journal for Descriptive Poetics and Theory of Literature* 1 (1976): 105–128.

Benveniste, Emile. *Problems in General Linguistics.* Translated by Mary Elizabeth Meek. Miami Linguistics Series 8. Coral Gables, FL: University of Miami, 1971.

Berlin, Adele. *The Dynamics of Biblical Parallelism.* Bloomington and Indianapolis: Indiana University Press, 1992.

Bloom, Harold. *The Anxiety of Influence.* Oxford: Oxford University Press, 1973.

———. *A Map of Misreading*. Oxford: Oxford University Press, 1975.
Brock, S.P. "The Psalms of Solomon." Pages 649–682 in *The Apocryphal Old Testament*. Edited by H.F.D. Sparks. Oxford: Clarendon, 1984.
Brooke, George J. "4Q500 1 and the Use of Scripture in the Parable of the Vineyard." *Dead Sea Discoveries* 2 (1995): 268–294.
———. "The Book of Jeremiah and its reception in the Qumran Scrolls." Pages 183–205 in *The Book of Jeremiah and its Reception*. Edited by A.H.W. Curtis and T. Römer. Bibliotheca ephemeridum theologicarum lovaniensium 128. Leuven: Uitgeverij Peeters, 1997.
Brown, Schuyler. "Deliverance from the Crucible: Some Further Reflexions on 1QH III. 1–1." *New Testament Studies* 14 (1967–1968): 247–259.
Brown, W.P. *Seeing the Psalms*. Louisville: Westminster John Knox Press, 2002.
Brownlee, William H. "Messianic Motifs of Qumran and the New Testament." *New Testament Studies* 3 (1956–1957): 12–30, 195–210.
———. *The Meaning of the Qumrân Scrolls for the Bible: with Special Attention to the Book of Isaiah*. New York: Oxford University Press, 1964.
Burke, Kenneth. *Language as Symbolic Action: Essays on Life, Literature, and Method*. Berkeley, CA:University of California Press, 1966.
———. *A Rhetoric of Motives*. Berkeley, CA: University of California Press, 1969.
———. *The Rhetoric of Religion: Studies in Logology*. Berkeley, CA: University of California Press, 1970.
Campbell, Jonathan G. *The use of Scripture in the Damascus Document 1–8, 19–20*. Beihefte zur Zeitschrift für die alttestamentliche Wissenschaft 228. Berlin: de Gruyter, 1995.
Carmignac, Jean. "Remarques sur le texte des hymnes de Qumrân." *Biblica* 39 (1958): 139–155.
———. "Localisation des fragments 15, 18 et 22 des hymnes." *Revue de Qumran* 1 (1958–1959): 425–430.
———. "Compléments au texte des hymnes de Qumrân." *Revue de Qumran* 2 (1959–1960): 267–276, 549–558.
———. "Étude sur les procédés poétiques des Hymnes." *Revue de Qumran* 2 (1959–1960): 515–532.
———. "Les citations de l'ancien testament, et spécialement des poèmes du serviteur, dans les hymnes de Qumran." *Revue de Qumran* 2 (1959–1960): 357–394.
———. "Les éléments historiques des Hymnes de Qumrân." *Revue de Qumran* 6 (1960): 205–222.
———. "Les hymnes." Pages 129–282 in *Les textes de Qumran, traduits et annotés*. By J. Carmignac and P. Gilbert. Paris: Letouzey & Ané, 1961.
———. *Christ and the Teacher of Righteousness*. Baltimore: Helicon Press, 1962.
Chamberlain, John V. "Another Qumran Thanksgiving Psalm." *Journal of Near Eastern Studies* 14 (1955): 32–41.
———. "Further Elucidation of a Messianic Thanksgiving Psalm from Qumran." *Journal of Near Eastern Studies* 14 (1955): 181–182.
Charlesworth, James H., et al. *Graphic Concordance to the Dead Sea Scrolls*. Tübingen: Mohr; Louisville: John Knox Press, 1991.
Charlesworth James H., and Elisha Qimron. *The Dead Sea Scrolls: Hebrew,*

Aramaic and Greek Texts with English Translations, Vol. 1, Rule of the Community and Related Documents. Princeton Theological Seminary Dead Sea Scrolls Project. Tübingen: Mohr; Louisville: John Knox Press, 1994.

Charlesworth, James H. "A Prolegomenon to a New Study of the Jewish Background of the Hymns and Prayers in the New Testament." *Journal of Jewish Studies* 33 (1982): 1–21.

———. "An Allegorical and Autobiographical Poem by the Moreh Haṣ-Ṣedeq (1QH 8:4–11)." Pages 295–307 in *Sha'arei Talmon: Studies in the Bible, Qumran and the Ancient Near East Presented to Shemaryahu Talmon*. Edited by. M. Fishbane and E. Tov. Winona Lake: Eisenbrauns, 1992.

Chazon, Esther G. "Review: B. Nitzan, *Qumran Prayer and Religious Poetry*." *Dead Sea Discoveries* 2 (1995): 361–365.

———. "The Use of the Bible as a Key to Meaning in Psalms from Qumran." Pages 85–96 in *Emanuel: Studies in Hebrew Bible, Septuagint and Dead Sea Scrolls in honor of Emanuel Tov*. Edited by S.M. Paul et al. Vetus Testamentum Supplement 94; Leiden: Brill, 2003.

Collins, John J. "Patterns of Eschatology at Qumran." Pages 351–375 in *Traditions in Transformation, Turning Points in Biblical Faith*. Edited by B. Halpern and J.D. Levenson. Winona Lake: Eisenbrauns, 1981.

Collins, Terence. *Line-Forms in Hebrew Poetry*. Rome: Biblical Institute Press, 1978.

Craigie, Peter C. *Psalms 1–50*. Word Biblical Commentary 19. Waco: Word Books, 1983.

Cross, Frank Moore. *The Ancient Library of Qumran and Modern Biblical Studies*. Garden City, N.Y.: Doubleday, 1958.

Culler, Jonathan. "Prolegomena to a Theory of Reading." Pages 46–66 in *The Reader in the Text*. Edited by S. Suleiman and I. Crosman. Princeton: Princeton University Press, 1980.

Daise, Michael A. "Biblical Creation Motifs in the Qumran Hodayot." Pages 293–305 in *The Dead Sea Scrolls: Fifty Years after Their Discovery. Proceedings of the Jerusalem Congress, July 20–25, 1997*. Edited by L.H. Schiffman, E. Tov, and J.C. VanderKam. Jerusalem: Israel Exploration Society in cooperation with the Shrine of the Book, Israel Museum, 2000.

Davies, Margaret. "Reader Response Criticism." Pages 578–580 in *A Dictionary of Biblical Interpretation*. Edited by R.J. Coggins and J.L. Houlden. London: SCM, 1990.

Davies, Philip R. *Behind the Essenes*. Brown Judaic Studies 94. Atlanta, Ga.: Scholars Press, 1987.

Davila, James R. "The Hodayot Hymnist and the Four who Entered Paradise." *Revue de Qumran* 17 (1996): 457–478.

Delcor, Matthias. *Les Hymnes de Qumran (Hodayot): Texte hébreu, introduction, traduction, commentaire*. Paris: Letouzey, 1962.

Dombrowski-Hopkins, Denise. "The Qumran Community and the 1Q Hodayot: a Reassessment." *Revue de Qumran* 10 (1981): 331–364.

Douglas, Michael C. "Power and Praise in the Hodayot: A Literary Critical Study of 1QH 9:1–18:14." Ph.D. diss., University of Chicago, 1998.

———. "The Teacher Hymn Hypothesis Revisited: New Data for an Old Crux." *Dead Sea Discoveries* 6 (1999): 239–266.

Dupont-Sommer, A. "La mère du Messie et la mère de l'Aspic dans un hymne de Qoumrân." *Revue de l'histoire des religions* 147 (1955): 174–188.

———. "Le Livre des Hymnes découvert près de la mer Morte (1QH): Traduction intégrale avec introduction et notes." *Semitica* 7 (1957): 1–120.

———. *The Essene Writings From Qumran*. Translated by G. Vermes. Oxford: Blackwell, 1961.

Eagleton, Terry. *Literary Theory: An Introduction*. 2nd ed. Oxford: Blackwell, 1996.

Emerton, J.A. "The Odes of Solomon." Pages 733–752 in *The Apocryphal Old Testament*. Edited by H.F.D. Sparks. Oxford: Clarendon, 1984.

Eshel, Esther. "Self-Glorification Hymn." Pages 421–432 in *Qumran Cave 4.XX: Poetical and Liturgical Texts, Part 2*. Edited by E. Chazon et al. Discoveries in the Judaean Desert 29. Oxford: Clarendon, 1999.

Evans Craig A., and James A. Sanders, eds. *Paul and the Scriptures of Israel*. Journal for the Study of the New Testament Supplement 83. Sheffield: JSOT Press, 1993.

Fish, Stanley. "Interpreting the Variorum." Pages 311–329 in *Modern Criticism and Theory: A Reader*. Edited by D. Lodge. London: Longman, 1988.

———. *Is There a Text in this Class?* Cambridge, Mass.: Harvard University Press, 1980.

Fishbane, Michael. *Biblical Interpretation in Ancient Israel*. Oxford: Clarendon Press, 1985.

Fitzmyer, Joseph A. "The use of Explicit Old Testament Quotations in Qumran Literature and in the New Testament." *New Testament Studies* 7 (1961): 297–333.

Fletcher-Louis, Crispin H.T. *All the Glory of Adam: Liturgical Anthropology in the Dead Sea Scrolls*. Studies on the Texts of the Desert of Judah 42. Leiden: Brill, 2002.

Foucault, Michel. *Discipline and Punish: The Birth of the Prison*. Translated by Alan Sheridan. New York: Random House, 1995.

———. "Technologies of the Self" pages 16–63 in *Technologies of the Self A Seminar with Michel Foucault*. Edited by Luther H. Martin, Huck Gutman and Patrick H. Hutton; London: Tavistock, 1988.

Fowler, Robert M. "Who is 'The Reader' in Reader Response Criticism?" *Semeia* 31 (1985): 5–23.

Fox, Michael V. "The Identification of Quotations in Biblical Literature." *Zeitschrift für die alttestamentliche Wissenschaft* 92 (1980): 416–431.

Frechette, Christopher G. "Chiasm, Reversal and Biblical Reference in 1QH 11.3–18 (= Sukenik Column 3): A Structural Proposal." *Journal for the Study of the Pseudepigrapha* 21 (2000): 71–102.

Frennesson, Björn. *"In a Common Rejoicing": Liturgical Communion with Angels in Qumran*. Studia Semitica Upsaliensia 14. Uppsala: Acta Universitasis Upsaliensis, 1999.

Frey, Jörg. "Flesh and Spirit in the Palestinian Jewish Sapiential Tradition and in the Qumran Texts: An Inquiry into the Background of Pauline Usage." Pages 367–404 in *The Wisdom Texts from Qumran and the Development of Sapiential Thought*. Edited by C. Hempel, A. Lange and H. Lichtenberger. Bibliotheca ephemeridum theologicarum lovaniensium 159. Leuven: Uitgeverij Peeters, 2002.

Fujita, Shozo. "The Metaphor of Plant in Jewish Literature of the Intertestamental Period." *Journal for the Study of Judaism* 7 (1976): 40–44.

Furniss, Tom, and Michael Bath. *Reading Poetry: an introduction*. Harlow: Pearson Education, 1996.

García Martínez, Florentino, and Eibert J.C. Tigchelaar. *The Dead Sea Scrolls Study Edition*. 2 vols. Leiden: Brill, 1997.

Gaster, T.H. *The Scriptures of the Dead Sea Sect*. London: Secker & Warburg, 1956.

Geller, Stephen A. *Parallelism in Early Biblical Poetry*. Missoula: Scholars Press, 1979.

Gordis Robert. "Quotations in Wisdom Literature." *Jewish Quarterly Review* 30 (1939/40): 123–147.

———. "Quotations as a Literary Usage in Biblical, Oriental and Rabbinic Literature." *Hebrew Union College Annual* 22 (1949): 157–219.

Greene, Thomas M. *The Light in Troy: Imitation and Discovery in Renaissance Poetry*. New Haven: Yale University Press, 1982.

Greenfield, J.C. "The Root 'GBL' in Mishnaic Hebrew and in the Hymnic Literature from Qumran." *Revue de Qumran* 2 (1959–1960): 155–162.

Greenstein, Edward L. "How Does Parallelism Mean?" Pages 41–70 in *A Sense of Text*. Jewish Quarterly Review Supplement. Edited by S. Geller. Winona Lake: Eisenbrauns, 1982.

Haberman, A.M. מגילות מדבר יהודה Tel Aviv: Machbarot Lesifruth, 1959.

Hays, Richard B. *Echoes of Scripture in the Letters of Paul*. New Haven & London: Yale University Press, 1989.

Hinson, Glenn. "Hodayoth, III, 6–18: In What Sense Messianic?" *Revue de Qumran* 2 (1959–1960): 183–204.

Hoffman, Yair. "The Technique of Quotation and Citation as an Interpretive Device." Pages 71–79 in *Creative Biblical Exegesis: Christian and Jewish Hermeneutics through the Centuries*. Edited by B. Uffenheimer and H.G. Reventlow. Journal for the Study of the Old Testament Supplement 59. Sheffield: JSOT Press, 1988.

Holland, Dorothy, William Lachicotte, Jr., Debra Skinner, and Carole Cain. *Identity and Agency in Cultural Worlds*. Cambridge, MA: Harvard University Press, 1998.

Hollander, John. *The Figure of Echo: A mode of allusion in Milton and after*. Berkeley: University of California Press, 1981.

Holm-Nielsen, Svend. *Hodayot: Psalms from Qumran*. Acta Theologica Danica 2. Aarhus: Universitetsforlaget I Aarhus, 1960.

———. "The Importance of Late Jewish Psalmody for the Understanding of Old Testament Psalmodic Traditions." *Studia Theologica* 13 (1960): 1–53.

Howard, David M., Jr. "Recent Trends in Psalms Study." Pages 329–368 in *The Face of Old Testament Studies*. Edited by D.W. Baker and B.T. Arnold. Grand Rapids: Baker Books, 1999.

Jakobson, Roman. "Linguistics and Poetics." Pages 173–190 in *Style in Language*. Edited by T. Sebeok. Cambridge, Mass.: MIT Press, 1960.

Jameson, Fredric. *The Political Unconscious: Narrative as a Socially Symbolic Act*. Ithaca, NY: CornellUniversity Press, 1981.

Jastrow, M. *A Dictionary of the Targumim, the Talmud Babli and Yerushalmi, and the Midrashic Literature, Vol 1*. New York: Putnam's, 1886.

———. *A Dictionary of the Targumim, the Talmud Babli and Yerushalmi, and the Midrashic Literature, Vol 2*. New York: Putnam's, 1903.

Jauss, H.R. "Literary History as a Challenge to Literary Theory." Translated by E. Benzinger. *New Literary History* 2 (1970): 7–37.

Jeremias, Gert. *Der Lehrer der Gerechtigkeit*. Studien zur Umwelt des Neuen Testaments 2. Göttingen: Vandenhoeck & Ruprecht, 1963.

Jeremias, J. "Theophany in the OT." Pages 897–898 in *The Interpreters Bible Dictionary, supplementary volume*. Edited by G.A. Butterick. New York: Abingdon Press, 1962.

Kister, Menahem. "Biblical Phrases and Hidden Biblical Interpretations and Pesharim." Pages 27–39 in *The Dead Sea Scrolls. Forty Years of Research*. Edited by D. Dimant and U. Rappaport. Jerusalem: Magnes Press, 1992.

Kittel, Bonnie Pedrotti. *The Hymns of Qumran: Translation and Commentary*. Society of Biblical Literature Dissertation Series 50. Chico: Scholars Press, 1981.

Klein, Ralph W. *1 Samuel*. Word Biblical Commentary 10. Dallas: Word Books, 1998.

Kosmala, Hans. "The Three Nets of Belial." *Annual of the Swedish Theological Institute* 4 (1965): 91–113.

Kraft, Charles F. "Poetic Structure in the Qumran Thanksgiving Psalms." *Biblical Research* 2 (1957): 1–18.

Kristeva Julia. *Desire in Language: A Semiotic Approach to Literature and Art*. Edited by L.S. Roudiez. Translated by T. Gora, A Jardine, and L.S. Roudiez. New York: Columbia University Press, 1980.

———. *Revolution in Poetic Language*. Translated by M. Waller. New York: Columbia University Press, 1984.

Kugel, James L. *The Idea of Biblical Poetry: Parallelism and its History*. New Haven and London: Yale University Press, 1981.

Kuhn, Heinz-Wolfgang. *Enderwartung und gegenwärtiges Heil: Untersuchungen zu den Gemeindeleidern von Qumran mit einem Anhang über Eschatologie und Gegenwart in der Verkündigung Jesu*. Studien zur Umwelt des Neuen Testaments 4. Göttingen: Vandenhoeck & Ruprecht, 1966.

Kuhn, Karl Georg. et al. *Konkordanz zu den Qumran Texten*. Göttingen: Vandenhoeck & Ruprecht, 1960.

Lange, Armin. "Wisdom and Predestination in the Dead Sea Scrolls." *Dead Sea Discoveries* 2 (1995): 340–354.

Laperrousaz, E.-M. "La mère du Messie et la mère de l'aspic dans les hymnes de Qumran: Quelques remarques sur la structure de '1QH' III, 1–18." Pages 173–185 in *Mélanges d'histoire des religions offerts à H.-C. Puech*. Edited by P. Levy and E. Wolff. Paris: Presses Universitaires de France, 1974.

Laurin, Robert B. "The Question of Immortality in the Qumran 'Hodayot'." *Journal of Semitic Studies* 3 (1958): 344–355.

Leenhardt, Jacques. "Towards a Sociology of Reading." Pages 205–224 in

The Reader in the Text. Edited by S. Suleiman and I. Crosman. Princeton: Princeton University Press, 1980.

Licht, Jacob. "The Doctrine of the Thanksgiving Scroll." *Israel Exploration Journal* 6 (1956): 1–13, 89–101.

———. *The Thanksgiving Scroll: A Scroll from the Wilderness of Judaea. Text, Introduction, Commentary and Glossary*. Jerusalem: Bialik Institute, 1957.

Lim, Timothy H. in consultation with P.S. Alexander. *The Dead Sea Scrolls Electronic Reference Library, Vol 1*. Oxford: Oxford University Press and Leiden: Brill, 1997.

Lohfink, Norbert. *Lobesänge der Armen*. SBS 143. Stuttgart: Katholisches Bibelwerk, 1990.

Lohse, Eduard. *Die Texte aus Qumran: Hebräisch und Deutsch*. Darmstadt: Kösel-Verlag, 1964.

Lotman, Yury. *Analysis of the Poetic Text*. Ann Arbor: Ardis, 1976.

———. *The Structure of the Artistic Text*. Ann Arbor: University of Michigan, 1977.

Lundbom, J.R. *Jeremiah 1–20: A New Translation with Introduction and Commentary*. The Anchor Bible. New York: Doubleday, 1999.

Mansoor, Menahem. *The Thanksgiving Hymns: Translated and Annotated with an Introduction*. Studies on the Texts of the Desert of Judah 3. Leiden: Brill, 1961.

Martin, Malachi. *The Scribal Character of the Dead Sea Scrolls*. Bibliothèque du Muséon 44. Louvain: Université de Louvain, Institut Orientaliste, 1958.

Merrill, Eugene H. *Qumran and Predestination: A Theological Study of the Thanksgiving Hymns*. Studies on the Texts of the Desert of Judah 8. Leiden: Brill, 1975.

Milik, Józef T. "35. Recueil de cantiques d'action de grâces (1QH)." Pages 136–138 in *Qumran Cave 1*. Edited by D. Barthélemy and J.T. Milik. Discoveries In The Judaean Desert 1. Oxford: Clarendon, 1955.

Morawe, Günter. *Aufbau und Abgrenzung der Loblieder von Qumran*. Theologische Arbeiten 16. Berlin: Evangelische Verlagsanstalt, 1961.

Muilenburg, James. "The Linguistic and Rhetorical Usages of the Particle כי in the Old Testament." *Hebrew Union College Annual* 32 (1961): 135–159.

Murphy O'Connor, Jerome. "The Judean Desert." Pages 119–156 in *Early Judaism and its Modern Interpreters*. Edited by R.A. Kraft and G.W.E. Nickelsburg. Atlanta, Ga.: Scholars Press, 1986.

Nelson's Electronic Bible Reference Library[TM]. Nashville: Nelson Electronic Publishing[TM], 1997.

Newsom, Carol A. "The Case of the Blinking I." *Semeia* 57 (1992): 13–23.

———. *The Self as Symbolic Space: Constructing Identity and Community at Qumran*. Studies on the Texts of the Desert of Judah 52. Leiden: Brill, 2004.

Nickelsburg, George W.E. *Resurrection, Immortality, and Eternal Life in Intertestamental Judaism*. Harvard Theological Studies 26. Cambridge, Mass.: Harvard University Press, 1972.

———. "Currents in Qumran Scholarship: The Interplay of Data, Agendas, and Methodology." Pages 79–99 in *The Dead Sea Scrolls at Fifty*. Edited by R.A. Kugler and E.M. Schuller; Atlanta, Ga.: Scholars Press, 1999.

———. *1 Enoch 1: A Commentary on the Book of 1 Enoch, Chapters 1–36; 81–108*. Hermeneia. Minneapolis: Fortress Press, 2001.

Nielsen, Kirsten. *There is Hope for a Tree: The Tree as Metaphor in Isaiah*. Journal for the Study of the Old Testament Supplement, 65. Sheffield: Sheffield Academic Press, 1989.

Nitzan, Bilhah. *Qumran Prayer and Religious Poetry*. Translated by J. Chipman. Studies on the Texts of the Desert of Judah 12. Leiden: Brill, 1994.

———. "The Concept of the Covenant in Qumran Literature." Pages 85–104 in *Historical Perspectives: from the Hasmoneans to bar Kokbha in light of the Dead Sea Scrolls, Proceedings of the Fourth International Symposium of the Orion Center for the Study of the Dead Sea Scrolls and Associated Literature*. Edited by D. Goodblatt. Studies on the Texts of the Desert of Judah 37. Leiden: Brill, 2000.

O'Connor, M. *Hebrew Verse Structure*. Winona Lake: Eisenbrauns, 1980.

Pardee, Dennis. *Ugaritic and Hebrew Poetic Parallelism: A Trial Cut ('nt I and Proverbs 2.)* Vetus Testamentum Supplement 39. Leiden: Brill, 1988.

Patte, D., *Early Jewish Hermeneutic in Palestine*. Society of Biblical Literature Dissertation Series 22. Missoula: Scholars Press, 1975.

Penner, Ken. "Realized or Future Salvation in the Hodayot." *Journal of Biblical Studies* [http://journalofbiblicalstudies.org] 2:1 (2002).

Perri, Carmela. "On Alluding." *Poetics* 7 (1978): 289–307.

Perri Carmela., G. Carugati, P.W. Costa, M. Forndran, A.G. Mamaeus, E. Moody, Z.L. Seligsohn, L. Vinge, and F. Weinapple, "Allusion Studies. An International Annotated Bibliography, 1921–1977." *Style* 2 (1979): 178–227.

Porter, Stanley E. "The Use of the Old Testament in the New Testament: A Brief Comment on Method and Terminology." Pages 79–96 in *Early Christian Interpretation of the Scriptures of Israel: Investigations and Proposals*. Edited by C.A. Evans and J.A. Sanders. Studies in Scripture in Early Judaism and Christianity, 5. Sheffield: Sheffield Academic Press, 1997.

Puech, Émile. "Un hymne essénien en partie retrouve et les béatitudes: 1QH V 12–VI 18 (= col. XIII–XIV 7) et 4QBéat." *Revue de Qumran* 49 (1988): 59–88.

———. "Quelques aspects de la restauration du Rouleau des Hymnes (1QH)." *Journal of Jewish Studies* 39 (1988): 38–55.

———. "Restauration d'un texte hymnique a partir de trois manuscrits fragmentaires: 1QH^a xv 37–xvi 4 (vii 34–viii 3), 1Q35 (H^b) 1, 9–14, 4Q428 (H^b) 7." *Revue de Qumran* 16 (1995): 543–559.

———. *La croyance des Esséniens en la vie future: immortalité, résurrection, vie éternelle?* Etudes bibliques 22. Paris: Librairie Lecoffre, J. Gabalda, 1993.

Qimron, Elisha. *The Hebrew of the Dead Sea Scrolls*. Harvard Semitic Studies 29. Atlanta, Ga.: Scholars Press, 1986.

———. "A New Reading in 1QH XV 15 and the Root GYL in the Dead Sea Scrolls." *Revue de Qumran* 14 (1989–1990): 127–128.

Rabin, C. "Jubilees." Pages 1–139 in *The Apocryphal Old Testament*. Edited by H.F.D. Sparks. Oxford: Clarendon, 1984.

Reike, Bo. "Da'at and Gnosis in Intertestamental Literature." In *Neotestamentica et Semitica*, edited by E.E. Ellis and M. Wilcox, 245–255. Edinburgh, 1969.

———. "Remarques sur l'histoire de la form (Formgeschichte) des texts de Qumran." In *Les manuscrits de la mer Morte: Colloque de Strasbourg 25–27 Mai 1955*, edited by Jean Daniélou, 38–44. Paris: Paris University Press, 1957.

Ringgren, Helmer. *The Faith of Qumran: Theology of the Dead Sea Scrolls*. Translated by Emilie T. Sander. Expanded edition edited with a New Introduction by J.H. Charlesworth. New York: Crossroads, 1995.
Sandmel, Samuel. "Parallelomania." *Journal of Biblical Literature* 81 (1962): 1–13.
Schiffmann, Lawrence H. *Reclaiming the Dead Sea Scrolls: The History of Judaism, the Background of Christianity, the Lost Library of Qumran*. The Anchor Bible Reference Library. New York: Doubleday, 1995.
Schuller, Eileen M. "The Cave 4 Hodayot Manuscripts: A Preliminary Description." *Jewish Quarterly Review* 85 (1994): 137–150.
———. "A Thanksgiving Hymn from 4QHodayot^b (4Q428 7)." *Revue de Qumran* 16 (1995): 527–541.
———. "381. 4QNon-Canonical Psalms B." Pages 87–172 in *Qumran Cave 4.VI: Poetical and Liturgical Texts, Part 1*. Edited by E. Eshel et al. Discoveries in the Judaean Desert 11. Oxford: Clarendon, 1998.
———. "Hodayot." Pages 69–254 in *Qumran Cave 4.XX: Poetical and Liturgical Texts, Part 2*. Edited by E. Chazon et al. Discoveries in the Judaean Desert 29. Oxford: Clarendon, 1999.
Schultz, Richard L. *The Search for Quotation: Verbal Parallels in the Prophets*. Journal for the Study of the Old Testament Supplement, 180. Sheffield: Sheffield Academic Press, 1999.
Silberman, Lou H. "Language and Structure in the Hodayot (1QH3)." *Journal of Biblical Literature* 75 (1956): 96–106.
Silverman, Kaja. *The Subject of Semiotics*. New York: Oxford University Press, 1983.
Skehan, Patrick W., and Alexander A. Di Lella, *The Wisdom of Ben Sira*. The Anchor Bible 39. New York: Doubleday, 1987.
Skehan, Patrick W., Eugene Ulrich, and Peter W. Flint. "Psalms." Pages 1–169 in *Qumran Cave 4.XI: Psalms to Chronicles*. Edited by E.C. Ulrich et al. Discoveries in the Judaean Desert 16. Oxford: Clarendon, 2000.
Sonne, Isaiah. "A Hymn against Heretics in the Newly Discovered Scrolls," *Hebrew Union College Annual* 23 (1950): 275–313.
Stanley, Christopher D. "The Social Environment of 'free' Biblical Quotations in the New Testament." Pages 18–27 in *Early Christian Interpretation of the Scriptures of Israel: Investigations and Proposals*. Edited by C.A. Evans and J.A. Sanders. Journal for the Study of the New Testament Supplement 148. Studies in Scripture in Early Judaism and Christianity 5. Sheffield: Sheffield Academic Press, 1997.
———. "The Rhetoric of Quotations: An Essay on Method." Pages 44–58 in *Early Christian Interpretation of the Scriptures of Israel: Investigations and Proposals*. Edited by C.A. Evans and J.A. Sanders. Journal for the Study of the New Testament Supplement 148. Studies in Scripture in Early Judaism and Christianity 5. Sheffield: Sheffield Academic Press, 1997.
Stegemann, Harmut. "Methods for the Reconstruction of Scrolls from Scattered Fragments." Pages 189–220 in *Archaeology and History in the Dead Sea Scrolls: The New York University Conference in Memory of Yigael Yadin*. Edited by L.H. Schiffman. Journal for the Study of the Pseudepigrapha: Supplement Series 8. Sheffield: Sheffield Academic Press, 1990.

———. "The Material Reconstruction of 1QHodayot." Pages 272–284 in *The Dead Sea Scrolls: Fifty Years after Their Discovery. Proceedings of the Jerusalem Congress, July 20–25, 1997.* Edited by L.H. Schiffman, E. Tov, and J.C. VanderKam. Jerusalem: Israel Exploration Society in cooperation with the Shrine of the Book, Israel Museum, 2000.

———. "The Number of Psalms in 1QHodayot[a] and Some of Their Sections." Pages 191–234 in *Liturgical Perspectives: Prayer and Poetry in Light of the Dead Sea Scrolls. Proceedings of the Fifth International Symposium of the Orion Center for the Study of the Dead Sea Scrolls and Associated Literature, 19–23 January, 2000.* Edited by E.G. Chazon with the collaboration of R. Clements and A. Pinnick. Studies on the texts of the Desert of Judah 48. Leiden: Brill, 2003.

Steudel, Annette "Assembling and Reconstructing Manuscripts." Pages 516–534 in *The Dead Sea Scrolls after Fifty Years. Volume 1.* Edited by P.W. Flint and J.C. VanderKam. Leiden: Brill, 1998.

Strugnell, John and Eileen M. Schuller. "Further 'Hodayot' Manuscripts from Qumran?" Pages 51–72 in *Antikes Judentum und frühes Christentum: Festschrift für Harmut Stegemann.* Edited by B. Kollmann, W. Reinbold, and A. Steudel. Berlin: De Gruyter, 1999.

Sukenik, Eleazar L. מגילות גנוזות סקירה רישונה. Jerusalem: Magnes Press, 1948.

———. מגילות גנוזות סקירה שנייה. Jerusalem: Magnes Press, 1950.

———. *The Dead Sea Scrolls of the Hebrew University.* Jerusalem: Magnes Press, 1955.

Suleiman, Susan. "Introduction: Varieties of Audience-Orientated Criticism." Pages 3–45 in *The Reader in the Text.* Edited by Susan. Suleiman and I. Crosman. Princeton: Princeton University Press, 1980.

Tanzer, Sarah Jean. "The Sages at Qumran: Wisdom in the 'Hodayot'." Ph.D. diss., Harvard University, 1986.

Thiering, Barbara. "The Poetic Forms of the Hodayot." *Journal of Semitic Studies* 8 (1963): 189–209.

Turner, Victor. *Schism and Continuity in an African Society.* Manchester: Manchester University Press, 1957.

———. "Social Dramas and Stories about Them." Pages 137–164 in *On Narrative.* Edited by W.J.T. Mitchell. Chicago: University of Chicago Press, 1981.

VanderKam, James C. *Textual and Historical Studies in the Book of Jubilees.* Harvard Semitic Monographs 14. Missoula: Scholars Press, 1977.

Vermes, Geza. *The Dead Sea Scrolls in English.* London: Pelican Books, 1962.

Vries, Simon J. de. "The Syntax of Tenses and Interpretation in the Hodayoth." *Revue de Qumran* 5 (1964): 375–414.

Wallenstein, Meir. *Hymns from the Judean Scrolls.* Manchester: The University Press, 1950.

———. *The Nezer and the Submission in Suffering Hymn From the Dead Sea Scrolls: Reconstructed, Vocalised and Translated with Critical Notes.* Istanbul: Nederlands Historisch-Archaeologisch Instituut in het Nabije Oosten, 1957.

Watson, Wilfred G.E. *Classical Hebrew Poetry: A Guide to its Techniques.* Journal for the Study of the Old Testament: Supplement Series 26. Sheffield: JSOT Press, 1984.

———. *Traditional Techniques in Classical Hebrew Verse*. Journal for the Study of the Old Testament: Supplement Series 170. Sheffield: Sheffield Academic Press, 1994.
———. "Hebrew Poetry." Pages 253–285 in *Text in Context: Essays by Members of the Society for Old Testament Study*. Edited by A.D.H. Mayes. Oxford: Oxford University Press, 2000.
Waugh, L. "The Poetic Function and Nature of Language." *Poetics Today* 2/1a (1980): 57–82.
Wernberg-Møller, P. "The Contribution of the Hodayot to Biblical Textual Criticism." *Textus* 4 (1964): 145–173.
Wheeler, Michael D. *The Art of Allusion in Victorian Fiction*. London and Basingstoke: The Macmillan Press, 1979.
Williams, Gary Roye. "Parallelism in the Hodayot from Qumran." Ph.D. diss., Annenberg Research Institute, 1991.
Wimsatt, W.K. Jr. and Monroe C. Beardsley. "The Intentional Fallacy." Pages 3–20 in *The Verbal Icon: Studies in the Meaning of Poetry*. Edited by W.K. Wimsatt. Lexington: University Press of Kentucky, 1954.
Wise, Michael O. *The First Messiah: Investigating the Savior before Jesus*. New York: HarperSanFrancisco, 1999.

INDEX OF MODERN AUTHORS

Abegg, M.G., 7 n.17, 61 n.88, 62, 76 n.60, 106 n.156, 107 n.159, n.162, 118 n.210, 119 n.212, 151 n.73, 156 n.88, 177 n.164, n.165, 179 n.169, 193 n.41, 206 n.80, 219 n.141
Allen, L.C., 115, 121 n.218, 158
Alter, R., 39 n.15, 40
Aune, D.E., 179, 180
Avigad, N., 3

Baillet, M., 227 n.170
Bakhtin, M.M., 25
Bardtke, H., 3 n.6, 13
Barthes, R., 56
Bath, M., 37, 38, 48, 50, 51, 52 n.62, 53, 56, 235
Baumgarten, J.M., 170
Beal, T.K., 56 n.73
Beardsley, M.C., 48
Becker, J., 4 n.9, 7, 14, 63 n.1, 137 n.9, 207
Ben Porat, Z., 45 n.40
Benveniste, E., 27
Berlin, A., 37, 38, 72 n.41
Bloom, H., 51, 52, 53
Brock, S.P., 152 n.75, 179 n.170
Brooke, G.J., 94 n.110, 152 n.74, 168 n.145
Brown, S., 194 n.48
Brown, W.P., 181
Brownlee, W.H., 105 n.151, 107 n.159
Burke, K., 25, 28, 29 n.109

Campbell, J.G., 128
Carmignac, J., 1 n.1, 3 n.6, 4 n.7, n.8, 6, 18, 21, 24, 51, 61, 137 n.9, 160 n.107
Chamberlain, J.V., 192 n.40, 193 n.45, 203 n.74

Charlesworth, J.H., 4 n.8, 17 n.52, 62, 136, 151
Chazon, E., 7 n.16, n.17, 9 n.22, 23, 24, 35 n.1, 229, 230 n.176
Collins J.J., 110 n.180, 205, 206, 222 n.152
Collins, T., 40
Craigie, P.C., 200 n.67
Cross, F.M., 17
Culler, J., 55 n.72

Daise, M.A., 151 n.71
Davies, M., 49 n.54
Davies, P.R., 15, 16, 110 n.181, 128, 129, 133
Davila, J.R., 136
Delcor, M., 3 n.6, 4 n.7, 21, 137 n.9
Di Lella, A.A., 87
Douglas, M.C., 7 n.17, 15, 16, 26, 33, 34, 58, 95, 96, 98, 99 n.131, 104 n.146, n.147, n.148, 107, 108, 116 n.206, 119, 126, 127, 129, 132, 133, 135, 136, 137 n.9, n.12, 138 n.17, n.26, 139 n.29, 150, 151 n.70, n.72, 155, 157 n.95, 159 n.104, 162 n.117, 163 n.125, 166, 175, 176, 176 n.161, n.162, 177, 178, 182, 186, 187 n.20, 189 n.29, 190 n.31, 191 n.36, 193 n.45, n.47, 198, 206, 207, 209 n.97, 210 n.105, 212, 214 n.118, 215 n.120, 216, 218 n.136, 228
Dupont-Sommer, A., 3 n.6, 4 n.8, 137 n.9, 185, 190 n.31, 191, 193 n.45

Eagleton, T., 37, 41 n.22
Eliot, T.S., 48
Emerton, J.A., 179 n.170
Eshel, E., 35 n.1, 227 n.170, 230 n.175

Evans, C.A., 42 n.25, 43 n.34, 44 n.38, 54 n.67

Fish, S., 57, 58 n.77
Fishbane, M., 4 n.8, 50, 51 n.58, 52, 53, 136 n.6
Fitzmyer, J.A., 42 n.28, 43, 44
Fletcher-Louis, C.H.T., 106, 213 n.112, 215, 220 n.146
Flint, P.W., 7 n.15, 61 n.88, 204 n.78
Foucault, M., 25
Fowler, R.M., 50
Fox, M.V., 43
Frechette, C.G., 1, 185, 190, 193, 194 n.48, 196, 199, 201 n.71, 202, 203, 204 n.77
Frennesson, B., 208, 215 n.120, 226, 227
Frey, J., 94
Fujita, S., 170 n.148, 178
Furniss, T., 37, 38, 48, 50, 51, 52 n.62, 53, 56, 235

García Martínez, F., 7 n.17, 12, 47 n.47, 59, 110 n.177, 123 n.223, 128 n.243, 138 n.24, n.26, 139 n.30, 168 n.144, 169 n.146, 171 n.149, n.150, 193 n.41
Gaster, T.H., 3 n.6
Geller, S., 40
Gordis R., 43
Greene, T.M., 55, 81
Greenfield, J.C., 46 n.44
Greenstein, E., 40

Haberman, A.M., 12, 19
Hays, R.B., 44 n.38
Hinson, G., 185, 190, 199, 200
Hoffman, Y., 42 n.29, n.33
Holland, D., 26 n.97
Hollander, J., 48, 51 n.59
Holm-Nielsen, S., 1, 3 n.6, n.7, 7, 12, 13, 14, 21, 24, 46 n.44, n.45, 47, 51, 60 n.84, 61, 63, 67 n.27, 69 n.32, 71 n.37, 72 n.44, 73 n.48, n.51, 76, 93, 97 n.122, 98 nn.126–130, 99 nn.131–133, 100 n.137, 101 n.142, 102 n.143, 105 n.152, 107, 107 n.165, 108 n.170, 110 n.181, 111, 115, 132, 137 n.9, n.12, 138 n.17, n.27, n.28, 142 n.48, n.49, 143 nn.52–54, 144 n.55, 151 n.70, 152 n.76, 156 n.89, 157, 157 n.91, n.93, 160, 163, 164 n.130, 173, 174, 176 n.161, 182, 183, 186, 187 n.12, n.13, 188 n.21, n.22, 193 n.45, 203 n.74, 207, 210 n.101, n.103, n.104, 211 n.106, n.107, 222 n.157, 223
Howard, D.M. Jr., 40 n.19

Jakobson, R., 37 n.8
Jameson, F., 32, 114 n.195
Jastrow, M., 46 n.45
Jauss, H.R., 57
Jeremias, G., 4, 5, 7, 14, 63 n.1, 137 n.9, 207
Jeremias, J., 225, 226

Kister, M., 113, 123, 162 n.118
Kittel, B.P., 1, 14, 17 n.53, 18, 19, 20, 21, 23, 24, 34, 36, 39, 40, 45 n.42, 51, 59, 105 n.149, 135, 196, 197, 208, 212, 214, 214 n.118, 215, 216, 217, 218, 228
Klein, R.W., 201 n.72
Kosmala, H., 222 n.150
Kraft, C.F., 17, 18
Kristeva J., 56
Kugel, J., 38 n.12
Kuhn, H.-W., 4 n.9, 7, 14, 24, 63 n.1, 64, 137 n.9, 164 n.130, 207, 213 n.111, 226
Kuhn, K.G., 62

Lange, A., 94
Laperousaz, E.-M., 193 n.45
Laurin, R.B., 213 n.111
Leenhardt, J., 57 n.76
Licht, J., 3 n.6, 4 n.7, 12, 17, 22, 24, 59 n.81, 65 nn.11–13, 65 n.15, n.17, 66 nn.18–23, 71 n.37, 72 n.44, 97 n.118, n.120, 103, 137 n.9, n.15, 138 n.19, n.20, n.24, 139

n.30, n.31, n.35, 140 nn.36–37, 163 n.125, 187 n.12, n.14, 209 n.97
Lim, T.H., 12 n.35, 59 n.81, 110 n.180
Lohfink, N., 212
Lohse, E., 12, 19
Lotman, Y., 37, 41
Lundbom, J.R., 75

Mansoor, M., 3 n.6, 4 n.7, 12, 60 n.84, 98 nn.126–130, 101 n.140, 106 n.157, 110 n.176, 138 n.28, 142 n.49, 143 nn.53–54, 151 n.70, 188 n.22, 193 n.45, 203 n.74, 214, 214 n.119
Martin, M., 187 n.15
Merrill, E.H., 27, 64, 71 n.37, 85, 94
Milik, J.T., 137 n.11
Morawe, G., 3 n.6, 4 n.7, 14, 137 n.9, 207
Muilenburg, J., 194 n.48
Murphy O'Connor, J., 14

Newsom, C.A., 7 n.17, 8, 16, 24–34, 54, 57 n.74, 58, 64, 70 n.34, 71, 72, 81, 83 n.81, 84, 87, 90, 91, 96, 100 n.137, 104 n.148, 107, 108 n.168, 111, 112 n.187, 113, 114, 116, 119 n.211, 122, 126, 136, 174, 175, 185, 186 n.7, 187 n.20, 191, 195, 197, 207, 212, 215, 216, 218, 220, 234
Nickelsburg, G.W.E., 4 n.7, 5 n.9, 14 n.43, 90 n.97, 181, 223 n.158, 224, 225 n.164, 226 n.168
Nielsen, K., 152 n.77, 155 n.85
Nitzan, B., 14, 22–24, 94 n.110

O'Connor, M., 40

Pardee, D., 40
Patte, D., 1
Penner, K., 213 n.111
Perri, C., 44, 45, 48, 49, 51, 53
Porter, S.E., 42, 43
Puech, E., 5–8, 10 n.28, 12, 26 n.99, 35 n.2, 59 n.81, 64, 65 nn.9–11, 66 notes, 67 n.28, 69, 70, 72 n.44, 84, 89, 96, 131, 136, 137–140 notes, 151 nn.71–72, 163 n.125, 174 n.155, 186, 207, 208, 209 n.94, 209 n.96, 213 n.111, 214 n.118

Qimron, E., 65 n.14, 211 n.107

Rabin, C., 85 n.89
Reike, B., 25
Ringgren, H., 71 nn.37, 38, 73 n.51

Sandmel, S., 54 n.66
Schiffmann, L.H., 5 n.10, 122, 151 n.71
Schuller, E.M., 4 n.7, 7 n.17, 9–11, 12, 35 n.1, n.2, 59 n.81, 65 n.8, 89, 97 nn.115–117, 131, 137 n.10, 174 n.155, 186 n.8, 187 nn.16–20, 189 nn.28–30, 198 n.59, 208 n.93, 209 n.95, 218 n.136, 227 n.170, 229
Schultz, R.L., 1, 41, 42, 52, 53, 54, 55 n.71
Silberman, L.H., 185, 190, 191, 192 n.40, 193 n.45, 198
Silverman, K., 27
Skehan, P.W., 87 n.91, 204 n.78
Sonne, I., 105 n.153
Stanley, C.D., 43 n.34, 54
Stegemann, H., 5, 6, 7, 8, 9, 10, 11 n.34, 12, 36 n.3, 59 n.81, 64, 65 n.7, n.9, 70 n.36, 76 n.60, 83, 96, 105 n.149, 136, 174, 186, 187 n.9, 208
Steudel, A., 7 n.15, 11 n.3
Strugnell, J., 9, 11
Sukenik, E., 1 n.3, 2, 3, 5, 6, 7, 8, 12, 59 n.81, 64, 65 n.9, n.16, 96, 97 n.120, 106 n.157, 136, 139 n.30, n.31, 186, 187 n.10, n.13, n.15, 188 n.21, 208, 209 n.94, n.97, n.98
Suleiman, S., 55 n.72, 57 n.76, 58

Tanzer, S.J., 13, 27, 64, 68 n.30, 69, 82, 83, 84, 93, 94, 96, 103 n.146, 126, 127, 133, 135, 136, 137 n.9, 175, 182, 207
Thiering, B., 18, 185, 190

Tigchelaar, E.J.C., 7 n.17, 12, 47 n.47, 59, 110 n.177, 123 n.223, 128 n.243, 138 n.24, n.26, 139 n.30, 168 n.144, 169 n.146, 171 n.149, n.150, 193 n.41
Turner, V., 16

Ulrich, E., 61 n.88, 204 n.78

VanderKam, J.C., 5 n.10, 7 n.15, 85 n.88, 151 n.71
Vermes, G., 3 n.6, 4 n.7, n.8
Vries, S.J. de, 98 n.126, 105 n.151

Wallenstein, M., 136, 137 n.9, n.16, 139 n.31, 140 n.39, n.40, 141 n.41, 142 n.49, 151 n.70, n.72, 153 n.80, 156 n.89, 159 n.104, 161, 162, 174, 214 n.118
Watson, W.G.E., 38, 39, 40, 60, 72 n.47, 74 n.53, 149 n.64
Waugh, L., 38 n.9
Wernberg-Møller, P., 1 n.1, 61
Wheeler, M.D., 55, 79
Williams, G.R., 20, 40, 141 n.41, n.42, 144 n.55, 155 n.84, 163 n.127, 189 n.29, 198, 210 n.102, 214 n.118
Wimsatt, W.K. Jr., 48
Wise, M., 167 n.143

INDEX OF TEXTS

Old Testament/Hebrew Bible

(Verse numbers are given according to the NRSV with Hebrew Bible equivalents in brackets)

Genesis
1:1–2:25	73
2:5	75 n.56
2:7	46
2:8–10	150 n.69, 169
2:9	152
3:1–24	155 n.85
3:18	158 n.102
3:19	47
3:24	156
6:1–4	221 n.148
9:12	65 n.17
13:10	150 n.69
27:4	75 n.56
37:1–50:26	181
42:21	76 n.58

Exodus
1:19	75 n.56
2:1–10	75
6:6	77 n.63
7:4	77 n.63
10:7	75 n.56
11:6	219
15:1–18	204 n.77
15:10	157
24:16	218, 223
28:30	106 n.157
32:11	118 n.210
34:1–35	119
34:29	105 n.151
40:34–35	202 n.72

Leviticus
8:8	106 n.157
9:23–24	202 n.72
19:13	72 n.45
20:1–27	121 n.218
26:1–46	128
26:40	117, 124

Numbers
1:9	178
6:25	105 n.152, 106
11:12	167 n.141
11:33	75 n.56
14:41	116 n.205
21:18	110, 181
27:21	106 n.157

Deuteronomy
4:34	118 n.210
5:15	118 n.210
6:6–7	109
14:13	222
18:9–22	119
27:15–26	80
28–32	128
28:46	77, 78, 80
29	119, 121, 132
29:14–19 [13–18]	120
29:17–20 [16–19]	112, 121
30:2	132
30:15–20	89
32:8	221 n.148
32:22	218, 224
33:2	106 n.155, 165 n.135, 225
33:8	106 n.157

Joshua
—	120 n.214
7:5	161 n.112

Judges

5:4–5	225
13:5, 7	75 n.55
16:17	75 n.55
18:10	76 n.58
19:19	76 n.58

Ruth

4:10	173
4:15–16	167, 173, 178

1 Samuel

1:1–28	75
2:8	225 n.164
2:10	204 n.77
3:7	75 n.56
4:14	198 n.60
4:19	195, 201
4:19–22	201 n.71
18:18	162 n.122
28:6	106 n.157

2 Samuel

4:9	76 n.58
7:10	178
22:1	201, 229
22:2–20	200, 204 n.77, 220, 229
22:5	162 n.120, 172, 195, 200, 201, 220, 222
22:5–6	163 n.124, 195, 201
22:8–16	204
22:18, 49	201 n.69
22:50–51	203
24:14	125 n.230

1 Kings

1:29	76 n.58
2:33	76 n.58
5:24	151 n.74
18:41	198 n.60
22:22	221

2 Kings

19:3	195, 172 n.151, 201 n.68

1 Chronicles

16:9	163 n.126
21:13	125 n.210
28:9	163 n.128

2 Chronicles

15:7	72 n.45
18:20	221
32:8	72 n.43
32:21	115 n.201, 165 n.132

Ezra

2:63	106 n.157
4:42	206
8:52	169
9:1–10:6	124, 125
9:2	124
9:4	117 n.208, 214
9:6–15	117 n.207
9:6	214
9:7	115 n.201, 214, 165 n.132
9:13	214
9:15	214
10:2	215, 221
10:6	117 n.208, 214

Nehemiah

1:5–11	117 n.207
7:65	106 n.157
9:1–37	125
9:5–38	117 n.207, 117 n.207
9:6–37	125
9:17	125 n.231, 145 n.60
9:19	125 n.230
9:27	125 n.230
9:28	125 n.230
9:31	125 n.230

Job

1:6	221 n.148
2:1	221 n.148
3:4	106 n.155
7:10	76 n.58
9:6	225 n.164
10:3	106 n.155
10:9	46

10:22	106 n.155	18:3 [4]	166
12:9–10	72 n.43, 74	18:4 [5]	195, 200 n.66, 212, 218, 220, 222
12:10	78, 92, 130		
13:16	43, 44		
14:7–9	154 n.82	18:5 [6]	220, 222 nn.151, 153
17:5	112	18:7 [8]	220
17:7, 13	162 n.121	18:7–15 [8–16]	219, 225, 226
20:16	193 n.42	18:8 [9]	220, 221, 223
21:10	196 n.54	18:13 [14]	219, 220
26:6	213 n.113, 224 n.160	18:14 [15]	204 n.77
28:22	224 n.160	18:15 [16]	225 n.164
28:28	93	18:16 [17], 19 [20]	220
29:19	153 n.80	19:8	105 n.152
30:3	163 n.124, 176	20:1 [2]	149 n.64
31:12	224	20:8 [9]	114, 118 n.209
31:18	75 n.55	20:9 [10]	149 n.64
31:21–22	161, 176	22:2 [3]	162 n.121
33:6	46	22:9 [10]	75 n.55, 131 n.247
33:28	213 n.110	22:10 [11]	75, 75 n.55, 131 n.247
36:22–39:40	205		
36:22	157	22:10–11 [11–12]	166 n.139
37:4–5	204 n.77	22:14 [15]	161 n.112
37:15	106 n.155	26:1–12	217 n.135
38:1–39:30	199, 204, 205	26:4	112 n.188
38:7	221 n.148	26:7	215, 220
38:8–10	199	26:11–12	213, 220
38:16	199	26:12	45 n.42, 221 n.146
38:17	199	27:10	166
38:27	163 n.124, 176	28:5	72 n.44
		29:1	215 n.121, 221 n.148
Psalms		29:3	204 n.77
1	74, 181	29:3–10	219 n.142
1:1, 6	149 n.64	30:1–3	213 n.110
1:2	93	31:7 [8]	76 nn.58, 59
1:3	159, 169	31:7–8 [8–9]	166
5:6	107 n.165	31:10 [11]	162 n.121
6:7–8	162 n.121	31:11–12 [12–13]	108
10	116 n.205	31:13 [14]	109
10:10	210 n.99, 216, 221	31:17 [18]	105 n.152
11:1	108 n.170	31:22 [23]	101 n.142, 118 n.209
12:2	112	33:11	111 n.186
16:10	213 n.110	34:9	76 n.58
17:4	72 n.44	36:4	77 n.62, 92
17:7	144 n.57	36:9	154 n.81
18:1–19 [20]	200 n.67, 200, 229, 230, 233	37	216 n.129
		37:11	221
18:2 [3]	166 n.138	37:23	87 n.93

38:11	162	88:11 [12]	224 n.160
42	160, 171	89:1–52 [53]	135 n.3, 221
42:5, 6, 11 [6, 7, 12]	160	89:5–7 [6–8]	215 n.121
42:7 [8]	160 n.111, 171, 201 n.68	89:6 [7]	221 n.148
		89:7 [8]	115
43:1	165 n.134	92:12	169
44:16	115 n.201, 165 n.132	93:4	172 n.151, 201 n.68
44:23	163 n.128	94:1	106 n.155, 165
46:2–4	204 n.77	94:12–23	172
46:6	219 n.143	94:14	173
48:6–7 [7–8]	206	94:19	148 n.63, 163, 164, 172, 173, 232
49:15	213 n.110		
50:2	106 n.155, 165 n.135	97:2–6	219 n.142
51	117 n.207	101:2–3	92
51:5 [7]	117	102:6	162 n.121
58:3	75	103:4	213 n.110
62:2 [3]	166 n.138	103:20	156
67:2	105 n.152	104:2–5	225 n.164
68:33	219 n.143	104:4	156, 221 n.149
69:13 [14]	75	105:2	163 n.126
69:21 [22]	110	106:1–48	117 n.207
71:6	75 n.55	106:7	144 n.57
71:6–7	166 n.139	106:20	109 n.173
72:7	76 n.58	107:1–43	198, 204
73:3	107 n.165	107:18	77 n.62
74:1	163 n.128	107:23, 27	198
75:3 [4]	225 n.164	107:26	223
75:5 [6]	107 n.165	107:33	204 n.78
77:1–20 [21]	160, 171	107:35	204 n.78
77:3 [4]	160 n.109	109:20	72 n.44
77:6 [7]	143 n.51, 160 n.109	118:1, 29	149 n.64
77:7 [8]	163 n.128	119	29, 30, 135 n.3
77:7–12 [8–13]	163	119:27	163 n.126
77:17 [18]	219 n.143	119:89–91	92
77:17–20 [18–21]	219 n.142	119:118	121 n.215
78:1–72	135 n.3	119:154	165 n.134
80:1–19 [20]	178	119:156	125 n.230
80:1 [2]	106 n.155, 165	130:4	125 n.231, 145 n.60
80:8–15 [9–16]	152 n.76, 158 n.101	139:13	75 n.55, 166 n.139
80:12–13 [13–14]	154, 155 n.83	143:11	76 n.58
82:1, 6	215 n.121	144:2	166 n.138
82:5	225 n.164	145:5	163 n.126
82:6	221 n.148	145:12	116
88:1–18 [19]	147 n.62, 160, 171	150:1, 6	149 n.64
88:3–5 [4–6]	160 n.109, 171		
88:7 [8]	160 n.111, 171, 201 n.68	*Proverbs*	
		2	40 n.19

INDEX OF TEXTS 257

3:18	154 n.81	7:25	158 n.102
4:10–27	89	9:5	202
5:13	157	9:6	3, 53, 196, 201, 203
6:4	112 n.189	9:18	158 n.102
7:21	112 n.189	10:17	158 n.102
8:29	225 n.164	10:23	220 n.144, 226
10:6	72 n.45	10:33–34	179
10:11	154 n.81	11:1	147, 147 n.61, 153 n.78, 154, 169, 173, 179
11:18	72 n.45		
11:28	169		
11:30	154 n.81, 169	12:3	154 n.81
13:12	154 n.81	13:4	198 n.60
13:14	154 n.81	14:4	210 n.100, 216, 221
14:27	154 n.81	14:19	153 n.78
15:4	154 n.81	16:2	108 n.170
15:11	213 n.113, 224 n.160	17:11	160, 167 n.143, 176
16:9	79 n.66, 87 n.93	17:12	198 n.60, 204 n.77
16:22	154 n.81	18:2, 7	156 n.89, 167 n.143
16:29	77 n.62, 92	19:1	225
19:21	111	24:17	111, 222
20:24	87 n.93	24:18	225 n.164
21:23	76 n.58	26:21	225
27:8	108 n.170	27:2–13	158 n.101
27:20	213 n.113, 224 n.160	27:4	158 n.102
28:12	143 n.51	28:1–13	122
28:27	76 n.58	28:7	111, 123
		28:11	111, 113, 123, 126
Ecclesiastes	107 n.165	28:17	157 n.96
8:1	105 n.152	28:22	220 n.144, 226
		29:10–12	155 n.86
Song of Songs		29:16	46, 79 n.67
4:8–15	155 n.85	30	128
		30:6	193 n.42
Isaiah		30:8–14	122
1:18	172 n.152	30:9–11	108 n.166
3:13	172 n.152	30:10	107, 109, 112 n.189
5	152 n.74, 155 n.83	30:11	128
5:1–7	158, 169, 170, 179	30:12	167 n.143
5:2	158	30:18–26	166
5:4	158	30:20	157
5:5	155 n.83	30:26	178
5:6	158, 158 n.102	30:27	218
6:9	155 n.86	31:3	72 n.43
6:15	155	32:6	99 n.133, 110, 123 n.222
7:14	185		
7:23	158 n.100, 158 n.102	32:13	158 n.102
7:24	158 n.102	33:3	198, 198 n.60

34:9	218	48:8	75, 75 n.55
34:17	217 n.134	49:1	75, 75 n.55
35:1–2	158	49:4	72 n.45, 78 n.65
35:7	150 n.68	49:5	75, 75 n.55, n.56
37:3	172 n.151, 195, 195 n.49, 201, 202	49:8	75 n.57
		49:10	150 n.68
38:17	213 n.110, 214 n.113	49:13–15	173, 183
40–66	167, 168, 183	49:15	166, 178
40:3	123 n.224	50:2	204 n.78
40:10	72 n.45, 78 n.65, 225	50:4	147, 161, 177
		50:4–9	171, 181, 183
40:11	167 n.143, 225	50:7	172 n.152
40:13	167 n.143	50:7–9	173
40:21	225 n.164	51:3	137 n.12, 152
40:24	154 n.82, 158 n.98	51:6	76 n.58
40:28	214 n.115	51:22	172 n.152
41:1–29	172 n.152, 173	52:13–53:12	181
41:11–12	165, 173, 178	53:1–4	147, 155, 159, 171, 183
41:17–20	147, 168, 173, 183		
41:18	150 n.68, 204 n.78	53:2	159 n.105
41:19	151, 151 n.73, 151 n.74, 158, 168	53:3	108, 114, 123 n.222, 172
41:24	193 n.43	53:3–4	159, 160
41:25	46	53:4	163 n.124, 172
41:29	167 n.143	54:17	167 n.143
42:3	115, 123 n.222	56:4–6	118, 123 n.222
42:5	78	57:14–21	123, 124
42:6	105	57:15	162 n.118
42:13	162 n.119, 225	57:17	113, 123, 128, 167 n.143
42:14	193 n.44		
43:1, 7	73 n.49	57:18	123
43:8	155 n.86	57:20	156 n.89, 167 n.143, 223
43:18–21	202 n.72		
43:26	172 n.152	59:4–5	197, 201
44:2, 24	75, 75 n.55, n.56	59:5	167 n.143, 193 n.42, 193 n.47, 203
44:3	150 n.68		
44:24	78	59:12–15	117 n.207
44:18	155 n.86	59:15–19	225
45:9–12	73	60:13	151, 151 n.73, 152 n.74, 168
45:9–19	78, 79		
45:9	79 n.67	60:13–61:3	168, 183
45:12	78	60:21	152, 152 n.75, 153, 153 n.78, 153 n.79, 154, 167 n.143, 168, 169, 177, 179
45:17	76 n.58		
45:18	73 n.50, 92 n.104		
46:2–3	166 n.140		
46:3	75 n.55		
46:3–4	166, 173	61–62	80

INDEX OF TEXTS

61–65	78, 79	10:12	73, 78, 92
61:2	75, 75 n.57, 78, 79	10:13	198, 204, 219 n.143
61:3	147 n.61, 152 n.75, 153, 168, 179	10:23–25	80
61:8	72 n.45, 78 n.65, 80 n.69	10:23	56, 71, 73, 77, 78, 79, 82, 87, 88, 89, 91, 92, 95, 117, 124, 130, 131, 234
62:11	72 n.45, 78 n.65		
63:7–64:12	125		
63:7	125 n.230	11:1–17	80
63:15–64:12	80, 131, 172	11:3–5	80, 81
63:15	76, 78, 118, 123 n.222, 125, 148 n.63, 163, 172, 173, 219, 232	11:10	80 n.73
		11:16–17	178
		12:1–4	78
		12:3	76, 78, 79, 80
63:15–16	167 n.141, 173, 183	13:21	194, 201
63:17	172, 173	14:7–9	117 n.207
64:4–11	117 n.207	14:14	121 n.215
64:8	79 n.67, 80 n.70, 167 n.141	14:19–22	117 n.207
		15:18	160, 172, 176
65:1–16	80	17:5–8	158, 169
65:2	77, 78, 92	17:5	72 n.43
65:7	72 n.45, 78 n.65	17:8	147, 153, 159
65:8	80 n.71	17:13	154 n.81
65:12	80 n.72, n.73	18:1–12	73, 78, 79, 92
66:7	195, 195 n.52, 201, 203	18:6	79 n.67
		20:9	160, 172
66:7–13	167 n.141	23:9–40	121
66:10–13	173, 178	23:15–17	121 n.217
66:11	164 n.129	23:16	121 n.218
66:12	164 n.129	23:18	115 n.199
66:15–16	225	23:20	112, 113, 121
		23:22	115 n.199
Jeremiah		23:27	112
1:5	74, 75, 78, 79	24:6	178
2:8	109	25–27	128
2:11	109, 121 n.216, 126	25:16	111
2:13	154 n.81	25:30	219, 219 n.143
2:21	158 n.101, 178	25:30–31	225
3:4, 19	167 n.141	28:7–9	121 n.218
4:6	201 n.70	29:13	105 n.153
4:31	194, 201	30:15	160, 176
5:21	155 n.86	30:24	113 n.194
6:25	142 n.49	31:16	72 n.45, 78 n.65
7:19	115 n.201, 165 n.132	31:27–28	178
8:5	121 n.215	31:33	109 n.172
9:12–16	121 n.217	31:37	225 n.164
10–12	81	32:23	77 n.62

260 INDEX OF TEXTS

32:41	178	15:1–8	179
33:1	73 n.50	16:59–63	117, 125
33:2	92, 92 n.104	16:41	77 n.63
47:2	157 n.92	17:1–24	179
51:7	111 n.184	17:7	153 n.79
51:15	73 n.50	19:10–14	179
51:16	198, 219 n.143	20:27–44	117 n.208, 125
51:20	116 n.205	20:43	117
51:55	219 n.143	20:47 [21:3]	157 n.94, 218
		21:7 [12]	161, 171
Lamentations		22:28	115 n.201
1:2	162 n.121	25:11	77 n.63
1:3	162 n.121	28:22	77 n.63
2:11	162 n.121	28:26	77 n.63
2:18	162 n.121	29:20	72 n.45
3:15	177 n.164	30:14	77 n.63
3:17	164, 173	30:19	77 n.63
3:18	173	31	152 n.77, 153, 155, 169
3:21–66	173		
3:21	173	31:4	153 n.79
3:22	173	31:6	154
3:24	173	31:7	141 n.42
3:29	173	31:12–13	154
3:31–32	163	31:14	152
3:31	163 n.128, 173	32:23	151 n.70
3:32	173	33:17	113 n.192
3:58–59	173	34:29	153 n.79
		36:16–37	125
Ezekiel		36:31	77 n.62, 117
5:10	77 n.63	40–47	158
5:15	77 n.63	43:1–5	202 n.72
7–11	128	47:1–12	158, 170
7:17	161	47:12	159
7:18	165 n.132		
9:2	116 n.205	*Daniel*	
11:9	77 n.63	—	120 n.214
12:21	121	4:9 [12]	154
13:1–14:11	121	9:4–19	125
13	112	9:7	115 n.201, 117 n.208, 165 n.132
13:3	121 n.218		
13:8–11	122	9:8	115 n.201, 165 n.132
13:9	115	9:9	125 n.231, 145 n.60
13:10	115	9:18	125 n.230
14:3	112, 122	9:27	220 n.144, 226
14:4	112	10:16	195
14:7	112	11:7	153 n.78
14:7–8	121 n.218	12:1–3	181

Hosea

—	118, 120, 120 n.214, 132, 134, 234
4–5	128
4:1–6:3	120
4:6	121
4:7	109 n.173
4:14	108, 126
6:3	105, 106, 121, 156, 157 n.91, 234
9:11	75 n.55
10–11	128
10:8	158 n.100, n.102
10:12	107 n.159
13:13	172 n.151, 201 n.68
14:6	158 n.98

Joel

2:1–11	226
2:2	219
2:7	219
2:11	219
2:23	107 n.159, 156, 157 n.90, n.91
3 [4]:9–16	226
3 [4]:16	219

Amos

1:2	219 n.143, 225
4:13	74 n.52
7:4	218, 224
9:1–4	223 n.157

Jonah

2	199, 205
2:3 [4]	172 n.151, 201 n.68

Micah

1:2–7	225
1:4	117
1:6	153 n.79
5:2	185
6:2	225 n.164
7:8–10	165 n.134

Habakkuk

1:4	115
2:5	129
2:15	110, 111, 114, 129
2:16	111
3:3–15	225

Zephaniah

1:15	163 n.124, 176
2:9	158 n.100
3:17	76 n.58

Haggai

2:15	75 n.56

Zechariah

9:14	225
12:1	74, 78, 92, 130
14:3–4	225

Malachi

—	120 n.214
1:4	216, 221
2:6	213 n.112, 220 n.146
3:1–5	225

Apocrypha

Judith

16:15	225

Wisdom of Solomon

—	181
1–5	90 n.97
5:5	221
5:21–23	225
15:7	93
15:7–11	86

Wisdom of Ben Sira

10:2	107 n.163
15:11–16	29, 30, 87
15:11–20	87
16:18–19	225
24	169
24:23	93
24:30–33	180
33:7–13	30, 86

33:13 93
43:16–17 225

Prayer of Manasseh
— 117 n.207

OT Pseudepigrapha

Jubilees
— 85 n.88, 92
1:16 179
1:20 222 n.153
3 152 n.74
5:26 85
7:34 179
16:26 179
21:24 179
22:20 179
36:6 179

1 Enoch
— 224
1:3–9 227
10:16 179
14 221
17–18 222, 223
17:4–5 227
17:5 223 n.158, 224
18:2 225 n.164
23:1–24:1 227
24:4–25:5 169
25–32 179 n.171
62:4–5 206
84:6 179
93:1, 2, 14 179
94–104 181
102:1–3 227

Testament of Abraham
— 224

Testament of Asher
— 90 n.97

Testament of Levi
— 179

18:11 179 n.171
19 222 n.153

The Apocalypse of Ezra
— 224

Psalms of Solomon
14:3 152, 179

Odes of Solomon
11:18 179 n.170

4 Ezra
4:42 206
8:52 169

Assumption of Moses
10:36 225

New Testament

Luke
16:26 224 n.161

Romans
9:21 93
9:27–28 220 n.144

Philippians
1:19 43, 44, 48

Hebrews
10:37–38 44 n.36

Revelation
12 185, 206

Dead Sea Scrolls and Damascus Document

CD (Damascus Document)
— 91, 125, 128, 133, 170, 179
I–VIII 91
I 1–II 1 127, 128, 133

INDEX OF TEXTS 263

I 3–8	171	VI 26	74 n.54
I 3–11	123	VI 30	215 n.120
I 7	179	VI 31	126 n.236
I 11	91, 107 n.159, 113, 127	VII	119 n.212
		VII 14	26 n.99
I 14	91	VII 14–39	63 n.1, n.2, 90 n.100, 91 n.101
I 18	122 n.219		
II	84	VII 18	215 n.120
II 3	91	VII 21–VIII ?	36, 63–95, 119, 129–130, 133, 232
II 15	91		
III 16	169 n.146, 181 n.174		
VI 4–7	110	VII 21–38	31, 35, 63, 82, 83
IV 10–19	111, 221	VII 25–27	117
IV 19	122 n.219	VII 28–37	27, 30, 82
V 4–7	128	VII 34	215 n.124
V 18–19	222 n.153	VIII 11	130
VI 3–7	181 n.174	IX 3–41	27, 46 n.43, 71, 72 n.46, 82, 84, 94
VI 4	169 n.146		
VI 15	222 n.156	IX 9	72 n.46
VIII 12	115, 122 n.219	IX 9–36	27
VIII 18	122 n.219	IX 19	71
IX 3–41	82	IX 23	46 n.43, 215 n.125
XIV 2	222 n.151	IX 25–28	215 n.124
XVI 2–4	85	X	119 n.212
XIX–XX	91	X 5–21	31, 32, 126, 127, 133
XIX 25	115, 122 n.219	X 13	107 n.162
XIX 31	122 n.219	X 14	124 n.229, 156 n.89
XX 25–26	106 n.155	X 15	107 n.162, 124 n.229, 127 n.238
XX 32	107 n.159		
		X 16	107 n.162, 127 n.237
1QH^a (Hodayot)		X 17	122 n.219
IV 24	42 n.29	X 18	198 n.61
IV 29–37	29, 30	X 19	127 n.239
V 12	84 n.85	X 21	108 n.167, 126 n.236
V 12–38	84	X 22–32	17 n.53, 18, 21, 28, 29, 51
V 12–VI 18	82, 84, 90, 91 n.101		
V 18	26 n.99, 27	X 23	222 n.151
V 18–38	82 n.76	X 25	127 n.239
V 18–VI 18	90, 91 n.101	X 27	98 n.128
V 19	27	X 28	217 n.133
V 25	72 n.46	X 29	198 n.61
V 31–32	215 n.124	X 30–31	193 n.47, 221 n.146
V 34	156 n.88	X 32	45 n.42
VI 19–33	19 n.60, 26 n.99, 30, 91 n.100, n.101	X 33	107 n.162, 127 n.237
		X 34	122 n.219
		X 38	126
VI 24	71	XI 6–19	1 n.3, 3, 28, 29,

	36, 144 n.56, 185–206, 232–233	XIII 27–28	154 n.81, 176 n.161
		XIII 28	127 n.239
		XIII 30	176
XI 4	105 n.150	XIII 31	177
XI 8–9	162 n.120	XIII 32	163 n.124, 176, 205
XI 8–12	162 n.120, 163 n.124	XIII 34	106 n.155, 166 n.135
XI 17	217 n.133	XIII 35	76 n.59
XI 20	226 n.166	XIII 37	115 n.201
XI 20–37	14, 17 n.53, 28, 29, 36, 157 n.95, 205, 207–230, 232	XIII 38	177
		XIII 41	127 n.239
		XIV 6–22	127 n.241
XI 21	164 n.130	XIV 9	164 n.130, 221 n.147, 177, 226 n.166
XI 23, 24	215 n.120		
XI 25	46 n.43, 215 n.124	XIV 9–16	226
XI 27	222 n.151	XIV 10	123 n.226, 127, 177
XI 29	112 n.188, 127 n.239	XIV 12	76 n.60, 127, 131, 177
XI 30	127 n.239		
XI 33	124 n.229, 127 n.239, 156 n.89	XIV 13	119 n.212
		XIV 16	107 n.162, 127 n.237, n.238
XII 6–XIII 6	8, 13, 17 n.53, 31, 32, 36, 46 n.43, 63, 76 n.60, 82, 87, 89, 95–134		
		XIV 19	156 n.88
		XIV 21–33	176 n.162
		XIV 22–39	127 n.241
XII 7	106 n.155, n.156, 166 n.135	XIV 24	123 n.226, 127, 127 n.239
		XIV 25–38	206
XII 8, 10	107 n.162, 127 n.237	XIV 31–41	226
XII 11	119 n.212, 126 n.236, 127 n.239	XV	119 n.212
		XV 4	127 n.238
XII 14	127 n.239	XV 5	177
XII 18, 19, 22	123 n.226	XV 6	106 n.155, 166 n.135
XII 24	13, 106 n.155, n.156, 166 n.135	XV 7	206
		XV 9–28	174, 177, 178
XII 25	13, 123 n.226	XV 23–24	13
XII 26	210 n.99	XV 27	106 n.155, 166 n.135
XII 30	46 n.43, 215 n.124	XV 29–36	17 n.53, 76 n.60, 82, 84, 87, 89, 131, 178
XII 31	131		
XII 34–35	161 n.112, n.115		
XII 37, 38	76 n.60	XV 33	76 n.60, 131
XIII	119 n.212	XV 35	215 n.124
XIII 4	76 n.60	XV 37	112 n.188
XIII 7–21	17 n.53	XV 37–XVI 4	10 n.28, 76 n.60, 131
XIII 13	119 n.212	XV 38	76 n.60, 131
XIII 22–XV 8	31, 32, 76 n.59, 76 n.60, 126, 127, 135 n.3, 174, 177, 178, 205, 226, 233	XVI	10
		XVI 5–XVII 36	36, 76 n.59, 76 n.60, 135–184, 232

XVI 7	176 n.161	XX 7–39	84, 90 n.100
XVI 7–12	176 n.162	XX 7–XXV 33	174
XVI 16	124 n.229	XX 29	46 n.43, 47
XVI 28, 29	177 n.164	XX 30–36	47, 215 n.124
XVI 29	176	XX 35	46 n.43
XVI 32	177	XXI	119 n.212, 222 n.151
XVI 34	132 n.248, 177	XXI 2–29	82 n.76, 83, 84
XVI 37	124 n.228	XXI 5	215 n.124
XVI 38	177 n.164	XXI 15	106 n.156
XVII	876 n.60	XXII 10	46 n.43, 164 n.130, 221 n.147
XVII 6	176		
XVII 8	76 n.60, 177	XXII 14	215 n.124
XVII 13	177	XXII 23	163 n.124
XVII 14	221 n.147, 177, 226 n.166	XXIII 7	106 n.155, 166 n.135
		XXIII 12	107 n.162, 127 n.238
XVII 14–36	136	XXIII 13	46 n.43
XVII 16	46 n.43	XXIII 16	124 n.227
XVII 20, 22	115 n.201	XXV 10	26 n.99, 91 n.100
XVII 26	127 n.237	XXV 34	84 n.85
XVII 28	76 n.59	XXVI 15	215 n.120
XVII 30	131	XXVI 37	127 n.238
XVII 31	127 n.237	XXVII 10	215 n.124
XVII 34	76 n.60, 177		
XVII 38–XVIII 14	19, 28, 82 n.76, 83, 84	*1QH^b (1Q35)*	
		—	6, 9, 10 n.28, 35, 89, 131 n.246, 137
XVIII 5–14	215 n.124		
XVIII 14	28	1	10 n.28
XVIII 15–XIX 5	84	2 1–2	137
XVIII 23	76 n.60, 131	9–14	10 n.28
XVIII 32	156 n.88		
XIX 5	83	*1QM*	
XIX 6	46 n.43, 215 n.124	—	227, 228
XIX 6–17	13, 17 n.53, 19 n.60	I 16	106 n.155
XIX 7–30	84	V 11	193 n.41
XIX 7–18	82 n.76, 83	X 16	71 n.38
XIX 13–17	18, 226	XII 1–4	227
XIX 14	131	XIII 11	222
XIX 17	215 n.120		
XIX 25	115	*1QS (Rule of the Community)*	
XIX 29	106 n.155, 166 n.135	—	13, 14, 30, 32, 57 n.74, 115
XIX 31–XX 6	82 n.76, 83 n.79, 84		
XIX 31–XX 39	82 n.76, 83	I 16–II 12	227
XX 6–12	18	I 16–II 25	22 n.78, 105, 115, 117, 222, 227
XX 7	26 n.99, 83 n.79, 84 n.85		
		I 22–II 1	117 n.207
XX 7–21	10, 10 n.28, 46 n.43, 47	II 2	105 n.152
		II 5	222 n.153

II 24–25	115 n.198	*1Q14 (1QpMic)*	
III–IV	84	8–10 6	107 n.159
III 9–10	129		
III 16–17	130	*1Q16 (1QpPs)*	
III 13–IV 26	84, 90, 129–130	9–10 3	177
VII 15–25	32		
VIII 4–6	169, 171, 179	*1Q26 (1QInstruction)*	
VIII 13	123 n.225	—	94
VIII 14	168		
IX 4	131	*1Q27 (1QMysteries)*	
IX 12–XI 22	27, 28, 82, 84, 87, 88, 91, 92, 129–130, 156, 179, 215, 222	—	94
		4Q37 (4QDeut^j)	
		—	221 n.148
IX 16	222 n.156		
IX 19–20	123 n.225	*4Q163 (4Qpap pIsa^c)*	
IX 22	222 n.156	—	122 n.219
X 1–22	82		
X 5–22	87	*4Q169 (4QpNah)*	
X 15	156	—	122 n.219
X 16–17	130		
X 19	222 n.156	*4Q171 (4QpPs^a)*	
XI 2	88	—	107 n.162, 127 n.238, 216 n.129, 221
XI 7–8	227 n.171		
XI 8	179		
XI 9	130		
XI 10–11	88, 92, 129	*4Q173 (4QpPs^b)*	
XI 17	88	1 4	107 n.159
XI 20–22	88, 215		
XI 22	46 n.43, 130	*4Q184*	
		—	107 n.162
1QSb			
—	106 n.158	*4Q185*	
		—	93
1QapGen ar			
VI 1	193 n.41	*4Q216 (4QJub^a)*	
		VI 3	156 n.88
1QpHab			
—	107, 110, 111, 128, 129	*4Q256 (4QS^b)*	
		XX 3	156 n.88
1QIsa^a			
		4Q258 (4QS^d)	
—	123, 153 n.79, 156 n.89, 167 n.143, 210 n.100	X 3	156 n.88
		4Q265	
		7 12, 14	156 n.88

4Q266 (4QD^a)
— 122 n.219, 177

4Q267 (4QD^b)
9 V 5   222 n.151

4Q280 (4QCurses)
2 2   222 n.154

4Q286 (4QBer^a)
— 219 n.141, 222

4QMysteries
— 94

4Q301 (4QMyst^c)
— 76, 85, 94

4Q368
— 107 n.162, 127 n.238

4Q374
— 107 n.162, n.163, 127 n.238

4Q381 (4QNon–Canonical Psalms B)
— 229, 230 n.175

4Q392
— 106 n.156

4Q400–407 (4QShirShabb^{a–h})
— 22 n.78

4Q403 (4QShirShabb^d)
— 106 n.156, 219 n.141

4Q404 (4QShirShabb^e)
5 4   106 n.156

4Q405 (4QShirShabb^f)
23 II 10   219 n.141

4QInstruction
— 94

4Q416 (4QInstruction^b)
2 III 17   193 n.41

4Q418 (4QInstruction^d)
— 107 n.162, 156 n.88, 179, 193 n.41

4Q418a (4QInstruction^e)
25 2   156 n.88

4Q426
— 107 n.162

4Q427 (4QH^a)
— 9, 10, 35, 65, 65 n.8, 107 n.162, 163 n.125, 219 n.141, 227

4Q428 (4QH^b)
— 9, 10, 11, 35, 46 n.43, 76 n.60, 89, 131, 156 n.88, 186, 208, 219 n.141, 222 n.151, 227 n.170

4Q429 (4QH^c)
— 9, 11, 176

4Q430 (4QH^d)
— 9, 97

4Q431 (4QH^e)
— 9, 11, 227 n.170

4Q432 (4QH^f)
— 9, 11, 97, 137, 186, 187 nn.16–20, 189 nn.28–29, 198 n.59, 208, 209 n.95, 218

4Q433 (4QHodayot–like A)
— 156 n.88

4Q468
— 107 n.162

4Q471b (4QSelf–Glorification Hymnᵃ)
— 10, 35

4Q484
7 1 156 n.88

4Q491 (4QMᵃ)
— 224

4Q491c (4QSelf–Glorification Hymnᵇ)
— 10, 227 n.170

4Q500
— 152 n.74, 168 n.145, 170 n.147

4Q502
— 22 n.77

4Q504–506 (4QDibHamᵃ⁻ᶜ)
— 23, 156 n.88, 219 n.141, 224

4Q507–509 (4QFestival Prayersᵃ⁻ᶜ)
— 22 n.78, 23, 131

4Q511 (4QShirᵇ)
— 177 n.165, 219 n.141

4Q512
— 22 n.77

4Q525 (4QBeat)
— 84 n.85, 93

4Q544
2 3 222 n.154

4Q577
8 1 156 n.88

5Q10
— 107 n.162

11Q5
— 198

11Q11
— 224

11Q14
— 156

11Q17 (11QShirShabb)
— 22 n.78

11Q19
— 177

11Q21
— 177

8HevXIIgr
— 110 n.180